The SCOTTISH GOVERNMENT YEARBOOK 1985

edited by
DAVID McCRONE

First published 1984

Published by

Unit for the Study of Government in Scotland
Department of Politics
University of Edinburgh
31 Buccleuch Place

ISBN O 9508369 0 7

Printed by
Research Centre for Social Sciences – Service Unit

SCOTTISH BUSINESS EDUCATION COUNCIL

SCOTTISH TECHNICAL EDUCATION COUNCIL

**SCOTBEC/SCOTEC amalgamate this year
to form a new
Scottish Vocational Education Council**

SCOTVEC

**Under this new body a new National Certificate
will be awarded made up of
modules or units of study.**

For further information on the National Certificate
and on
SCOTVEC
please contact:

**The Publicity Department
SCOTBEC
Freepost
EDINBURGH EH3 0HD**

**The Chief Officer
SCOTEC
38 Queen Street
GLASGOW G1 3DY**

Scottish Government Yearbook 1985

TABLE OF CONTENTS

The Yearbook is edited on behalf of the Unit for the Study of Government in Scotland at The University of Edinburgh. Additional copies of the Yearbook, backcopies of the eight previous volumes and further information about The Unit's activities can be obtained from Mrs. Helen Ramm at 31 Buccleuch Place, Edinburgh Eh8 9JT, Scotland.

A COMMENTARY

THE EDITOR

Once the dust settled on the district election result in May 1984, the Government party in Scotland was left in control of the bastions of Berwickshire, Bearsden and Milngavie, Kyle and Carrick, and Eastwood. These districts represented 5% of the Scottish electorate; Labour districts accounted for 74%.

Defeat on this scale, however, does not appear to have dented the self-esteem of George Younger and his Scottish Office team. They have continued to implement Whitehall policies without significant deviation, insisting the while that they have successfully protected, even promoted, Scotland's interests.

In this year's *Yearbook*, we pay special attention to the current state of housing policy, and health policy in Scotland. Despite Labour's control of so many districts, and rearguard action by some, government housing policy has been implemented without much fuss. Health policy, too, reflects central government initiatives, Labour and Tory, since the 1970s. There is little especially Scottish about the character or impact of these policies, despite continuing evidence that Scotland's health problems are peculiar and chronic.

Given the unpopularity of the Government in Scotland, why so little conflict? Certainly, Scottish local authorities have been in the shade of the GLC, Liverpool and Sheffield these past twelve months. Apart from mutterings that they were at the receiving end first, few Scottish local authorities seem willing to take on the Government. Why should this happen? First of all, we can grouse that the Metropolitan (English) media don't notice, and even if they do, they don't understand (a traditional and complacent view of ours). Secondly and more importantly, Labour has failed to mount an integrated challenge. Lothian stood alone because

Strathclyde mistrusted the motives of the East Coasters, and weren't doing too badly out of the Scottish Office. Dundee was ignored. No-one understood them anyway, and wasn't it the biggest village in Scotland? Thirdly, the Scottish Office came into its own as a weapon of Whitehall. Honed nicely by previous Labour administrations to provide a comprehensive basket of services, the Scottish Office has proved to be a marvellous instrument for controlling Scottish local authorities. While it is not too difficult for Liverpool to cock a snook at the cumbersome Department of the Environment (which hasn't all the Scottish Office powers anyway), it's more difficult for Scottish local authorities to oppose St Andrew's House. The Scottish Office has evolved for ninety-nine years into a peculiar weapon of Government, administratively devolved, but democratically unaccountable, a perfect device for a colonial viceroy to employ.

Paradoxically, the weakness of the Tories in Scotland is Younger's strength. He doesn't have to worry much about dissident Tory authorities because there aren't many. Elections aren't won or lost for the Tories in Scotland. It's far-fetched to imagine the Tories winning a majority of Scottish seats as they did in 1955. Scotland's politics aren't those of Quebec; and Thatcher is no Mulroney. Younger's successes – essentially defensive, the protection of Ravenscraig and of 'Locate in Scotland' bureaux – are traded against the privatisation by Trafalgar House of Scott Lithgow and the RCG offshore construction yard at Methil. His Cabinet colleagues allow him some victories in return for curbing the local authorities, and using the monetarist vocabulary. The saga of Ravenscraig will keep him occupied, and he will be faced with problems from sectors of the economy he has not had to worry about before. He lost a major battle over Regional Aid, but put his customary brave face in things. The 'real' crisis of Scottish agriculture promises to be a thorn in his flesh and that of the Tory Party particularly thirled to the farming lobby in Scotland. Whisky can no longer be counted on as an invisible earner of a highly visible asset. The Scottish Office (and the SDA) bangs the drum for Silicon Glen in the hope that publicity hype will attract in enough hi-tech companies to generate a critical mass. Hood and Young's definitive survey of Scottish Industry* shows the parlous state of much of it. Engineering companies have failed to capitalise on oil-related work, and to adjust to new product and market opportunities. Resource-based industries – forestry, fishing and food processing – are conservative, and give poor returns on capital. Even the electronics industry has difficulty holding its own in employment terms. Between 1971 and 1983, employment in electronics had increased by 14%, while manufacturing employment fell by 38%. Still, electronics only accounts for 10% of manufacturing employment (p.298). Much relies, the editors conclude, on a strong interventionist role for the Industry Department of Scotland (IDS) and the SDA, but these are not the political times for such a message. The Scottish Office pursues an intervention-by-stealth policy up to the limits allowed by government policy. As a consequence, IDS is forced into a reactive rather than a proactive role. The dropping of 'economic planning' from its title in 1983 was more than symbolic. The SDA, too, has evolved a role more agreeable to government and business in Scotland as a consequence of eschewing its previous front-loading strategy. The authors of this impressive survey conclude that while the openness of the Scottish economy, and its strong linkages with the rest of the UK is a real constraint, more – Keynesian – intervention is required, and even an 'enhanced Scottish dimension', which would allow an independently determined industrial policy for Scotland.

This definitive report will provide ammunition for Younger in his battles with the Department of Trade and Industry, and the Treasury, but also for his political opponents. Labour will be a major beneficiary, but will continue to find it difficult to play the tartan card now that support for the SNP is off the floor of the opinion polls. The Alliance, with around a quarter of the electorate, is unsure how to use this asset in Scotland. Besides, its local government strength is negligeable, and that is where the battles will be fought in the year to come.

The slumbering giant of Strathclyde has now put its foot down, aided by Dick Stewart's succession to the COSLA presidency. It promises to use its weight to block the new round of Scottish Office cuts. Intriguingly, Lothian, run by a minority Tory administration, looks set to do something similar, though in a more douce way. Brian Meek's Tories on the whole don't speak the language of the New Right, and promise to defend services. George Younger will recognise their voices as more akin to his own, but will be tied by Party and Cabinet loyalty. He is, after all, a team player. There are cracks in the opposition to be exploited again. The four cities (now all Labour) show signs of wanting to run their own campaign to the annoyance of other Labour districts. No-one is more experienced or skilled at this game of divide and rule than George Younger; he has had to be. But the road ahead is rocky, and the opposition seems to have had enough. He is fortunate that there are no more elections in 1985 (so is Brian Meek), but the battle which is developing is likely to be an extra-electoral one.

The Scottish Office, celebrating its centenary, will be playing contradictory roles to two audiences. To Scotland, it will have to show its interventionist capabilities. To London, it will have to be a true privatiser. It will need to call up all the skills of its venerable ghosts to ride these two horses at once.

The *Yearbook* will watch this trick with interest, and will report on it in twelve months' time. Meanwhile, we hope that this edition will shed more light on the governance of Scotland. The editor is indebted to all the contributors, and particularly to Chris Allen, Hamish Henderson, Allan Macartney and Richard Parry for continuing to provide their valuable reviews for readers.

Helen Ramm continues to cope with annual changes in technology, and is indispensable to the production of the Yearbook. John Nimmo and his staff work marvels with our copy, and meet our needs admirably. Above all, we are indebted to readers and subscribers without whom there would be no Yearbook.

*N. Hood and S. Young (eds.) *Industry, Policy and the Scottish Economy*, Edinburgh University Press, 1984.

November, 1984

THE DISTRICT ELECTIONS OF 1983: A 1 + 3 PARTY SYSTEM

JOHN BOCHEL
DEPARTMENT OF POLITICAL SCIENCE
UNIVERSITY OF DUNDEE

DAVID DENVER
DEPARTMENT OF POLITICS
UNIVERSITY OF LANCASTER

Introduction

On the face of it, the main interest in local elections should focus on the results in each authority for these have local consequences such as party control of the administration, policy orientations, patterns of expenditure and so on. But for good or ill perhaps most attention today is devoted to the overall performances of parties. This may be inevitable. Local elections are widely interpreted as important and reliable between-general-election indicators of trends in the popularity of major parties. Underlying this is the assumption that local electoral behaviour is largely 'nationalised' in that it reflects voters' concern with national issues, personalities and governmental performance. There is considerable evidence that this assumption is, on the whole, valid.

Both of these focuses are justified in an era in which many local authorities and their associations are in conflict with central government. The political complexion of individual local authorities has assumed more than its usual importance and, unlike public opinion polls, local elections are real tests of opinion and may be held to reflect, to some extent, concern about what is happening to local government.

The District elections of 1984 were the first electoral test for the parties in Scotland since the 1983 General election. That election had seen a dramatic fractionalisation of the party system in respect of voting. Labour, long the dominant party, slumped from 41.6 per cent of the popular vote in 1979 to 35.1 per cent, its poorest performance since the war, the SNP also fell back to only 11.7 per cent, a far cry from the heady days of October 1974 when it came second with over 30 per cent. Although the Conservatives won the election with an increased majority their share of the vote in Scotland was, at 28.4 per cent, their second lowest since 1945. Only the SDP/Liberal Alliance could be said to have advanced, with 24.5 per cent of the Scottish vote compared with only 9 per cent for the Liberals in 1979. The fractionalisation was, however, mainly of votes. Labour still held 41 (−3) of the Scottish seats, the Conservatives 21 (−1) whilst the SNP retained their 2. But the Alliance did advance on previous Liberal performances with 8 seats (+5).

The second half of 1983 saw a modest improvement in the national position of Labour as reflected in opinion polls. The accession to the leadership and deputy leadership of Neil Kinnock and Roy Hattersley proved to be a mild tonic. Labour's progress at this stage was at the expense of both the Conservatives and the Alliance. The former's support drifted slightly downward and the latter's fell back to hover at around the 20 per cent level. In Scotland the SNP continued in the doldrums. The District elections would show whether these trends would appear in actual voting behaviour.

It was not only the fortunes of parties relative to the 1983 General election that was of interest. Comparison with the District elections of 1980 was also important. These were held at a time of Conservative and SNP unpopularity and had resulted in a massive Labour dominance of local government in Scotland where they had outright control of twenty-four Districts and minority control of one other. In contrast the Conservatives controlled only five Districts with a majority and formed a minority administration in two others. (The remaining Districts were controlled by Independents). Would the 1984 District elections result in the other parties making a dent in Labour's near hegemonic position in Scottish local government, or would they strengthen Labour's hold further and legitimise the challenge of some authorities to central government policies?

Important and interesting though relatively short-term trends in party support are, there are other, more fundamental movements in Scottish local elections that demand and deserve examination, for example, changing patterns of party competition, increasing partisanship, and the decline of Independents, turnout and so on. We propose to analyse these first.

Candidates and Contests

Before the emergence of the Alliance local elections in Scotland were already more complex than in England and Wales. We had, in effect, in local as in national elections, at least a three-, and perhaps a four-party system. The rise of the Alliance certainly added to the complexity and, so far as candidates went, instituted a four-party system.

TABLE 1

Candidates at District Elections 1974-1984

	1974	1977	1980	1984
Conservative	539	543	547	571
Labour	753	719	765	830
Liberal/Alliance	148	136	153	417
SNP	269	465	439	493
Others	207	187	122	120
Independent	644	521	426	402
Total	2559	2571	2452	2833

Table 1 shows that all of the major parties increased their numbers of candidates, but it is obvious that the major change compared with previous elections was the extensive challenge mounted by the Alliance parties. A mere 153 Liberal candidates in 1980 increased to 400 Alliance candidates in 1984.

The rise in the number of major party candidates reflects, in a small way, the fact that boundary changes increased the number of District wards from 1,124 in 1980 to 1,151 in 1984. More important is the slow, but steady incursion of party candidates into areas that have hitherto been characterised by non-Partisan local politics. After the 1980 elections we classified 32 Districts as 'Partisan' (those dominated by parties), 14 as 'non-Partisan' (those dominated by Independents) and 7 as 'Intermediate' (those in which there is significant but not dominant intervention by parties) in their form of local politics. (See J.M. Bochel and D.T. Denver, *The Scottish District Elections of 1980*,Election Studies, University of Dundee, Dundee 1980). Although the same Districts remain in the three categories it can be seen from Table 2 that the proportion of Independent candidates declined in each category between 1980 and 1984. The decline was especially marked in Intermediate Districts, but even the formerly solidly Non-Partisan Districts had a significant number of party candidates in 1984. Overall, only 14.2 per cent of all District candidates in 1984 were Independents compared with 17.4 per cent in 1980, 20.3 per cent in 1977 and 25.2 per cent in 1974. This is a massive change in a ten year period.

TABLE 2

Percentage of Candidates Independent 1980-1984

	1980 %	1984 %
Partisan Districts (32)	4.0	3.3
Intermediate Districts (7)	54.4	41.3
Non-Partisan Districts (14)	87.8	80.4

These changes in candidatures have, of course, consequential effects on patterns of perty competition at ward level and these are illustrated in Table 3 and 4. Table 3 shows firstly the proportion of wards in which only Independent or 'Other' candidates (e.g. Ecology, Communist, Independent Labour, etc.) were seeking election. This proportion remained steady from 1974 until 1984 when there was a significant fall to 17 per cent. The second feature of the Table is the decline, over the decade, in the proportion of wards in which a candidate of a major party (that is, Labour, Conservative, SNP, Liberal/SDP) faced competition from at least one Independent or 'Other' candidate, this has fallen from 13 per cent to 9 per cent. Together these two items indicate an increase in the level of party competition in Scottish local government. The third item in the Table further illustrates this increase in party competition; the proportion of wards in which at least two major party candidates opposed one another has

TABLE 3

Patterns of Competition in District Wards, 1974-1984

	1974 %	1977 %	1980 %	1984 %
Ind/Others Only	22	22	21	17
Major Party v Ind/Others	13	11	9	9
Major Party Contest	56	59	61	65
Major Party Uncontested	9	8	9	9
	(N = 1110)	(N = 1117)	(N = 1124)	(N = 1148)

increased steadily since 1974. The proportion of seats in which a major party held or gained seats unopposed has remained steady at around 9 per cent over the ten year period.

This phenomenon of increasing party activity in Scottish local elections seems likely to continue. It is largely a consequence of the 1974 reorganisation of local government which swept away small burghs and rural authorities with a tradition of Non-Partisan local politics and replaced them with larger Districts with both an urban and rural content. These are less well suited to the more intimate, personal characteristics of non-partisan politics. In addition the Conservative party has changed its attitude to participation in local government. Before 1974 the task of opposing Labour was, for the most part, left to an assortment of ratepayers, moderates, progressives, etc. as well as Independents. Since 1974 the Tories have increasingly taken up the challenge themselves. As their base in urban areas contracts it seems likely that they will seek to retain a substantial foothold in local government by replacing Independents in Non-Partisan Districts. Certainly, since 1974 the number of Conservative candidates has consistently increased. Similarly, the SNP and the Alliance parties have, for much the same reasons, increased the numbers of their candidates. Labour, which already dominates the larger Districts, is in the comfortable position of seeking new worlds to conquer.

It is now only in small (in population) authorities on the periphery of Scotland – the Highlands, Borders and Dumfries and Galloway – that Non-Partisan politics predominates; but even here there was, in 1984, a significant decline in the number of Independent, and an increase in the number of party, candidates.

It is not only the increasing partisanship in District elections that is a feature of 1984. Table 4 demonstrates a major change in the nature of major party contests. Not many years ago the British party system was considered to be an archetypical two-party system. It is true that in the first (1974) District elections two-party, Conservative v Labour contests were the most common, but even then they accounted for less than two-fifths of party contests. By 1977 three-party, Conservative v Labour v SNP contests were the commonest and there were almost as many Labour v SNP contests as there were Conservative v Labour. This, broadly speaking remained the position in 1980.

In 1984 however, with the Liberal/SDP Alliance mounting a major challenge, the situation changed. For the first time fewer than half of party contests were straight fights (40 per cent) and only 12 per cent were single Conservative v Labour contests. The proportopn of three-way contests

TABLE 4

Party Contests in District Wards 1974-1984

Two-Way Contests	**1974** %	**1977** %	**1980** %	**1984** %
Conservative v Labour	39	24	26	12
Labour v SNP	20	22	23	16
Others	9	10	9	12
All Two-Way	68	56	58	40
Three-Way Contests	%	%	%	%
Conservative v Labour v SNP	17	30	26	17
Conservative v Labour v Lib/All	13	5	8	15
Others	1	2	2	7
All Three-Way	31	37	36	39
Four-Way Contests	%	%	%	%
Con v Lab v Lib/All v SNP	3	6	6	21

increased to 39 per cent mainly because of a sharp rise in the number of Conservative v Labour v Alliance confrontations. Even more striking is the increase in the proportion of four-way contests. This was 3 per cent in 1974, and 6 per cent in 1977 and 1980. In 1984 more than 20 per cent of party contests involved all four parties. At least insofar as candidates are concerned the 1984 elections confirmed the increasing complexity of the Scottish party system demonstrated by the results of the 1983 General election.

The increased level of party competition in 1984 resulted in an increase in the proportion of wards contested from 74 per cent to 78 per cent despite the fact that, following boundary changes, the number of wards had increased and thus more candidates had to be found. Table 5 shows the percentage of wards contested at each set of District elections since 1974 with separate figures for the Partisan, Non-Partisan and Intermediate Districts referred to earlier.

In Partisan Districts the proportion of wards contested has remained consistently high since reorganisation and is increasing – to a record 92 per

TABLE 5

Percentage of District Wards Contested 1974-1984

	1974 %	1977 %	1980 %	1984 %
Scotland	80	78	74	78
Partisan Districts (32)	88	88	90	92
Intermediate Districts (7)	53	61	49	59
Non-Partisan Districts (14)	61	47	27	36

cent in 1984. The figures for Intermediate and Non-Partisan Districts are distinctly more variable. After an initial surge of enthusiasm in 1974, the latter have never had more than half of their wards contested and despite an improvement in 1984 only 36 per cent of wards were contested. If the incursion of parties into these Districts continues, however, fewer wards are likely to remain uncontested.

As in previous elections, Independents were the major beneficiaries of unopposed returns in 1984 (Table 6). Labour consistently wins more seats unopposed than the other parties.

TABLE 6

Winning Party in Uncontested Wards 1974-1984

	1974	1977	1980	1984
Conservative	23	41	29	22
Labour	73	42	61	64
Liberal/Alliance	1	3	7	7
SNP	4	7	6	8
Independent	122	154	184	145
Others	–	–	3	1
Total	223	247	290	247

Turnout

Levels of turnout at local elections are notoriously low. Table 7 shows that the trend of declining turnout that we have noted in previous years continued in 1984, albeit at a slower pace. The smallest decline since reorganisation may owe something to increased party competition, but

TABLE 7

Turnout at District Elections 1974-1984

1974	1977	1980	1984
%	%	%	%
51.4	47.8	45.7	44.4

the position is far from healthy. As usual, there are considerable variations in turnout between and within Regions. Again Grampian Region as a whole had the lowest turnout at 35 per cent, not one of its five Districts polled as much as 40 per cent of the electorate. Only two other Districts, Roxburgh and Wigtown, fell below 40 per cent. The Central Region continued to top the turnout league with 48.4 per cent and within it, Stirling polled 54 per cent – by far the highest for any District in which all seats were contested.

There is no ready explanation for consistently low or relatively high turnout in some areas. Patterns and styles of party activity are fairly uniform throughout the country and some wider social-cultural explanations have to be sought.

The Performance of the Parties

Table 8 shows the share of the votes obtained by each party at each set of District elections since 1974. As we have cautioned in previous analyses

TABLE 8

Party Shares of the Votes 1974-1984

	1974	1977	1980	1984	Change 1980-84
	%	%	%	%	
Con	26.8	27.2	24.1	21.4	−2.7
Labour	38.4	31.6	45.4	45.7	+0.3
Lib/All	5.0	4.0	6.2	12.8	+6.6
SNP	12.4	24.2	15.5	11.7	−3.8
Ind	14.1	9.8	6.7	6.8	+0.1

of local election results, these are 'raw' figures which take no account of variations in the number of candidates of each party or unopposed returns. Nonetheless the message of the figures in clear. In 1984 the Conservatives, despite a record number of candidates, fell back to their lowest level of support at local level since the reorganisation of local government in 1974. This was, indeed, the poorest Conservative performance at *any* nationwide election in Scotland for many years (certainly since 1974, probably since 1945). In contrast, Labour polled marginally better, despite greatly increased competition, and from an already high base, than they did in 1980. This was their best local election performance since reorganisation and their highest nationwide share of the vote since the 1966 General election. Despite an increase of 6.7 percentage points in their share of the vote the Alliance performance must have been a disappointment to them. They put forward 264 more candidates than in 1980, but although their share of the vote doubled the return was relatively poor. The figures seem to confirm the electoral decline of the SNP who, like the Conservatives, recorded their poorest performance since 1974.

As might be expected the decline in Independent and Other candidatures noted earlier is accompanied by a shrinking in their share of the vote from 17.5 per cent ten years ago to 8.4 per cent in 1984.

A more precise indication of trends in major party support in Scotland is given in Table 9 which shows the distribution of votes among the four parties in wards which had four-party contests, compared with the result of

TABLE 9

Trends in Major Party Support in Scotland

	Regional Election 1982 %	General Election 1983 %	District Election 1984 %
Conservative	27.8	28.5	25.8
Labour	38.9	35.2	45.9
Liberal/Alliance	23.3	24.6	17.5
SNP	10.0	11.8	10.8

the General election of 1983 and four-party contests in the Regional elections of 1982. On the basis of these figures the broad trends apparent in Table 7 are confirmed. There has clearly been a very substantial Labour recovery in Scotland accompanied by a decline in the fortunes of the Conservatives and a significant diminution in the attraction of the Alliance.

It is very obvious that the impression of intense party competition conveyed by an analysis of candidatures is not reflected in party support.

What we seem to have is a four-party system in which one party (Labour) is predominant, one (Conservative) is a moderate challenger and two (Alliance and SNP) are really minor challengers.

Support for this interpretation is found in a consideration of the number of seats won by parties in the 1984 District elections, details of which are given in Table 10. We have noted in the past that the first-past-the-post system produces distortions in the relationship between votes

TABLE 10

District Council Seats Won 1974-1984

	1974	1977	1980	1984	Change 1980-84
Conservative	241	277	229	189	−40
Labour	428	299	494	545	+51
Liberal/Alliance	17	31	40	78	+38
SNP	62	170	54	59	+5
Independent	345	318	289	267	−22
Others	17	22	18	11	−7
Total	1110	1117	1124	1149*	

* There were no candidates in three wards.

and seats. Parties doing well in terms of the popular vote gain a bonus in seats. Labour, as the predominant party in Scotland, tends to obtain more seats in Parliamentary and local elections than its share of the votes suggests it should. But in 1984 the bias in the electoral system did not distort Labour's share of the seats by much, especially when we remember that they took 64 seats unopposed for which no votes are counted. They advanced to 545 seats (47.3 per cent of the total from 45.7 per cent of the vote). By contrast the Conservatives gathered only 189 seats (16 per cent of the total from 21.4 per cent of the vote), by far their worst performance under the new system. Both the Alliance and the SNP made advances in the number of seats won, but they were even more severely punished by the electoral system. With 13 and 12 per cent of the votes respectively they won only 7 and 6 per cent of the seats.

With 267 seats won, Independents also had their worst election since reorganisation, but because of the number of seats won without a contest (mostly wards with small electorates) the decline in the proportion of seats they won (to 23 per cent) is less marked than their decline in votes (to 6.8

per cent).

The consequences of these changes in seats won was to increase further Labour's hold on power at local level in Scotland. Party control of the 53 seats is now as follows:

1. Majority Labour Control (25)

Aberdeen	Clackmannan	Monklands
Dundee	Stirling	Motherwell
Kirkcaldy	Falkirk	Hamilton
Dunfermline	Dumbarton	East Kilbride
West Lothian	Glasgow	Renfrew

2. Majority Conservtive Control (4)

Berwickshire	Kyle and Carrick
Bearsden and Milngavie	Eastwood

3. Majority Alliance Control (1)

North East Fife

4. Majority SNP Control (1)

Angus

5. Majority Independent Control (16)

Caithness	Ettrick and Lauderdale	Tweeddale
Sutherland	Argyll and Bute	Badenoch and Strathspey
Ross and Cromarty	Nairn	Wigtown
Skye and Lochalsh	Moray	Stewartry
Lochaber	Kincardine and Deeside	Annandale and Eskdale
		Inverness

6. No Overall Control (largest party in brackets) (6)

Banff and Buchan (Ind.)	Clydesdale (Lab.)
Nithsdale (Con.–SNP–Ind.)	Roxburgh (Ind.)
Perth and Kinross (Con.)	Gordon (Ind.)

A comparison of the pattern of control of the 53 Districts in 1980 and 1984 is given in Table 11.

Labour lost control of Kyle and Carrick to the Conservatives but gained Edinburgh and Stirling (where in 1980 they formed the largest party). The result is that Labour now controls authorities containing 74 per cent of the Scottish electorate. The Conservatives are now in charge of only four small authorities containing 5 per cent of the Scottish electorate. It is worth noting too that the number of authorities where Independents hold a majority of seats has slipped from 20 to 16 and these contain only 10 per cent of the electorate.

TABLE 11

Party Control of Districts

	1980	1984
Majority Labour Control	24	25
Majority Conservative Control	5	4
Majority Lib/Alliance Control	0	1
Majority SNP Control	0	1
Majority Independent Control	20	16
No Overall Control	4	6

Conclusion

Five major points can be made in conclusion to this analysis of the 1984 District elections in Scotland.

1. There continues to be an advance on the part of political parties at local level in Scotland. There were fewer Independent candidates than evern before; they gained a smaller share of the votes and fewer seats.

2. The Labour party has made a substantial recovery since the General election. They gained more votes and more seats and control more authorities than ever.

3. The Conservative party is in a weaker position in Scotland than it has been in living memory.

4. The SNP are at a lower ebb than they have been since their dramatic arrival on the Scottish electoral scene in the 1960s.

5. The Alliance failed to make a major impact upon the Scottish electorate in 1984. Despite their increase in votes and seats the Alliance do not look like shaking the party system in Scotland.

When commenting upon the results of the Scottish Regional elections in 1982 we asked in our title whether Scotland was heading 'towards a four-party system'. The results of the 1984 District elections suggest that there is indeed a four-party system but not one of four equals. Rather, as we indicated earlier, it is now a system in which a dominant party is challenged to some extent by one other and to a small extent by two others.

THE 1984 EUROPEAN ELECTION IN SCOTLAND

JOHN BOCHEL
DEPARTMENT OF POLITICAL SCIENCE
UNIVERSITY OF DUNDEE

DAVID DENVER
DEPARTMENT OF POLITICS
UNIVERSITY OF LANCASTER

The second election for the European Parliament was held in June 1984, just one month after the District elections in Scotland and a year after a Westminster election in 1983. It is probably fair to say that the main popular and media interest concentrated on the fortunes of the parties rather than on the substantive issues, and that is also the limited concern of this paper.

The principle interest was whether the recovery in Labour's fortunes since 1983 and the decline in Conservative, Alliance and SNP support suggested by opinion polls, and confirmed by the District elections, would continue. But first it is worth comparing the result of the second European election with the first held in 1979. Table 1 compares party performances at the two European elections. In 1984 Labour made substantial progress, the Conservatives lost a lot of ground and the SNP suffered, on this calculation, a small setback. Perhaps the most striking is the poor performance of the Alliance, up only 1.7 percentage points over the Liberal only performance in 1979.

The first European election is widely regarded as somewhat freakish and may not form a good basis for comparison. It took place soon after a considerable Conservative victory in a Westminster election, and at a time of serious demoralisation for Labour and the SNP. Divided as it was on the whole European issue, Labour failed to take the election seriously and as a

TABLE 1

Party Shares of the Vote: European Elections 1979 and 1984

	1979 %	1984 %	Change 1979-1984 %
Conservative	33.7	25.7	−8.0
Labour	33.0	40.7	+7.7
Liberal/Alliance	13.9	15.6	+1.7
SNP	19.4	17.8	−1.6

consequence it suffered, doing considerably worse than at the General election. In contrast, the 1984 election was held under a new Labour leadership determined to use the occasion as a test of the popularity of the Conservative government.

It is perhaps more useful to compare the results of the 1984 European election with the Westminster election of 1983 (Table 2). Again Labour

TABLE 2

Party Shares of the Vote: 1983 General Election and 1984 European Election

	1983 General Election %	1984 European Election %	Change 1983-1984 %
Conservative	28.4	25.7	−2.7
Labour	35.1	40.7	+5.6
Liberal/Alliance	24.5	15.6	−8.9
SNP	11.8	17.8	+6.0

made substantial progress between the two elections and the Conservative vote declined slightly from an already low level. Two surprises are reflected in the Table – the abrupt decline, by almost 9 percentage points, in the Alliance share of the votes, and the significant increase of 6 percentage points in the SNP share. The firmness of these trends can be tested by a comparison of the European elections results with those in the 1984 District elections held a month earlier. The calculations in Table 3 for the District

TABLE 3

Party Shares of the Vote: District Elections and European Election 1984

	District Elections (Four-Party Contest) %	European Election %	Change %
Conservative	25.8	25.7	−0.1
Labour	45.9	40.7	−5.2
Alliance	17.5	15.6	−1.9
SNP	10.8	17.8	+7.0

election are based only on those wards which were fought by the four main parties. (Those wishing to make comparisons with the total shares of the vote will find the necessary data in our paper on the District elections). The major feature of Table 3 is confirmation of a continuing disappointing performance for the Alliance. The striking increase in the SNP share is more puzzling. It is difficult to believe that the party devoted more resources to the European than to the District elections, but the groundwork laid a month earlier may have paid off (although the same might be said of the Alliance). It seems unlikely that opinion shifted substantially in one month during which there were no new major domestic issues in view.

In the 1979 European election the Conservatives won five of the eight European seats in Scotland, Labour won only two and the SNP one. In 1984 the position was reversed for Labour and the Conservatives who won five and two respectively, the SNP retained its one seat. Labour now holds Glasgow, Lothians, Mid Scotland and Fife, Strathclyde East and Strathclyde West. The Conservatives hold Scotland North East and Scotland South.

It is not possible to talk about gains and losses because of extensive boundary changes, but the 1983 Westminster results can be aggregated to estimate the pre-election status of the European seats (Table 4). Given these, there was no real surprises in individual constituency results, with perhaps, the exception of the Highlands and Islands. As Table 4 shows this was a seat in which the Alliance had a lead over the Conservatives. (In the General election the SNP obtained only 21.7 per cent of the aggregate vote in the seven constituencies comprising the European seat. Alliance candidates had also won four of the seven Westminster seats). Despite the

TABLE 4

Pre-election Status of European Seats Based on 1983 General Election Results

	%
Glasgow	32.1 Labour lead over Alliance
Lothians	4.2 Labour lead over Conservatives
Mid Scotland and Fife	6.1 Labour lead over Conservatives
Strathclyde East	28.6 Labour lead over Alliance
Strathclyde West	6.3 Labour lead over Conservatives
Scotland North East	12.7 Conservative lead over Labour
Scotland South	3.6 Conservative lead over Labour
Highlands and Islands	3.0 Alliance lead over Conservative

statistical evidence it was generally considered that the battle here would be between the Alliance candidate (Russell Johnston, Liberal MP for Inverness, Nairn and Lochaber) and the SNP candidate (Winnie Ewing, the incumbent European MP). Those who watched the results programme on BBCTV will recall that the computer, stubbornly, throughout the night, predicted an Alliance victory. The computer could not take account of the advantages of incumbency for a publicity conscious MP, or the possible resentment by the electorate at Johnston's readiness to relinquish a Westminster seat to which he had been elected only a year before, or of the charisma and campaigning skills of Winnie Ewing. In the event she won a stunning victory.

Elsewhere the results reflected the standing of the parties in the polls and the estimates based on the 1983 General election. Labour professed disappointment at not winning Scotland South, but it would have been a major upset if they had done so. As it is this is now a highly marginal seat (1.9 per cent Conservative lead over Labour). There were fears in the Labour camp that low turnout would adversely affect them, but this seems to have been far from the case. In every constituency Labour did better than in 1983. The Alliance did not win a seat and indeed slipped badly in every one of the eight constituencies. On estimated status they had one first place, two second places and five third places. In the election they ended up with one second place, three third and four fourth places. The promise of 1983 had quickly evaporated. The SNP lost two deposits and the Alliance one in Scotland.

Turnout remains a problem for those who value the European elections as an affirmation of commitment to Europe. In 1979 Scotland had, with 36.6 per cent, a slightly higher turnout than the United Kingdom as a whole (32.7 per cent), but in 1984 the differential had virtually disappeared. The 32.7 per cent turnout in Scotland was considerably lower than for the District elections (44.4 per cent). North East Scotland, which contains the Grampian Region, had, predictably, the lowest turnout (28.7 per cent) and the Highlands and Islands the highest (38.4 per cent).

The 1984 European election, then, confirmed Labour's dominance in Scotland and the continuing weakness and diminishing appeal of the Alliance. The SNP made more progress than any other party, but the basis of that progress and its soundness as a predictor for the future are difficult to estimate. Labour is clearly in a much stronger position in Scotland (with 40.7 per cent of the votes) than in Britain as a whole (36.5 per cent of the votes) and the Conservatives are very much weaker in Scotland (25.7 per cent of the votes in Scotland compared with 40.8 per cent in Britain as a whole). The Alliance too, on the basis of the election results, has obviously more appeal South of the Border than in Scotland. The implications for British politics are intriguing.

THE YEAR AT WESTMINSTER

JAMES NAUGHTIE
THE SCOTSMAN

One of the most interesting statements made by George Younger as Secretary of State for Scotland in 1984 was not made to the Commons, but to his party conference in Perth. With the Prime Minister about to head north to address the traditional, unchanging, ecstatic rally and to affirm her faith in her style of government, Younger decided to be bold (an attitude which, his critics say, does not come naturally to him). He spoke about his conduct of business in the Scottish Office and drew a clear distinction – and one he had never before made in these specific terms – between the business of government in Scotland and at Westminster.

Bold? Certainly. The assertion that, as he put it, Scotland was run from Edinburgh and would continue to be so as long as he was Secretary of State, was a quite calculated message to his party and those outside it, not to mention Mrs Thatcher herself. Such displays of independence – even those that turn out to be purely rhetorical – have been known to presage removal from the Cabinet, and always to bring a new frost to relationships with Downing Street. Yet here, a few months before a Government reshuffle in which he hoped for a move to a UK Department, Younger was arguing publicly on the centre of the stage at his own party conference that Scotland had special problems which needed to be assessed and tackled from Edinburgh, not from London. It is hardly a revolutionary view, of course – indeed the point could hardly be more obvious after the latest round of industrial closures and troubles, but the significance was in the timing of Younger's speech and in the confidence with which he dissassociated himself publicly from the prevailing mood in the Cabinet. At a time when the cry "Whitehall knows best" was echoing again around Westminster (particularly in relation to Mrs Thatcher's problems with local authorities which refused to do the Government's bidding), Younger was saying openly: "Edinburgh knows best".

Sceptics – cynics, indeed – noted at the time that Younger's speech had the air of a valedictory about it. His opening passage in which he said that this was the fifth time he had addressed the conference as Secretary of State sounded like a groan, albeit a polite and gentlemanly one. It was known to everyone in the hall who was interested that he wanted out: a successor, in Malcolm Rifkind, was now "ready" in the way these things are managed in Whitehall, and all that was now needed was a suitably senior Cabinet post to be made available to the long-serving, loyal and decent George. So, the argument goes, his tiredness induced some indiscretion: why not boast about the independence of his regime at St Andrew's House and take head-on the criticism (familiar to any Scottish Secretary in a Tory Government) that he was an insignificant figure in Cabinet discussions. The evidence about Younger's approach to politics suggests that is a naive approach. It was a quite careful speech.

Politically, the Government has used the growth of new industries in Scotland to try to take the sting out of the Opposition's attack on employment: arguing, in effect, that all prosperity would flow from Silicon Glen. This fragile argument was not very well analysed, at least publicly, by the Opposition. Still concentrating (naturally) on the defence of jobs, it seemed difficult for Labour in particular to turn its attention fully to the dubious assumptions and forecasts in Younger's argument about the growth of high-tech industry and its potential benefits for Scotland. But it was his great theme, and it was a key element in the Perth speech. He tried, as politically he had to, to portray the Scottish Office as a bastion of fairness and commonsense, holding off the worst effects of the recession and turning its attention to building for the future. Never mind that the evidence of good times ahead was patchy, to say the least – sounds of confidence from Ministers were to be the keynote of the Scottish Office's defence. So, Younger began to argue not simply that the picture was brighter than the Opposition was suggesting but that the reason for it was that in St Andrew's House there were none of the blinkers which were so prominent on his colleagues south of the border.

It was splendid stuff for the party, of course. The *amour propre* of the Scottish Tories in being worthy defenders of Scotland was reinforced (and more effectively than by some of the gimmicks they have employed in recent years – the only question about most of them being whether they were more embarrassing to the public at large or the party itself). On the Right-wing fringe, however, there was unhappy muttering. The Scottish Office was incurably "wet" they said, indeed the "wettest" in Whitehall (an interesting Freudian slip – or was it? – from one of Younger's critics at the conference, in private). And what was the evidence? Principally, the urge to intervene imbedded in the newly-named Industry Department for Scotland. Younger, though operating within financial restraints imposed by a Treasury team faithfully implementing Mrs Thatcher's view, had a different *approach*. Though his willingness to claw back grant from "overspending" authorities – even when the mechanics, and some of the results, became politically embarrassing – was welcome enough to the Right, his industrial strategy was not.

In looking at the Scots at Westminster it is the Younger approach that is the key in 1984. The legislative programme, though it had its moments of party conflict and its embarrassments for the Government from time to time, was not the main battle waged across the Commons chamber. The industrial scene cast its shadow again. First, there was the Scott-Lithgow affair.

The crisis, with thousands of jobs at risk in the threatened closure of the yard, had all the familiar ingredients – the prospect of social disaster in a wide area dependent on the yard, the strange behaviour of the head of a nationalised industry (in this case Graham Day of British Shipbuilders), the accusations of Scottish Office complacency from the Opposition benches and the battle with Whitehall to win approval for "oiling the wheels" of a rescue operation. No-one involved could have felt anything but an acute sense of deja-vu as the saga unfolded, with a hopeful sign one day, a setback the next, and finally a solution which, though it was hailed by Ministers as proof that private enterprise could save jobs where the public purse could not, was hardly a triumph.

Throughout the weeks of negotiation, with the Opposition pressing hard for a Government "initiative" and Scottish Office officials (desperately, most of the time) juggling figures with potential purchasers and with British Shipbuilders, one of the mysteries was the attitude of Norman Tebbit, the Trade and Industry Secretary. Not for the first time he was assuming the guise of the Hard Man, the Wrecker. In short, the forces of darkness concentrated in one man. He was believed anxious to restrict the Government's involvement in any rescue deal, for political reasons. He wanted a private rescue about which he could boast and which he could use as evidence of the failure of public stewardship and the ever-ready strength of the private sector to save jobs which would otherwise disappear. But Tebbit was playing a clever game. He knew better than most that the Government had a huge financial commitment, whether it liked it or not, and that what mattered from his point of view was the rhetoric, and the way the "rescue" of at least part of the yard was presented. One of the most fascinating aspects of Tebbit's performance at the Trade and Industry Department has been the contrast between the public style and his willingness to sign cheques which, at least in his speeches to party conferences and even in the Commons, he would previously have denounced, perhaps for not being what Mrs Thatcher likes to call "honest money".

The contrast with Younger was marked. Where Tebbit was (a little) more co-operative behind the scenes than in public, Younger had to fight off political criticism on every television programme and in every newspaper week after week. He had to display enthusiasm for intervention at every turn, even if it was the sort of intervention deeply unsatisfactory to the Labour Party. In terms of the Thatcherite lexicon it was still a word to be regarded with some suspicion, but it had to be used. It was a rough patch for Younger. The attack from Labour and the Alliance over the future of the Clyde, and the evident unease among many Scottish Tories (Anna McCurley, the new MP for Inverclyde and Renfrew West, was well aware of the social consequences of complete closure at Scott Lithgow), was pressed home effectively, with Donald Dewar leading his troops as Shadow Scottish Secretary with considerable style and force, and Ministers appearing bogged down in a sea of industrial troubles – no sooner had Ravenscraig won a little more time than Scott Lithgow was teetering on the brink. The miners' strike was still to come.

In the end, the rescue of some jobs could be presented by Younger as a triumph (but only because the landscape in most of the rest of Scotland was so bleak, and dark). The episode demonstrated his strengths and weaknesses well. First, he was certainly inhibited by the prevailing philosophy around the Cabinet table which allowed more Government intervention than some Ministers liked to admit but always insisted that it be accompanied by an overwhelming sense of guilt, as if it was never to be regarded as anything other than a painful act of last resort. the Government's handling of the Scott Lithgow affair could be dressed up as merely the exercise of Ministerial influence to facilitate the injection of substantial private funds into an unemployment blackspot and therefore defensible: in fact it was much more. The Scottish Office was engaged in an old-fashioned piece of industrial intervention, without the cash. The style – the approach to the problem and the establishment of a specialist team in St Andrew's House to examine every option for a rescue – was exactly the same as before. Younger can admit such things go on – indeed, he has to – Tebbit can not. It is always bound to be an uneasy contrast between the public face of Government in Whitehall and in Edinburgh.

There was another scare a little later on, when a threat was revealed to the operation of the Locate in Scotland Bureau's activities, working with the Scottish Development Agency and the Scottish Office as an engine for investment from overseas. There is no doubt that the leak – of an impending Whitehall battle – was useful to Younger, once again portrayed in Scotland as being *contra mundum,* fighting for his rights. Once again the dark figure of Tebbit was seen on the horizon, complaining about the cost of LIS and its alleged "unfairness" to other parts of the UK. Whether it was the public row that saved LIS we don't know – but it certainly helped. The Opposition's outcry in the Commons was in a sense less important than the near-unanimous cry of pain from the Tory side at the prospect of the end of the bureaux overseas. The old scene was staged again: Younger pressed from all sides to defend Scotland against the Whitehall barbarians and, after an agonising week or two, being seen to have survived yet again.

The question hovering behind it all is this: has Younger made a difference or has he done what any reasonably competent Minister would have done in the same circumstances? There is no doubt that any Tory Secretary of State, faced with the party's limited support in the Scottish group at Westminster, is susceptible to peculiar pressures which his colleagues in the Cabinet sometimes find it hard to understand. To that extent, anyone in Younger's position would have to defend publicly attitudes not normally adopted by the Tebbits. The policies, dictated centrally (whatever Younger says), restrict his room for manoeuvre. The Scottish Office budget does not float freely according to the whim of the Secretary of State. But within the framework established by the Prime Minister and the Treasury there is some elbow room, particularly in the matter of style. It is that which has been Younger's most valuable asset. Though he has been consistently accused of complacency, he has succeeded in presenting the image of a Secretary of State willing to tussle with Cabinet colleagues – and even Mrs Thatcher – to get as much as he can for Scotland. It is not a bogus image: he has had rough times, and severe disputes with colleagues and it is largely because of them that he has won the respect of Tebbit and others who may not like the style of the Scottish Office but recognise that Younger can be a feisty opponent.

One of the factors contributing to the successful presentation of Younger, and little-known outside St Andrew's House, has been the arrival as head of the Scottish Information Office – the Scottish Office's PR and information unit – of Fred Corbett, one of Whitehall's shrewdest information officers. He came to Edinburgh from the Northern Ireland Office, where the business of public relations is fraught indeed. Corbett, a genial Ulsterman, has been a vital influence in presenting the Scottish

Office's case on issues like the Scott Lithgow affair and his influence on Younger (with whom he has a trusting relationship) appears to have been considerable. Certainly, the Scottish Office's efforts to present an independent image – to the extent, for example, of organising high-powered lunches in London for editors and executives of Fleet Street newspapers to meet Younger and hear his views – have had some success. As a by-product, Younger's own profile has become sharper.

From the Opposition point of view, naturally, that picture is false. They see the last year as one of disaster in Scotland, principally on the industrial front – and that has been their main concern in the Commons. The seemingly endless string of redundancy announcements – with such disasters as Bathgate standing out – provided them with plenty ammunition. Dewar led Labour with flair and dedication. (His capacity for work is enormous: perhaps it leads him to delegate too little to his colleagues and it is something many of his friends have warned him about.) Jim Craigen, one of his lieutenants, was a particularly diligent committee man, in a rather earnest way, giving a bit of weight to their arguments over some legislation which was hardly earth-shaking but which needed scrutiny. On the Alliance benches there was evidence of a much more vigorous challenge to the Government than has ever been seen from the Liberals alone.

Malcolm Bruce, Jim Wallace and Archy Kirkwood, as the new Liberals, were very active (with Bruce leading them) and on the SDP bench Charles Kennedy showed a forceful style which belied his unfortunate title as the Baby of the Commons (he was only 23 when elected in Ross, Cromarty and Skye). So they had a bit of fire in their bellies, though their inexperience showed from time to time, as was inevitable.

One of the reasons for a better Opposition performance during the year was the state of the Government front bench. Younger's stature – paradoxically, in view of the economic developments in Scotland – increased. The same cannot be said of his Ministerial colleagues. Lord Gray of Contin (the scalp claimed by Kennedy in the general election) was not a great success in his new role. And Younger's junior Ministers in the Commons were not as powerful a team as he would have liked, either. John Mackay showed again that he has a sharp political eye, and tongue (MacTebbit, his Tory colleagues call him) but Michael Ancram and Allan Stewart dealing with local government and home affairs, and industry and education respectively, were less successful at appearing confident in the presentation of their case. Ancram, faced with local authorities now well-used to the annual ritual of grant claw back and all the ritual posturing that goes with it, gave him a rough time. Stewart's role as Industry Minister was largely usurped by Younger, at least in the public eye.

Ancram's major piece of legislation was the Rating and Valuation Act, giving Younger new powers to control rate levels. There was less fuss – outside the Commons committee room, at least – over this measure than over the English and Welsh ratecapping proposals, largely because since 1981 the Scottish Office's controls over local government spending had become an established part of the scene. It made it no less horrendous a measure to the Opposition, but it took some of the steam out of it. The Tenants Rights Etc. (Amendment) Act extended the right to buy council houses and included exceedingly controversial measures on right-to-repair grants which provided the Opposition forces with one of their main targets of the session.

The Inshore Fishing Act, the Roads Act and the Tourism (Overseas Promotion) Act provided moments of controversy, but hardly touched on the central political questions of the year.

It was the running of the Scottish economy, as usual, that seemed most important to MPs of all persuasions, as unemployment remained high, the number of closures increased, and the search for overseas investment continued. Younger had some success in staving off some of the worst consequences – but it was against a gloomy background. It says much for his resilience as a politician that he survived it all, despite the constant attack. He had little good news – only some news that was better than it might have been. The world of Scottish politics allows a Secretary of State to present himself as Scotland's fighter in the Cabinet, and this he did.

His critics would say it was a false claim. But his Cabinet colleagues would accept it is an accurate description. His confidence clearly increased, despite the gloom and doom. That was the background to his speech in Perth, where he asserted that element of independence. It brought scornful denials from the Opposition who pointed to the bleak industrial landscape and denounced it as a confidence trick – but it was the culmination of a five year stint in St Andrew's House in which he can justly claim to have won some victories. That may not be much in the sweep of history when it comes to be written, but without him it might have been worse. A backhanded compliment? Certainly, but a compliment nonetheless. Thanks to Younger, *some* nightmares never come to pass.

TWO NATIONS?
Regional Partisanship and Representation at Westminster 1868-1983*

R M PUNNETT
READER IN POLITICS,
UNIVERSITY OF STRATHCLYDE

The 1979 and 1983 general elections seemed to confirm two popular assumptions about British electoral politics – that there is a distinct polarization between 'Tory' England and 'radical' Scotland and Wales, and that the size of England means that Conservative Governments are thrust upon unwilling Scots and Welsh by the English majority. Certainly, in 1979 the Conservatives won 59% of the seats in England and 53% in the United Kingdom as a whole, but won only 31% of the Scottish seats and 37% of the Welsh seats. Although Labour support in Scotland and Wales, as elsewhere in the United Kingdom, declined in 1983 as compared with 1979, Mrs Thatcher's 1983 'landslide' still left Labour with 57% of the seats in Scotland and 53% in Wales.

Thus the immediate post-election reaction of *The Scotsman* in June 1983 was that[(1)]:

> "As usual, Scotland is distinctive and different...Here in Scotland it is the Conservative Party which has fallen below 30% of the vote... how many Scots can believe that they are being fairly treated when they get a Government which has only 21 of the 72 Scottish MPs?"

Similarly the *Glasgow Herald* observed that[(2)]:

> "The elections have confirmed a separate voting pattern in Scotland and have also made it more complicated...70% of the Scottish vote was for non-Government candidates, and almost by definition this must bring the Scottish dimension to the fore again."

NORTH
MIDLANDS
SOUTH

But while the current partisan commitments of the component nations of the United Kingdom support the popular images of 'radical' Celts and 'Tory' English, what of the broader historical picture?

In comparison with elections over the longer term was the polarization between England and Celtic Britain exceptionally pronounced in 1979 and 1983, and were these elections typical in producing a Labour-dominated Scotland and Wales within a Conservative-dominated United Kingdom? Over the years has the English Tory commitment been more consistent, and more pronounced, than the radical commitment of the Scots and Welsh? Is the contemporary Scottish and Welsh support for Labour more marked than their earlier support for the Liberals? In which particular elections have the contrasts between the partisan preferences of English, Scots and Welsh been most marked? To what extent has England's partisan commitment been reproduced in the United Kingdom as a whole? Just how often have Scotland and Wales 'backed a loser' by electing more opposition MPs than government MPs?

These and other questions will be examined in this chapter through an analysis of the partisan commitments of the component parts of the United Kingdom over the longer term – specifically the period since 1868. Three particular matters will be dealt with. In Section One the consistency and intensity of each nation's partisan commitment since 1868 will be examined, and in Section Two those elections in which Britain has been most conspicuously 'two nations' will be identified. In Section Three the extent to which, over the years, an English pattern of partisan commitment has been reproduced in the country as a whole will be considered. In the concluding Section some of the implications of the historical patterns that emerge will be discussed.

I. Radical Celts and Tory English?

Over the years how consistent and how intense has each nation been in its partisan commitment? Table I shows the extent of each nation's partisanship, as measured by the average share of seats achieved by the region's dominant party in elections in each of five sub-periods since 1868. The sub-periods were achieved by dividing the pre-1914 and post-1945 periods so that each spans five to seven elections, and retaining the inter-war years as a single period. Here and throughout the paper the 1918 election is excluded from consideration because the nature of the contest on that occasion, between the Lloyd George Coalition and the several Opposition groups, defies analysis on conventional party lines. This leaves twenty-nine elections from Gladstone's victory in 1868 to Mrs Thatcher's in 1983.

TABLE I

Party Dominance in Component Nations of the UK: General Elections 1868-1983 (By Period) [a]

Period (and Number of Elections)	UK		England		Scotland		Wales		Ireland[b]	
	Dominant Party by Nation and Period (Average % of seats)									
1868-86 (5)	Lib	51.6	Con	54.8	Lib	76.2	Lib	75.4	Nat[c]	70.0
1892-1910 (6)	Con	45.4	Con	55.7	Lib	71.0	Lib	82.9	Nat	80.5
1922-35[d] (6)	Con	60.6	Con	65.2	Con	43.0	Lab	53.3	Union	86.1
1945-59 (5)	Con	50.5	Con	51.0	Lab	51.0	Lab	74.3	Union	83.3
1964-83 (7)	Con	494	Con	54.4	Lab	60.0	Lab	69.1	Union	87.6
1868-1983 (29)	Con	50.1	Con	56.4	Lib/ Lab	58.5	Lib/ Lab	70.0	Union	85.8[c]

a Excludes 1918 election which defies analysis on conventional party lines.

b Northern Ireland from 1922

c Nationalist figure includes various 'Home Rule' factions for the elections of 1868-80

d Conservative figures include National Liberal and National Labour for 1931 and 1935.

e That is, the average for Northern Ireland 1922-83

Source:
D.E. Butler and A. Sloan, *British Political Facts 1900-79*, London, 1980; F.W.S. Craig, *British Parliamentary Election Results 1932-85*, London, 1977; F.W.S. Craig, *British Parliamentary Election Results 1885-1918*, London, 1974.

Analyses across time always raise questions of comparability, and this is certainly the case with a study of parties and elections over 115 years. The 'Conservative' label that is used here throughout the period embraces the Conservative Party of Disraeli, the Unionists (including the Liberal Unionists) at the turn of the century, the National Conservatives (and National Liberals and National Labour) of the 1930s, and the post-1945 Conservative party in its Churchillian, Butlerite and Thatcherite forms. In effect, 'Conservative' covers a succession of parties in organisational and ideological terms. The term 'radical', which is transferred from the Liberals of the pre-1914 period to Labour in the post-1918 period, covers an even more fundamental organisational distinction, and an even greater ideological spread, than is the case with the Conservative label[(3)].

Nevertheless, throughout the period under consideration it is possible to distinguish between a broadly right-of-centre 'Tory' party , and a broadly left-of-centre 'radical' party. It is this broad Tory-radical distinction that forms the basis of the analysis that follows.

The use of seats rather than votes as the measure of party performance will inflate somewhat the extent of a region's partisan commitment, given the tendency of the plurality electoral system to reward the winning party in a given region with more seats than it has earned in votes. Nevertheless, it is the regional composition of the parties' representation in Parliament, rather than their grass-roots strength, which determines the party that holds office, and which provides on the floor of the House a daily reminder of the regional contrasts between the parties.

The several extensions of the franchise have increased the electorate from approximately 16% of the adult population in 1868 to almost all adults today (now defined as those over 18 rather than 21). Similarly, the movement of population, and successive constituency boundary revisions to take note of this, mean that the constituencies are not distributed throughout the country in the way that they were in earlier periods. The electoral system, however, has retained its essential 'single-member constituency' and 'first-past-the-post' features throughout the period under consideration, so that the longer term comparisons are meaningful.

It can be seen from Table I that over the 1868-1983 period as a whole the popular images of radical Scotland and Wales and Tory England are broadly accurate. In Scotland the 'left' party (Labour since 1922 and the Liberals before that) has won an overall majority of seats in twenty-one of the twenty-nine elections, has won a simple majority in another two and achieved a 'draw' in another[(4)].

The Scottish radical commitment, however, has varied in its intensity over the years. Between 1868 and 1910 the Liberals won a large majority of Scottish seats in every election except 1900. Indeed the Whigs or Liberals won a majority of Scottish seats in every election from 1832 to the end of the century. Between 1922 and 1955 the Scots were more ambivalent, and the Conservatives won a majority of Scottish seats as often as did Labour. Since 1959 Scotland has returned to its nineteenth century pattern of 'consistent radicalism', giving a majority of seats to Labour in each of the last eight elections.

Scotland's commitment to Labour has not equalled the extent of its nineteenth century attachment to the Liberals. Labour's best performance in Scotland was in 1966, when it won almost two-thirds of the seats. The Liberals, in comparison, won over two-thirds of the seats in eight of the eleven elections between 1880-1910, and won over four-fifths of the seats in five of them.

Wales has been even more consistently and intensely radical in its commitment than has Scotland. The left party has won a majority of Welsh seats in all twenty-nine elections since 1968, and has averaged over 70% of the seats. As in Scotland, however, Labour has been unable to achieve quite the degree of success in Wales that the Liberals sustained before 1914. Only in 1964 and 1966 has Labour won more than three-quarters of the Welsh seats, whereas the Liberals managed this in eight of the nine elections between 1880 and 1910. From its 1966 peak of almost nine-tenths of the Welsh seats, Labour's performance in Wales has deteriorated in each of the last five elections, and in 1983 reached its lowest level since 1935. That said, Wales has sustained a remarkably consistent patttern of 'left' party dominance throughout the period.

Only England has been characterised by a consistent pattern of Conservative party dominance. The Conservatives have won a majority of English seats in twenty of the twenty-nine elections since 1868. Since 1885 the Liberals or Labour have won an *overall* majority of English seats only on three occasions (1906, 1945 and 1966).

The Conservatives achieved their greatest level of success in England at the end of the nineteenth century and in the 1930s. In post-war election wins the level of Conservative success in England has fluctuated within a fairly narrow band: even in 1983 the Conservatives won a smaller proportion of English seats than in most of their pre-1945 wins.

In 1983 the Conservatives did win a bigger share of English seats than Labour won of Scottish or Welsh seats, but generally the English have been less intense in their commitment than have the Scots and Welsh. Only on seven occasions have the Conservatives managed to win two-thirds of the English seats. Six of these elections were before 1945, and three were between 1886 and 1900.

Thus in partisan terms Great Britain has indeed long consisted of the 'two nations' of Tory England and radical Wales and Scotland. What is more, Ireland has constituted a 'third nation' characterised by an idiosyncratic pattern of dominance by 'home-grown' parties. In Northern Ireland the Unionists have won at least three-quarters of the seats in every election since 1922, and have averaged almost nine-tenths of the seats. The Nationalists were almost as successful in the all-Ireland elections of 1885 to 1910, winning around four-fifths of the seats on each occasion.

The broad images of Tory England, radical Wales and Scotland and idiosyncratic Ireland, however, need to be qualified in two important respects. First, the dominance of a party within 'its' nation has been far from total. The Unionists did win all the seats in Northern Ireland in 1924, 1959 and 1964, and the Liberals came close to doing so in Wales in 1892 and 1906. Apart from these cases, however, each region has given at least 10% (and usually much more than 10%) of its seats to parties other than its dominant party in every election since 1868.

Labour (and earlier Liberal) success in Scotland and Wales has never been so complete as to deny the Conservatives a Celtic foothold. In 1979 and 1983 the Conservatives won almost a third of the combined Scottish and Welsh seats, and even in 1923 (the Conservatives' worst performance in Celtic Britain in a 'winning' election[(5)]) they won a sixth. Over the years the Conservative Party in Parliament has been disproportionately English, but has been far from exclusively so.

Equally, Tory England has always made a considerable contribution towards the Parliamentary majorities of Labour and Liberal governments. The Liberal governments' share of English seats ranged from just under half (in 1910) to over two-thirds (in 1906). Labour, in its election victories, has never won less than a quarter of the English seats, and has twice (1945 and 1966) won an overall majority of English seats.

Thus the nations of the United Kingdom have been *predominantly*, but not *exclusively*, Tory, radical and idiosyncratic in their respective commitments. Whichever party has been in power, the Government and the Opposition sides of the House have consisted of a regional mix – although (as is discussed in detail in Section II) the precise extent of the mix has varied from one Parliament to another.

The second major qualification to the national partisan images is that they do not necessarily apply to all of their regional sub-divisions. The notion of radical Scotland, for example, does not extend to Edinburgh or the rural north-east. Within Tory England, London normally returns a large majority of Labour MPs. Unionist dominance in Northern Ireland has distinct regional limits. In Wales there are some rural constituencies that have invariably resisted the radical tide.

Regional sub-divisions, of course, can be extended almost indefinitely. Within Tory Edinburgh, there are some Labour strongholds; within these Labour areas there are some staunchly Conservative pockets; and within them will be some predominantly Labour inner-pockets. The principal concern here is with the broad national sub-divisions of the United Kingdom. Nevertheless, the sheer size of England demands that it be sub-divided.

Table II shows for the regions of the south, midlands and north of

England the dominant party's average share of seats in each of the five sub-periods since 1868. The choice of these three broad divisions of England was partly pragmatic, in that election results for these particular regions were readily available for most of the period, and could be calculated for the rest of it[(6)]. South, midlands and north, however, are widely recognized regions of England, even though they are entirely unofficial divisions, and their boundaries are somewhat arbitrary[(7)].

TABLE II

Party Dominance in Component Regions of England: General Elections 1868-1983 (By Period) [a]

Period (and Number of Elections)		Dominant Party by Region and Period (Average % of seats)							
		England		South		Midlands		North	
1868-86	(5)	Con	54.8	Con	61.6	Lib	50.1	Lib	54.5
1892-1910	(6)	Con	55.7	Con	65.2	Con	56.8	Lib	50.5
1922-35[b]	(6)	Con	65.2	Con	74.2	Con	65.9	Con	52.9
1945-59	(5)	Con	51.0	Con	64.4	Lab	61.0	Lab	60.3
1964-83	(7)	Con	54.4	Con	70.8	Lab	49.6	Lab	64.2
1868-1983	(29)	Con	56.4	Con	67.7	Con	52.7	Lib/ Lab	53.0

a Excludes 1918 election which defies analysis on conventional party lines.

b Conservative figures include National Liberal and National Labour for 1931 and 1935.

Source:
D.E. Butler and A. Sloman, *British Political Facts 1900-79,* London, 1980; F.W.S. Craig, *British Parliamentary Election Results 1932-85,* London, 1977; F.W.S. Craig, *British Parliamentary Election Results 1885-1918,* London, 1974.

Of these three regions of England, the south provides much the clearest example of party dominance. In the period under consideration the Conservatives have won a large majority of seats in the south of England in each election except 1868, 1906 and 1945. The extent of the Conservatives' strength in the south of England has been almost as great as that of the Liberals and Labour in Wales. In all, the Conservatives have won three-quarters of the seats in the south in ten of the twenty-nine elections, and have averaged over two-thirds of the seats.

The midlands region has produced the most balanced pattern of party competition, with the Conservatives winning a majority of seats in seventeen of the elections since 1868, and the 'left' party in twelve. This overall pattern, however, is a product of two contrasting periods. Before 1945 the Conservatives were clearly dominant in the midlands. They won a majority of seats in thirteen of the seventeen elections, and in eight of them won over 60% of the seats. Since 1945 Labour has been more successful, winning a majority of seats in eight of the eleven elections. In 1979, however the Conservatives achieved their largest share of the seats the midlands since 1935, and improved on this in 1983.

In the north of England the 'left' party has won a majority of seats in twenty of the twenty-nine elections. Again, however, there is a clear distinction between the pre-1945 and post-1945 periods. In the elections of 1868-1935 the north of England was the least consistent of all the regions, usually changing its allegiance at every other election, but since 1945 Labour has won a clear overall majority of seats in the north of England in each election. Thus in the north of England, as in the midlands, Labour has a better electoral record than had the Liberals before 1914 – the reverse of the pattern that is found in Wales and Scotland.

It is clear from Tables I and II that, taking the 1868-1983 period as a whole, there is a distinct south to north slope in the extent of the regions' commitment to the Conservatives. From the south of England, where the Conservatives have won a majority of seats in all except three of the elections since 1868, the extent of Conservative success declines northwards.

This overall pattern, however, has not persisted throughout the period. The south of England has been the Conservatives' strongest region in all five sub-periods, but the other regions have changed position on the 'most Tory – least Tory' continuum from period to period. In the 1868-86 period the Liberals were marginally more successful in Scotland than in Wales; since 1945 Labour has usually done better in Wales and the north of England than in Scotland; in the 1945-59 period Labour did better in the midlands than in either Scotland or the north.

The extent of the Conservatives' success between the wars was unusual. In each region the Conservatives averaged a bigger proportion of seats in the inter-war period than in any other, and only in that period were there more regions with a Conservative commitment than with a 'radical' commitment. Thus while the Conservatives' 'southern strength and northern weakness' is a long-established feature of British electoral behaviour, the precise nature and extent of that pattern has varied over the years.

II. Two Nations

In which particular elections have the partisan contrasts between

English and Celts been most marked? An indication of this is given in Table III which shows for each election since 1868 the proportion of seats achieved in England on the one hand, and in Celtic Britain (that is, Scotland and Wales taken together) on the other, by the party that won the election. The elections are ranked according to the extent of the contrast between the winning party's levels of success in these two parts of Britain. Table III thus provides an 'index of Anglo- Celtic electoral polarization' for the period since 1868.

The range between the extreme points in the 'index of polarization' in Table III is considerable. At one end of the scale the Conservatives in 1922 won almost four times as many seats in England as in Scotland and Wales, and in 1923 and 1892 they won almost three times as many. In 1945, however, Labour came close to doing equally well in each of the two parts of Great Britain. The 1945 election was thus doubly distinctive – as the election in which the Anglo-Celtic polarization was least pronounced, and as the one election since 1868 in which the 'left' party won a bigger proportion of seats in England than in Wales and Scotland.

For the most part, Conservative wins have been accompanied by a greater degree of polarization between England and Celtic Britain than have the 'left' party wins. Labour's seven wins, together with the Liberal win of 1906, fill the bottom eight (that is, least polarized) places in Table III, while Conservative wins fill twelve of the fourteen top (most polarized) places. Indeed, the only Conservative victories that are in the lower half of the rankings are their wins of 1951 and 1955. In these two elections the Conservatives won a majority of seats in Scotland as well as in England, and this helped to produce (by the standards of Conservative wins) a relatively low level of Anglo-Celtic polarization.

The other elections that are conspicuously 'out of place' in the rankings are the Liberal wins of January and December 1910. After their triumph throughout Great Britain in 1906, Liberal support in 1910 slumped in England but was sustained in Scotland and Wales. Indeed, in Scotland the Liberals won more seats in January 1910 than in 1906. This produced in 1910 a much greater contrast between the two parts of Great Britain in the extent of the winning party's success than was the case in any of the other 'left' party victories since 1868.

In general, then, it is the left party wins that have reduced the contrasts between England and Celtic Britain while within this pattern Labour wins have minimised the differences even more than did Liberal wins. For the most part, Labour in its victories has achieved much the same level of success in England as did the Liberals in their victories. In Wales and Scotland, however, Labour has done appreciably less well than did the Liberals, averaging 'only' 62.2% of the Scottish and Welsh seats in its seven victories, compared with the Liberals' average of 83% for their six

TABLE III

Anglo-Celtic Polarization in Regional Success of Winning Party: General Elections 1868-1983[a]

Winning	Party	Winning Party's Share of Seats: England	Winning Party's Share of Seats: Scotland & Wales	Index of Polarization (Larger share as a proportion of smaller share)	Rank Order: Con Wins	Rank Order: Lib/Lab Wins	Rank Order: All
1922	Con	63.5	17.9	3.55	1		1
1923	Con	45.4	17.0	2.67	2		2
1892	Con	57.2	22.1	2.59	3		3
1983	Con	69.2	31.8	2.18	4		4
1886	Con	73.0	33.7	2.17	5		5
1970	Con	57.1	28.0	2.04	6		6
1910J	Lib	41.2	82.7	2.01		1	7
1910D	Lib	41.0	80.8	1.97		2	8
1895	Con	75.2	38.5	1.95	7		9
1979	Con	59.3	30.8	1.93	8		10
1900	Con	72.8	40.4	1.80	9		11
1874	Con	62.1	35.2	1.76	10		12
1959	Con	61.6	35.5	1.74	11		13
1924	Con	73.0	42.5	1.72	12		14
1880	Lib	56.5	89.0	1.58		3	15
1868	Lib	53.6	81.3	1.52		4	16
1885	Lib	52.2	76.9	1.47		5	17
1935[b]	Con	74.0	50.9	1.45	13=		18=
1955	Con	57.1	39.3	1.45	13=		18=
1951	Con	53.6	38.3	1.40	15=		20=
1931[b]	Con	89.7	64.2	1.40	15=		20=
1964	Lab	48.1	66.4	1.38		6	22
1966	Lab	55.8	72.9	1.31		7	23
1906	Lib	67.1	87.5	1.30		8=	24=
1974F	Lab	45.9	59.8	1.30		8=	24=
1929	Lab	46.6	58.5	1.26		10	26
1974O	Lab	49.4	59.8	1.21		11=	27=
1950	Lab	49.6	59.8	1.21		11=	27=
1945	Lab	64.9	58.5	1.11		13	29

a Excludes 1918 election which defies analysis on conventional party lines.

b Includes National Liberals and National Labour.

victories. It is this factor that has produced the generally lower level of Anglo-Celtic polarization for the Labour wins than for the Liberal ones.

The extent of the polarization between England and Celtic Britain was much less pronounced in the Conservative wins of the 1930s and 1950s than in their earlier and later victories. In all, seven of the ten most polarized Conservative victories date from the 1920s or earlier, while the three most recent Conservative victories fill the other 'top ten' places. In 1970 and 1979 the Conservatives won almost exactly twice as many seats in England as in Scotland and Wales, and in 1983 they won more than twice as many. Even so, the extent of the polarization in 1983 was still much less marked than in the Conservative victories of 1892, 1922 and 1923.

The broad Anglo-Celtic division, of course, ignores the marked differences in the partisan commitments of the English regions that were revealed in Table II. Despite the overall English commitment to the Conservatives it is only the south of England that over the years has been consistently 'Tory': the midlands have been ambivalent, while the north of England (at least in the last forty years) has been predominantly 'radical'. Thus in addition to the Anglo-Celtic division of Great Britain there is a clear partisan division between 'Tory' south Britain (that is, the south and midlands of England) on the one hand, and 'radical' north Britain (that is, the north of England, Scotland and Wales) on the other.

In which elections has this polarization between 'north Britain' and 'south Britain' been most pronounced? Table IV provides a measure of this, showing for elections since 1868 an 'index of north Britain – south Britain electoral polarization' based on the winning party's share of seats in the south and midlands of England on the one hand, and the north of England, Scotland and Wales on the other. The elections are ranked according to the extent of the contrast between the winning party's performance in these two parts of Great Britain.

As with the Anglo-Celtic index, it is Conservative victories that have produced the greatest polarization between north Britain and south Britain, and 'left' party victories that have produced the least marked polarization. Conservative victories occupy five of the top six (most polarized) places in the rankings, while Liberal and Labour victories ocupy four of the bottom five (least polarized) places. That said, each party's victories are distributed rather more evenly among the rankings in Table IV than is the case in Table III.

With both parties the pattern has been for the degree of polarization between north and south Britain to increase over the last forty years. In each of its post-war victories Labour has won around two-thirds of the seats in north Britain (though it did rather better than this in 1966), but in south

TABLE IV

North-South Polarization in Regional Success of Winning Party: General Elections 1868-1983[a]

Winning	Party	Winning Party's Share of Seats: South Britain[b]	North Britain[c]	Index of Polarization (Larger share as a proportion of smaller share)	Rank Order: Con Wins	Lib/ Lab Wins	All
1979	Con	71.9	31.7	2.27	1		1
1983	Con	81.5	37.4	2.10	2		2
1922	Con	72.0	36.5	1.97	3		3=
1910J	Lib	33.8	66.7	1.97		1	3=
1970	Con	66.6	33.9	1.96	4		5
1923	Con	51.9	21.1	1.92	5		6
1910D	Lib	34.8	64.3	1.85		2	7
1974F	Lab	35.5	64.9	1.83		3	8
1892	Con	63.9	35.3	1.81	6		9
1964	Lab	38.4	67.5	1.76		4	10
1886	Con	81.5	47.3	1.72	7		11
1974O	Lab	39.2	66.8	1.70		5	12
1959	Con	69.2	42.0	1.65	8		13
1929	Lab	37.6	61.4	1.63		6	14
1880	Lib	50.9	79.5	1.56		7	15
1895	Con	81.8	52.7	1.55	9		16
1924	Con	80.6	52.1	1.53	10		17
1966	Lab	47.7	72.6	1.52		8	18
1951	Con	60.1	39.1	1.51	11		19
1955	Con	63.1	42.7	1.48	12		20
1874	Con	65.7	44.3	1.47	13		21
1950	Lab	42.9	61.1	1.44		9	22
1900	Con	77.5	54.3	1.43	14		23
1935[d]	Con	80.6	57.8	1.39	15		24
1885	Lib	52.0	68.6	1.32		10	25
1868	Lib	53.5	65.7	1.23		11	26
1931[d]	Con	92.0	77.3	1.19	16		27
1945	Lab	60.2	68.1	1.13		12	28
1906	Lib	67.5	74.8	1.11		13	29

a Excludes 1918 election which defies analysis on conventional party lines.

b That is, south and midlands of England.

c That is, Scotland, Wales and north of England.

d Includes National Liberals and National Labour.

Britain Labour's share of the seats has declined from 60% in 1945 to not much more than a third in 1974. It is this variation in Labour's fortunes in the south and midlands of England, rather than in the country as a whole, that has been the key to the size of the party's post-war victories and to the extent of the polarization between north and south in those victories.

The pattern of increased polarization between north and south Britain is even more pronounced in the case of Conservative victories. From 1931, when the Conservatives did very well in both parts of Britain, successive Conservative wins have produced increasingly polarized results, and their victories of 1970, 1979 and 1983 fill three of the top five places in the rankings.

The particular extent of the polarization between north and south Britain in 1979 and 1983 was the product of exceptionally poor Conservative performances in north Britain, rather than unusually good performances in the south. Only in 1923 did the Conservatives do worse in north Britain (in a 'winning election') than they did in 1979, and their improved performance in north Britain in 1983 still left them with a smaller share of northern seats than in most of their wins.

The extent of the increase in the polarization that has taken place over the last fifty years is emphasised by the contrast between the Conservative 'landslides' of 1983 and 1935. In both elections the Conservatives won a similarly large share of the total seats in Great Britain(8) – 69% in 1935 and 63% in 1983 (whereas in the 'super-landslide' of 1931 they won almost 90%). In south Britain the Conservatives did slightly better in 1983 than in 1935, but in north Britain they managed little more than a third of the seats in 1983 compared with almost 60% in 1935.

Taking Tables III and IV together, three particular points emerge. First, whether north and south are defined as 'England and Celtic Britain' or as 'south Britain and north Britain', Conservative victories have tended to produce a greater degree of polarization than have Labour and Liberal victories. Second, the most recent Conservative victories have produced a greater degree of polarization than have other elections in the post- war period, though in the case of the Anglo-Celtic divide the 1970, 1979 and 1983 elections have not exceeded the very high levels of polarization that prevailed in the Conservative victories of 1892 to 1923. Third, in 1979 and 1983 Britain was more conspicuously 'two-nations' if the two are defined as north Britain and south Britain rather than as England and Celtic Britain. Indeed, over the post-war period as a whole, the north Britain – south Britain divide has replaced the Anglo-Celtic divide as the most conspicuous regional electoral cleavage within Great Britain.

III. English Dominance

To what extent has an English pattern of partisan commitment been reproduced in the United Kingdom as a whole? Even allowing for the over-representation of Scotland and Wales in the House of Commons, England still accounts for some four- fifths of the seats. Thus a party that managed to win just under two-thirds of the English seats would have an overall majority in the Commons even if it did not win any seats at all outside England. Equally, even in the unlikely event of a party winning every seat in Scotland, Wales and Northern Ireland, it would still need to win over a third of the English seats to achieve an overall majority.

In 1979 and 1983 the Conservatives won a majority of the seats in the south and midlands of England, but not in Scotland, Wales, Northern Ireland, or the north of England. Just how unusual is this pattern? How often since 1868 have 'radical' Wales and Scotland been deprived of a Labour or Liberal government by Conservative success in England, and which of the nations, and which of the English regions have most often given a majority of seats to the party than won the election?

Taking the 1868-1983 period as a whole, England has not imposed its particular pattern of party dominance on the rest of the United Kingdom. The regional patterns of partisan commitment that were described in Section One have qualified each other to a remarkable degree. Within England the persistent Conservative success in the south has been qualified by the success of the 'left' party in the north of England and (at least in the post-1945 period as a whole) the midlands. In combination, these regional patterns have produced in England as a whole a less marked pattern of party dominance than is found in the other nations of the United Kingdom. In its turn, this relative English ambivalence has *qualified*, but not *nullified*, the more pronounced partisan commitments of the other component nations.

In the United Kingdom as a whole, there has been a relatively even pattern of party competition since the 1860s. The Conservatives have won sixteen of the twenty-nine general elections since 1868, twelve of the twenty-two since 1900, and six of the twelve since 1945. There is, however, a clear distinction between the inter-war period on the one hand, and the pre-1914 and post-1945 periods on the other. Between the wars, in what was essentially a transitional period of Liberal decline and Labour emergence, the Conservatives won large overall majorities in the Commons in four elections, achieved a simple majority in a fifth, and even denied Labour an overall majority in its one inter-war victory of 1929.

Before 1914 and since 1945, in contrast, the distinct national patterns of party dominance combined to produce a broadly even party balance of power in the United Kingdom as a whole. In the 1868-1914 period the Liberals won six elections to the Conservatives' five, and each party was in office for almost exactly the same amount of time. Similarly, since 1945 Labour and the Conservatives have each won six elections, and have held office for similar amounts of time.

Thus over the longer term the United Kingdom pattern of party competition has *not* been a coy of the English pattern, and the political complexion of United Kingdom governments has *not* simply been a reflection of the English partisan commitment. The point is emphasised by Table V, which shows the frequency with which each region has 'backed the winner', in the sense of giving a majority of its seats to the party that won the election.

TABLE V

'Backing the Winner' and 'Being in Office': Regional Support for the Winning Party 1868-1983[a]

	Elections When Region Backed Winning Party[b] (N)		Region's Time 'In Office' (as % of the period)[c]	
	1868-1983 (29)	1945-83 (12)	1868-1983	1945-83
England	24	9	88.7	89.5
North	22	6	79.1	45.7
Midlands	24	10	80.9	78.9
South	19	7	74.8	65.8
Scotland	19[d]	8[d]	72.2	65.8
Wales	13	6	48.7	45.3
Ireland[e]	11	4	33.9	34.2

a Excludes 1918 election which defies analysis on conventional party lines.

b That is, the region gave more seats to the party that won the election than to the main opposition party.

c That is, the region had more MPs on the government side of the House than on the opposition side.

d Includes 1951 when Labour and Conservatives won the same number of seats in Scotland.

e Northern Ireland since 1922

The significance of being 'on the winning side', of course should not be over-stated. Unless a region gives all of its seats to the losing parties it makes some contribution to the government's overall representation in Parliament. Nevertheless, there is a clear distinction between a region giving only a minority of seats to the party that wins the election, and actually 'backing the winner' by giving it a majority of seats. The distinction is not *constitutionally* significant, but can be significant in other practical respects.

The likelihood of a particular region 'backing the winner' in successive elections will be determined partly by the region's size, and partly by the flexibility of its commitment. The more populous the region, the greater the contribution that it will make to the overall result of the election, and thus the greater the likelihood that it will be on the winning side. At the same time, however, a region with a relatively small electorate could be on the winning side in every election if it was sufficiently flexible in its partisan commitment to transfer its support to the party that was nationally ascendant at a particular time. Given uniform partisan flexibility, every region could give a majority of its seats to the winning party in each election, and each government could claim to have been endorsed by every region of the country.

It can be seen from Table V that each region has had some success in backing the winner, but no region has been consistently successful in this respect. There has been a clear contrast between the Scots and English on the one hand, and the Welsh and Irish on the other. The consistent Irish support for their home-grown parties since 1885 has meant that they have been on the winning side only in the case of the Liberal wins of 1868 and 1880, and the nine Conservative wins between 1922 and 1970 when the Conservative-Ulster Unionist alliance was in operation. Consistent Welsh suppport for the 'left' party has meant that Wales has been on the winning side in only half the elections since 1868.

In contrast, Scotland has been on the winning side in two-thirds of the elections over the period as a whole, and England in four-fifths. Indeed, since 1900 the Scots have done almost as well as the English in this respect. Although the English and Scots have exhibited distinct partisan commitments, and have backed 'their' party in each of its election victories, their loyalties have been sufficiently flexible for them to give a majority of seats to the 'other' party in half of its victories. Although the Scots have failed to back the Conservatives in their last four victories, and did not do so in any of the Conservative victories in the nineteenth century, they did give a majority of seats to the Conservatives in six of their eight victories between 1900 and 1955.

England's ideological flexibility was most apparent at the beginning of the period, and England contributed a majority of seats to the winning party in all nine elections between 1868 and 1906. Since then England has backed the loser in five of the twenty elections – January and December 1910, 1950, 1964 and February 1974. It is not surprising that England, with the bulk of the sats in the Commons, has been on the winning side in most elections. What is perhaps surprising is that England has failed to back the winner (or *determine* the winner) in as many as a quarter of the elections this century.

Thus the political complexion of United Kingdom governments has not simply been a reflection of the English commitment. Still less, over the longer term, have United Kingdom governments been a reflection of the commitment of the south of England. Of the three English regions, the north and midlands have been sufficiently flexible to give a majority of seats to the winning party in (respectively) three-quarters and four-fifths of the elections since 1868. In contrast, the south of England's commitment to the Conservatives (broken only by the Liberal and Labour landslides of 1868, 1906 and 1945) has meant that it has been on the winning side less often than the other two more ambivalent English regions.

In effect the south of England's support for the Conservatives has been sufficiently *consistent* to prevent a majority of southern seats going to the left party in its winning years, but has not been sufficiently *intense* to overcome on every occasion the left party's strength in north Britain. Thus, far from the south of England determining the political complexion of United Kingdom governments, the south has had to live with governments to which it has contributed only a minority of its seats in almost half of the elections since 1945, and in more than half since 1964.

IV. CONCLUSIONS

The answers to the questions that were raised at the beginning of this paper can now be summarised.

1. While the images of 'Tory' England, 'radical' Scotland and Wales, and 'idiosyncratic' Ireland have been broadly accurate over the longer term, there are distinct limits to their validity. In particular, Scotland's radical image needs to be qualified in that Wales throughout the period, and the north and midlands of England since 1945, have averaged a larger proportion of 'left' party seats than has Scotland. While Labour has done appreciably better in Scotland since 1959 than it did between 1922 and 1955, it has still not matched the level of success achieved by the Liberals in Scotland in the nineteenth century.

2. Although throughout the period Great Britain has indeed consisted, in partisan terms, of 'two nations' (with Ireland as a separate 'third nation'), the extent of the polarization between Tory south and radical north has varied according to just how 'north' and 'south' are defined. The polarization between England and Celtic Britain was more pronounced in the period of Liberal-Conservative competition before 1914 than it has been in the modern period of Labour-Conservative competition, while the reverse is true of polarization between 'south

Britain' (that is, the south and midlands of England) and 'north Britain' (Scotland, Wales and the north of England). There was a greater degree of polarization between south Britain and north Britain in 1979 and 1983 than in any other general election since 1868.

3. An English pattern of Conservative party dominance has not been reproduced in the United Kingdom as a whole. The Scots have given a majority of seats to the party that won the election almost as often as have the English, and the supposedly dominant south of England has been on the losing side in more general elections than have the north, midlands or Scotland. Rather than reflecting an English pattern of Conservative dominance, the United Kingdom as a whole has had its own distinctive pattern of relatively even two-party competition.

It has to be emphasised again that the regional patterns that have been described in this paper are based upon the *seats won* by the parties, and thus reflect regional representation in Parliament rather than the regional distribution of electoral support. The British first-past-the-post electoral system distorts the relationship between votes and seats by giving the dominant party in any particular region a larger share of seats than it has 'earned' in votes. It thereby magnifies regional partisan differences. The regional contrasts would be reduced somewhat if the established electoral system was replaced by one that achieved a more precise relationship between the parties' votes and seats. The tendency for the established electoral system to exaggerate regional differences, however, is generally under-stated in debates about the desirability of electoral reform.

A major consequence of the regional patterns that have emerged from the established electoral system over the years is that successive British governments have been regionally unrepresentative to a quite marked degree. The government side of the House has been disproportionately 'southern' whenever the Conservatives have been in office, and disproportionately 'northern' when Labour or the Liberals have been in power. In none of the elections since 1868 has a party won a majority of seats in all six of the regions of the United Kingdom that have formed the basis of this analysis, and not since 1880 has a party achieved a majority of seats in each of the four nations. Even if idiosyncratic Ireland is excluded from consideration, only twice (1906 and 1945) has a party won a majority of seats in all five regions of Great Britain, and only on six occasions (all of them Liberal or Labour victories) has a party won a majority of seats in the three nations of Great Britain.

Within this general pattern of narrowly-based governments, however, the 1979 and 1983 elections produced a government with a particularly limited regional base. Since 1979 the Conservative benches have been even more disporportionately 'southern' than usual. For the first time since 1892 the winning party achieved a majority of seats in just two of the six regions of the United Kingdom. Not since at least the 1850s have the south and midlands of England (as in the 1979 and 1983 Parliaments) accounted for three quarters of the MPs on the Government side of the House. In all, less than 10% of Conservative MPs elected in 1979 and 1983 came from Scottish and Welsh seats (the smallest proportion since the 1920s), and only 16% came from the north of England (the smallest proportion for a hundred years or more).

Constitutionally, of course, a government's position is unaffected by the extent of its regional support: a government holds office because it is supported by a majority of MPs, regardless of their regional origins. Politically, however, it is clearly undesirable for a government to have an exceptionally narrow regional base. Despite some temptation for a Government to woo those areas in which it is electorally weak, a region that has a disporportionately small number of MPs on the government side of the House is likely to be at a disadvantage in the Parliamentary battle for government favours. Certainly, regional justice is not seen to be done if a government does not have a broad regional base. This matters more today than in the nineteenth century, or even before 1945, because the electorate is now more sensitive to regional disparities. For the most part regional inequalities are regarded as undesirable, and the government of the day is seen as having an obligation to do something about them. The notion of 'regional mandates' is popular, and the government's legitimacy is questioned by groups that are dominant in particular regions.[9]

Given these considerations a regionally dominant party that today finds itself persistently in opposition might be tempted to 'play Parnell' and, like the Irish Nationalists in the 1880s, seek to emphasise its role as a champion of regional interests by obstructing the proceedings of Parliament. It might even be tempted to follow Sinn Fein's tactics after the 1918 election of boycotting Westminster and meeting as a regional assembly.

Clearly, the parallels between the 1980s and the 1880s, or 1918, cannot be taken too far. Among other things, the Irish Nationalists and Sinn Fein had specific and limited legislative objectives; they did not seek to present themselves as an alternative government of the United Kingdom; they held a bigger proportion of Irish seats than Labour holds of Scottish, Welsh or north of England seats; Parliamentary procedures in the nineteenth century gave greater opportunities for disruption than they do today. What is more, regional MPs who pursue such tactics ostracise themselves from the established processes of Parliamentary Opposition, and may undermine their party's credibility as a responsible United Kingdom force.

Nevertheless, as a means of drawing attention to regional discontents, the Parnell and 1918 Sinn Fein options might be attractive to a frustrated Opposition which feels that although it has lost two successive elections, it is nevertheless the true voice of large areas of the United Kingdom. Certainly the prospect of a Labour-dominated Scotland within a Conservative-dominated United Kingdom, prompted Scottish Labour MPs to consider such tactics even in the last Parliament.

Regardless of whether Opposition MPs choose to adopt the Parnell or Sinn Fein options, or simply use the more conventional processes of inter-party debate to highlight the exceptional narrowness of the Conservative Government's regional base, the current situation has clear dangers for the established system of Parliamentary representation. The possibility is that, in the face of an extended period of office by an exceptionally narrowly based government, whole regions will become disillusioned with their continued under-reprepresentation on the Government benches and will prefer direct action to Parliamentary action as the means of bringing pressure to bear on Ministers.

In the past the significance of the regionally unrepresentative nature of British governments has been reduced by the fact that our governments have tended to be relatively short-lived. As has been shown elsewhere,[(10)] the parties alternate in office much more regularly in Britain than in other European and Anglo-American countries. In Britain over the last 150 years there has been a change of party or parties in office every four years on average;[(11)] there have been only four governments that have survived for more than eight years;[(12)] and 'Conservative' and 'non-Conservative' governments have held office for broadly equal amounts of time.

Thus over the years each region has seen 'its' party in office at fairly frequent intervals. It is true that Wales and the north of England were 'in opposition' (in the sense of having more MPs on the Opposition side of the House than on the government side) for the whole of the 1951-64 period of Conservative government, but that was an atypical experience. For the most part, since at least 1868 each region of Great Britain has alternated regularly between being 'in office' and being 'in opposition'.

It remains to be seen whether this pattern will continue in the immediate future. There are three main possible scenarios. The next general election might return a revived Labour Party to office with a regional pattern of support similar to that of the 1960s, thereby giving Scotland, Wales and the north of England 'their turn' in having a majorityof their MPs on the Government side of the House. Alternatively, the established pattern of regional partisanship might not survive the strains to which it has been subjected in recent years. It is at least possible that the SDP-Liberal Alliance will threaten Conservative dominance in the south, and Labour dominance in north Britain, while the nationalist parties remain in the wings as other potential threats to Labour's current strength in Scotland and Wales. If the mould of regional party dominance is indeed broken in the 1980s and 1990s, and Britain experiences a succession of hung

Parliaments as a result, a coalition might emerge that will be broadly based regionally as well as ideologically.

A third distinct possibility, however, is that the Conservatives are currently launched upon an extended period in office, that a third successive victory will confirm them in office into the 1990s, with government benches that are at least as disproportionately southern as in the present Parliament. It should be realised that for the Conservatives to win a further general election with a majority of seats only in the southern half of England would be an unprecedented development. In their other long spells in ofice, in the 1950s, 1930s and at the turn of the century, the Conservative benches were much more regionally representative than in the 1979 and 1983 Parliaments. Certainly, Scotland returned a majority of Conservative MPs in 1900, 1924, 1931, 1935 and 1955 (and tied with Labour in 1951), and over the last hundred years Scotland has had the experience of being 'on the losing side' for no more than one Parliament at a time. In the context of the increased regional awareness of recent years, an extended period of office for a Conservative Government that holds only a minority of seats in Scotland, Wales and the north of England might well impose greater regional strains upon the political system than it has experienced since the Irish troubles of the 1880s.

References

* An earlier version of this paper appeared as *The Anglo-Celtic Partisan Divide,* Strathclyde Papers on Government and Politics, No.16, University of Strathclyde, 1983. I am grateful to William Miller, Jeremy Moon, Campbell Sharman and Alex Smith for their comments on the earlier draft.

1. *The Scotsman* (leading article) 11 June 1983.

2. *Glasgow Herald* (leading article) 11 June 1983.

3. For the details of party classifications, and a comment upon the problems involved in party labelling, see F.W.S. Craig *British Parliamentary Election Results 1832-1885,* London 1977, pp.xv and 622.

4. That is, 1951 when Labour and the Conservatives won the same number of seats in Scotland.

5. By a 'winning election' is meant (here and throughout the chapter) an election in which the party in question won more seats than any other party – even though it may not have won an absolute majority of seats, may not have received most votes, and may not have formed the Government. Thus the Conservatives' won the 1923 election, in the

sense that they achieved more seats than any other party, though Baldwin's government was in a minority in the new Parliament and was soon defeated by a combination of Liberal and Labour MPs.

6. See D.E. Butler and A. Sloman *British Political Facts 1900-79*, London, 1980, p.145 for the regional results of 1900-79. Regional results for earlier elections calculated from F.W.S. Craig, *British Parliamentary Election Results 1832-85*, London 1977, and F.W.S. Craig, *British Parliamentary Election Results 1885-1918*, London, 1974.

7. The definition of these regions and their boundaries is that used by Butler and Sloman *British Political Facts*, p.212. That is, the north is composed of the 'old' counties of Cheshire, Lancashire, Yorkshire and the counties to their north; the midlands consists of Hereford, Worcestershire, Warwickshire, Northants, Lincolnshire, Notts, Leicestershire, Staffordshire, Salop and Derbyshire; the south consists of the rest of England (including London).

8. That is, excluding Northern Ireland and, in 1934, all the University seats.

9. See R.M. Punnett 'Regional Partisanship and the Legitimacy of British Governments' *Parliamentary Affairs*, 1984 pp.140-58, for a fuller discussion of these points.

10. R.M. Punnett 'Must Governments Lose? British Inter- Party Competition in Comparative Perspective', *Parliamentary Affairs*, 1981, pp.392-408.

11. For these calculations a 'change of government' is confined to a change in the party composition of the government : changes of Prime Minister within the same party are ignored.

12. That is, the Unionist Government 1895-1905, the Liberal Government 1905-15, the National Government 1931-40 and the Conservative Government 1951-64.

Scottish central bureaucracy since the Scottish Office was founded a century ago. Over so long a period, we can only use relatively 'gross' indices, and those in a pretty 'broad brush' treatment, for we are limited to data that are available in a roughly consistent form over the whole of that time. In the section after that (Section III), we come to the era of attempted retrenchment in the 1970s and 1980s to date, and compare in finer detail the way in which the Scottish Office and its component departments changed over that time, in relation to developments in 'Whitehall'. A few concluding remarks are offered in the final section.

II THE BACKGROUND : LONG-TERM GROWTH OF SCOTTISH CENTRAL BUREAUCRACY(3)

When the Scottish Office was created in 1885, it did not move into uninhabited territory. Apart from UK or GB-wide departments with offices in Scotland, a traditional administrative apparatus already existed, in the shape of the Lord Advocate's Department, the Exchequer Office, the offices surrounding the law courts, the Registrar-General's Office, the Department of the Registers, and the National Gallery of Scotland (in possession of an annuity dating from the Treaty of Union). This group of small departments, which we can loosely term the 'eighteenth-century' bureaucracy of Scotland, has remained more or less separate from the Scottish Office to this day; and since 1885 this group has been augmented by the National Library of Scotland, the National Museum of Antiquities and the Scottish Record Office (formerly part of the Department of the Registers). We shall call this set of departments the 'independents'.

Beside this group, there were a number of autonomous central boards and departments for Scotland (not necessarily *in* Scotland), many of them paralleling Irish agencies, which have subsequently become part of the Scottish Office. In 1885 there were the Fishery Board (DAFS), the Lunacy Commission (SHHD), the Board of Supervision for the Relief of the Poor and for Public Health (SHHD), the Prison Commissioners (SHHD) and the Scotch Education Department (SED); to which were later added the Crofters Commission (DAFS), the Local Government Board (SDD), the Board of Agriculture (DAFS), the Highlands and Islands Medical Service Board (SHHD) and the Scottish Board of Health (SHHD). We shall call this group of departments, which existed as distinct departments or boards in or for Scotland prior to their incorporation in the Scottish Office, the 'kernel' departments. In 1885 the Scotch Education Department (with its HQ in London and its schools inspectorate in Edinburgh) dwarfed the rest of this group in terms of the budget which it controlled; and the Prison Commissioners dwarfed the rest in terms of numbers of staff employed.

TABLE 1

Indicators of Growth in Scottish Central Bureaucracy, 1885-6 to 1984-5.

Year	'Kernal' Scottish Office Departments[1] Total staff[4]	Gross budget estimates as % UK civil	% of budget on staff salaries	'Independent' Scottish Departments[2] Total staff	Gross Budget estimates as % UK civil	Gross Budget estimates as % Sc. kernal	% of budget on staff salaries
1885-6	583	2.6	11.5	n.a.[3]	0.74	28.9	64.6
1895-6	660	3.8	9.7	n.a.[3]	0.63	16.6	70.0
1905-6	790	4.0	7.5	n.a.[3]	0.35	9.1	86.0
1915-6	1290	3.2	7.7	n.a.[3]	0.21	6.7	84.2
1925-6	1989	3.4	5.8	n.a.[3]	0.09	2.9	86.5
1935-6	2332	4.4	3.6	838	0.06	1.4	85.5
1945-6	3653	3.9	4.5	1005	0.05	1.4	86.9
1955-6	5449	4.2	3.0	1018	0.02	0.6	83.5
1965-6	7422	6.4	2.4	1457	0.03	0.5	80.9
1975-6	9869	7.3	2.3	2537	0.03	0.5	74.1
1984-5	10583	6.7	2.1	3487	0.06	1.0	55.2

Source: Budget Estimates.

[1] Those department now forming part of the Scottish Office which existed prior to their incorporation in SO as distinct departments/boards in or for Scotland (Prison Commissioners/Prisons Dept., Lunacy Commission/General Board of Control, Fishery Board, Local Government Board, Scottish Education Department, Board of Agriculture, Scottish Board of Health, Highlands and Islands Medical Service Board, Crofters Commission (1886-1911), Board of Supervision for the Relief of the Poor and for Public Health).

[2] Those departments not forming part of the SO but existing as distinct departments, boards in or for Scotland (QLTR/KLTR, Lord Lyon Office, Exchequer Office, Lord Advocate's Dept., Procurator Fiscal Service, Pensions Appeal Tribunals, Scottish Law Commission, Crown Office, Signet Office, Clerk of Admission of Notaries, Scottish Courts Administration, General Register Office, Department of the Registers, National Gallery Scotland, National Library of Scotland, National Museum of Antiquities, Scottish Record Office).

[3] Figures for staff numbers employed in the Procurator Fiscal Service and Sheriff Courts Service were not published in budget estimates for these years.

[4] This includes prison staff and staff of the state mental hospital, but excludes staff of the Common Health Services Agency (covering ambulance, blood transfusion and other health services supplied on a Scotland-wide basis); the staff involved are paid directly from SHHD's budget and the numbers involved are considerable (over 4,500 in 1984/5), but staff numbers are not detailed in budget estimates throughout the period taken here.

The development of the two groups of departments, the 'independent' departments and the 'kernel' departments later absorbed into the Scottish Office, has taken rather different paths over the century.

Let us take the Scottish Office group to start with. Several commentators on the growth of the Scottish Office[(4)] have emphasized the way that it has eaten into what was formerly the administrative territory of UK or GB ministries, while yielding very little of its own territory. Such a process of transfer of functions, taking place over a long period, might be expected to show up in an increased 'share of the cake' going to the Scottish departments (whatever kind of 'cake' it may be), and a rise in the place of the Scottish Office in the 'pecking order' of central government departments. The same supposition might be drawn from the oft-noted progression of the Scottish Secretary from the status of a minister sometimes excluded from a Cabinet seat to one assured of a Cabinet seat from 1892 and of senior Cabinet rank from 1926[(5)].

This expectation is certainly confirmed in relation to spending power. If we express the budgetary estimates of the 'kernel' Scottish Office departments as a proportion of the UK Civil Estimates (that is, excluding military spending, which presents complications owing to open-ended military estimates during war periods), there is a noticeable and steady growth in the proportion over the century up to the mid-1970s. In 1885 this group of departments accounted for less than 3 per cent of UK gross estimated (civil) spending, and though there were falls in both World Wars, the proportion had more than doubled by the 1960s and nearly trebled by the mid-1970s. The proportion fell back somewhat in 1984-5; but there is no doubt that the Scottish Office 'share of the cake', in terms of spending, has grown significantly over the past century.

If we turn from budget to the other major measurable resource of government bureaucracies – manpower – the picture is rather different. Numbers of staff in the 'kernel' departments certainly grew steadily for most of the century – in fact, they doubled approximately every twenty years from 1885 to 1975, describing a 'natural growth' curve of remarkable elegance until the late 1970s, when numbers flattened out and began to fall back a little. But if we express the numbers as a proportion of total UK civil servants, as best we can, the Scottish Office departments' share of the cake show a less steady expansion. There is no consistent run of comparable figures for total UK civil servants from 1885 to date, so the comparison can only be rough-and-ready. But from what figures are available, it would appear that, up until World War II, the Scottish Office was running to keep still, in the sense that staff growth in the Scottish Office kernel departments no more than kept pace with the general growth in numbers of civil servants in the UK. Their staff comprised roughly 0.6 per cent of the UK total in the 1890s, and this proportion did not rise (and even fell) until the 1960s, rising to approximately 1 per cent in 1984-5.[(6)] Now a rise of 0.4 per cent on rough-

FIGURE 1 GROWTH TRAJECTORIES

Numbers of Staff in 5 Selected Staff Groups 1885 - 1983 /4

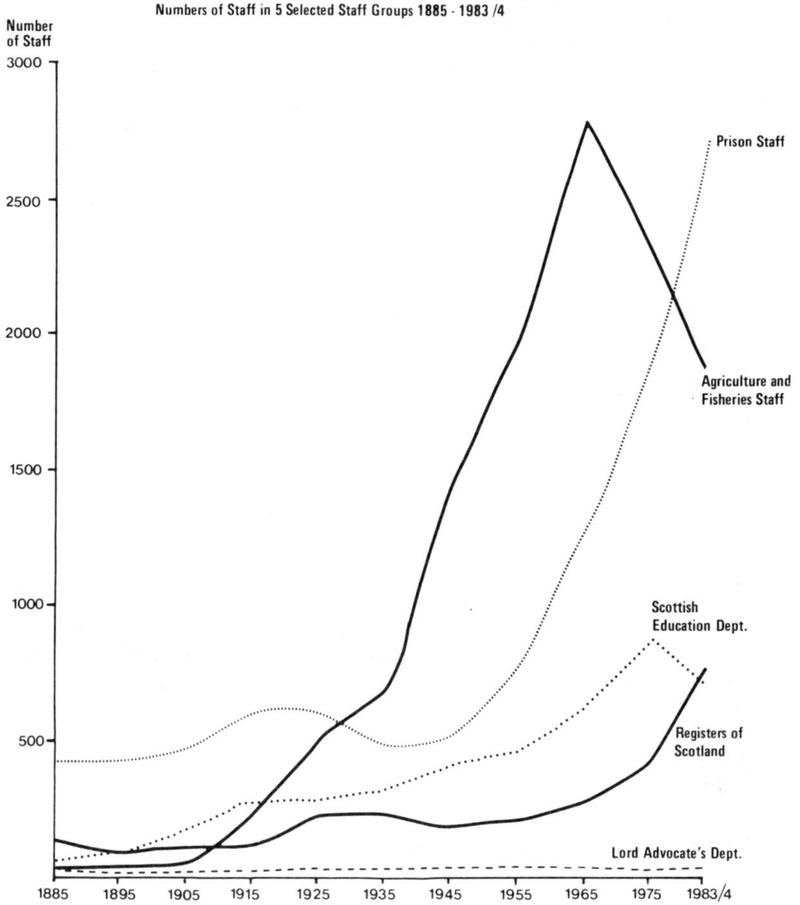

Number of Staff

3000
2500
2000
1500
1000
500

Prison Staff
Agriculture and Fisheries Staff
Scottish Education Dept.
Registers of Scotland
Lord Advocate's Dept.

1885 1895 1905 1915 1925 1935 1945 1955 1965 1975 1983/4

Source. Budget Estimates and Scottish Office Staff Returns

and-ready figures of this type is not exactly a difference that you can measure with a foot-rule. We conclude that any acceleration of staff growth in the Scottish Office kernel departments, in relation to the UK civil service as a whole, appears to be very slight; to the extent that it has taken place at all, it is a phenomenon only of recent years, not of the century as a whole.

Take these two histories together (spending and staff numbers), and it is clear that the Scottish Office departments nowadays utilize their budgets on things other than paying bureaucrats, compared with their early days. They have increasingly adopted a 'money-moving' style of operation, spending money on grants and contracts, rather than themselves employing staff to carry out operations directly. In 1885, the kernel Scottish Office departments collectively spent over 11 per cent of their gross budget on staff salaries; that figure fell fairly steadily over the subsequent century, to about 2 per cent in 1984-5. this, however, does not make the Scottish Office distinctive in its pattern of development: it reflects an overall UK trend towards 'chequebook government'.

While all the kernel Scottish Office departments have grown in staff and spending over the century, in the aggregate and individually, that growth has by no means been uniform among the component departments, with each retaining its original share of the overall expansion. Markedly differential growth has occurred, as can be seen for staff numbers in five selected units (three 'kernel', two 'independent') in Figure 1, and the same is true of spending. Take, for example, the two dominant elements among the kernel departments in 1885: the prisons administration and the SED. Prisons accounted for over threequarters of the staff numbers in this group of departments in 1885 and nearly 15 per cent of spending: by 1984/5, prison staff were just a quarter of the whole, and spending on prisons about 1 per cent. For SED the picture is less clear-cut. Its share of the spending of the group rose from 65 per cent in 1885 to 91 per cent in 1905, but then fell to below 50 per cent by 1945. Subsequently, the development of block grants to local authorities took the bulk of the direct funding of local authority schools out of SED's hands, leaving it, by 1984/5, with about 4 per cent of the spending of the Scottish Office group of departments. Similarly, SED staff numbers rose from 10 per cent of the group total in 1885 to 22 per cent in 1915, but fell back subsequently, ending up as a rather smaller proportion than it had been in 1885. Plainly, there is no simple 'proportional growth law' in operation here, to explain the increase in size of these bureaucracies.

Turning to the other group of Scottish departments, which we called the 'independents': over the bulk of the period since 1885, the picture (in contrast to that for the 'kernel' departments) is one of stagnation and relative decline, in both budget and staff numbers, whether measured against the rest of the Scottish departments or against the UK total. As can be seen from Table 1, some degree of recovery took place for this group between 1975-6 and 1984-5, with a 37 per cent increase in staff and an increase in budgetary shares. (The growth points in the group were the Department of the Registers, where a new land registration system meant a doubling in staff numbers, and the Procurator Fiscal service and Scottish Courts Administration, reflecting increased emphasis on 'law and order' activities since 1979.) But in the overall period between 1885 and 1984-5, the budgets of the 'independent' group as a proportion of UK gross (civil) estimates fell from 0.74 per cent to 0.06 per cent; and as against the budgets of the 'kernel' Scottish Office departments, fell from nearly 29 per cent to 1 per cent. There is no complete record of staff numbers for the 'independent' group until the 1930s (Procurators Fiscal and Sheriff Court staffs were not enumerated in the regular civil service style until then); but what can be said with certainty is that in 1885 the staff of the 'independent' Scottish departments together amounted to at least half of the total of the kernel Scottish Office departments (and in all probability considerably more than half), whereas by 1984/5 the proportion had fallen to less than a third. Figure 1 includes an example of a department from this group (the Lord Advocate's Department) which has not grown at all in absolute staff numbers over a century.

As Table 1 shows, the 'independent' Scottish departments seem to be coming late to the shift towards a 'money-moving' style of operation. Although the percentage drop in the proportion of gross budget spent on officials' salaries between 1885 and 1984 is exactly the same for the 'kernel' Scottish Office departments and the independents, most of the change to a more money-moving style for the latter group comes in a sudden drop between 1975-6 and 1984-5 rather than in a steady change over decades; indeed the proportion of budget spent on staff salaries for the 'independent' group actually rose in the first twenty years from 1885 and remained above the 1885 level until the 1980s. The overall proiportion of budget devoted to official salaries by the independents remains much higher than that of the Scottish Office kernel departments, at over 50 per cent as against about 2 per cent.

How are we to explain this difference between the two groups of Scottish bureaucracies over the century since 1885? Perhaps it is that the 'policy space' inhabited by the eighteenth-century bureaucracy did not include much room to expand. That is, agencies reflecting an eighteenth-century philosophy of government administration – that the implementation of public policy is a matter of enacting laws, and providing an apparatus of law courts to enforce them (plus a few bits of machinery for enumerating the population, registering land titles, guarding the nation's art treasures and so on) – have fewer inbuilt tendencies to expand (even as the nation grows larger or richer), than agencies reflecting the nineteenth-century administrative philosophy of providing a specialized bureaucracy for the self-conscious implementation of each succeeding policy.

Alternatively, perhaps the eighteenth-century bureaucracy was simply 'crowded out' of what might otherwise have been its natural expansion space by competition from the nineteenth-century group.[7] (Hanham describes the opposition put up by successive Lords Advocate to proposals for creating a Scottish Office in the nineteenth century, and the eclipse of the Lord Advocate as a political potentate by the Scottish Secretary after the latter office had been created.) Or perhaps the different trajectories of growth displayed by the two groups of agencies reflects a general 'sclerosis' which is sometimes alleged to affect long-established organizations.[8] Yet again, perhaps departments which spend the bulk of their budgets on the employment of bureaucrats (as is certainly the case with the Scottish independents) are inherently less likely to display growth over a long period, simply because growth is in staff, an unpopular form, than are 'money-moving' bureaucracies, which (we might suppose) attract a constituency of hopefuls and dependents who have reason to welcome expansion in budgets, without attracting the attention of the manpower-savers. These are but speculations, which cannot be examined further here.

III THE FOREGROUND : THE SCOTTISH OFFICE IN AN ERA OF RETRENCHMENT

From that very sketchy background of the development of the Scottish Office over a century, we move to the foreground of history. After nearly a century of bureaucratic growth, the Scottish Office from the middle 1970s faced a climate of sustained attempts at retrenchment in the public sector. Accordingly, in this section, we examine what changes have taken place in the Scottish Office in relation to the attempts to cut public spending since 1976 (from now on, we look at the Scottish Office only, excluding the 'independent' group). Has its place in the Whitehall 'pecking order' changed, and, to the extent that any real cuts have taken place, how have those cuts been accommodated in its own structure?

The Scottish Office in the Whitehall 'Pecking Order'

Kellas and Madgwick[9] remark that the Scottish Office (together with the Welsh Office) is 'still obviously quite low in the Whitehall pecking order'; but they do not specify *how* low, nor whether it is moving up or down or constant, nor what 'league tables' they have in mind. Nor do they say how retrenchment might change the Scottish Office's ranking, although a climate of financial pressure is a good test of a bureaucratic pecking order, since marginal or peripheral departments are likely to suffer disproportionately from cutbacks as their fundamentally more powerful bureaucratic brethren seek to protect their own positions. A lightweight department may find itself classed as an administrative luxury, liable to suffer extra cuts during 'hard times'. Indeed, if the Scottish Office *were* that kind of lightweight, it might be in a particularly vulnerable position, since it shares bureaucratic 'turf' in many of its areas of operation with other UK or

GB departments.

Table 2 shows the position of the Scottish Office in four leagues over the past fifteen years or so, in relation to nine other major government departments which have been in existence in more or less unchanged form since 1971 (DHSS, DOE, MoD, Home Office, Welsh Office, MAFF, DES, Treasury, Department of Employment). The leagues are: share of total civil service staff, share of top staff (that is, posts graded at Under-Secretary level or above), share of total spending and the ranking of departmental Ministers in the Cabinet. Ranking the Scottish Office against a set of constant comparators screens out some of the short-term variations in its rank relative to *all* departments which derive from the waxing and waning of the less stable Whitehall empires such as the DTI group.

TABLE 2

Scottish Office Ranking relative to 9 other major Government Departments (1971-83)

Year	Cabinet	'Top' staff	Total staff	Gross actual spending
	Ranking			
1971	7	n.a.[1]	7	5
1972	7	5	7	4
1973	7	4	7	4
1974	7	4	7	4
1975	8	4	7	4
1976	7	4	7	4
1977	5	4	7	4
1978	5	4	7	4
1979	5	4	7	4
1980	7	4	7	4
1981	7	4	7	4
1982	7	4	7	4
1983	6	4	7	n.a.[2]

1 No common grading structure for 'top' staff before 1972.

2 Appropriation Accounts for 1983-4 not yet available at time of writing.

In fact, the Scottish Office's ranking in the Whitehall pecking order for these four leagues is not particularly low, nor has it fallen back during 'hard times'. Its position in three of the leagues is relatively stable: the ranking of the Scottish Secretary in the Cabinet is slightly more volatile, but no more so than that of many of the major departmental ministers. The department's position is high and stable in the league tables for top staff numbers ('brass') and for gross expenditure; at number four in both of those leagues, it comes immediately behind the 'big three' bureaucratic giants in Whitehall (i.e. MoD, DHSS and DOE). Its place in the pecking order does not alter significantly in these leagues as between the period of overall government spending and staff growth in 1971-6 and the period of attempts at retrenchment from 1976 to 1984. It has held its position during hard times.

Another aspect of pecking order, but one which does not quite so readily lend itself to 'league tabling' after the manner of Table 2, is that of the social exclusivity of senior officials – their 'top drawer rating', as it were. On this factor, Scottish Office bosses (i.e. Permanent Secretaries and the heads of the six departments) do stand out as a group from the bosses of the thirty or so other major UK government departments over the period 1971 to 1984, in that noticeably fewer of the Scottish Office bosses came from a 'top-drawer' secondary education, as can be seen from Table 3. A minority of them attended private fee-paying schools as against a majority of the other UK departmental bosses; none of them attended either Clarendon schools (the nine most exclusive public schools in England) or their Scottish equivalents (which we took to be Gordonstoun, Fettes, Glenalmond, Strathallan and Merchiston Castle) as against a substantial minority of the other departmental heads. The proportion of those with an Oxbridge (undergraduate) university education is also much smaller among Scottish Office bosses than among other departmental bosses (but that conventional index of social status is perhaps ambiguous in this case, given that about half of Scottish Office bosses have a Scottish university background). Nor is there much sign of these characteristics changing over the past fifteen years, for either group.

How much should be built on this is doubtful. Scottish Office bosses do seem as a group to come from less exclusive social backgrounds than other major UK departmental bosses in general and in that sense might perhaps count as 'quite low in the Whitehall pecking order'. On the other hand, Scottish Office bosses as a group are not quite proletarian bureaucrats *a la* Lenin; like most elites in Britain, they are as a group 'male, middle-aged and middle-class' and disproportionately drawn from the higher-status academies rather than the general run of local authority schools. Moreover, their relative isolation from the old-boy-network of Oxbridge and Britain's top private schools has not apparently kept down the Scottish Office's position in the pecking orders shown in Table 3.

Structural Changes

Apart from considerations of 'pecking order', how far has the structure of the Scottish Office changed in an era of retrenchment, and in what

TABLE 3

Social Exclusivity : Scottish Office and other bosses, 1971-84

Scottish Office Permanent Secretaries and Departmental Heads compared to Permanent Secretaries and Departmental Heads of the 33 biggest Central Goverment Departments[1]: Educational Background of those appointed between 1971 and 1984.

	Scottish Office 'bosses' %	Bosses of other departments %
Secondary Schooling:		
Private fee-paying schools[2]	35.3	56.1
Non-fee-paying schools	53.0	36.4
University (undergraduate degree):		
Oxbridge	47.1[3]	65.4
Scottish universities	53.0	4.7

[1] This covers all major UK government departments, but excludes small registry offices, art galleries and museums etc. (i.e. small departments analogous to the Scottish 'independents').

[2] 'Private fee-paying schools' here means independent and Headmasters' Conference schools as listed in *Whitaker's Almanac*.

[3] Scottish Office figure sums to more than 100 per cent because some Scottish Office bosses did undergraduate degrees at Oxbridge as well as at Scottish universities.

directions? We will briefly consider the effect of retrenchment on the Scottish Office in terms of five broad aspects of bureaucratic structure, namely

- specialists-to-generalists ratio
- Chiefs-to-Indians ratio
- ratio of 'core' to 'peripheral' operations
- blue-collar to white-collar ratio
- departmental shares of the cake *within* the Scottish Office

(a) Specialists-to-generalists ratio. Our earlier study showed the Scottish Office departments to be significantly different from other British government departments in terms of extent of specialism – as measured by a higher proportion of staff employed in special departmental grades and in professional, technological and scientific grades, as against general administrative grades. We attributed this characteristic to a 'small country' or *multum in parvo* effect. We concluded that it reflected the administrative implications of delivering a similar standard of public services to a population which is small in relation to that of England and Wales or of the UK as a whole, in that it meant a *relatively* large number of discrete specialisms were required.

If that interpretation was correct, the *multum in parvo* effect should persist during retrenchment. Indeed, if the specialist-intensiveness of the Scottish Office departments does indeed reflect the irreducible minimum of central administrative specialists who are needed to deliver a complex range of modern public services, even in a small country, we would expect that the proportion of such specialists would tend if anything to *rise* as absolute staff numbers fall during a period of cutbacks. This expectation appears to be confirmed, in that the degree of relative specialism of the Scottish Office departments in the sense described above did increase a little from the mid-1970s to 1984: the proportion of 'specialists' in that sense to total staff (including prison staff) rose from just under 40 per cent in 1975 to nearly 50 per cent in 1984.

(b) Chiefs-to-Indians ratio. Another distinctive feature of the Scottish Office as a department which was revealed by our earlier study was a high proportion of staff in 'top' grades (i.e. Under-Secretary grade and above) and 'middle' grades (grades equivalent to Assistant Secretary to HEO inclusive), as against central government departments in general. To some extent, this characteristic, too, may reflect a 'small country' or *multum in parvo* effect (even a small ship needs a captain and officers) and also – perhaps more importantly – from the nature of the Scottish Office as a fairly 'policy-heavy' department working for Ministers who are 400 miles away for most of the time and who are obliged to take an interest in matters relating to Scottish affairs which go well beyond their formal administrative responsibilities. If this is a correct interpretation, we would expect this characteristic top- and middle-heaviness to persist during retrenchment, as with 'specialists', and we would be surprised to see proportionately heavier cuts in the upper as against the lower ranks.

Indeed, as applied to the 'specialists', we might expect the proportion of higher-paid staff to drift *upwards* in such circumstances. Those on the bureaucratic shop-floor or 'coal-face' often complain that it is they who suffer disproportionately from cutbacks, as against the middle and upper ranks. Policies relying on no (or limited) replacement of staff who leave to do the job of reducing staff numbers (instead of deliberately dismissing staff) often take their heaviest toll in the lower ranks, where natural turnover tends to be somewhat higher, and exceptions are almost invariably made to such policies in respect of the topmost posts.[10]

In general, some such effect does seem to have been at work in the Scottish Office. Excluding prison staff (who have been explicitly protected from civil service manpower cuts since 1979) and the staff of the state hospital at Carstairs, the proportion of Scottish Office staff in the 'middle' ranks (in the sense described above) rose a little between 1975 and 1983 from 32 per cent to 35 per cent, and those at the bottom (i.e. on grades equivalent to EO and below) fell back from 67 to 65 per cent of the total. The effect is very marked in DAFS and SED, where the proportion of 'middle' to 'bottom' staff changed by 5 per cent or more over this period, and it is less sharp but still noticeable for SHHD and Central Services. SDD tends to pull the overall average change down, because of its assumption of responsibility for managing ancient monument sites in Scotland from PSA in 1978, which brought in a large number of lower-graded staff. We will return to the position of the individual departments shortly.

In some ways, this overall tendency to increasing middle- heaviness may represent the 'rational bureaucratic' response to cuts (i.e. if you can't increase your absolute staff numbers, hire proportionately more staff in higher grades if you can). Moreover, it may be easier to follow such a pattern of cutbacks in the Scottish Office than in departments which have large numbers of individual clients to be served by counter staff in local branch offices, since the Scottish Office is in general centralized in Edinburgh. (By combining figures supplied in a House of Commons answer by Mr Hayhoe (HC Deb 31/10/83, c.186) with 1981 Scottish census data, it can be shown that staff numbers of other government departments operating in Scotland are much more closely correlated with population per hectare by local authority districts in Scotland ($r^2 = 0.78$) than are numbers of Scottish Office staff ($r^2 = 0.41$).)

(c) Ratio of 'Core' to 'Peripheral' Operations. It is sometimes said (for instance by Glennerster in Hood and Wright (1981), ch.8) that a climate of retrenchment will lead bureaucracies to attempt to protect what are deemed to be the core of their operations (for instance, full-time staff, headquarters apparatus) as against what may be deemed to be marginal or peripheral activities – grants or contracts to outsiders, trainees or part-timers, publicity and research, branch offices. If we follow the logic of that kind of argument, we might expect producer group pressures to lead to disproportionate cutbacks in payments to outside groups or institutions as against staff salary costs in a climate of retrenchment.

We noted in our earlier study that Scottish Office departments were significantly more 'money-moving' in their style of operation than the general run of Whitehall departments, in that they spent a smaller proportion of their budget on the salaries of their own staff and correspondingly more on other items such as grants and contracts – indeed, as was shown in Section II, this is a characteristic that the Scottish Office departments have shown in an increasingly marked degree over the past century (and Whitehall in general has been moving in this direction for at least forty years). If the argument about pressures for 'protecting the bureaucratic core' has any force in this case, we might expect to see that historical trend going into reverse from the early 1970s to the early 1980s.

Table 1 above showed no real evidence for any such effect, in that the proportion of budget set aside for staff salaries of the 'kernel' Scottish Office departments was in fact fractionally smaller in 1984-5 than in 1975-6. Nor does the picture change greatly if we look at actual expenditure rather than budgeted amounts, on a year-by-year basis rather than at intervals of a decade, and exclude prison and other staff who have been protected from cutbacks since 1979. The proportion of actual expenditure by the Scottish Office going on staff salaries of the six core departments (excluding prisons, state hospital, etc.) did not in general rise over the period 1971-2 to 1982-3; in fact, it fell slightly, from 1.7 per cent in 1971-2 to 1.3 per cent in 1982-3. So it does not appear as if the bureaucratic core of the Scottish Office has positively been protected by eating into the proportion of its budget passed out to other groups: the proportions have remained more or less constant, however calculated.

'Protecting the core', however, is not only or necessarily to be equated with the protecting of staff salary budgets as against other spending. A maxim sometimes applied to bureaucratic responses to pressures for retrenchment is that 'when money is short, information is vulnerable', meaning that agencies cut down on promotional and research activities in order to protect the 'core' of their operations.

To the extent that any such effect can be observed for the Scottish Office, it would take an extremely keen eye to detect it. The sums budgeted for public relations spending by or on behalf of the Scottish Office did indeed drift down slightly as a proportion of total Scottish Office estimates over the decade 1971-2 to 1982-3[(11)], but the change is relatively small and, since only a tiny fraction of the Scottish Office's spending is officially counted as going on 'information' in this sense (much less than 1 per cent of total spending), not much could anyway be released for the relief of the 'core' by savings on this item. The same in general applies to Whitehall as a whole.

The picture for research and development expenditure appears to be broadly the same, from what published figures are available.[(12)] That is, less than 1 per cent of Scottish Office expenditure goes into research and development as recorded in official statistics, and though R and D expenditure fell very slightly as a proportion of total Scottish Office spending between 1973/4 and 1981/2, pressure on other aspects of Scottish Office spending could hardly be stemmed by major cutbacks on this item alone: at most, it can only be a symbolic gesture.

One item of outside spending which *has* fallen noticeably as a proportion of total Scottish Office spending during retrenchment is rate support grant to local authorities. RSG (not including Housing Support Grant for this purpose) increased as a proportion of total Scottish Office spending during the 'years of expansion' in the early 1970s, rising from just under one-third in 1971-2 to over 40 per cent in 1975-6, but then fell back to just under one-third again in 1982-3. How clearly this fits the 'protecting the core' theory, however, is debatable, since (a) it might be argued that cutting local government spending was deliberate Cabinet policy at this time rather than discretionary behaviour by self-regarding bureaucrats; and (b) the proportion of Scottish Office spending 'lost' to local authorities over the period of retrenchment has not been appropriated in a correspondingly higher proportion of spending on the salaries of Scottish Office administrators: rather, it seems to have been redistributed into *other* types of 'outside' spending.

(d) Blue-collar to white-collar staff ratios. One feature which we might expect from a bureaucracy going through a period of retrenchment is the replacement of services once performed by specially-employed blue-collar staff (so-called 'industrial' civil servants) by services provided on contract by outside enterprises. Part of the general Whitehall story over recent decades (and certainly since 1976, as a response to pressures for staff cuts) has been a continuous thinning of the ranks of 'industrial' or blue-collar civil servants and their substitution by services provided on contract. In the middle 1950s there were four industrial civil servants for every six non-industrial or white-collar civil servants; by the 1980s, there was only one industrial civil servant for every five non- industrials.

However, the Scottish Office did not appear to follow this trend to anything like the same degree as its Whitehall counterparts in the 1970s and 1980s. Its blue-collar labour force in fact *increased* substantially between 1975 and 1983, both absolutely and as a proportion of total staff, as can be seen from Figure 2. As Figure 2 shows, the increase largely reflects the importation of responsibility for ancient monuments from PSA in 1978; but even since 1980, numbers of blue-collar staff have not been reduced by a greater proportion than numbers of white-collar staff. It is interesting to speculate on the reasons why the Scottish Office has not up to now followed the same path as its Whitehall counterparts in respect of laying off blue-collar workers. A possible explanation is that many industrial staff in the Scottish Office work (in fairly small numbers) in close conjunction with a variety of 'policy' or scientific establishments, or in tasks such as fishery patrols that are not readily 'contractable out' to private security enterprises, so that the only major substitution of contract work for the employment of blue-collar civil servants in the Scottish Office to date has been in the realm of contract cleaning.

FIGURE 2
'BLUE COLLAR' STAFF COMPONENT OF SCOTTISH OFFICE DEPARTMENTS
Cumulative percentage share of Scottish Office Total staff)

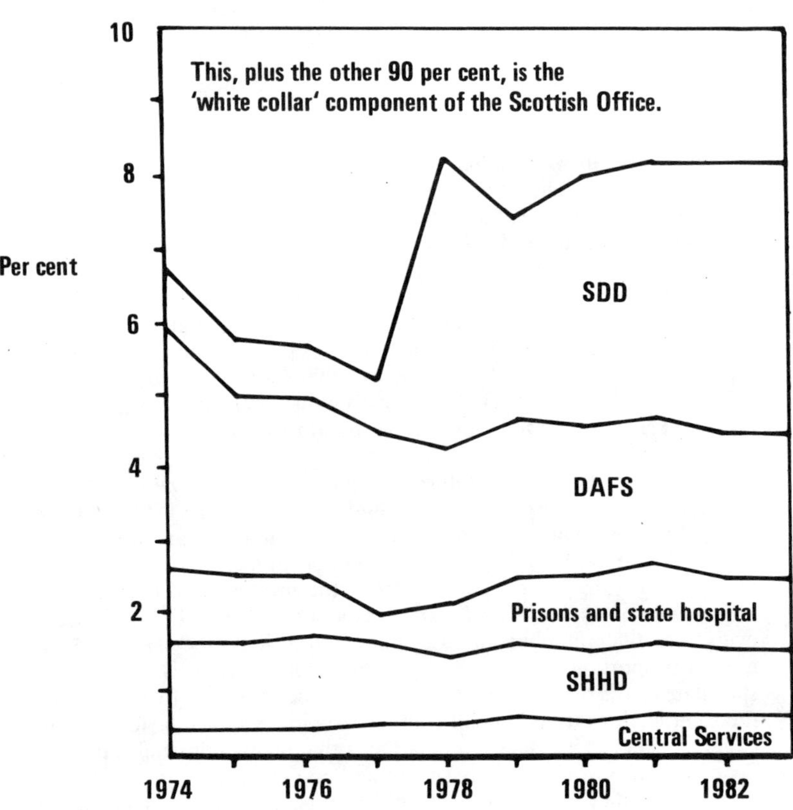

(e) Departmental Shares of the Cake – Proportionate Sacrifice or Selective Cuts? In contrast to the idea that public bureaucracies seek to protect their 'cores' by disproportionate cutbacks on types of activity deemed by producers to be 'peripheral' (a view for which not much evidence can readily be found in the case of the Scottish Office, with the possible exception of rate support grant) is the idea that cutbacks tend to be accommodated by strategies of 'equal misery'. It is often assumed that the reflex reaction of public bureaucracies towards pressures for retrenchment – at least in the first instance – is to distribute cutbacks equally among their component parts (cf. Hood and Wright, 1981). Each unit is called upon to produce the same percentage sacrifices in staff and budget, in order to avoid the delays and bitter in-fighting that may result from attempts to impose cuts in a selective fashion. So we might expect the long-term pattern of 'unbalanced growth' of the Scottish Office which was remarked upon in Section II (that is, the fact that its component parts have not grown in strict proportion to one another over the long term) to change into a pattern of strict proportionality during a period of retrenchment intended to keep the Scottish Office's total size constant or to make it smaller.

To a considerable extent, 'equal misery' in this sense does seem to have prevailed among the component departments of the Scottish Office during retrenchment. Figure 3 shows shares of total Scottish Office staff and budget for the individual departments over the period 1973-4 to 1982-3; and, as can be seen, none of the departments quite went from riches to rags relative to the others, or *vice-versa*.

Nevertheless, the picture is not one of *totally* 'equal misery'. The nearest to a riches-to-rags story is that of DAFS, whose share of total Scottish Office staff and spending slumped by 6 per cent and 3 per cent respectively over the period shown in Figure 3. The nearest to a rags-to-riches story is that of SHHD, whose share of Scottish Office spending rose by 7 per cent over the same period, while the share of total Scottish Office staff accounted for by SHHD's prison staff increased by over 5 per cent (though the staff of SHHD on its own fell back very slightly as a proportion of the Scottish Office total). No doubt if it were possible to disaggregate these figures into 'Home' and 'Health', it could be shown that SHHD's fortunes reflect in large part the decision of the Conservative government since 1979 to protect law and order activities from spending cutbacks, although the trend is observable before 1979, as can be seen from Figure 3.

Other changes in the intra-Scottish Office pecking order are harder to detect. However, three further points are perhaps worth noting about the behaviour of the separate departments within the Scottish Office group in response to pressures for retrenchment – differences in behaviour which can be masked by considering the Scottish Office as an aggregate unit. First, it is interesting to note that it is those departments which have slumped in the league *both* in staff and budget shares of the Scottish Office

FIGURE 3 CUMULATIVE PERCENTAGE SHARES OF TOTAL SCOTTISH OFFICE STAFF AND SPENDING

(a) SPENDING

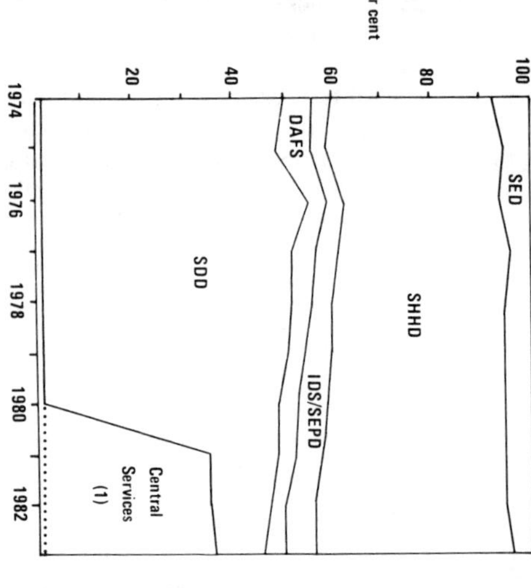

(b) STAFF

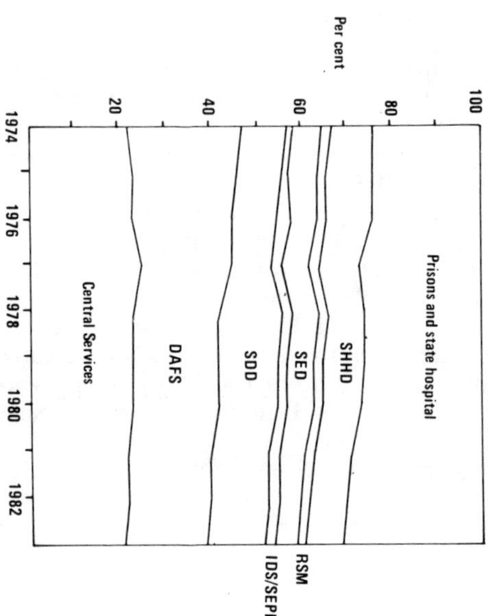

(1) The rise reflects assumption of responsibility for rate support grant by CS from SDD; the dotted line shows CS's share excusive of rate support grant

'cake' (that is, DAFS and SED) which have been the ones in which the greatest increase has taken place in the proportion of middle-grade to lower-grade staff. Changes in the proportion of staff by grade level for each of the six departments between 1975 and 1983 are summarized in Figure 4. Second, as is shown in Figure 5, DAFS and SED are also the only two departments in which the proportion of 'specialists' (in the sense described earlier) to general administrative staff increased over the five years 1979 to 1983. Clearly, it would be risky to build much on this, since the changes are slight and the picture is to some degree base-year-sensitive. But this perhaps points in the same direction as our earlier findings, in that it seems to be lower-grade, non-specialist staff who are exposed to proportionately greater cutbacks when the pressure is on for retrenchment.

Third, a point about blue-collar ratios. We noted earlier that the Scottish Office in aggregate has not apparently followed the general 'Whitehall' trend of cutting back disproportionately on blue-collar industrial staff as against white-collar staff as a means of getting overall staff numbers down. Does this reflect a common response among the four Scottish Office departments which employ blue-collar staff (CS, DAFS, SHHD, SDD)? To some extent, the aggregate Scottish Office figure reflects what has happened to SDD, which in 1978 imported large numbers of blue-collar staff from PSA in connection with its acquisition of responsibility for maintaining ancient monuments. But even if, to avoid that complication, we take the picture only from 1978 to 1983, there is little sign of change. Industrial staff did fall slightly in two of the departments involved (DAFS and SHHD) and rose slightly in the other two (CS and SDD). But the change was less than one and a half per cent in all cases, meaning that none of the four departments has vigorously pursued a retrenchment strategy of exposing blue-collar staff to disproportionate cuts. Figure 6 shows industrial staff in each department as a proportion of total Scottish Office industrial staff between 1974 and 1983. It seems possible that there is some general 'Scottish effect' (whether it be relating to the size of the country or to administrative culture) reflected in these relatively uniform responses, and not just an average concealing very different retrenchment strategies at departmental level.

IV SUMMARY AND CONCLUSION

Over the period considered here, the Scottish Office has moved from a background of nearly a century's growth to a foreground of nearly a decade's retrenchment. Pressure for curbing growth in the civil service had flattened the 'natural growth' curve described by the staff of the Scottish office from the 1880s to the mid-1970s. But the Scottish Office has apparently maintained its place in the pecking order relative to a group of other major departments on a number of indices. Perhaps this is because of its 'broad portfolio' of responsibilities, some of which have proved to be 'growth stocks' (prisons, law and order), to some degree offsetting losses in

FIGURE 4
RATIO OF 'MIDDLE' TO 'BOTTOM' GRADES
IN MAIN SCOTTISH OFFICE DEPARTMENTS

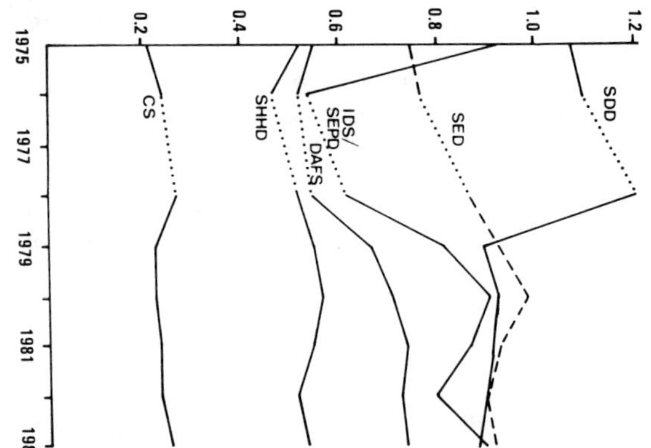

FIGURE 5
RATIO OF 'SPECIALISTS' TO ADMINISTRATION
GROUP OFFICIALS IN MAIN SCOTTISH OFFICE DEPARTMENTS

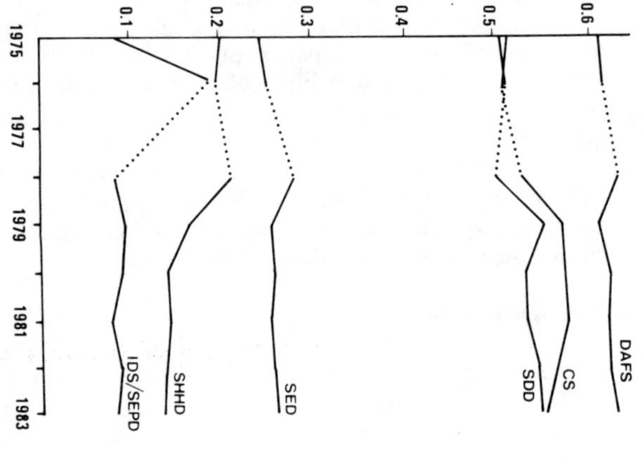

FIGURE 6
'BLUE COLLAR' STAFF COMPONENT
OF SCOTTISH OFFICE DEPARTMENTS
(Cumulative percentage share of Scottish
Office industrial staff)

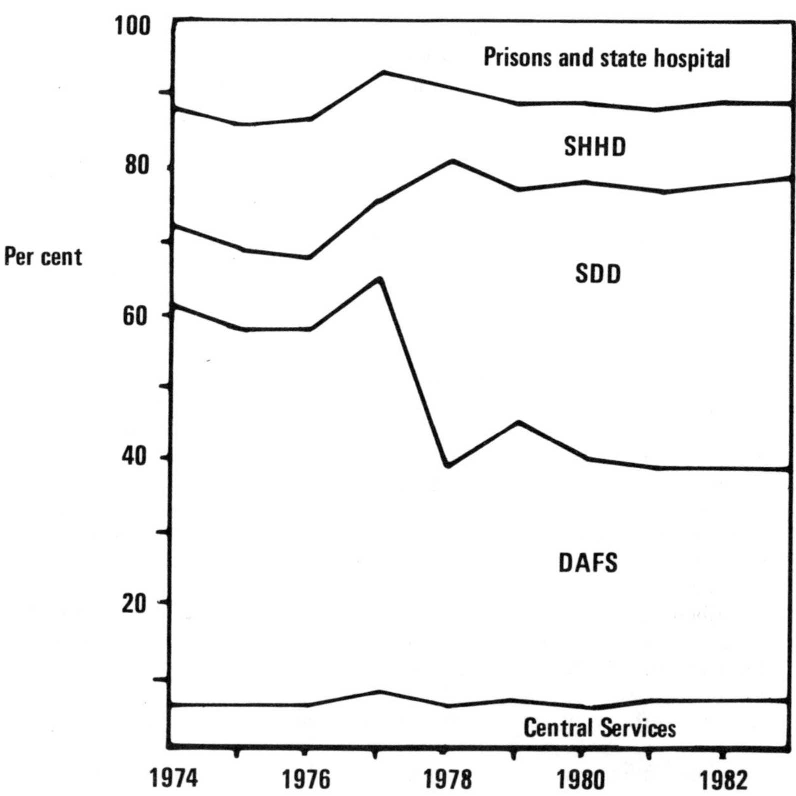

other sectors of the portfolio during a period of overall attempts at retrenchment. Over the past decade or so the Scottish Office has retained distinctive characteristics such as a high proportion of staff in top and middle ranks, a high proportion of staff in 'specialist' grades and a high proportion of spending devoted to items other than the salaries of its own staff; indeed, some of these features appear to have become somewhat more marked under pressures for retrenchment.

To some extent, 'equal misery' seems to have prevailed among the Scottish Office's component departments during a period of cutbacks, though the fortunes and behaviour of the individual departments have not been completely identical. In general, though, the evidence of the extent to which producer group pressures (i.e. pressures reflecting the interest and convenience of producers rather than consumers of public services) have dominated the response to retrenchment is somewhat mixed and in some cases effects are hard to see, given that bureaucratic structures change slowly. Much depends on how much significance one is willing to read into relatively small changes in percentage shares, and this is unavoidable. A week may be a long time in politics; a decade or so is not necessarily very long in the life of a bureaucracy.

Might the growth in numbers of Scottish Office bureaucrats have levelled off in time, even without retrenchment, as the department reached some kind of natural limit either of maximum politically controllable size for a heterogeneous and top-heavy department or of major Scottish-related functions easily appropriable from other central departments? We cannot say. It is a common enough observation that bureaucracies tend to develop rapidly in their early years, then level off into a more sedate pace of change and place increasing emphasis on protecting what they have as against finding new worlds to conquer (Dowas 1967,[13] goes so far as to propose this as a 'Law of Increasing Conservatism'). The Scottish Office, however, did not follow this pattern in exact or classical style – for instance, its staff numbers grew at a fairly constant, not a decreasing, rate for 90 years before levelling off, and its budgetary advances likewise continued over a very long period. Moreover, the fortunes of the Scottish 'independents', as described in Section II, seem to indicate that very long-established bureaucracies can grow vigorously late in their lives. We are thus doubtful if there are any infallible laws of bureaucratic development from which the future of the Scottish Office can be predicted.[14] The only thing that can be said with certainty about the future is that it hasn't happened yet.[15]

This inquiry has been restricted to the readily measurable and countable aspects of Scottish Office administration. In future work, we hope to do a little more in the same vein, in developing some comparisons between the Scottish departments and central government departments more generally, in terms of responses to pressures for retrenchment. But we would be the first to admit that the approach taken here has its limits, cannot easily get at the 'fine grain', and that many intangible or qualitative, but nevertheless important, aspects of bureaucratic change cannot be encompassed by it. Not all administrative analysis can be done 'by numbers', especially when the numbers are taken from 'unobtrusive' inquiry, as has been the case here. Even so, it is the only way of telling some parts of the story.

Notes and References

1. The term 'Scottish Office' is used here in the sense that it acquired after 1939, to denote the Scottish departments under the direct control of the Secretary of State (Royal Commission on Scottish Affairs Vol I *Memoranda Submitted to the Royal Commission by the Scottish Departments,* Edinburgh, HMSO 1953, p.65). The reseach on which this paper is based is funded by ESRC grant No. E00232018. We are grateful to HM Treasury and the Scottish Office for supplying us with some of the figures on which this analysis is based. We are also grateful to Bruno Frey, Keith Hartley, James Kellas, Charles Raab and two Scottish Office officials for comments on an earlier draft of this paper.

2. C.C. Hood, A. Dunsire and K.S. Thomson 'Comparing the Scottish Office with "Whitehall" : A Quantitative Approach' *British Journal of Political Science,* 1979, Vol 9, (pp.257- 80). C.C. Hood, and A. Dunsire, *Bureaumetrics,* Farnborough, Gower 1981, (pp.209-32).

3. This does not purport to be a general account of the history of the Scottish Office such as is given by Sir D. Milne, *The Scottish Office*, London, Allen and Unwin, 1957, or by J.G. Kellas, *Modern Scotland,* revised ed., London, Allen and Unwin 1979, (pp.88-113)

4. D. Milne *op.cit.* pp.19-20

5. J. Kellas *op.cit.* p.96

6. For this comparison, post office and telecommunications staff have been included with civil service staff throughout the period. Prior to World War II the figures used for comparison with the Scottish Office kernel departments' staff are Abramovitz and Eliasberg's figures for UK civil central government employment: M. Abramovitz and V.F. Eliasberg, *The Growth of Public Employment in Great Britain* Princeton, Princeton University Press 1957 (p.25, Table 1,and p.34, Table 2)

7. H.J. Hanham 'The Creation of the Scottish Office 1881-87' *Judicial Review* 1965 Vol 10 Part 3, (pp.243-4)

8. H. Kaufman, *Are Government Organizations Immortal?* Washington,

Brookings Institution 1976, (p.68)

9. J.G. Kellas and P. Madgwick 'Territorial Ministries: The Scottish and Welsh Offices' in P. Madgwick and R. Rose (eds) *The Territorial Dimension in United Kingdom Politics,* London, Macmillan 1982, (p.16)

10. C.C. Hood and M. Wright (eds.) *Big Government in Hard Times,* Oxford, Martin Robertson, 1981 (pp.208-217)

11. These figures are taken from tables which used to appear regularly in the Chief Secretary to the Treasury's Memorandum on the Supply Estimates, showing spending on information by major departments and also the sums budgeted by the Central Office of Information for information services to each department. The funding basis of the COI has now been changed, and comparable figures are not available for the most recent years.

12. These figures are based on summaries of departmental spending on research and development which appeared in *Economic Trends* July 1979, July 1980, August 1981, August 1982 and September 1983.

13. A. Downs, *Inside Bureaucracy*, New York, Wiley, 1967.

14. C. Pollitt, *Manipulating the Machine: Changing the Pattern of Ministerial Departments 1960-83*, London, Allen and Unwin, 1984, (pp.16-18)

15. S. Brittan 'The Future Hasn't Yet Happened' *Financial Times* 5.1.84

POLITICAL ECONOMY OF SCOTCH WHISKY

LYNNE F BAXTER
MANCHESTER BUSINESS SCHOOL
UNIVERSITY OF MANCHESTER

The next few years represent a critical period in the development of the Scotch Whisky Industry. The phenomenal post second World War growth in production and sales has now evened out. The industry has begun to shed labour, and D.C.L. has closed its plants in Glasgow and South Queensferry in mid-1984. The seemingly unassailable position of Scotch as the leading quality spirit has been challenged by 'white' ones such as vodka and rum. The company share has altered as well, with Distillers Company Limited, the giant which constitutes half the industry being eclipsed by Bells on the home market, and seriously challenged by Seagrams and Hiram Walker in the overseas ones. It will be interesting to see whether D.C.L., currently undergoing an organisational shake-up and change of leadership, is properly questioning its assumptions or merely contemplating its navel. It will also be interesting to see whether the tired old assumptions used by the majority of companies in their advertising campaigns, usually aimed at middle-aged tweed-bedecked ex-army types, will be phased out in favour of more upmarket images suitable for a wider target area. In the following article I shall examine the gap between advertising myth and corporate reality, and attempt to set some current issues in context.

Scotch Whisky is unique to Scotland. Because it is unique with a pleasing distinctive flavour – perhaps something to be proud of – it has long been used as a symbol of Scottishness, what makes Scots different from the rest. Scotch has been called variously the essence of Scotland, Scotland's life blood, the national drink (note how much mileage a well known soft drinks manufacturer has got out of being 'your other National Drink' – nobody questions what is number 1). Scots are well acquainted with the product, but are far from acquainted with the industry which gave the product such a high profile.

A quick glance through most colour supplements and one will soon pick up that Scotch Whisky advertising makes full use of other plainly recognisable symbols of Scottishness such as tartan, glens, deer, and quaint homely Scots expressions. Romantic, bellicose and masculine images abound. In addition, if one was to sift through a selection of the books that are available on Scotch, one would find the focus of the books firmly on the late 19th Century.

The reason for the books' attention to this era is that it was the time when, after the perfection of bottling and blending, Scotch became a consistent, marketable product for a wider market, and it was pushed very hard by some very colourful characters. Luckily for them, Prince Albert, Queen Victoria and Sir Walter Scott had made Scotland a fashionable place, and if one couldn't actually go there, one could capture the essence by drinking Scotch. However just because a symbol is recognisable, does not make it accurate, and if the widespread Scottish myth of Highland, kilted, warlike natives clashed with the urban, trousered, housetrained reality, then it is not difficult to imagine the huge discrepancy there is between the same symbols and reality now. When Scotch was drunk by kilted folk in glens, it was a very crude single malt produced by anyone on a small scale, not matured, and treated with far less reverence than single malt is today. With the obvious fiscal and commercial possibilities there, the ordinary man was progressively barred from distilling his own batch by legal restrictions on still size and grain tax. In the Lowlands, the Coffey continuous still (as opposed to the previous batch production still), and vatting and blending were perfected, and so by the second half of the century a consistent, quality, wide-appeal liquor was produced. The rise of whisky as a British, and then world drink was due to trousered urban folk, with the focus of power firmly in urban centres such as Perth, Edinburgh, Glasgow and London, not in Speyside or Islay. They were not much like 'craftsmen' or 'skilled in their art' but rather businessmen who made use of the convenient, easily recognisable images to emphasise the Scottishness and age of their product in their very successful marketing campaigns.

Tartanry and kailyard gave a comforting if false picture of the urban Scots past, but also helped create a sense of inferiority in the minds of the Scots urban dwellers and fostered ambiguous set of emotions in the English. They were attracted by the beauty of the scenery and spectacle of the kilt but also felt contempt for the one step removed savagery of it all. It is possible to draw links between those attitudes then and now, in the political sphere with the seventies' devolution referendum and in more general themes in the media.

The Scotch Whisky Industry in promoting its product has made use of the Scots myth. It has also created through this a new one of its own. Using advertising from the last century has meant that the real nature of the ownership and structure of the industry is not widely known. This has led to a complacency in the minds of both people and government, causing the former to be widely disturbed by D.C.L. redundancies; and the latter's laissez-faire attitude (except in matters of taxation). Non-intervention has seen the ownership of the industry polarize and now consist of large non-Scots companies for whom Scotch is just one product amongst many, and certainly not integral to their psyche, or their life blood, as it is supposed to be to Scotland.

The most successful era in terms of sales and production is the post World War Two era, which the myth and its perpetrators have masked. Information on this era and its most problematic phase – the seventies – is scant. The next section provides a brief account.

Sales and Production Since the Second World War

Since the Second World War, the growth of sales and value of whisky has escalated at an amazing rate; that this rate has reached a plateau in the late seventies is due to a bit of sanity creeping in.

More recent figures show the current falter in progress. The hiccups between 1974 and 1976 –

	Home Releases		Exports	
Calendar Year	Quantity in litres of pure alcohol	Per-centage of total	Quantity in litres of pure alcohol	Per-centage of total
1971	28,771,000	13.6	182,501,000	86.4
1972	32,653,000	15.5	178,411,000	84.5
1973	39,825,000	16.4	203,577,000	83.6
1974	45,075,000	16.5	227,336,000	83.5
1975	42,410,000	15.3	234,274,000	84.7
1976	48,438,000	16.9	238,303,000	83.1
1977	40,248,000	14.2	243,633,000	85.8
1978	48,812,000	15.1	274,073,000	84.9
1979	52,536,000	16.7	262,421,000	83.8
1980	50,159,000	16.7	249,917,000	83.3
1981	47,711,000	16.3	244,239,000	83.7
1982	44,751,000	15.1	251,277,000	84.9
1983	44,561,000	16.4	227,844,000	83.6

Source: Scotch Whisky Association 2

N.B. The above figures do not include shipments to the Channel Islands, where duty was paid there. In 1980 these shipments totalled 590,341 litres of pur alcohol.

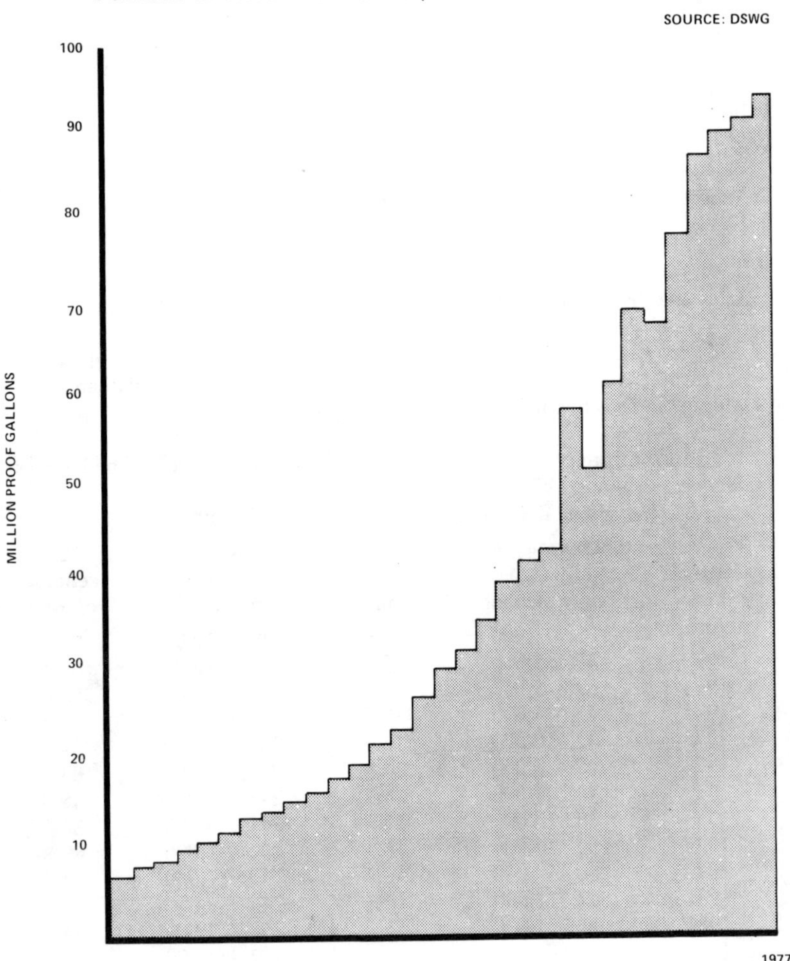
VOLUME OF WHISKY EXPORTS (MILLION PROOF GALLONS).
SOURCE: DSWG
MILLION PROOF GALLONS
100
90
80
70
60
50
40
30
20
10
1947
1977

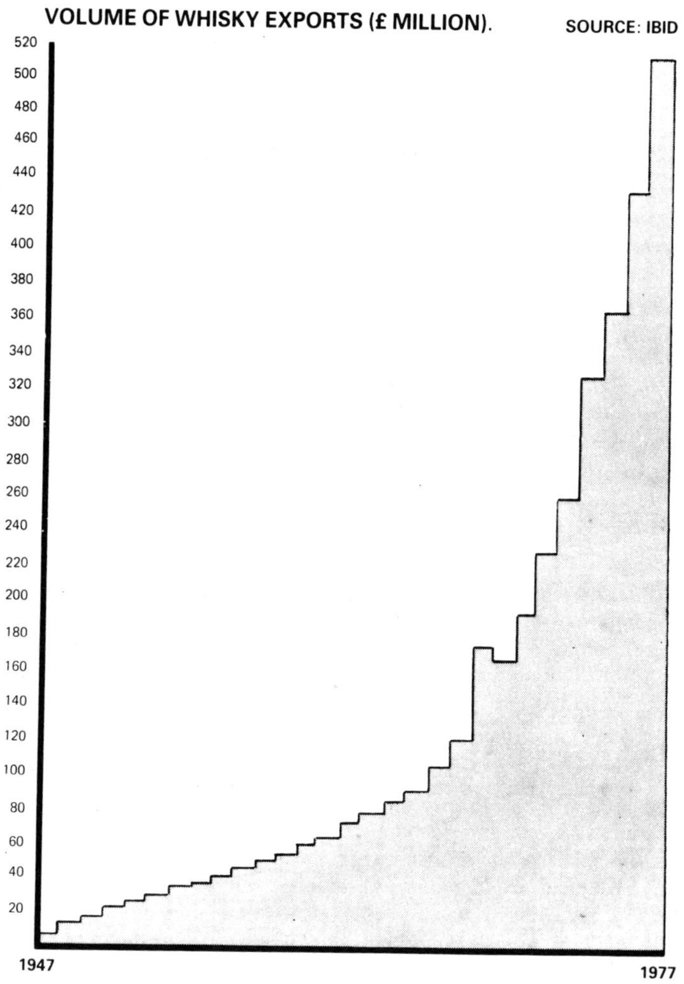
VOLUME OF WHISKY EXPORTS (£ MILLION).
SOURCE: IBID
520
500
480
460
440
420
400
380
360
340
320
300
280
260
240
220
200
180
160
140
120
100
80
60
40
20
1947
1977

and again the next years are quite unusual. The growth in the home market and its marginally greater percentage take-up at home vis-a-vis export up since the seventies is counter intuitive. A commonsense interpretation of Scotch would have been that the market at home is saturated and that the greatest possibility for expansion would be overseas.

The Scotch Whisky Industry can be said to have had three discernible phases in its history.

Stage	Title	Type of Production Unit	Company	Product/ Market
1 Pre 1860	'Cottage'	small malt distillery	none/ small	malt for local consumption in Scotland
2 1860-1925	'Company'	malt/grain distilleries	family	blends for Scotland and England
3 1925+	'Corporate'	as above in larger groupings	corporation/ multi-national	blends for world

The three stages have fairly arbitrary date parameters, but in the three eras, companies of the type described predominated, so although family Victorian capitalist-type companies were the norm, there still existed smaller units, and in the third era there are remainders from both previous phases.

Each progressive phase requires more capital than the previous one. As the stocks of malt grow, more money is tied up – for longer. By law whisky must be matured for three years as a basic minimum, but most companies work on nearer a six year budgetary cycle. The estimates tend to be on the generous side, so periodically there has been more malt than buyers. This has resulted in 'moth-balling', where distilleries are closed temporarily, and more recently cheaper than standard brands have been put on the market to get rid of indifferent quality malts which would not be worth maturing.

Only rarely have malt distilleries been sold as a result of a downswing in the economy or discrepancy between estimates and reality. Over-estimation is cyclical, say Moss and Hume. This can be seen from the following distilleries' statistics.

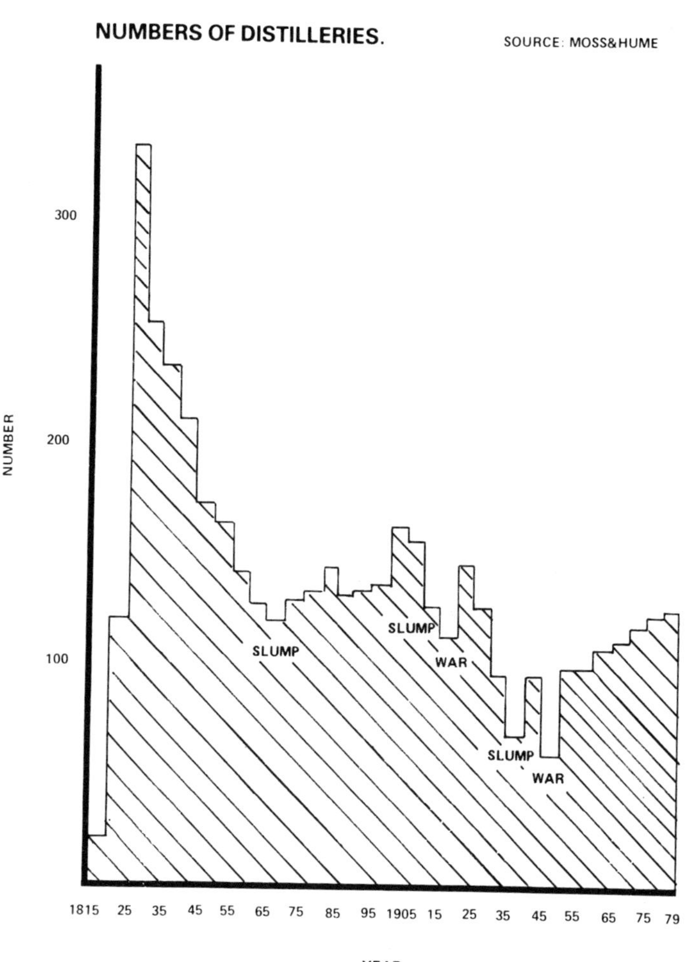
NUMBERS OF DISTILLERIES.
SOURCE: MOSS&HUME
NUMBER
300
200
100
SLUMP
SLUMP
WAR
SLUMP
WAR
1815
25
35
45
55
65
75
85
95
1905
15
25
35
45
55
65
75
79
YEAR

Seizure or Detection of Illegal Plants:–

1830	392
1835	764
1840	244
1845	148
1850	142
1855	73
1860	29
1865	9
1870	5
1875	2

The preceding table and graph show, in addition, how large number of 'illegal' stills were gradually stamped out and in their place grew a comparatively smaller number of licensed ones, which had to be of a certain capacity (20 gallons initially, in 1783), though subsequent increases were made rendering it practically impossible for a small farmer to supplement his income by this method. All was left strictly to the professionals.

Some companies such as J. & G. Grant have never progressed further than the basic unit malt distillery, Others are at the second stage, such as Arthur Bell's, though it is trying very hard to reach third phase 'status'. All this leads to a fairly complicated range of companies making up the current structure.

Because blends include many malts (the exact number is secret), and few companies own sufficient for their own needs, a complex network of swopping, selling and brokerage has grown up. Many of the smaller distilleries produce 'fillings' for other companies' blends. In order to obtain the various malts needed, it would be possible to buy straight from the desired distillery, exchange some of one's own malt for it, or buy it from brokers who are independent of any company. There exist historically important relationships between certain companies – an example would be Robertson & Baxter's special relationship with Highland Distillers, where Robertson & Baxter depend on this relationship heavily to fulfil commitments.

The result of these interactions is that the industry is galvanised to a greater degree than could be said if they did not have to interact with each other so often. However, it would be wrong to over-emphasise those relationships as there remain divisions in interests and policies which cause discordant notes occasionally (as over the Bulk Malt issue).

Tables I and II show the breakdown of companies by number of distillers, and distilleries by country of ownership. Table I shows clearly the dominance of D.C.L. In addition, it shows how sixteen companies own 88% of malt distilleries – control is in few hands. Of these sixteen, only five could be said to be Scottish companies mainly interested in Scotch Whisky (Highland, Bells, Wm. Grant, MacDonald and Martin, and Stanley P Morrison).

Table II further underlines the lack of Scottishness of the Scotch Whisky Industry. However, the figures would be more in Scotland's favour if D.C.L. was counted as Scots. Its status is very difficult to determine. Half of its turnover is in Scotch, half elsewhere (vodka, gin, et al); it is registered in Scotland, its Head Office is in Scotland, but it conducts much of its business in London.

Control rests with these few companies. They all act in the 'best' interests of their company or parent company. Particularly in the cases of the foreign multi-nationals, this is not always in the best interests of Scotch.

TABLE I

Company (country if not U.K.)	**Malt Distilleries**	**Grain Distilleries**
D.C.L.	45	5
Hiram Walker (Canada)	9	1
Seagrams (Canada)	9	
Invergordon (Hawker Siddely)	6	1
Highland Distillers	5	
A. Bell & Sons	5	
Whitbread	4	1
Grand Metropolitan	4	
Wm. Grant & Sons	3	1
Lonhro	3	
Allied Breweries	2	
Scottish & Newcastle	2	
Barton Brand (U.S.A.)	2	
McDonald & Martin Distillers Ltd.	2	
Stanley P. Morrison	2	
Speyside (half Swiss/U.S.)	1	1
total for above companies	104	10
single distilleries*	14	4
a grand TOTAL of	118	14

* These include Tomatin, Macallan-Glenlivet, North British Distillery (grain), Robertson & Baxter, Destilerias-y-Crienze (Spain), Omnia-Liumburg (Belgium), Pernod Richard (France), Publicker (U.S.A. – grain).

Source: J.K. Thompson 2

TABLE II

Distilleries by Ownership

Control	Malt Distilleries No.	Malt Distilleries Per Cent	Grain Distilleries No.	Grain Distilleries Per Cent
Scottish	26	22.0	3	21.4
* U.K.	67	56.8	7	50.0
Foreign	25	21.2	4	28.6
Total	118	100.0	14	100.0

* D.C.L. has been included in the U.K. figure. this has been hotly disputed by the D.C.L. themselves. The previous Chairman, J.R. Cater, tried to transfer power back from London over a number of years.

The Scotch Whisky Association is the trade body, but, in effect, it is no more than a glorified advertisement agency and statistics collator. It does not have much in the way of power over its members; if any action requires to be taken, it must be done with a consensus of all members. Thus, when a quality standard – say, no artificial colouring being added – is muted, if one company refuses to countenance it, the whole proposal has to be rejected. The S.W.A. does not even award quality prizes – a fairly innocuous activity introduced at exhibitions last century,which would, none-the-less, make good advertising. (And perhaps it would make certain companies more quality orientated than they have been of late.) In addition, not all companies belong to the Association.

The unions, too, are in a fairly weak position. The workforce is scattered over the country and the section which would be easiest to organise, namely those in the bottling halls, is composed largely of women, and moreover recently women in fear of losing their jobs, due to the adoption of new technology, and the depression. The fact is that the Scotch Whisky Industry ranked 70 out of 75 in a survey on manning levels (J K Thompson, 1979). It is a process industry, dispersed geographically in small units – hence there are grave difficulties in organising workers. Often in the past, when there has been a strike, it has been almost 'convenient for management', taking place in the slack season (summer) in bottling factories. With stocks high, the workforce going on strike stopped the management paying them 'for nothing'.

The Government and E.E.C.

The government will not legislate against practices widely accepted as damaging to Scotch's future. Instead it confines its activities to taxation.

TABLE III

Total tax as a proportion of retail price in main markets:

	April '78
U.K.	78%
Canada	66%
France	62%
Belgium	57%
Italy	51%
Australia	50%
Spain	50%
Germany	44%
Japan	41%
U.S.A.	38%
Venezuela	35%

Source: Distilling Sector Working Group (DSWG)

TABLE IV

Approximate amount of duty on a normal measure of five kinds of alcoholic beverage each containing approximately the same amount of alcohol.

	Present Duty per Measure
2oz. British Fortified Wine	7.84p
½ pint of Beer	7.15p
3½ oz. Imported Table Wine	10.62p
2 oz. Imported Sherry	9.22p
1 oz. Scotch Whisky	16.43p

Source: S.W.A. 1

Note – The duty-paid price per measure is subject to Value Added Tax at the current rate of 15%.

The preceding two tables illustrate how discrimination operates at an international level : Britain charges more tax on her own product than other countries do on a foreign one, and within Britain whisky pays a far higher tax than other drinks: note especially the 'foreign' drink of wine.

This duty was paid, up until recently (1982), after the whisky was made, but before it was sold. Now deferral of duty is in operation. With the often mentioned finance operating requirements as difficult as they are, the additional burden of duty before the produce is sold seemed unduly harsh.

However the Scotch Whisky Combine carried out examinations of the major corporations, such as Grand Metropolitan, Whitbread, D.C.L. et al and found that through various reliefs and deferrals the end tax payment was minimal. So when large whisky companies complain about their exorbitant tax bill, one should keep in mind that this would only be the case if they actually paid it, which they do not in full.

An E.E.C. decision in the seventies regarding dual pricing has seriously affected Scotch Whisky's reputation and market chances. Exporting Scotch Whisky to a foreign country has traditionally meant that one picks a local to be one's agent in the country, and sells the Scotch to him cheaper than the going rate, providing the local undertakes to promote (advertise) Scotch substantially. But the E.E.C. did not like two prices for the same product and banned it.

The options available to the companies were twofold: to have one price for both home and away markets and let 'parallel exports' run free, i.e., home-based wholesalers exporting abroad without needing to advertise, hence selling the whisky cheaper than the sole distributor, who was contractually obligated to advertise; or to withdraw a brand which does better abroad than at home from the home market and selling it only abroad. The latter option was temporarily taken up by D.C.L. for two of their brands, Johnnie Walker Red Label, and Haig 'Dimple'. These brands did sell well in the U.K., but the prospect of the erosion of sales abroad was felt to be more serious, so they were withdrawn. This resulted in D.C.L's overall showing in the U.K. market falling substantially. They brought out a new brand 'John Barr', which is said to be very similar to Red Label, but despite a massive promotion, sales were very disappointing. Recently this matter was resolved when 'Red Label' was re-introduced onto the home market.

Markets

Over the years an interesting structure has grown up in the carve-up of markets. (Certain companies produce for certain markets, see over). The British market standard sector is very difficult to penetrate with a new brand:

TABLE V

U.K. Whisky Market, Brand shares 1981:–

Bell's	24%
Teacher's (Allied)	15%
Famous Grouse (Highland Distillers)	8%
Haig (D.C.L.)	8%
Claymore (D.C.L.)	8%
White Horse (D.C.L.)	7%
Grant's Standfast	6%
Whyte & Mackay (Lonhro)	5%
Others	19%
	100%

Source: Mintel and trade estimates.

U.S. WHISKY MARKET.
SOURCE: DSWG
TOP SIX BRANDS BOTTLED IN SCOTLAND
OTHER BRANDS BOTTLED IN SCOTLAND
BULK (BOTTLED IN THE U.S.) SCOTCH
MILLION PROOF GALLONS
50
40
30
20
10
1964
65
667
67
68
69
70
71
72
73
74
75
76

Apart from 'Grouse' and 'Claymore', the rest of these brands have been around since the turn of the century. Bell's success has been largely since the Second World War, and especially in the seventies where the market share has risen from 13% in 1972 to the above figure (24%) in 1981. 'Grouse' and 'Claymore' are not really 'standard' brands. 'Grouse' is priced dearer than the standard brands, which makes its success all the more remarkable. The secret of its success is, in effect, no secret; it is a quality taste presented well. 'Claymore', it is agreed, is a *sub*standard brand, which was introduced to dispose of some surplus malts which were not worth retaining.

Hiram Walker's brand Ballantines and Seagram's 100 Pipers, Passport and even Chivas Regal are little known in Britain, but sell well on the export market. I have been unable to obtain breakdowns for Hiram Walker's or Seagram's Scotch Whisky market areas, but I do not think it unreasonable to transfer the proportions over from Seagram's overall market areas to their whisky operations.

D.C.L's more equal home/export ratio is largely due to history. Dewar's for example, were the first to export overseas. Tommy Dewar's travels set up links with the U.S. and colonies, which have meant that Dewar's was the brand most associated with whisky. (like biro for ballpoint pen and sellotape for sticky tape). Brand loyalty seems to rule supreme and it is terribly difficult to gain a slice in a new market. D.C.L. were the only corporation selling overseas for long enough. They have not made any attempt to buy foreign companies to augment their range of drinks to the extent Seagram's have. The companies they own abroad act for their British products, or tie in with the British market. Consequently it would be not wholly correct to describe them as transnational.

Another hindrance for Scotch Whisky reaching its fullest sales potential is the 'portfolio' method of sales, and the conflicting interests within the larger companies. Although Scotch in foreign markets is assigned to a sole distributor, that sole distributor is often sole distributor for other spirits and drinks – even whiskies. The larger the company's portfolio of drinks, the less likely it is going to devote special attention to Scotch. The same process occurs internally in large corporations. The goal is overall profits. One section will not press its own products, if it will affect another's.

Foreign Ownership and Bulk Exports

The following section will examine two major issues of the seventies which illustrate the lack of congruence between furthering some companies' profits and furthering Scotch Whisky as a product.

AREAS OF MARKET.

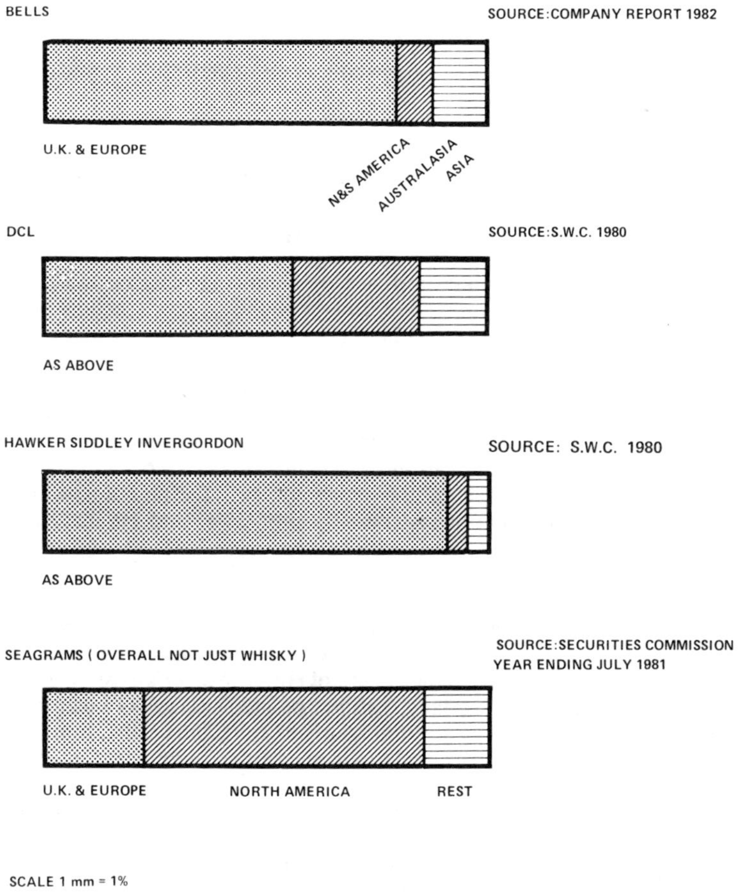

BELLS

SOURCE:COMPANY REPORT 1982

U.K. & EUROPE

N&S AMERICA

AUSTRALASIA

ASIA

DCL

SOURCE:S.W.C. 1980

AS ABOVE

HAWKER SIDDLEY INVERGORDON

SOURCE: S.W.C. 1980

AS ABOVE

SEAGRAMS (OVERALL NOT JUST WHISKY)

SOURCE:SECURITIES COMMISSION
YEAR ENDING JULY 1981

U.K. & EUROPE

NORTH AMERICA

REST

SCALE 1 mm = 1%

The first issue I will concentrate upon is the attempt by Hiram Walker-Gooderham and Worts Ltd., (to give them their full title), to take over Highland Distillers, which resulted in a Monopolies Commission Report. This would have meant a considerable increase in the concentration of control, especially non-Scottish control.

The second issue is that of Bulk Shipping, which incorporates two strands : Bulk Blend and Bulk Malt exporting. Each of the two practices give rise to differing results, as well as similar ones. They both, it is asserted, result in less employment in Scotland either now or in the future, and erode Scotch's 'quality' image.

Hiram Walker's take-over bid (it was the central company H W- G & W, not Hiram Walker, Scotland) was made in 1980, and contributed to the Bulk Shipping argument in that part of the reason for the strong feelings against the take-over was that Hiram Walker are among those who bulk export, and with the take-over, this may have increased. Many of the arguments concerning bulk exporting were set out in widely available print for the first time in the Report. It represents publicity certain sections of the trade would have rather done without.

It is ironic that Hiram Walker-Gooderham & Worts Ltd., was initially financed by Scottish money. As I have previously mentioned, their Scotch interest lie mainly with the export trade; they have no well-known home brand, whereas Highland Distillers with its hugely successful 'Famous Grouse' has a firm slice of the home market. Despite the taxation problems, the home market is still very profitable, and Hiram Walker wanted to exploit it.

'Famous Grouse' had grown in popularity to such an extent that Highland Distillers were going to embark on an export drive for this brand. Hiram Walker's were under the impression that the merger would facilitate its progress, as it could have the benefit of Hiram Walker's existing market knowledge. However, Highland Distillers pointed out that 'Grouse' would become part of a very thick portfolio, already containing a blend similar to Grouse, namely Ballantines, and this would lead to a conflict of interest.

Hiram Walker also put forward financial reasons for the takeover: they could bring to Highland Distillers' aid all the clout of a multi-national. The riposte was that Highland Distillers were on a perfectly sound financial footing, and in addition were not involved in any other industry, which would drain capital from the whisky division, (Hiram Walker have substantial oil and gas interests).

The merger would have made Hiram Walker virtually self-sufficient in malt, but Highland had longstanding commitments to fulfil with other companies, and if Hiram Walker appropriated it all for themselves, there would have been serious disruptions to the various networks, which in turn would have led to disruption to blends perhaps creating a domino effect. Vis-a-vis Highland's 30% interest in Robertson and Baxter; the relationship went much further than that, as Highland supplied many 'fillings' for R & B's blends. If Hiram Walker had decided to alter the contracts, the results would have been disastrous for R & B.

Although there are around 118 malt distilleries of 4 geographically based taste distinctions, within these, particularly the largest Highland category, there are additional quality bands. The Report brought to light the point that, although polarisation of ownership as a whole was going to be concentrated further with the merger, polarisation would be particularly acute with respect to the top quality bracket. Hiram Walker's share would rise from two to five, but the 'big three' of D.C.L., Seagram's and Hiram Walker's slice would rise from twenty two to twenty five out of thirty-three,(76% as opposed to owning 58% of all malt distilleries).

Views were submitted by interested third parties, such as the Ministry of Agriculture, Fish and Food, who deal with the Whisky Industry (not the Scottish Office), the Scottish Economic Planning Department, the Scottish Development Agency, the Highlands and Islands Development Board, the S.T.U.C., and Whisky companies. The arguments of these bodies focussed around the points of control within the industry, bulk malt exporting and Hiram Walker's size and lack of Scottishness.

The merger would have made Hiram Walker's the second largest company. It may have used this clout to buy up more independents (or others might take an approval of the merger by the commission as being a 'green light', as the S.T.U.C. put it for them to buy up the other independents). Hiram Walker's seat of power is in Canada. That is where the major decisions are taken, not Scotland. Therefore they would not have been slanted in favour of Scotland or Scotch's interests. The arguments against Hiram Walker's range of brands swamping Scotch's interests are compounded by their foreign base.

Lastly, Hiram-Walker are one of the main perpetrators of Bulk Malt exporting. Their take-over of Highland Distillers would have made additional exporting more likely, and this was especially serious as Highland's distilleries were of premier quality.

Thankfully for Scotch, the Commission agreed with the majority and recommended that the merger was not in the public interest. The government rubber stamped it, and Highland Distillers remained as it wanted to be: independent! This Report has put a stop to further accumulation by foreign companies of malt distilleries as a whole, but it came too late to stop Seagram's takeover of The Glenlivet, Scotland's 'best' malt.

The ideal product of Scotch Whisky to be sold from the Scottish point of view is that of a blend or single malt blended, bottled and packaged in Scotland. This ensures the maximum employment for Scots both directly and indirectly involved, and guarantees the purity of the product until it reaches the customer.

However, since the turn of the century, and the opening up of the world market, the cost of transport and discriminatory taxation policies of the foreign governments has resulted in standard grade bottled in Scotland produce being priced abroad comparable to deluxe (and even higher) on the home market. Obviously this restricts the number of prospective customers. The companies tried to cut costs: a clear area where savings could be made was in the space taken up by bottles and packaging, hence the advent of bulk blend shipping. This reduced costs considerably, and was encouraged by foreign governments as a way of developing their own bottling facilities, so discriminatory taxation does not apply to the bulk product. The following table illustrates the benefits of exporting blends in bulk.

Average price of blended Scotch Whisky per gauge proof gallon for the year 1977:–

	World	**U.S.A.**
Bottled in Scotland	£6.71	£6.47
Bulk Blends	£2.30	£2.05

Source: DSWG

It need not be stressed too often that bottling and blending require the most labour of any section of production of Scotch and the packaging industry also benefits. Brazil goes a step further making it more lucrative to ship malt and grain separately. Blending, bottling and packaging are all carried out in Brazil itself. The N.E.D.C. Distilling Sector Working Group says that if the companies did not take advantage of this process, a bottled in Scotland brand would cost £20.

By far the most controversial act in respect of bulk blends was the old Wine Gallon Assessment Tax, which used to operate in the biggest market for Scotch, the U.S.A.

> 'Under this arrangement, imports of Scotch Whisky in bottles were subject to duty as if they were 100° Proof (American). Since Scotch Whisky, bottled in Scotland, is commonly sold at 86° Proof (American), the duty on bottled imports was higher than was justified by the spirit content.'(D.S.W.G.,78)

In effect, the U.S. government were taxing water, and raising the cost of Scotch, vis-a-vis its American competitors of the same strength. The result of this was that it became cheaper to ship whisky (blended) in bulk to America at 100° Proof (U.S.) and bottle and water it down there.

The arguments against bulk blends centre round the points that the practice creates employment in the country of destination, but not in Scotland, and that because water is added, or some more of the process is carried out, quality may be sacrificed.

Even the most cursory glance at the previous table should convey to the reader that bulk blends are cheaper than their bottled in Scotland counterparts, and that along with the bottling and blending section, constitute the greatest employment opportunities. This is sufficient incentive for a government to promote it's own bottling and blending industry and for companies to bulk export blends. However, the employment statistics also form the main component of the argument *against* bulk exporting.

TABLE VI

Export of Scotch Whisky and Northern Irish Whiskey* to the Major Overseas Markets in 1983

(Volume figures in million litres of pure alcohol)

	% of export market 1983	Malt		Grain	Blend		Total	Value £ million
		Bottle	Bulk		Bottle	Bulk		
USA	29.89	0.62	0.59	0.02	37.35	29.53	68.11	224.46
EEC*	24.74	2.19	2.52	0.62	39.38	11.65	56.36	227.70
France	*9.26*	*0.50*	*1.16*	*0.29*	*13.34*	*5.81*	*21.10*	*78.91*
Italy	*4.84*	*1.32*	*0.17*	*0.01*	*9.26*	*0.26*	*11.02*	*54.21*
Fed. Rep. Germany	*3.68*	*0.15*	*0.29*	*0.20*	*4.32*	*3.42*	*8.38*	*32.41*
Belgo-Lux	*2.59*	*0.07*	*0.21*	–	*3.99*	*1.62*	*5.89*	*23.40*
Others	*4.37*	*0.15*	*0.69*	*0.12*	*8.47*	*0.54*	*9.97*	*38.77*
Japan	10.53	0.13	16.09	0.01	7.72	0.04	23.99	70.13
Australia	2.83	0.08	0.03	–	0.73	5.62	6.46	15.76
Spain	3.23	0.03	1.46	–	5.86	0.02	7.37	26.89
South Africa	3.52	0.03	0.10	0.01	7.82	0.06	8.02	34.71
Venezuela	1.43	–	0.04	–	3.21	–	3.25	22.59
Canada	1.92	0.09	0.01	–	3.69	0.58	4.37	19.87
	78.09	3.17	20.84	0.66	105.76	47.50	177.93	642.11

*Exluding U.K.

The main countries blends are exported to are the U.S.A., some European Countries, Australia, New Zealand, Canada, South Africa and Brazil and Argentina. These also constitute, in the main, the major export markets for all varieties of Scotch Whisky. The proportion of bulk blends to all varieties of Scotch is illustrated in the following table.

Calendar Year	Bulk Blend (Million Proof Gallons)	% of Total Exports
1971	17.2	24.5
1972	15.8	23.0
1973	17.5	22.3
1974	18.7	21.4
1975	21.8	24.1
1976	18.6	20.3
1977	19.2	20.5

Source: DSWG

The above table shows how, during the seventies bulk blend exporting *fell* from almost a quarter of all exports of Scotch to a fifth. However, the percentage is back up to 26.7 of exports to what the S.W.A. considers the major overseas markets.

One would expect this to have fallen with the removal of the Wine Gallon Assessment Tax in the United States (by far the largest market for Scotch). Bottled in America produce is recognised as Scotch Whisky, but not of the highest quality. The carve up of the market is illustrated overleaf.

In 1980, the Wine Gallon Assessment Tax was changed so that bottled in Scotland produce was not discriminated against. Observers confidently expected a reduction in the quantity of bulk blends destined for the American market. What actually happened could not have been predicted by even the most pessimistic: the top firms raised their prices to nullify the withdrawal of the Wine Gallon Assessment Tax.

The reason that this was so unexpected was that whenever arguments against bulk blend exporting to the U.S. came up, the Wine Gallon Assessment Tax was put up as the villain of the piece. If the Wine Gallon Assessment Tax was removed 'then it is certainly likely that after a few years, the majority of Scotch blended whisky currently exported in bulk will be replaced by bottled exports'(Thompson, 1979, p.4.)

The author, John K. Thompson, asserts that the higher transport costs of bottled in Scotland produce would be offset by the cheaper bottling and blending costs of bottling in Scotland. He notes that if the Tax differential was not removed or the differential pricing was maintained by some other method, and if Bulk Blends were stopped, they would not be replaced to any great extent by bottled-in-Scotland produce.

The N.E.D.C. Distilling Sector Working Group said that the trends shown on the previous diagram might be reversed if bulk blend exporting was made less profitable.

	Litres Pure Alcohol	£	Value/Litres Pure Alcohol
Jan.-Oct. 1979 Bottled Blends	42,346,000	125,517,860	£2.96
Jan.-Oct. 1980 Bottled Blends	36,248,000	125,066,000	£3.45
Jan.-Oct. 1979 Bulk Blends	25,683,330	24,036,360	£0.95
Jan.-Oct. 1980 Bulk Blends	27,738,000	26,440,000	£0.95

Source: S.W.C.R.

However, one should be able to abstract from this that the price of bottled-in-Scotland produce has gone up, whereas Bulk Blends have remained the same.

No concrete effort has been made to change the proportion of bottled in Scotland produce to Bulk produce. Why? The Scotch Whisky Combine argues that company profits have improved by keeping the Bulk Blends at the same level. Another reason could be that three out of the top seven Scotch brands sold in 1981 are owned by North American Corporations, who also own the major competitors to Scotch (e.g. Bourbon, Canadian Whisky, Vodka and Gin). The result of reducing bulk Scotch is that it would be contravening their policy of a 'finger in every pie' with regard to the market place and reducing their work force in the main market/base – the U.S. – which would not be a politically sound thing to do. The 1983 figure for Bulk Blend exports stands at 29.53 million litres of pure alcohol.

The fact remains that most companies which export Bulk Blends do so to other parts of their own companies, e.g., Seagram has bottling plants in all the main markets. This means that they gain a first-hand knowledge of the respective market place, and yet more control of the journey from the inception of Scotch to the customer's mouth, on a world basis. In this light, Seagram and Hiram Walker especially represent the archetypal multinational corporation. It is company profits as a whole which matter, not that of the subsidiaries.

So the foreign governments' policy of fostering their own bottling and (in the case of Brazil) blending facilities provide their countries with employment and revenue, but for the most part profits go overseas.

From the Scottish point of view, Bulk exports of blends allow more people access to Scotch. If Bulk Blend exporting ceased tomorrow, with the current taxation discrimination, the amount of Scotch sold would fall, as would the numbers needed to be employed in Scotland to produce whisky. Less people would be able to buy the more expensive bottled-in-Scotland produce.

When statistics showing the results of having all Scotch bottled in Scotland are given, they are usually followed by a caveat which states the above, but even given that, there would be a net increase in employment in Scotland, and this is, of course, the main plank of the argument against Bulk Blend exporting.

The following table illustates the employment situation with respect to Bulk Blends.

Direct Employment Effect of Ending Bulk Exports
(by number of employees)

		Bulk blended whisky			
		1978		**1979**	
Sub-sector	**Av. output per employee**	**Minimum**	**Maximum**	**Minimum**	**Maximum**
Malting distilling	23,911 pg	–159	–46	–140	–40
Grain distilling	45,011 pg	–254	–73	–222	–64
Warehousing	85,025 pg	–179	–51	–156	–45
Blending	36,412 pg	–419	–120	–366	–105
Bottling	7,241 pg	+902	+2406	+790	+2106
Administration	38,057pg	–401	–115	–351	–100
Total direct employment change		–510	+2001	–445	+1752

Source: J.K. Thomson (3)

This table illustrates that the largest area for employment, the bottling and blending areas, could be expanded yet further if bulk blend exporting ceased. Whilst it is naive to imagine that companies would in fact implement this across the board, it is not quite so naive to presume that it is in the government's interest to persuade common market countries to withdraw discriminatory taxation practices, thus minimising additional costs for exports to the companies. The two main arguments for bulk blend exporting, namely discriminatory taxation and transport costs would be mitigated and more jobs would be created.

However, even given this, it must be remembered that there exists excess capacity in the bottling halls, and new technology is ever increasingly cutting down manpower – or to be more accurate woman-power. A spokesman for Chivas Regal (Seagram) said that the whole of the Bulk Blend exports for the United States could be accommodated on his line with perhaps 50 more employees. It can hardly be disputed, however, that more employment in Scotland would result from the cessation of Bulk Blends, even in part in the bottling and blending section of the industry, and of course, the spin-off industries of glass-making and packaging.

Companies may argue that if Bulk Blends are stopped, bottled exports will probably not wholly replace them. This is certainly true in distant markets, but untenable as far as Europe is concerned. The reason is that the companies are *not* likely to change a lucrative procedure off their own bat. Government intervention or public uproar would be necessary, but neither appears to be forthcoming.

Public uproar is much more the order of the day with Bulk Blend exporting's sister problem, namely Bulk Malt exporting. There exists a famous Radio Clyde interview with W S McCann, Managing Director of Hiram Walker in the mid seventies, which focussed attention on this problem. Bulk Malt exporting does not have the same profile as Bulk Blend exporting. The practice is not as widespread with respect to quantity or number of companies involved. Whereas Bulk Blend exporting is done by D.C.L.(with half the industry's malt distilleries in it's power), along with nearly every other major exporting company, Bulk Malt exporting is confined to a few overt, largely non-Scottish corporations, Seagram, Hiram Walker, Long John (Whitbread) and Lonrho, and two Scottish companies in particular, Stanley P. Morrison and Tomatin. An alternative method of buying malt is indirectly through the brokerage system. For example, Bells only uses 50% of the malt it produces in its own distilleries, the rest is either swopped or sold to brokers. Once in the hands of brokers, anyone can buy it.

Calendar Year	Bulk Malt (Million Proof Gallons)	% of Total Exports
1971	3.3	4.7
1972	4.1	5.9
1973	6.2	8.0
1974	7.1	8.1
1975	8.0	8.8
1976	8.0	8.7
1977	8.4	9.0
1983 (S.W.A.)	20.8	17.7

Source: DSWG (These figures refer only to major markets.)

There is also a discrepancy between the countries importing Bulk Blends and Bulk Malt. The trade is heavily centred on Japan (see below) and has grown quite steadily throughout the seventies.

Thus the amount sold is not very large, but as the Distilling Sectór Working Group says:

> 'The admix question has escalated into being not only an industrial and economic problem, but also in Scotland, an issue of social and political significance' (Report p.12)

Bulk Malt is not bottled in foreign countries as single Scotch Malt. It is admixed with local spirits (of any description) and renders them palatable. The reasons for selling malt in Bulk to foreigners is that it earns a substantial amount of money. (£22 million in 1977, source: DSWG). 40% of Malt distilleries would be affected if this trade ceased in rural areas of Scotland where even minor loss of employment is felt far more seriously across the whole community. Bulk Malt, it is said, also whets people's appetite for Scotch. This argument is very weak, as the Scotch content is not mentioned on the bottle, and the result of an admix may vary greatly from any Scotch taste, so the chance of any Japanese progressing up the market after a bottle of Suntory is highly unlikely. In most cases, if the customer wanted Scotch, he'd buy Scotch in the first place.

The arguments against Bulk Malt exporting are said to be couched in emotional, hence untenable language. Often authors seem to me to misrepresent the case. The major selling point for Scotch as a world drink is that it is unique and of high quality. Suntory of Japan, for example, is a huge company, well capable of going multi-national, and one of the major reasons it has got so large is that it sells products which would not do as well if it was not for their Scotch Malt component. The analogy can be drawn between the U.S. bolts which hold together the U.S.S.R's nuclear missiles, and British shipbuilders teaching the Koreans all they knew. It is said Suntory will not expand outside Japan. Why then do they sponsor golf tournaments in G.B.,(The World Matchplay of Wentworth) and the U.S. Bulk Malt exports create competitors who would be comparatively toothless without them.

The main use of Scotch whisky in Japanese whiskies is in the Special Class; 'sales of this class constitute a high proportion (47% in 1976) of the Japanese market and these Special Class whiskies do compete in price, and, to an extent, in quality, with Scotch blends' (DSWG p.13).

Why then, do the specific companies export Bulk Malt? With Stanley P Morrison and Tomatin, for example, they have no major blend that could be harmed by exporting malt. For other companies, it is a lucrative method of soaking up any 'surplus to requirements' Scotch. For Seagram and other multi-nationals the reason is less clear-cut, until one realises that Seagram owns half of a major Japanese whisky company, Kirin, and has interests in Suntory. One arrives back to the portfolio idea; Seagram want overall success. It does not matter to them which of their companies earns the most: they want *overall* profits to be good.

This Bulk Malt can be seen to be restricting the growth of proper Scotch exports especially in the lucrative market of Japan. It is interesting that there is no longer trade in Bulk Blend exporting to Japan, which would at least be 'Scotch'. Mr Grindal of the Scotch Whisky Association said that in Japan Scotch sells because of its quality image. Japanese whisky is of lower prestige than Scotch. Bulk Blends would erode further the image of up-market brands of Scotch, as do dual priced exports, (resulting from the E.E.C. decision). Thus, from a Scottish point of view, Scotch Malt exports undermine existing and future export potential; although currently it may actually increase jobs, or rather if one was to call a halt to the process immediately, there would be a net loss of jobs. In the future, these products, which at the top end of their scale and bottom of Scotch's overlap, will lessen the potential for growth in sales and indeed erode the existing market for Scotch.

During the seventies, several measures were mooted to curtail this practice. The unions, for example, aired the matter at their conferences. The focus was on Bulk Malt, which has less of an adverse impact on jobs than Blends. The D.S.W.G. report prompted the group to try and get the companies involved to limit this exporting at least – with no concrete results.

Legislation by a British government would be practically impossible to implement as Thompson says:

> 'First any quantitive instructions or ending of bulk exports would be contrary to G.A.T.T., and would probably lead to retaliatory action by other countries. Second, as the U.K. is a member of the E.E.C., the government or any company is not permitted to place quantitative restrictions on exports'(p.13).

Monitoring of any voluntary measure taken by companies is also problematic mainly because of the brokerage system. A company can sell 'fillings' to a broker, who in turn can sell it again to anyone. Seagram, for example, exports to its own companies.

The major point I would want the reader to abstract from this is that a suitable control mechanism does not exist for the industry. The Government cannot or will not act except to cream off excise. The industry Association has no power; it operates by consensus or not at all, and only consists of part of the industry anyway.

Many people compare the Scotch situation to another spirit – cognac. The comparison is not always valid as the amount of cognac sold is only a fraction of that of whisky, but the organisation overseeing it could be used as a model (or rather could have been).

The Bureau National de Cognac is a quasi-autonomous governmental organisation, which sets and enforces rules for the constituents and grades of cognacs. There are several categories of cognac available – price is only a loose indicator. The same could apply in effect to Scotch, sectors showing the predominance of Islay or Speyside malts in a blend and grades ranging from standard through to deluxe and so on, which are well known in the trade, but as of yet are not so well known by the customer. The Bureau sets prizes and promotes the standard of cognac. This is not the case with the Scotch Whisky Association, which only becomes involved in advertising at a generic level. Around the turn of the century, gold medals were awarded for quality and were greatly coveted, but these were awarded by Trades Exhibitions – not just purely Scotch ones, but rather exhibitions for any form of industry. But once these lapsed, so did the competitions for quality.

Scotch Whisky is far larger an industry and less rare a product, but it shares with cognac its uniqueness of taste and restricted geographical location suitable to produce it.

The French government's attitude to cognac can be transferred to a more general attitude to its industry : numerous instances can be cited of protectionist or quasi-protectionist behaviour (a current one would be its treatment of Japanese video recorders). Japan too has well-known import restrictions. However, our government's 'laissez-faire' attitude has prevailed in the case of this industry, and I would propose that this has been exacerbated by the lack of public awareness of the goings-on of the Scotch Whisky Industry.

The government appears to be rather hypocritical with regard to the Scotch Whisky Industry : it creams off the largest slice of tax of any of the countries where Scotch is sold, yet is not prepared to protect or even further the Industry's prospects. Recently the S.D.A. wanted to join with the S.W.A. in a generic advertising campaign in America : however the then Scottish Minister responsible, refused the money saying "we don't back winners"!

Thus it can be seen that indulging in Bulk Malt exporting can be determined by the type of company involved. The main exporters of malt are non-Scots multi-nationals and small Scots producers. The point is that there is no control mechanism over these companies' actions, although Scotch is supposed to be special in its economic capacity and also in its social significance to the Scots' people. So, processes which almost everyone acknowledges as damaging, go on and one wonders whether this would have been allowed to happen, if the public was not blinded by rather 'out-of-date' publicity and advertising.

Conclusions

Scotch has few rivals in the construction and maintenance of the perverted image the Scottish Nation has of itself. The product of whisky is so recognisably Scottish around the world and within Scotland. However, the associated images used in the advertising, such as tartan, kilts and sturdy army pipers in beautiful Highland glens, cast up the idea that Scots are half- tamed savages, country yokels or infantrymen rather than officers. The imagery of the 'Scottish Myth' harkens back to a 'Golden Age', which soothes the dour experience of the grey urban Scots who now constitute the overwhelming majority. The Scotch Whisky Industry has employed such symbols to telling effect in their sales drives. This has carried over to the images the natives hold of the industry: a plurality of small, Highland based, Scottish companies. But the art and skill so often emphasised *must* have been modified, in order to produce the huge gallonage which has to satisfy even the home market. A craft industry run in bothies simply could not have achieved such world dominance.

The industry is a multi-million pound process industry. It has grown from a craft industry to its current size in a century and a half. In that time, the numbers involved in making the product and controlling its industry have shrunk as the capital requirements have rocketed. This has resulted in the three stages of development, as previously described. These three stages coincide with many other industries. The industry's growth has been stunningly normal. There is nothing in the least magical or wonderful about the production process or the industry.

The product itself has been romanticised beyond belief. In the eighteenth century, 'fire-water' would be a more accurate label; it was nothing to wax lyrical about. Over the years, it has been made blander and more consistent to capture a wider, regular custom. The ingredients are so few, and it is sheer luck which has brought this 'resource' to Scotland, and 'hard nosed' businessmen who have made it prominent. It is certainly true that Scotch is a unique drink, with an unusual flavour, which has wide appeal, but this should not blind people to the fact that it is an essentially simple product, produced by large sophisticated companies, who, on on the whole, lack the romantic view that Scots have of their 'National Drink'! The common man used to make it rather like his wife would make jam until the law instigated a process of exclusion, which forbad him from distilling a batch, when required. This process has continued until non-Scottish ownership is said to exceed Scottish.

Since the Second World War, growth has been so phenomenal that it has made people forget about the slumps during the 1850's, the 1890's, the 1920's, and now the 1980s. Due to the estimations of stocks so many years in advance, and the fact that Scotch is subject to the crises in capitalism, just like any other commodity, it has cyclically slumped. This has brought much distress in the very small rural communities where the malt distillery is the focus for economic activity. Over the years, new technology has eroded work at the urban work places, especially the bottling halls. What are deemed exigencies of the markets, usually foreign ones, have given employment to foreigners at the expense of Scots and made foreign hootch palatable, to the extent that it has become eligible to challenge Scotch's position. These processes are not new and they have happened in other industries such as shipbuilding. What is clear is that if Scotch were French, it is unlikely that this would have happened.

Pubic awareness of the industry is minimal, even subliminal. The images used in current advertising might have been true once, but certainly aren't now. They are geared at middle-aged men, but they only occupy a small section of the possible custom. Recently, whisky has been losing out to white, neutral spirits, such as vodka and less neutral ones, such as rum and gin. I would suggest this has a lot to do with the wider target of appeal in their advertising. It is in this direction that Scotch should be going in the future. Scotch sells on an image of quality. Tartanry et al is often 'tacky' and this could be another reason for abandoning it.

An understanding of the current 'problems' of the Scotch Whisky Industry can only be achieved by examining its history, structure and trading practices. Only then can one put such issues as Bulk Malt exporting into perspective. This practice seems iniquitous to Scots, but, because Seagram, for example, own both companies involved, the seller and buyer, it makes sound business sense.

In a few years time we will be able to see if the Scotch Whisky Industry has analysed itself properly in the light of its recent 'problems'. D.C.L.'s change in chairmanship could lead to a new more aggressive or modern posture which could lead to its recapturing its home and foreign market share, or it might come to nought, and the company continue its slow slide away from prominence.

Source Material

Allan, R., *The Whisky Barons*, London.
Barnard,A., *The Original Scotch*, London, 1944.
Bruce Lockhart, Sir R., *Scotch*, London, 1951.
Cooper D., *Whiskies of Scotland*. London, 1978.
Daiches, D., *Scotch Whisky*, London, 1977.

Dewar, T., *A Ramble Round the Globe*, London, 1884.
House, J., *The Pride of Perth*, Perth, 1982.
Laver, J., *The House of Haig*, Markinch, 1958.
Macdonald, A., *Whisky*, 1930.
McDowall, R.J.S., *The Whiskies of Scotland*, London, 1971.
Moss,M.S., & Hume,J.R., *The Making of Scotch Whisky*, Edinburgh, 1981.
Murphy, B., *The World Book of Whisky*, Glasgow, 1978.
Newman, P., *King of the Castle*, U.S. 1980.
Robb, J.M., *Scotch Whisky, A Guide*, London, 1950.
Ross, J., *Whisky*, London 1970.
Sillet,S.W., *Illicit Scotch*, Aberdeen, 1965.
Simpson, Bill et al., *Scotch Whisky*, London, 1979.
Wilson, Ross, *Scotch Made Easy*, London, 1959.
Scotch, The Formative Years, London, 1970.
Scotch, It's History and Romance, Newton Abbot, 1973.

Reports

Company:
Bell's 1982.
D.C.L. – since inception, lodged in Edinburgh
S.W.A. – since inception, lodged in Edinburgh
Seagrams '10K' form lodged in Washington D.C.
Scotch Whisky Association 1 *Statistical Reports*, 1980, 81,82.
2 *Questions and Answers* (Edinburgh 1981)
3 Advertising leaflet: Scotch Whisky of the Land and of the People.
Thompson, J.K.,1 *Ownership and Control of the Scotch Whisky Industry*, The Fraser of Allander Institute Discussion paper 17.
ibid 2, *Should Scotland Export Bulk Whisky?* The Scottish Council for Development and Industry. December, 1979.
ibid 3, 'Bulk Exports of Scotch Whisky', in *Scottish Journal of Political Economy,* Vol.27, No.3, Nov.1980.
The Scotch Whisky Combine Report : *Bulk. The Real Reason* Jan/Feb. 1981.
Economic Associates *Whisky in Bulk : The Export Trade*. London, August 1976.
Mintel, *'Spirit 2'* May 1982.
Targett, D., Strategies in Scotch Whisky in Journal of Long Range planning.
N.E.D.C. Distilling Sector Working Group Report, 1978.

Various pieces by the S.T.U.C., including Annual Reports, Monopolies Commission Report on the Hiram Walker Takeover bid 1980.

The Bulletin of Scottish Politics, No.2, Spring 1981, pp.56-86.

Private Interviews

Mr. J.B. Ashworth, Chivas Bros. Mr. Moncrieff, Long John International. Mr. Grindal, S.W.A. Mr. Harrison, S.T.U.C. Mr. J. Firn, S.D.A. Mr. J.K. Thompson, The Scottish Investment Trust.

THE REAL CRISIS OF SCOTTISH AGRICULTURE

DUNCAN CAMPBELL
DEPARTMENT OF SOCIOLOGY
UNIVERSITY OF EDINBURGH

Scottish and British agriculture has over the past fifty years undergone a transformation so profound that it is barely recognisable from the past. State support, technological innovation, new practices, new products have all transformed the agrarian economy and society of Scotland, and, in many places, the face of the land itself. This article attempts to identify and evaluate the most important economic and political developments bearing upon Scottish agriculture in the Seventies and Eighties. We start, however, with a brief history of agriculture support policies in Britain.

The "Great Depression" to 1939

British agriculture reached its zenith of prosperity in the 1860s. Around 1875 it entered a period of sustained depression – of falling product and land prices, lower rents and untenanted farms – which was to continue for almost forty years, ending only with the outbreak of world war. It was in this period that farming finally ceased to be Britain's major industry, unable to compete with imports of cheap grain and meat from Latin America, Australia, New Zealand and the American prairies. The effects of what became known as the "Great Depression" were most marked in the wheat growing areas of England. Scottish farming, being more dependent on stock activities and with only a small-scale involvement in wheat production, survived the shock of the depression better. If Symon is to be believed this was due also in no small measure to the moral sturdiness and resourcefulness of the Scottish farmer, who countered adversity by,

> "....industry, thrift, an excellent rotation system, attention to the breeding and management of livestock, sound labour organisation, skill and pride in farm craft, and the combination of agricultural

science, so far as was then known, with practice."[1]

Not that Scottish agriculture was without its difficulties. The effects of the depression were probably most severe on the uneconomically small units of the eastern glens, as well as on that cold, infertile central plateau that stretches from Midlothian in the east to Dunbartonshire in the west. Above all, the depression severely affected the viability of hill sheep farming, particularly in the Highlands where the glens, having already been emptied of people, were now cleared of sheep. A concomitant of this sectoral decline was a rising demand for moors for sporting purposes by the magnates of the new, industrial Britain. This large-scale appropriation of land for the recreation and pleasure of the few is a symbolic and literal blight on the face of Scotland that has yet to be expunged. Elsewhere, farmers survived as best they could in face of the official indifference engendered by the prevailing ideology of economic laissez-faire and the imperative of cheap (imported) food for an expanding industrial workforce.

Agricultural fortunes improved briefly during and immediately after the First World War as the exigencies of conflict forced a reluctant and faltering government to impose price controls and guarantee product prices. Scottish agriculture responded rapidly to this stimulus, with the acreage under grain growing by over 20% in two years. Soon after the Armistice Lloyd George was heard to declare that never again would the industry be left to sink or swim. In 1921, as world prices tumbled, its war-time system of agricultural support was dismantled. Depression returned with renewed force. Prices did gradually recover until, in 1929, another and more severe slump recurred. Everywhere land reverted to grass; many farms bore an air of neglect and decay; rural poverty was endemic. By 1939,"the damage done to the industry had been immense and, often, in the poorer areas irreparable. Where the permanent equipment of the marginal land farms had been allowed to fall into gross decay; so impoverished had much of this land become that it had degenerated into an agricultural slum, occupied in the main by old and infirm persons. These, by pursuing the least productive form of farming – the rearing of store sheep – managed somehow, and often with outside aid, to maintain themselves on a low standard of living. Impoverished farms with many derelict fields were to be seen everywhere in the poorer areas, silent but eloquent testimonies to the depression in agriculture".[2]

Grasping this history of neglect, indifference and betrayal is vital to an understanding of the collective mentality of farmers. A sense of beleaguered adversity, of threat from an ignorant, uncaring urban mass, "backs-against-the-wall" rhetoric, an unquenchable belief in the dignity and indispensability of their calling are characteristic elements of the self-image and public pronouncements of farmers. If the effects are often risible, inducing only cynicism in the hearer, they nonetheless have a very real historical basis.

World War Two to 1973

The sustained support and management of agricultural markets dates largely from the Second World War, though some aspects date from the inter-war years – principally, the de-rating of agricultural land, the formation of the Milk Marketing Boards[(3)], and the introduction of some limited support and subsidies for wheat, barley, oats and beef.

The outbreak of war immediately accorded agriculture the status of a strategic industry. Overwhelmed by governmental advice and aid, farmers once again rapidly expanded output. In Britain, in the three years from 1938-9 to 1941-2 the value of gross output rose by two-thirds. In Scotland the area under tillage was increased by 639,000 acres in four years, with wheat and barley production more than doubling. The farmers' contribution to British victory was substantial and indispensable, providing them with "a moral account on which they were able to draw heavily when the war had ended",[(4)] as well as giving the NFU a key weapon in its propaganda armoury.[(5)]

This time around state support was consolidated and extended beyond the years of wartime emergency. A number of factors came into play. In the first place it was obvious that food shortages were going to last well beyond the end of the war itself, while it was hoped that sustained agricultural output would relieve the currrency and balance of payments crisis attendant upon the ending of Lend-Lease. The election of a reforming Labour government was not without consequence either. The widespread rural poverty of recent memory could lay claim to its egalitarian sympathies, while agriculture could also serve to exemplify the value and benefits of a managed economy. So begins the curious and ironic tale of Labour's involvement with Britain's farmers.[(6)]

The first piece of post-war agricultural legislation was the Hill-Farming Act of 1946 which provided support for farm improvement in the hills. However the centrepiece of the post-war agricultural settlement was undoubtedly the Agriculture Act of 1947. The Act undertook to provide "proper remuneration" for farmers and farmworkers and an "adequate return" on invested capital by providing price guarantees for (and here follows a sentence of majestic and fruitful ambiguity) "such part of the nation's food and other agricultural produce as in the national interest it is desirable to produce in the United Kingdom".

At first, while wartime controls were still in operation, farmers were paid a fixed price for their produce by the government. From 1953 and until entry into the EEC a "deficiency payments" system of price control operated. Imported food was by and large free to enter the country, with farmers being repaid the difference between a guaranteed price and the market price actually obtaining when domestic produce was sold in competition with imports. In this way some of the institutions and forms of a free market were restored, albeit one whose parameters were largely defined by the state.

The short-run results on output of the new legislation were disappointing. Between 1945-6 and 1950-1 output at constant prices rose by only about 8.5%, a long way short of the official goal of a 60% increase by 1956. Understandably perhaps, farmers seem to have initially spent their increased incomes on personal consumption rather than on productive investment. The official response to this was the introduction of production grants in the Fifties with the aim of increasing "efficiency".[(7)] Grants were made available for, amongst other things, hill cows and sheep, fertilizer purchase, bringing pasture under the plough, hedgegrow removal and bracken eradication. By 1960-61 such payments accounted for nearly 40% of all public expenditure on agriculture. In conjunction with the high levels of relatively stable prices provided by guarantees, production grants soon made a dramatic impact on both the volume of output and the pattern of farming. The pace of mechanization increased sharply, fertilizer usage shot up, and crop yields improved markedly. In Scotland the total output of the main cereal crops (wheat, barley and oats) rose from 1,032,000 tons in 1950 to 1,200,000 tons in 1960 despite a fall of nearly 11% in the area devoted to these crops. The value of total agricultural output rose from £121,096 to £168,617 over the same period. But as world food prices fell during the 1960s, the costs of agricultural policy grew. The agriculture departments and the Treasury were also having to face the emerging problem of surpluses, particularly of milk, as growth in output spiralled far in excess of consumption. Attempts were made to control output, and to limit the Exchequer's liability, by imposing "standard quantities" on milk.[(8)] This policy achieved some short-term success, but the long-run trend was still towards growing output.

One of the most remarkable policy developments of the Fifties was contained in the Agriculture Act of 1957. The 1947 Act had required the

Agriculture Ministers[9] to conduct an annual review of the economic conditions and prospects of agriculture as the basis upon which economic guarantees would be settled for a specified list of commodities. (By requiring their active participation this review procedure greatly enhanced the power and influence of the NFUs). The 1957 Act required the government to keep the total value of its guarantees at not less than 97.5% of the previous year, a remarkable self-imposed constraint on its budgetary autonomy.

This system of support continued largely unchanged in its essentials until entry to the EEC in 1973. However the value of price support was held down throughout the Sixties, despite the clamourings for expansion in the latter half of the decade which received expression in Labour's "National Plan" of 1965.[10]

A new decade and a new government brought higher guaranteed prices, eventual entry into the EEC and a fundamental reorientation in our system of agricultural support.

The Common Agricultural Policy

The Common Agricultural Policy (CAP) is an institution of truly baroque complexity. Here only the briefest sketch of its operations will be attempted.

CAP expenditure (which in 1981 accounted for more than 67% of the total Community budget) is administered through the European Agricultural Guidance and Guarantee Fund (FEOGA, after its French title). FEOGA disburses its budget under two main headings:

(1) Price guarantees – which account for more than 95% of total expenditure.

Structural measures ("Guidance"), concerned with such matters as farm size, agricultural employment, investment etc.

Prices and markets are manipulated by a combination of internal price supports and external protection. Each year the Council of Ministers sets desired prices (variously known as "target", "guide", "basic" and "norm" prices) for a set list of commodities. The market is then manipulated, principally by levies on imported goods, in an attempt to achieve the desired prices. At a certain percentage (generally a little over 90%) below this price there is an intervention price at which intervention agencies are obliged to buy any produce offered to them. This surplus output may be variously,

(1) Stored – hence the EEC's surreal landscape of food mountains and lakes

(2) Destroyed

(3) Exported – with the aid of "export restitutions" to bring the price down to the world market price

Price guarantees are open-ended; that is, there have until recently been no restrictions on the quantities which may be sold into intervention. Further complexities (and expense) are engendered by Monetary Compensatory Allowances (MCAs), a system of internal subsidies and levies intended to iron out trade "distortions" caused by the absence of a common currency, floating exchange rates and divergent economic conditions among the member states.

Structural policy has never assumed its intended importance and now accounts for less than 5% of total FEOGA expenditure. Structural measures operative within the CAP include aids for farm amalgamation and capital investment on small farms. As far as Scottish agriculture is concerned the most important structural policy is the Less Favoured Areas Directive of 1975 which provides investment aid for farm modernisation in the hills and uplands as well as an annual livestock subsidy known as the Hill Livestock Compensatory Allowance (HLCA). In the area of structural policy member states retain a great deal of autonomy with regard both to the goals and level of support. There also still remain some purely national elements of price support; Britain's sheep variable premium being one such example.

The marked disproportion between the Guarantee and Guidance sections of FEOGA is of crucial importance in understanding the present crisis and future direction of the Common Agricultural Policy. It is an issue to which we shall return.

Entry to the EEC provided a spectacular bonanza for British farmers. Compared with the old British system guaranteed prices were higher under the new Community regime, and in the years following entry farm incomes rose dramatically as the following table shows.[(11)]

In both Scotland and England farm income rose steadily throughout the first half of the Seventies and, particularly in Scotland, managed to keep ahead of movements in the Retail Price Index. Incomes peaked in 1976/77 in Scotland and 1978/79 in England. Since then, apart from a brief improvement in 1981/82 (and 1980/81 in the case of England) they have steadily fallen, the decline being particularly marked in Scotland. The latest Annual Review(12) showed a drop in incomes in 1982/83 of 15% in the UK and 29% in Scotland. The divergent income trends in England and Scotland are in large part a result of differences in the main types of farming. Livestock and dairy farming are far more important in Scotland than in England(13), and it is these farm-types (and, in the main, the lower-income farmers) which have been disproportionately affected over the past few years.

As can be seen, the only farm-types to have maintained their real incomes are cereal and crop farms. Such variations in farm-type performance imply regional variations in agricultural profitability. In Scotland, as in England, there is a long-term trend towards increasing enterprise specialization and the geographical concentration of farm-types.(14) Thus arable production is particularly prevalent in the eastern Borders, East Lothian, Fife, Angus, the Mearns and the Laigh of Moray. In addition, there is in the North-east a particularly heavy concentration of arable with rearing farms – farms combining arable production with intensive livestock production (especially of pigs) – whose incomes are likely to have held up reasonable well. Dairy production, in contrast, is heavily concentrated in South-west Scotland where over one-third of all Scottish dairy farms are to be found.

Over fifty years of sustained support has helped transform Scottish and British agriculture. Production grants and the maintenance of price stability have encouraged capital investment, the increasing use of manufactured inputs (fertilizer, pesticides, machinery etc.) and turned the drift from the land into a floodtide. In 1951 Scottish agriculture employed 87,710 full-time workers; by 1981 the corresponding figure was 32,903, a fall of over 60%. There have been huge changes in production practices arising not just from technological innovation, but also from the application of an ever-growing body of scientific knowledge and expertise to the rationalization of crop production and animal husbandry. Land prices and yields have risen almost constantly since the fifties, at the same time as there has been an extension in the area of owner-occupied land. In 1945 around 31% of Scottish agricultural land was owner-occupied. By 1982 that figure had risen to 58%. The cereals acreage (a traditional indicator of agricultural prosperity) has expanded, from 1.18 million acres to 1.3 million

TABLE 1

Indices of Net Income per Farm: England and Scotland, 1970/1 – 1980/81
(1977/78 = 100)

	70/71	**71/72**	**72/73**	**73/74**	**74/75**	**75/76**	**76/77**	**77/78**	**78/79**	**79/80**	**80/81**
England	28	44	59	79	73	104	108	100	141	118	121
Scotland	26	41	64	70	83	143	154	100	99	80	75

Source: Taken from F.W. Furness "Some Features of Farm Income and Structure Variations in Regions of the United Kingdom", *Journal of Agricultural Economics*, Vol. 33, 1982, p. 295, Table 2.

TABLE 2

Real terms index numbers of average net farm income in the United Kingdom by main types of farming

	Dairy	**Less Favoured Areas Cattle and Sheep**	**Lowland Cattle and Sheep**	**Cereals**	**Other Cropping**	**Pigs & Poultry**
1977/78	100	100	100	100	100	100
1978/79	106	109	107	126	188	134
1979/80	66	50	48	92	181	94
1980/81	65	58	57	97	109	84
1981/82	81	101	66	93	157	96
1982/83	93	85	53	147	165	67

Source: *Annual Review of Agriculture* 1984, p. 44, Table B.

acres an increase of 10%. However improved yields have meant that total production has increased by well over 70%. New products have been introduced, perhaps the most famous, or notorious, being oilseed rape, whose bright yellow intrusions on the landscape have come to symbolize the wasteful extravagancies of the CAP. Almost unknown in Britain prior to EEC membership, its growth has been encouraged by hefty subsidies with the aim of providing a Community substitute for cheaper imported oils and animal feeds. Total UK production rose from 33 million tons per annum in 1972-74 to 580 million tonnes in 1982. In Scotland the area planted was so small, or even non-existent, that no returns were made in the Agricultural Census period to June 1982, when nearly 4,000 acres were reported to be under this crop.

This then is the backdrop against which current developments are being played out. It should be clear that the crucial decisions affecting the health and future of Scottish agriculture are made not in Edinburgh but, rather, in London and Brussels. It may also be noted that the superior staffing and budgetary resources of the English and Welsh NFU, together with that organisation's proximity to the metropolitan centres of power, gives it rather more power and influence in government circles than is possessed by the Scottish NFU.[G(15)] As tensions and dissensions within the farmers' unions mount in response to actual and proposed cuts in support, this fact may assume an increasing practical significance. But it is time now to turn to a consideration of recent economic, social and political developments which have, or have been generally identified as having, especial significance for the future of Scottish and British agriculture.

Scottish Agriculture and the Land Issue

Agricultural production is ultimately inseparable from the land issue, from control over the use and abuse of one of our most basic productive resources. But our ignorance on this issue is boundless. Of course, since land confers wealth, prestige and not a little power upon its owners it is perhaps not surprising that so little is known about its use and ownership. Such silences insinuate the powerful presence of a class which has come to recognize the "advantages of discretion and ambiguity".[(16)] In the absence of an official register of landownership we are left with McEwen's splendid but still incomplete and increasingly outdated study of *Who Owns Scotland*[(17)], which shows the extent of private landownership in 1970. What is most remarkable is the extent to which the Scottish landed estate has maintained its position over a century of unprecedented economic. social and political change. Although ownership is certainly not as concentrated as it was in the last century its persistence in just a few hands remains startling. McEwen shows that 63% of the Scottish land area was in 1734 private estates of 1,000 acres or more. Fifty-three landowners with estates of more than 40,000 acres held 18% of Scotland's land, while the top 549 owned nearly half (49%) of the country.

The decisions of landowners can, and do, have a powerful impact on the economies of rural areas and the life chances of their residents. Thus attempts in the 1960s to revitalize the agricultural economy of Mull foundered in face of opposition from local landlords who preferred to turn what was by Highland standards good agricultural land over to sporting uses, in the process evicting farming tenants.[18] In a contrasting case study of the Luss Estates in Dunbartonshire, Bird[19] has documented the effects on the local community of an aggressively commercial approach to the land. The Laird's primary concerns were with achieving high returns from his property and ensuring its succession. To this end life-long tenancies for estate-workers were abolished, who then often faced eviction on the termination of employment; land was taken in hand as tenancies expired; estate houses were left empty for most of the year to be let to summer holidaymakers, while attempts to purchase land for council housing were repeatedly resisted. The result is the decline of the local community as its old occupational base is eroded and new and potentially revitalising developments are blocked.

The twentieth century as a whole, and particularly the post- war years, have seen a decline in the extent of the traditional landed estates, and thus the erosion of the previous three-tier hierarchy of landowner, tenant-farmer and agricultural labourer. Initially the reasons for this change lay in the operation of Engel's Law, which states that as overall incomes increase there is a long-run tendency for returns to agriculture to decline. Latterly, as agricultural support policies have mitigated the impact of this law, fiscal policies which discriminate against owners of let land and the income advantages which attach to direct farming have become more important. Some of this increase in owner-occupation is undoubtedly accounted for by the purchase of estate land by sitting tenants. But some of it (and naturally we don't know how much) results from the taking in hand of land by traditional owners. In the absence of a cadastral record of landholding, or detailed local studies, we cannot reliably say to what extent land has changed hands over the past century (and thus, too, how far the Scottish agrarian class structure has changed). On the basis of McEwen's figures and the continued concentration of landholding they reveal, the answer is perhaps "not all that much".

These changes have implied, too, an effective convergence of interest between landowners and farmers, with the result that on many issues the Scottish NFU and the Scottish Landowners' Federation are able to speak as one voice. There is no doubt that both organizations can exert quite considerable influence on the Scottish Office, but, once again, the mechanisms and channels through which such influence is exercised are largely invisible and unexplored. Here, as elsewhere in Scottish society, power is real but effectively anonymous. The linkages between landowners, farmers, the Scottish ruling class and the exercise of local and national political power is a fascinating, much needed and still unwritten study.[20]

By 1970 it seemed as if a new and fairly stable system of agricultural property relationships had emerged. But two developments during that decade were to threaten the future of private landownership: namely the emergence of financial institutions as major agents in the land market and capital taxation.

The Financial Institutions

The repetition is becoming increasingly tedious but – once again – our knowledge of this topic is patchy. However according to one of the more reliable recent estimates[21], financial institutions owned 82,400 acres of let agricultural land in Scotland (or 1.95% of the acreage of crops and grass). While substantial institutional involvement in farmland purchases in the arable counties of eastern England dates from the early Seventies, involvement in the Scottish farmland market is more recent. The Savills-RTP survey indicates that 82% (or 67,900 acres) of all institutional purchases of Scottish farmland have taken place since 1976.[22] That date is perhaps not entirely fortuitous. The Northfield Committee[23] reported that at one time there had been a reluctance to invest in Scotland because of the greater security of tenure afforded to tenants there, until such differences were largely removed by the Agriculture (Miscellaneous Provisions) Act of 1976. Matters have now changed so much that in 1982 34% of total British purchases were in Scotland, where stable capital values and increasing yields relative to the rest of Britain provided a considerable stimulus to investment.

Corroboration of the scale of recent institutional activity in the Scottish agricultural land market is provided by figures released by DAFS.[24] These indicate that in 1979-81 such institutions bought a total of some 44,000 acres of farmland. What is particularly interesting is the relative scale of their involvement in the Scottish land market. In 1979, 1980 and 1981 the institutions accounted for 8%, 12.5% and 10.6% respectively of all sales of land remaining in agriculture. These proportions are substantially higher than the 3.6% per annum given in the Northfield Report.[25] In the case of land sold out of agriculture for afforestation in these same years the institutions accounted for 45%, 36.2% and 67.5% respectively of all purchases.[26] Such information as exists suggests that the bulk of such purchases are concentrated in the eastern lowlands from Berwickshire to Nairn, not surprisingly, perhaps, in view of the institutions' well-known preference for large arable or mixed farms on prime land.

Transfers of land on the scale reported above, if sustained for any length of time, could lead to financial institutions coming to play an increasingly significant role in Scottish agriculture. Their importance, perhaps even their predominance, would be less likely to arise from owership of land per se, than from control over a disporportionate share of total production. In Scotland, as elsewhere in Britain, a small proportion of enterprises account for the bulk of total production. To give a few examples: in 1982 18% of all cereal growing farms produced 63% of total production, 46% of the total number of beef cattle were to be found in just 13% of herds, and 23% of dairy herds accounted for a little over half of the total number of dairy cattle.

If we take note, too, of the institutions' bias in favour of large, well-equipped farms on superior land, we might be well advised to give credence to the Centre for Agricultural Strategy's observation that while fewer than 865,000 acres changes hands in the UK every year,

> ".... it is inconceivable that a substantial proportion of UK farmland could pass into the hands of City institutions in the next decade. On the other hand, it is possible that, if financial institutions made a concerted effort and bought up the (150,000 acres) of large farms ..... coming on to the market each year, they could be responsible for just under 50% of UK agricultural production within 30 years"[27]

While institutional purchases in the UK have not been on this scale, the potential for control nonetheless remains very great indeed.

If our understanding of the activities and purchases of financial institutions as a whole is inadequate, then how much more so is our knowledge of who exactly owns what and where. McEwen's otherwise invaluable work is not particularly helpful in this instance, since it essentially presents a snapshot of Scottish landholding in 1970, before the current wave of institutional investment. The names, but often not much more, of some institutions are known: for example, the Commercial Union

Assurance Co. Ltd., the Prudential Assurance Company and the Post Office Superannuation Scheme. In any event it is quite probable that only a small number of individual institutions are involved in the Scottish agricultural land market. The Northfield Committee reported that while the number of institutions investing in farmland had risen considerably during the 1970s, these funds still remained in a small minority. No consensus existed among institutions over the purchase of agricultural land, though it was generally agreed that the necessarily long-term nature of investment in agriculture did not make it attractive either to mature funds or to those that needed to maintain a high level of liquidity.[28] But whatever the precise details of ownership may be, it is undoubtedly the case that the activities of the institutions "represent, potentially at least, one of the most significant developments in landownership in this country in the last fifty years".[29] Collectively they represent the fastest growing landowner in Britain, and as perhaps the most important agents in the contemporary British economy developments in their activities and investment decisions deserve to be carefully scrutinized. It has been argued that the emergence of the institutions as significant landowners signals the end of that long-run trend toward owner-occupied farming that followed upon the break-up of the large-landed estates in the aftermath of the First World War. We might thus be witnessing a new separation of the functions of landowner and farmer. Alternatively, the institutions might take land in hand and either farm directly or in partnership with specialised farming companies. If this were to happen on any scale, the corporate dominance of production characteristic of some sectors and regions of United States agriculture would become a feature of British farming.

Capital Taxation

The rise of the institutions was only one of a number of developments in the Seventies which threatened established property relations in agriculture. Land values, which had risen steadily throughout the Fifties and Sixties, spiralled dramatically in the Seventies, particularly in the years from 1972 to 1974 when land values doubled or even trebled. Almost overnight the asset-value of owner-occupied enterprises burgeoned, with the larger farmers on prime land becoming paper-millionaires. However, far from welcoming their good fortune, many farmers looked upon their new-found wealth with gloomy trepidation as the incoming Labour government of 1974 brought with it "penal" capital taxation in the shape of Capital Transfer Tax. This in conjunction with Capital Gains Tax (and – who could say? – the possibility of an annual wealth tax), seemed to place the inter-generational continuity of farming and land-holding in jeopardy, since on his death a farmer's survivors would be forced to sell land in order to meet crippling tax demands. Apart from the state, the most likely purchasers of such land would be the financial institutions who, unlike mere farmers, are immortal.

All these developments drew vehement, acrimonious and often bitter comment from the farming community and their spokesmen, never more so perhaps than when it was the activities of the institutions that were being called into question. There was plenty of scope for the habitual suspicion and defensive paranoia of farmers, with many coming to believe in

> "a vague conspiracy by the City and the government: the City institutions, by forcing up land prices, were imposing a crippling CTT burden on the individual landowner who was thereby forced to sell out to them"[30]

In point of fact it is far more likely that the movement of the institutions into land and their willingness to bid high prices was part of a wider confidence in land, which was itself a response to, inter alia, growing inflation rates, declining industrial profitability, looming economic crisis, a bumper harvest in 1973 under conditions of world shortage, not to mention the hopes inspired by entry into the EEC. If a villain must be found then it is probably "roll-over-relief" rather than the city institutions which should be arraigned.[31]

In the event matters have not turned out as badly as was first hoped or feared. In the first place, and partly as a consequence of the concessions progressively extended to owner-occupier and tenant farmers, capital taxation does not present an insurmountable problem to most farmers.

Using data derived from MAFF's Farm Management Survey, Peters[32] has estimated both the wealth and CTT liability of various groups of farmers. He reports that on the basis of net worth all full-time owner-occupier farmers fall among the top 6% of wealth owners. Small dairy farmers just make that level while large cropping and livestock farmers are easily in the top half per cent. On the income side farmers are on the whole in a less favoured position than with respect to wealth. All large farms and medium cropping farms would fall into the upper 1% of the distribution, medium size dairy and livestock farms into the upper 10% or incomes with small dairy and livestock farmers slipping down to about the fourth decile. However,

> "Despite this it can fairly be stated that owner-occupiers belong to a particularly wealthy sector of the community who are also

advantageously placed, though less markedly, in terms of income".[33]

In spite of this marked concentration of wealth, farmers are not particularly vulnerable to capital taxation. Peters suggests that the full CTT liability of small and medium dairy and livestock farms could for the most part be met out of income. But all other farms would be threatened if their maximum theoretical CTT and CGT liability had to be met. However, if a farmer is prudent enough to take sound financial advice and make maximum use of the concessions and loopholes available under the acts then he can, in most cases, ensure the transfer of his business. Tenant farmers have even fewer problems in spite of the fact that larger tenants have wealth sufficient to place them within the top second or third percentile in the national placings. However, it is likely that CTT will further encourage the decline of the traditional agricultural landlord since, as has been the case throughout the century, the owners of let land are treated far more harshly than owner-farmers. Consequently, more land is likely to be taken in hand or sold to sitting tenants or other buyers such as the financial institutions.

Agricultural Incomes

It seems clear, therefore, that farmers are a relatively wealthy and privileged group within British and Scottish society. Nor should the falling farm incomes of recent years necessarily lead us to modify that judgement. The agriculture departments' annual calculations of Net Farm Income (NFI) are important primarily as a resource for production-oriented economic studies of the industry or, and just as importantly, as a weapon in the negotiations, debates and battles between the NFUs and Government. While the are undeniable links between the incomes of individuals (or families) and the aggregate:

> "the situation is too complex for a simplistic view to be acceptable, and changes in the industry figure do not necessarily offer a valuable guide to what is happening to the incomes of farmers and their families".[34]

In particular industry figures are unsatisfactory in two main respects:

(1) Farm households may have income from sources other than farming. Hill, for example, has shown that only 63% of the total income of individuals and couples engaged in UK farming comes from business profits.[35]

(2) While, with appropriate modifications, Net Farm Income might make a useful indicator of incomes on tenanted farms, its ignoral of capital gains makes it of limited value in the case of owner-occupied farms. Farming spokesmen often like to pretend that capital gains are somehow unreal – existing only on paper – and are of little real consequence or benefit to the farmer. Of course, there are problems in realizing capital gains if wealth is held in land, but part of any gain in real net worth can be realized indirectly, for example through extra borrowing. At any rate:

"When a capital gain is realised there is a clear release of purchasing power to the person or family owning the asset. When capital gains are NOT realised by disposal ..... it is evident that unrealised gains still constitute part of real personal income. Unrealised gains represent the value of rights which the owner MIGHT HAVE exercised in consumption without diminishing the value of his wealth".[36]

Hill goes on to argue that if capital gains are taken into account then almost 50% can be added to UK Net Farm Income in 1976/77 (a year in which NFI was particularly high), raising the proportion of the sample with incomes of £10,000 and over from 45% to 65%.[37]

While the average figures for Scotland will be lower than the UK figures quoted here, there can be little doubt that as a group Scottish farmers are rather better off than the majority of their compatriots. In particular, the large east coast arable farmers must be among the wealthiest in Britain.

For many farmers, this prosperity is of comparatively recent origin. Bowers and Cheshire[38] have derived an income series for UK farmers and other occupational groups over the period 1935-77. At constant 1976 prices the "average" farmer's annual income rose fairly steady from £1,177 in 1938 (80% of average male manual wages and 152% of average agricultural worker wages) to £7,384 (209% and 281% respectively) in 1973-77. The change in farmers' economic status is dramatically obvious, fully bearing out the authors' assertion that farmers as a group "have moved from a position of absolute and relative poverty to a position of substantial prosperity".[39] It is equally obvious that this transformation has been effected primarily by the ever-burgeoning financial and administrative apparatus of state-support for agriculture. Not that its benefits have been evenly or equitably distributed. Far from it. Support policy as we shall see raises the incomes of farmers proportionately to their richness. And farm workers remain amongst the lowest paid and disadvantaged of all occupational groups, poverty and dependence being their all too-common lot. In 1983 average weekly wages for full-time male agricultural workers stood at £112.25 per week (including overtime payments and the value of perquisites), or 77% of the average Scottish male manual wage.

This digression upon farmers' income and wealth is not a purely academic exercise. Knowledge about such matters will naturally be relevant to an assessment of the position of farmers in the contemporary Scottish class structure. But it has, too, a direct importance for agricultural policy-making; or so one might naively presume.

Concern over the incomes of farmers has been a fundamental but ill-defined and poorly articulated component of the post-war agricultural policies of both the United Kingdom and the EEC. It has often been assumed that a gap exists between farm and non-farm incomes which should be closed (though commentators have typically been vague as to the magnitude of this gap). Such concerns lie behind the declared objectives of ensuring the "proper remuneration and living conditions for farmers and workers" of the 1947 Agriculture Act and the "fair standard of living for the agricultural community" of the Treaty of Rome. But there has been little attempt to translate such goals into detailed and coherent policy formulations. Any comprehensive and workable programme to eradicate agricultural poverty surely requires details of the sectoral and regional distribution of real incomes within agriculture, detailed knowledge of the structure of the agricultural industry (including patterns of tenure and landownership)and a knowledge of the linkages between agriculture and other sectors of the economy. In all these areas our knowledge is to a greater or lesser extent deficient. In the case of incomes, Hill points out that

> "Despite the importance of being able to assess the poverty and comparability aspects of agricultural policy ...... incomes have never been officially measured in ways which can be used to indicate in any meaningful manner the living standards of farmers".[(40)]

The ambiguities and lacunae of this policy area have proven advantageous to the farming unions, allowing them both to blur and elide very real differences in the circumstances of different groups of farmers and to present any kind of increase in total agricultural support as a step towards eradicating agricultural poverty. And, of course, concern over agricultural incomes has invariably focussed on farmers' incomes at the expense of farmworkers. There undoubtedly are relatively poor farms and farmers in Scotland, more so than in England. For example, many small and medium size general dairy farms have probably experienced severe financial problems in recent years, even before the imposition of quotas. But by far the largest number of marginal enterprises are to be found in the hills and uplands, where many farms are entirely dependent upon EEC and UK subventions for their survival. Indeed their precarious status and the vital contribution they make to the fragile local economy of many parts of Scotland has found official recognition in the classification of the so-called "Less Favoured Areas" which make up nearly three-quarters of the land area of Scotland. However, it nonetheless remains the case that the overall distribution of support is sharply skewed in favour of these high output/high income producers who are presumably least in need of it. In essence, support is biased towards large farms at the expense of the small and arable farmers rather than livestock farmers. Even in the hills and uplands large farmers benefit more from Hill Livestock Compensatory Allowances (which are paid on a headage basis) than their smaller counterparts.

As budgetary crisis deepens, and financial constraints tighten, then more detailed knowledge of, and more carefully specified policies with respect to, farm incomes will become essential if the income maintenance goals of the Treaty of Rome are to be realized and the hill and upland economy of Scotland sustained. Otherwise, farm support will remain, in the words of the European Commission, "a source of social inequality under the cloak of economic equality".[41] It is to the budgetary crisis of the Common Agricultural Policy and its potential effects upon Scottish agriculture that we now turn.

Crisis in the CAP

Attempts to limit agricultural output and support costs have been forced upon the EEC in response to growing food surpluses and the ever-rising costs of price guarantees. In Scotland, the value of production grants and price supports administered by DAFS went from £38.25m in 1975/6 to £78.9m in 1983. In 1981/82 the relevant figure was £72.23m or £3,036 for each of the 23,790 farmers listed in the 1981 population census.[42] Nor does this take into account the value of CAP price support. Over the past five years the annual budget of the Intervention Board for Agricultural Produce (IBAP), the body charged with the implementation of CAP price support in the United Kingdom, has risen at a frightening rate:

TABLE 3

Gross Annual Expenditure by IBAP, 1979-1983

	£m
1979	529.8
1980	762.5
1981	960.3
1982	1,225.9
1983	1,778.8

% Change 1979-1983 = 236%

Source: IBAP Annual Reports.

Bowers and Cheshire[(43)] have argued that in 1979 support was worth about £10,000 to every farmer in the UK (or £5,000 per farmer and worker) an estimate they consider to be fairly conservative. This represents a subsidy of between £60 and £80 for every agricultural acre in the UK (or 60-95% of the level of average rents). It is clear that the costs of the Common Agricultural Policy have, particularly in a period of low growth and high unemployment, simply become insupportable. To these budgetary pressures must be added those arising from the political tensions engendered by the inequitable distribution of the CAP's costs among the member states.[(44)] Within Britain one has also to take account of the influence of a renascent New Right and its detestation of state intervention and subsidy in all things economic. Certainly it is an open secret that certain members of the present Cabinet, including the Prime Minister, have little sympathy for the farmers.

So in April 1984, confronted by impending bankruptcy, the EEC took the hitherto unprecedented step of imposing curbs on production in the shape of milk quotas, with stiff levies being imposed on excess production. Support prices for a range of other commodities were also cut slightly. The farmers' response was vehement, bitter and often self-righteous. Demonstrations were organised, demands were made for the Agriculture Minister's resignation (and occasionally his head), while from within the NFUs we could hear mutterings of discontent over the leadership's supposed failure to protect the dairymen's interests. This well-orchestrated chorus of indignation made no difference to the quotas, but it did succeed in getting the Government to introduce 'redundancy' payments for farmers wishing to leave the industry. For a farmer with a herd of 30 cows this will be worth about £20,000; a 180 cow dairyman will receive £120,000.[(45)]

Despite these production restrictions, the EEC will still be faced with an estimated surplus of 12.5m tonnes of milk in the 1984/85 financial year, not to mention a budget which continues to lurch ever deeper into crisis. Further cuts in the value of price guarantees are therefore almost inevitable, with cereals and beef being high on the list of likely candidates for control at the 1985 price review. It is impossible to say just how harshly cuts will bite, or how they will be distributed across different sectors. Much will depend on general economic conditions within the Community, on the State of political relationships between member states and the sort of trade-offs they facilitate, and, of course, the balance of power within the farmers' unions both at the national level and within COPA, the Community's federation of farmers' unions. Here we may note that cereal farmers traditionally constitute a powerful and well organised bloc: they are certainly well represented within the NFUs.

Obviously, quotas and support price cuts, by raising the threshold of viability, will force many farmers out of business and act as a further stimulus to farm amalgamation and growing enterprise size. They are also likely to have an effect on the activities of financial institutions in the land market. Institutional purchases of farmland have been a response to high and stable levels of land prices. High land values have in turn been conditional upon state support for agriculture: support which has to a large extent been capitalized in land. In an econometric simulation Trail found that a 1% increase in farm support prices resulted, amongst other things, in an increase in farm income and land prices of around 10%.[46]

Given that the investment decisions of institutions have in the past shown themselves to be highly sensitive to short-run fluctuations in the agricultural land market, one might therefore expect a decline in price support and land values to be followed by the institutions disengaging themselves from the farmland market.

The hills and uplands

An issue of particular concern to Scotland will be the future of subsidies for the nation's hill and upland farmers, whose dependence on outside support has already been noted. Any redirection in the level of subsidy could deprive the local economies of these regions of one of their most crucial supports. Moreover, the major land-use problems of such regions are not those of over-production and environmental damage, but all too often, and particularly in the Highlands, the misuse, neglect and underdevelopment of potentially productive land by private landlords.[47] At least in the short-run, therefore, there are good grounds for maintaining agricultural support to these regions. However, in the long-run, if the social and economic viability of "marginal" regions is to be maintained (and, indeed, if large tracts of lowland Scotland and Britain are not to become the preserve of a privileged population of middle-class commuters who have taken over villages once populated by now displaced agricultural workers) greater consideration will have to be given to the respective goals and methods of agricultural policy and regional planning. In a study of the Orkneys, Slee[48] has pointed out the contradictory consequences of the lack of co-ordination between agricultural planning and regional and local planning. Thus one of the principal goals of the H.I.D.B. and the Orkney Islands Council has been the halting of depopulation. Agricultural policy-makers, on the other hand, have directed their energies towards tackling the perceived problems of agricultural "backwardness" and "low incomes" by, inter alia, providing generous advice, grants and subsidies for capital improvements. But by encouraging the substitution of capital for labour these policies only exacerbate the very problems of unemployment and depopulation which regional and local policies are attempting to combat. Thus, in the absence of alternative sources of employment, agricultural policy tends to bring about what Gerald Wibberley has termed the paradox of "strong agricultures but weak rural communities",[49] as agricultural modernization helps create local unemployment, depopulation, surplus rural settlements, rising costs of maintaining infrastructures etc. If the present crisis of the CAP is to be resolved without either a wholesale withdrawal of funds for agricultural support, or sacrificing the interests of the most vulnerable producers in favour of those of the most powerful, much greater consideration will inevitably have to be given to structural reform and policy. The directions in which this may lead are best indicated by the EEC's Mansholt Plan of 1968.[50] The Plan argued that because of the tendency of farm incomes to decline relative to the remainder of the economy (the aforementioned Engel's Law) farm income would be a perennial and ever more burdensome problem without an increase in the size of farms and a reduction in their number. It presented comprehensive proposals for reforming the structure of production. These included:

(1) the creation of more economic farms by the expansion and amalgamation of existing farms.

(2) the withdrawal of some land (about some 13m acres amongst the then Six) from cultivation, mostly for afforestation.

(3) regional development schemes to create new jobs in agricultural areas and so avoid depopulation.

(4) reductions in price guarantees, principally in the dairy sector which even then was experiencing acute surplus problems.

In face of vigorous opposition from the Community's farmers' organisations the Plan was shelved. The need for such a programme of comprehensive development and reform has never been greater and given that member states retain a great deal of autonomy in the area of structural policy, a start could be made by the UK government in devising and implementing such a programme. Indeed, if the presently conflicting goals of farm income support, the containment of exchequer commitment to agriculture and the maintenance of economically and socially viable rural communities are to be reconciled, then such programmes of integrated policy-making and regional economic diversification are essential. This does not mean, however, that we have to accept prevailing definitions of what "modernisation" and "development" entail. In the case of agricultural policy for example, a welcome change would be a shift of emphasis away from capital subsidies toward labour subsidies. Not only would this delay the rate of outflow of labour from agriculture, but, especially in the Lowlands, it would also help minimize the environmental damage which accompanies modern capital-intensive farming.

However, any attempt to implement successfully such a thorough-going programme of rural development must face up to two crucial problems. In the first place the power wielded by landowners must be attacked and their capacity to resist personally unwelcome change eroded. Secondly, if economic diversification is not to proceed via the establishment of externally controlled branch plants by footloose metropolitan or multinational companies then some attempt must be made to establish local control over such developments.

In the present political climate of governmental hostility to state intervention in the economy and indifference to the world beyond the golden vale of the south-east, such proposals inevitably have a utopian ring. However, here as in so many other respects so scandalous is Scotland's decline that nothing less than radical solutions and policies will do. In the meantime, the other political parties could usefully devote some thought to the problems facing rural Scotland.

References

1. J.A. Symon, *Scottish Farming*, Oliver & Boyd, 1959. p.197. One should not be too sceptical about such claims. Carter has attempted to show how the widely renowned quality of North-east husbandry was rooted in "the

social formation of improved agriculture: in the structural relations between classes in the rural North-east at the end of the agricultural revolution of the late eighteenth and early nineteenth centuries". Ian Carter, *Farm Life in North-east Scotland 1840-1914*, John Donald, 1979, p.10.

2. Symon, *op.cit.* p.239

3. The Milk Marketing Boards are essentially monopoly buyers and wholesalers of milk.

4. J.K. Bowers and Paul Cheshire, *Agriculture, the Countryside and Land Use*, Methuen, 1983, p.59.

5. The "strategic necessity" argument for self-sufficiency has a long and honourable history stretching back to the Corn Law debates. Of course the nature of the threat we are exhorted to protect ourselves against – blockade in war, world famine, disruption of food supplies in an area of international unstability – varies with time and context. The counter-arguments are by now equally well-rehearsed. They include, inter alia, the points that "security of supply" should be taken to mean the amount of production needed to survive, not the amount needed to maintain stable patterns of consumption; the growing dependence of agriculture on high-cost imported inputs, especially oil; that with the general situation in temperate foodstuffs that of surplus we are hardly faced with a major crisis; and that by introducing a crucial element of instability into the world agricultural market the Common Agricultural Policy actually exacerbates the problems of international economic and political instability it pretends to protect us from.

6. Indeed, in 1946 Attlee became the first British Prime Minister to attend and address the annual dinner of the NFU of England and Wales.

7. Once again a key term was left substantively undefined. In practice, "efficiency" seems to have come to mean increasing labour productivity and expanding total output.

8. "Standard quantities" stated the maximum output for which the Treasury would pay the guaranteed price. If producers exceeded this they were penalized by a dilution in the value of the guaranteed price. Standard quantities were also imposed on eggs and potatoes.

9. In Scotland this was the Secretary of State.

10. National Plan, Cmnd. 2764, 1965. Agriculture was to contribute to the solution of Britain's chronic balance of payments problems by an expansion in production, thus saving on imports. However expansion was not to absorb an excessive share of real resources which could be better used elsewhere. Over this stipulation the proposal came to grief. In Beresford's delicate phrasing, "Cost-benefit analysis, performed by the NFU's ever-resourceful team of economists, gave different answers from those reached by the Treasury". Tristram Beresford, *We Plough the Fields, Agriculture in Britain Today*, Penguin, 1975, p.58.

11. The income figures provided are calculations of Net Farm Income (NFI) as measured by the agriculture departments for the purposes of the Annual Review. As we shall see, they are not an unambiguous guide to the income and wealth of individual farmers.

12. Annual Review of Agriculture 1984 HMSO, 1984 Cmnd. 9137.

13. In England 53% of the agricultural land area is classified as "arable"; in Scotland only 18.6%. In Scotland in 1978 over one third of all full-time farms were classified as dairy farms, about the same proportion as cropping farms.

14. I.R. Bowler, "Regional Variations in Scottish Agricultural Trends", *Scottish Geographical Magazine* vol.92(2), 1975; "Regional Specialization in the Agricultural Industry", *Journal of Agricultural Economics*, vol.32(1), 1981.

15. See Graham K. Wilson, *Special Interests and Policymaking*. Wiley, 1977, Ch.3.

16. Howard Newby, *Green and Pleasant Land?*, Penguin, 1980, p.27.

17. John McEwen, *Who Owns Scotland*, 2nd Edition, Polygon, 1981.

18. See Ian Carter, "Community Development in Scotland: Promises and Problems" in M. Gaskin (ed.), *The Political Economy of Tolerable Survival*, Croom Helm, 1981. Also, James Grassie, *Highland Experiment: the story of the Highlands and Islands Development Board*, Aberdeen University Press, 1983, ch.4.

19. S. Elizabeth Bird, "The Impact of Private Estate Ownership on Social Development in a Scottish Rural Community", *Sociologia Ruralis*

Vol.22(1), 1981.

20. We lack even the kind of case studies of farmers' and landowners' control over local labour markets, housing, politics and planning which have been undertaken in East Anglia. See Howard Newby et al, *Property, Paternalism and Power*, Hutchinson, 1978. Also M. Mosely (ed.), "Power, Planning and People in Rural East Anglia", Centre for East Anglian Studies, 1982.

21. *Savills-RTP Agricultural Performance Analysis* for 1982, dated June 1983. Savills and RTP are firms extensively involved in the agricultural land market.

22. Nonetheless their figures are almost certainly under-estimates perhaps by as much as 50%.

23. *Report of the Committee of Inquiry into the Acquisition and Occupancy of Agricultural Land*, Chairman Lord Northfield, 1979 Cmnd. 7599, pp.317-18, para. 28.

24. A.M. Mackenzie "Land Sales and Financial Institutions", in DAFS *Economic Report on Scottish Agriculture 1981*, HMSO, 1982, pp.8-11.

25. Northfield, *op.cit.* p.66 Table 15.

26. Mackenzie, *op.cit.* p.10, Table 3. In area terms the institutions purchased 20,871 acres for afforestation in that three year period.

27. Centre for Agricultural Strategy, *Capital for Agriculture*, Report no.3, 1978, pp.42-43.

28. Northfield, *op.cit.*, p.323, paras.38 & 39.

29. Newby, *Green and Pleasant Land?, op.cit.*, p.59.

30. *Ibid.* p.63.

31. "Roll-over relief" was a term given to a concession granted by the Heath government to landowners who sold land at development prices for housing and industrial use. Provided that the money was invested in agriculture within three years, the resulting Capital Gains Tax could be avoided. Since development value was far greater than agricultural value, these landowners, who had large sums of liquid capital seeking a quick

investment, could afford to pay a premium on land equivalent to the foregone tax rate. The irony, of course, was that many of these landowners were themselves farmers who, having sold land to developers, were seeking either to re- establish themselves in farming or to expand their businesses.

32. G.H. Peters, "Some thoughts on Capital Taxation", *Journal of Agricultural Economics*, vol.31(3), 1980.

33. *ibid.* p.390. This is also before we consider sources of income and wealth outwith farming.

34. Berkeley Hill, "Farm Incomes: Myths and Perspectives", *Lloyds Bank Review*, no. 149, July 1983.

35. Berkeley Hill, "Information on Farmers' Incomes: Data from Inland Revenue Sources", *Journal of Agricultural Economics*, vol.35(1), 1984.

36. Berkely Hill, "Concepts and Measurement of the Incomes, Wealth and Economic Well-Being of Farmers", *Journal of Agricultural Economics* vol.33(3), 1982, p.317.

37. *ibid.* p.319 and pp.322-23.

38. Bowers and Cheshire, *op.cit.*, Ch.4., esp. pp.77-88. While the broad trend undoubtedly holds true for Scotland, the appropriate Scottish figures would probably be below the UK average. It should also be noted that the calculations are based on official estimates of Net Farm Income and so are subject to the limitations previously noted.

39. *ibid.*, p.86.

40. Hill, "Farm Incomes..." *op.cit.*, pp.40-41.

41. Commission of the European Communities,"Reflections on the Common Agricultural Policy", Brussels, 1980, quoted in Hill, "Concepts and Measurement ...", *op.cit.*, p.324.

42. This does NOT include expenditure under such headings as "educational, advisory, research and development services", or "assistance to marketing".

43. Bowers and Cheshire,*op.cit.* pp.98-102.

44. The CAP transfers resources from EEC countries which are net importers, such as Britain, to those that are net exporters, such as France. The net cost of the CAP to Britain was estimated by the House of Lords Select Committee on the European Communities (Session 1980/81) to have been £1,110m in 1979.

45. *The Scottish Farmer*, August 11 1984, p.46.

46. W.B. Traill, "The Effect of Price Support Policies on Agricultural Investment and Employment", *Journal of Agricultural Economics*, vol.33(1), 1982.

47. George Houston and John Bryden, *Agrarian Change in the Scottish Highlands,* Martin Robertson, 1976. Also, A.M. Armstrong and A.S. Mather, *Land Ownership and Land Use in the Scottish Highlands,* Department of Geography, University of Aberdeen, 1983; McEwen, *op.cit.* pp.80-108.

48. R.W. Slee, "Agricultural Policy and Remote Rural Areas", *Journal of Agricultural Economics,* vol.32(2), 1981.

49. Gerald Wibberley, "Strong Agricultures but Weak Rural Communities", *European Review of Agricultural Economics* vol.8(2), 1981.

50. Its official title was the "Memorandum on the Reform of Agriculture in the European Economic Community".

THE POLITICS OF COUNCIL HOUSING FINANCE

ARTHUR MIDWINTER
DEPARTMENT OF ADMINISTRATION
UNIVERSITY OF STRATHCLYDE

1. The Conservative Government and Council Housing Finance

The recently published Green Paper on Public Expenditure and Taxation[(1)] revealed quite clearly that council housing has borne the brunt of the Government's policy of cutting public expenditure. Public housing has been a central target in the attempt to roll back the state. There are several reasons why this should be so.

First of all, although the overall thrust of Conservative policy was to reduce public spending and taxation, several key areas of expenditure were not only exempt from such cuts, but intended to grow. The best examples are defence, with the commitment to grow by 3% per annum in real terms to reach the NATO average, and law and order. Health spending was to be maintained broadly in line with Labour's plans. With the rapid rise in unemployment, social security spending was to grow quite rapidly.

The end result in 1983, after the first term of the Thatcher Administration, was that local government and public housing had been the main target for spending cuts, and whilst local authorities had been successful in resisting the cuts in rate support grant, dramatic cuts in public expenditure on housing had been achieved (see Table 1).

Secondly, housing was also central to the Government's new vision of local democracy. Distrust of 'local corporatism' had resulted in a changed view of the virtues of local government as an institution, and an increased emphasis on individual rights.[(2)] Whilst the Tenants' Rights (Scotland) Act in many aspects fulfilled the policy aims of the previous Labour Government, the sale of council houses through the statutory right to buy (see David Alexander's article) was symptomatic of the new approach. Apart from the traditional Conservative vision of a property-owning democracy and the virtues of home ownership, there was the realisation that the propensity to vote Conservative was greater amongst working-class owner-occupiers than working-class council tenants.[(3)]

Table 1

Changes in Cost Terms in Government Expenditure Programmes since 1978-79

Defence	+23%
Agriculture, Fisheries, Food and Forestry	+40%
Law and Order	+33%
Health and Person Social Services	+16%
Social Security	+26%
Local Authorities	+10%
Trade and Industry	−29%
Public Housing	−34%

Thirdly, the nature of the council housing programme makes it administratively and politically convenient to cut. The growing literature on cutback management reveals the dominance of two strategies for coping with retrenchment and fiscal pressure. One is to increase income from other sources (charging) and the other is to cut capital expenditure, as it has less short-term consequences for the organisation. Housing was a suitable subject for such strategies. A large proportion of the public spending programme was on capital, and a major alternative source of income was available, namely council rents. We can expose these ideas further by examining the framework of council housing finance.

Control of housing capital expenditure in Scotland is effected through the Housing Plan system, and Section 94 of the Local Government (Scotland) Act 1973. The Government determines the overall resources available for housing and these are divided into two blocks, the housing revenue account (the HRA Block), which covers expenditure on council housing, and the non-housing revenue account (the non-HRA Block), which covers aid tothe private sector in the form of improvement grants and lending for house purchase and improvement. Local authorities have the power to transfer up to 10% of their allocations between blocks (*virement*), thus providing some flexibility for managing programmes. I have written elsewhere that this system has increased the degree of managerial freedom, whilst assisting in greater central control over expenditure.[(4)]

Scotland's heavy dependence on council housing has led to the programme forming a separate part of the accounts of District and Islands

Councils, unlike England and Wales where it is part of the Block Grant.[5] Revenue expenditure consists of *repairs and maintenance, administration and management,* and redemption and interest payments. Income arises from three main sources, government grant (Housing Support Grant), rents and contributions from rates. The HSG is related to the expenditure and rental income of each authority's Housing Revenue Account. It was introduced in 1979, with the declared intention of concentrating Housing Subsidies where the need was greatest. The Secretary of State estimates for each authority, the amount of (a) Eligible Expenditure and (b) Relevant Income. Eligible expenditure consists of

- annual loan charges reflecting the consequences of past capital expenditure;

- a standard amount per council house for management and maintenance expenditure together with specific weightings in respect of numbers of high rise dwellings in urban areas and in respect of the first 8,500 houses in the housing stock, and

- other expenditure.

Relevant Income comprises

- Standard Rents, that is rents before the deduction of any rebates granted;

- Rate Fund Contributions;

- Other income.

In assessing relevant income, the Secretary of State determines what he considers authorities can reasonably derive from rents and Rate Fund Contributions. The aggregate amount of the Housing Support Grant is the difference between Eligible Expenditure and Relevant Income. Concern to control all housing public expenditure, irrespective of its source of finance, and the treatment of housing as a separately financed service, has allowed the Government to link expenditure on capital with revenue, through the Housing Expenditure Limit system, in a way which is not possible with the Rate Support Grant. The scope for local discretion stems from the Rate Fund Contribution. The thrust of Government policy has been to reduce grants and ensure matching increases in rents, whilst maintaining the current level of Rate Fund Contribution. The HEL system operates so that any expenditure incurred via the Rate Fund Contribution in excess of government plans results in off- setting reductions in capital expenditure, whereby total public expenditure on housing is contained within the planned figure in the Public Expenditure Survey.

In practice, these mechanisms have allowed substantial reductions in the council housing expenditure programme, and also a change in priorities from public to private sector housing. Overall, the cut in capital expenditure between 1979 and 1983 was 33%.

Table 2

Capital Expenditure on Housing by Local Authorities (1979-83)
(1983 prices*)

*These figures have been recalculated using the retail price index.

	1979	1983	% Change
Housing Improvement and Standard Grants	£31.4m	£114.6m	+364%
HRA	£445.5m	£267.5m	– 40%
Loans	£43.4m	£29.3m	– 33%
Other Housing	£21.4m	£9.9m	– 54%
Total	£541.7m	£421.3m	– 33%

Source: Rating Review

The bulk of the reductions were in the HRA account, whilst grants to the private sector grew rapidly. (This was halted because of public expenditure pressures in 1984.) Table 3 reveals the extent to which spending priorities changed.

Table 3

Changing Priorities in Housing Capital Expenditure

	1979	1983
Housing Improvement and Standard Grants	5.7%	27.2%
HRA	82.2%	63.5%
Loans	8.0%	6.9%
Other Housing	4.1%	2.3%
Total	100.0%	100.0%

Source: Rating Review

The Government became sensitive to the impact of cutting capital expenditure on the construction industry, and in fact in 1983-84 a modest growth of 2% occurred over 1982-83, mainly in the HRA account. This was however the year of the General Election. The latest White Paper projections suggest a fall in capital expenditure of 2-3% in 1984-5.(6)

It is commonplace to equate cuts in expenditure with cuts in services. This is problematic in the analysis of council housing expenditure, and it is necessary to make a clearer distinction between the expenditure decisions of local authorities,and financing decisions.

It was noted earlier that there are three key sources of expenditure, loan charges, supervision and management, and repairs and maintenance. Two significant changes took place in the period 1979-83. First, the level of expenditure on loan charges dropped dramatically, by 23.8% in real terms. This is attributable to two factors, the policy of council house sales leading to debt redemption, and the favourable fall in interest rates since 1982. Secondly, however, expenditure on the other two elements in the equation has *risen* marginally in real terms.

Table 4

Housing Revenue Account Expenditure 1979-1983 (1983 prices)

	1979	**1983**	**% Change**
Loan Charges	£574.4m	£438.3m	−23.8%
Supervision and Management	£69.7m	£77.5m	+11.0%
Repairs and Maintenance	£191.1m	£198.5m	+ 3.8%
Total	£835.5m	£714.3m	−11.4%

Source: Rating Review

This is interesting, because the two elements which have grown are areas where there is much greater scope for local discretion. Therefore, although housing has borne the brunt of cuts in public spending, local authorities have increased *gross* revenue expenditure in areas under their control.

Turning to the financing decisions, we find that even more dramatic changes have taken place. Government has always been able to impose expenditure reductions by reducing funding, but seldom can there have been such a dramatic reduction in government support for a programme. The thrust of government policy was that reduction in HSG should be compensated for by increased rents. This policy has been reasonably successful. Whilst HSG has been cut by 72.1% in real terms, income from rents has rised by 25.7%, whilst the real increase in spending from the Rate Fund Contributions is a mere 6.0%. This resulted in a dramatic shift in the sources of funding council housing, as revealed in Table 5 below. The percentage of expenditure funded by rents has consistently grown, the percentage funded by HSG has consistently fallen, and the percentage funded by the Rate Fund Contribution has risen marginally.

Table 5

Financing of Council Housing

Year	Percentage Funded by		
	Rents	HSG	RFC
1979-80	47	39	14
1980-81	50	37	13
1981-82	59	25	16
1982-83	66	16	18
1983-84	71	11	18

Source: COSLA – Rate Support Grant and Housing Support Grant Scotland 1984-85.

By 1983, the Government could be well pleased with its progress towards its objectives in council housing finance.

2. Local Authority Responses

Decisions on financing council housing have long been a key issue which divides political parties. They represent explicit articulation of social and political values. In general, the Conservative Party is seen as the party of the owner-occupier and the small businessman. In housing finance, they exhibit a concern to protect the interest of the domestic and commercial ratepayer by limiting susidies to the Housing Revenue Account through the Rate Fund Contribution, whilst seeking to achieve 'economic' rents, i.e. higher and less subsidised than those which existed in 1979. As we have seen, this was reflected in Government policy since 1979.

The Labour Party is likewise seen as protecting special interests, i.e.those of the working-class council tenant. Council housing is seen as a low cost, equitable means of ensuring basic housing needs are met, and subsidies both via HSG and the Rate Fund Contribution are regarded as legitimate ways of redistributing wealth and providing good housing at a 'price people can afford'. In government from 1974-79, the Labour Government increased subsidies, and froze and then controlled rent increases. In the main, reliance was placed on central grants for subsidising the cost of council housing.

The question now is, is this basic partisan divide reflected at the local level? There are problems of analysis at this level, particularly the small number of Conservative councils, which requires careful consideration before generalisation can be justified. Moreover, there are a large number of Independent councils in Scotland, which it would be wrong to categorise as 'Conservative', but which can generally be regarded as 'non Socialist'.

In 1980, the Labour Party made sweeping gains in the local elections, winning control of twenty councils and retaining power of the six already under Labour control. The Conservatives lost overall control in two authorities, and outright control in one authority. The rural areas remained Independent. This permits some useful analysis of the impact of change in political control on council housing finance.

First of all, we can examine the issue in absolute terms. In Appendix One, the authorities with the highest levels of expenditure, and highest levels of grant, rental and rate fund income per house are listed. In terms of expenditure and grants, these are dominated by rural councils in Northern Scotland, where high building costs in areas of acute sparsity lead to higher spending, and therefore, higher grant.This is unaffected by the change of government in 1979. In each case, nine of the ten high spenders are high grant receivers in 1983 as in 1979. Berwickshire (Conservative controlled) is the only non-Independent council in this group.

High expenditure per house was also reflected in high rents per house in 1979. Five of the authorities who had the highest expenditure also had higher rents. Of the other five authorities, three were from the *lower* cost southern rural areas, one was Conservative controlled Edinburgh, and one was Liberal controlled Inverclyde. By 1983, considerable changes took place. Only five of the high rents councils were still in the group. Two rural councils in southern Scotland had entered the group, one northern rural council, and one Conservative and one Labour council.

Similar changes are recorded in terms of Rate Fund Contributions. In 1979, six of the ten authorities with high RFCs were northern Independent councils. By 1983, this had fallen to two councils. In 1979, two Labour and two Conservative councils also had high RFCs. By 1983, *seven* Labour councils were in the group, and only one Conservative council (Bearsden).

We can also examine this in relative terms. Local authorities operate within a framework of constrained choice. The theory of incrementalism suggests that part of those constraints is historic expenditure patterns.(7) But incrementalism has been shaped and developed in a period of growth. Cutback management in areas of financing rather than service provision, can result in relatively non-incremental charges. Until 1979, a relatively high and stable level of grant led to a more uniform pattern of housing finance. The abrupt and rapid erosion of Housing Support Grant (8) created environmental turbulence with key financing decisions to be taken locally which can be interpreted as reflecting local political choice.

Table 6 sets out the figures. I have included a *Labour Gains '80* category as it is change of control which past research suggests leads to changes of priorities and expenditure.[(9)] The figures are the average for the different categories.

Table 6

Financing of HRA Expenditure

Political Control	1979 Rents %	1979 Grant %	1979 RFC %	1983 Rents %	1983 Grant %	1983 RFC %
Conservative	50	35	14	86	5	9
Labour	48	33	19	76	4	20
Labour Gains '80	49	34	17	70	5	25
Independent	42	42	16	64	29	6
Scotland	47	39	14	71	11	18

There are several interesting trends. In partisan councils,the erosion of Housing Support Grant was most extreme. In Conservative controlled councils, there was a drop in the percentage funded by RFC from 13.6% to 10%, at a time when one might have expected it to increase. However, this conceals the variations in performance. Three of the five Conservative controlled councils eliminated their RFCs completely, and one reduced it drastically. The average is raised by Bearsden, who *increased* the RFC considerably. Moreover, in the two councils where the Conservatives lost control in 1980 (Angus and Edinburgh) RFC also rose. But the overall trend is clear. *Conservative councils reduced public subsidies through the RFC and increased rents,* in the latter case more than any other political groupings.

The opposite pattern is found in councils controlled by the Labour Party. Having fought the elections in 1980 on the basis 'Protect Yourself – Vote Labour', the most visible form of protection is to pass cuts in grant onto the rates rather than rents, as industrial and commercial rates contributes a majority of rateable income (56% in 1981-82). Thus the subsidy to council housing is drawn from private house owners and the business community, and council tenants are net beneficiaries.

Whilst as we have seen overall, Labour councils made increasing use of Rate Fund subsidies to compensate for loss in grant, considerable rent increases were still required, and considerable variation also occurred. In

Table 7

Changes in Council Housing Finance in Conservative Controlled Councils 1979-1983

	Rents % change	RFC % change	HSG % change
Perth	+44	Nil	−44
NE Fife	+39	− 8	−31
Berwickshire	+28	− 8	−20
Bearsden	+24	+ 5	−20
Eastwood	+44	−27	−17
Angus*	+37	+ 5	−42
Edinburgh*	+24	+ 9	−33

* Denotes minority administration from 1980.

1980, for instance, substantial increases in Rate Fund Contributions occurred in Dundee, where the Labour Party had promised a rent freeze, and in Stirling, where the RFC was already quite high. The most significant increases in RFCs were found in authorities where Labour gained outright control (e.g. Dundee, Cumbernauld, Renfrew, Inverclyde, Cunninghame, and Kyle and Carrick). These changes are recorded in Table 8, where the general trend is clearer. *Twenty of the twenty-five councils controlled by the Labour Party increased the RFC subsidy* to protect tenants from increases in rents caused by the *reductions in grants.*

The final group for analysis is Independent councils. These were most protected from cuts in grant, but we find two significant behaviour patterns occurring. In almost all councils, there was a tendency to *reduce* the *percentage* of finance provided by the rates, and secondly, the *extent* of the subsidy was much higher in district councils in the Highland Region than those in Borders, Dumfries and Grampian Regions. In general, councils facing the most severe grant loss incurred the greatest *increases* in rental income, with Lochaber, Inverness, Badenoch and Strathspey, and Nithsdale Districts providing spectacular exceptions to the rule.

The period 1979-83 was one of great turbulence in housing finance. It followed a period of stability, when increases in grant and a system of rent controls resulted in relatively common patterns in council housing finance. The Conservative Government's policy has been largely successful, but there have been diverse political responses locally. The Government argued that Rate Fund Contribution should remain stable. In fact, these have grown slightly, because Labour councils overwhelmingly refused to pass on the full impact of cuts in grant to council tenants. Two distinct patterns of response emerged. In Labour councils, the general response is

Table 8

Changes in Council Housing Finance in Labour Controlled Councils 1979-1983

	Rents % change	RFC % change	HSG % change
Aberdeen	+26	+ 7	−34
Dundee	+12	+19	−31
Kirkcaldy	+32	+ 8	−40
Dunfermline	+38	− 1	−37
West Lothian	+39	− 6	−33
Midlothian	+30	+ 6	−36
East Lothian	+30	+ 5	−35
Clackmannan	+26	+ 7	−33
Stirling	+15	+ 6	−21
Falkirk	+35	+ 4	−39
Dumbarton	+25	+ 8	−33
Glasgow	+13	− 3	−10
Clydebank	+22	No change	−22
Strathkelvin	+24	+ 4	−28
Cumbernauld	+13	+13	−26
Monklands	+22	− 7	−15
Motherwell	+22	+ 6	−28
Hamilton	+27	+ 1	−28
East Kilbride	+23	+ 6	−29
Renfrew	+18	+11	−29
Inverclyde	+10	+16	−26
Cunninghame	+15	+15	−30
Kilmarnock and Loudon	+20	+12	−32
Kyle and Carrick	+18	+17	−35
Cumnock and Doon Valley	+29	+ 4	−33

to *increase* Rate Fund Contributions and limit rent increase, in other councils, the opposite practice is found – rents are increased and Rate Fund Contributions limited. The traditional political divide emerges as a key factor in council housing finance.

3. Whither Now for Council Housing Finance?

At the time of writing (June 1984) further changes in housing finance are in the offing. First of all, the public expenditure projections suggest a

Table 9

Changes in Council Housing Finance in Independent Councils 1979-1983

	Rents % change	RFC % change	HSG % change
Caithness	+22	−10	−12
Sutherland	+21	− 7	−14
Ross and Cromarty	+21	−17	− 4
Skye and Lochalsh	+13	− 8	− 1
Lochaber	+20	− 4	−16
Inverness	+10	+12	−22
Badenoch and Strathspey	+21	−25	+ 4
Nairn	+13	− 2	−11
Moray	+31	−10	−21
Banff and Buchan	+32	− 5	−27
Gordon	+23	− 3	−20
Kincardine	+20	− 3	−17
Tweedale	+49	−16	−31
Ettrick	+37	− 5	−32
Roxburgh	+24	−12	−12
Wigtown	+33	− 5	−28
Stewartry	+23	− 6	−17
Nithsdale	+26	+ 7	−33
Annandale	+ 4	− 9	− 5

continuing decline in public expenditure on housing,[(10)] although the decline of capital expenditure is to be halted. This leaves two sources of target, Housing Support Grant (52.5m in 1984) and Rate Fund Contribution (143m in 1983). At the moment, Government plans for public spending over the next five years assume that overall it will remain broadly stable, but that economic growth will allow tax cuts in later years. However, that is based on a series of optimistic assumptions about the economy.[(11)] If these do not materialise, further pressure on public programmes will become necessary, and housing will be an obvious target.

This brings us to our second change. The Housing Expenditure Limit has proved successful in (a) controlling total expenditure on housing and (b) directing authorities towards rent increases. A recent Scottish Office document spells out the proposed changes thus.

> 'The HEL system has not however halted the overall trend for RFCs to increase, because a number of authorities have budgeted for RFCs

in excess of the limits specified by the Government. This has led to reductions in capital allocations which would otherwise have been given on the HRA block amounting to 38.5m in 1981-82, 51.6m in 1982-83, and 13.5m in 1983-84.

The Government therefore propose to replace the HEL system with a new system which will have statutory backing. Under this new system, the Government will set statutory limits to the contributions which local authorities may make from their rate funds to housing. This will enable greater accuracy in planning the component parts of housing public expenditure. ...'

The Thatcher Government has developed a great skill in presenting major changes in the constitutional rights of local authorities as minor administrative changes. This legislation is in fact a major change in the principles on which council housing has been conducted in this country, namely that council house rent levels should be decided locally. The democratic implications of the policy are clear enough – Central Government will decide how much each locality may subsidise its council housing programme – effectively nullifying the effect of the electoral process on what is in effect one of the three or four major strategic decisions a local authority takes. Unfortunately, the implications of this change have been overshadowed by the proposals for rate-capping, but there can be no doubt that it constitutes a major change in central-local relationships in housing.

So what does this mean for council housing? It means the future is highly uncertain. If the Treasury's optimistic assumptions fail to materialise, and further reductions in spending are sought, there is a limit to how far further savings can be attained in capital spending or Housing Support Grant. Already, 58% of the housing stock get no grant. Cuts in grant would fall in future on authorities with high costs, the rural authorities, or Glasgow. What is more likely is that the RFC will become the target. Cuts would then be concentrated on Labour councils, with little political repercussions for the Government. The implications for housing policy will be discussed by David Alexander. The thrust of the Government's financing policy has been a radical change in the structure of housing finance. Its council house sales policy has not changed dramatically the amount of Scots living in council housing. In 1979, local authorities owned 892,000 houses. In 1983, they still owned 875,000. Those on low incomes excepted, the high rent increases of recent years (growth of 25% in real terms) seem likely to continue, but their capacity to resist and influence those increases will be greatly reduced by the new legislation. The danger for the Government is of creating Clay Cross style situations for the most spurious of reasons. The small increase in Rate Fund Contributions cannot be seriously regarded as hindering public expenditure planning or macro-economic management. The new legislation is quite capable of producing political martyrs who will be able to point to the undemocratic nature of Government action. It will require quite sensitive political management by the Government to avoid scoring own goals.

APPENDIX ONE

Council Housing Finance

(a) Highest Expenditure

1979	1983
Ross and Cromarty (I)	Skye and Lochalsh (I)
Lochaber (I)	Lochaber (I)
Skye and Lochalsh (I)	Ross and Cromarty (I)
Inverness (I)	Badenoch and Strathspey (I(
Argyll and Bute (I)	Argyll (I)
Badenoch and Strathspey (I)	Gordon (I)
Sutherland (I)	Annandale and Eskdale (I)
Berwickshire (I)	Nairn (I)
Gordon (I)	Sutherland (I)
Moray (I)	Inverness (I)

(b) Highest Levels of HSG

1979	1983
Ross and Cromarty (I)	Ross and Cromarty (I)
Lochaber (I)	Badenoch and Strathspey (I)
Skye and Lochalsh (I)	Skye and Lochalsh (I)
Berwickshire (C)	Lochaber (I)
Gordon (I)	Annandale and Eskdale (I)
Argyll (I)	Argyll (I)
Sutherland (I)	Gordon (I)
Kincardine (I)	Kincardine (I)
Banff and Buchan (I)	Sutherland (I)
Badenoch and Strathspey (I)	Nairn (I)

(c) Highest Rental Income per House

1979	1983
Edinburgh (C)	Argyll (I)
Inverness (I)	Roxburgh (I)
Berwickshire (C)	NE Fife (C)
Inverclyde (Lib)	Stewartry (I)
Sutherland (I)	Edinburgh (C)
Ettrick and Lauderdale (I)	Wigtown (I)
Roxburgh (I)	Dunfermline (Lab)
Moray (I)	Berwickshire (C)
Annandale (I)	Annandale and Eskdale (I)
Argyll (I)	Badenoch and Strathspey (I)

(d) Highest RFC per House

1979	1983
Skye and Lochalsh (I)	Bearsden (C)
Eastwood (C)	Stirling (Lab)
Badenoch and Strathspey (I)	East Kilbride (Lab)
Ross and Cromarty (I)	Aberdeen (Lab)
Lochaber (I)	Lochaber (I)
Bearsden (C)	Skye and Lochalsh (I)
Argyll (I)	Hamilton (Lab)
Hamilton (Lab)	Cumbernauld and Kilsyth (Lab)
Glasgow (Lab)	Strathkelvin (Lab)
Sutherland (I)	Dumbarton (Lab)

(I) denotes Independent
(C) denotes Conservative
(Lib) denotes Liberal
(Lab) denotes Labour

APPENDIX TWO

The Pattern of Council Housing Finance

Authority	1979-80			1983-84		
	Rents	HSG	RFC	Rents	HSG	RFC
Berwickshire	44	48	8	72	28	0
Ettrick and Lauderdale	51	44	5	88	12	0
Roxburgh	51	36	13	75	24	1
Tweedale	52	31	17	99	0	1
Clackmannan	54	34	12	80	1	19
Falkirk	45	39	16	80	0	20
Stirling	53	21	26	58	0	32
Annandale	49	37	14	53	32	5
Nithsdale	66	33	1	92	0	8
Stewartry	54	36	10	77	19	4
Wigtown	59	36	5	92	8	0
Dunfermline	49	37	14	87	0	13
Kirkcaldy	57	40	3	89	0	11
North East Fife	55	37	8	94	6	0
Aberdeen	46	38	16	56	14	30
Banff	42	52	6	74	25	1
Gordon	37	49	14	60	29	11
Kincardine	43	48	9	53	31	6
Moray	44	46	10	75	25	0
Badenoch	34	38	28	55	42	3
Caithness	41	38	21	63	26	11
Inverness	51	42	7	61	20	19
Lochaber	29	49	22	49	33	18
Nairn	47	36	17	60	25	15
Ross and Cromarty	30	49	21	51	45	4
Skye and Lochalsh	34	37	29	47	36	17
Sutherland	40	42	18	61	28	11
Argyll	38	41	21	69	29	2
Bearsden	44	29	27	68	0	32
Clydebank	40	42	18	62	20	18
Clydesdale	51	33	6	89	0	11
Cumbernauld	58	26	16	71	0	29
Cumnock	51	33	16	80	0	20
Cunninghame	56	30	14	71	0	29
Dumbarton	44	33	23	69	0	31

Authority	1979-80 Rents	HSG	RFC	1983-84 Rents	HSG	RFC
East Kilbride	49	29	22	72	0	28
Eastwood	43	17	40	87	0	13
Glasgow	44	31	25	57	21	22
Hamilton	42	29	29	69	1	30
Inverclyde	53	38	9	63	12	25
Kilmarnock	55	32	13	75	0	25
Kyle and Carrick	56	42	2	74	7	19
Monklands	49	24	27	71	9	20
Motherwell	47	32	21	69	4	27
Renfrew	52	29	19	70	0	30
Strathkelvin	45	32	23	69	4	27
Angus	55	44	1	92	2	6
Dundee	59	31	10	71	–	29
Perth	56	44	0	100	–	–
Edinburgh	62	33	5	86	0	14
East Lothian	50	45	5	80	10	10
Midlothian	50	36	14	80	0	20
West Lothian	47	33	20	86	0	14
Scotland	47	39	14	71	11	18

REFERENCES

1. HM Treasury (1984), The Next Ten Years: Public Expenditure and Taxation into the 1990s, (Report), Cmnd. 9189.

2. Bulpitt, J. (1983), 'The Territorial Policies of the Thatcher Government', Paper presented to the PSA Workgroup on UK Politics, Oxford, August.

   Gyford, J. and James,M. (1983), *National Parties and Local Politics*, (Macmillan).

3. Kellner, P. (1984), 'The Traditional Labour Voter – and other Myths', *New Statesman,* 13 April.

4. Midwinter, A., Keating, M. and Taylor, P. (1984), 'The Politics of Scottish Housing Plans', *Policy and Politics,* Vol.12, No.2.

5. McCulloch, T.D. (1982), 'The New Housing Finance System', *Local Government Studies*, Vol.8, No.3, May/June.

6. Scottish Office (1984), Public Expenditure to 1986-87 – A Commentary on the Scotland Programme, (Report), Edinburgh.

7. Wildavsky, A. (1964), *The Politics of the Budgetary Process,* (Little, Brown).

8. Heald, D.A., Jones, C.A., and Lamont, D.W. (1981), 'The Rise and Fall of the Scottish Housing Support Grant', Paper presented to the UK Politics Workgroup, September 14-16.

9. Gibson, J., Davies, E., Game, C., and Stewart, J. (1983), 'The Influence of Local Politics, Expenditure Targets and Grant Changes on Local Authority Expenditure', University of Birmingham, Mimeo.

10. Scottish Office, *op.cit.*

11. The Fraser of Allander Institute (1984), *Quarterly Economic Commentary,* No.4, May, pp.40-41.

PUBLIC SECTOR HOUSING IN SCOTLAND: TRENDS AND PROSPECTS

DAVID ALEXANDER
DEPARTMENT OF HOUSING ADMINISTRATION
UNIVERSITY OF STIRLING

Introduction

The intention in this paper is to take Arthur Midwinter's analysis one step further. In his contribution, he examined trends in housing finance since 1979; this paper looks at the effect of those trends.

It begins with a summary of the main changes in housing policy. These have been achieved by financial and administrative controls rather than bylegislation, and have thus, for the most part, escaped public attention.

The paper then goes on to itemise the effect of these policies in various parts of the housing service, and, in so doing, painting with a very broad brush, a picture of Scottish housing at a specific point in time (July 1984). It concentrates on the public sector, and thus passes over some of the most significant developments, such as the upsurge and collapse of the improvement and repair grant programme. Within the public sector, the emphasis is placed on its largest component, council housing. The role of the Scottish Special Housing Association is the subject of a separate paper. Space does not allow more than passing reference to the housing association movement, which deserves a paper in its own right.

The concluding section is an indulgence in crystal-ball gazing. Recent changes have dramatically shifted the focus of debate on housing in Scotland, and the paper attempts, in a necessarily speculative fashion, to ask "where now?"

The Changes Summarised

The first task is to review the shifts in Government policy that have affected the public sector in housing in Scotland in recent years. In taking 1979 as the starting point for such a before-and-after analysis, the intention is not to hold the Conservative administrations of 1979 and 1983 responsible for all the changes that are currently in evidence. There is more common ground between the Conservative governments and their Labour predecessor than many care to recognise; for example, public expenditure on housing shows a clear downward trend since 1975, and much of the thinking of the Labour government defeated in the 1979 election was incorporated in the 1980 legislation. Nevertheless, 1979 does represent a convenient milestone if only because it marks an acceleration in the pace of change.

The major piece of legislation to reach the statute book since 1979 has been the Tenants' Rights etc (Scotland) Act 1980. The title of the legislation is significant, in that it departs from the long tradition of simply-named Housing Acts (or similar) both north and south of the border. The intention was to highlight the package of rights or reforms being introduced (principally) to the public rented sector. These included non-controversial matters such as the right to security of tenure and the right to a written lease, but, much more importantly, the right, conferred by Part I of the Act, for tenants to purchase their houses with discounts and the right to a mortgage.(1) This right, subsequently extended by amending legislation, far outweighs in importance the rest of the Act, in that it fundamentally alters the nature of the landlord-tenant relationship. But it must not be seen in isolation from other changes which have done as much if not more to alter the image of council housing.

Other housing legislation has not excited the same level of interest or controversy. The important, but legalistic, Matrimonial Homes (Family Protection) (Scotland) Act 1981 (which gave certain rights to partners in a marriage or relationship over the occupation of the home) began life in the House of Lords and never succeeded in capturing the imagination of a male-dominated Parliament. The UK-wide Social Security and Housing Benefits Act 1982 said remarkably little about the detail of the housing benefits scheme, instead delegating authority to the Secretary of State to make regulations which were not extensively debated in Parliament. Other far-reaching but technical changes have been introduced in predominantly non-housing legislation such as the Local Government (Miscellaneous Provisions (Scotland)) Act 1981 and the Rating and Valuation (Amendment) (Scotland) Act 1984, where public concern focused on the Secretary of State's power to curb local government expenditure generally.

But, with these exceptions, the policy shifts witnessed since 1979 have been the product of the manipulation of existing financial controls. The powers to limit capital expenditure and to withdraw Housing Support Grant, discussed by Arthur Midwinter, are not new. But they have been used since 1979 by the Scottish Office in such a way as to direct resources away from the public sector, in line with the twin prevailing orthodoxies of reducing public expenditure (as defined by the Treasury) and privatisation. These financial controls have been accompanied by a constant emphasis placed by Government ministers on the merits of owner-occupation, as manifested in Conference speeches and in Parliamentary Question Time. Meanwhile, the relative financial position of owner-occupiers has been improved, partly by way of incentives to low-cost house purchase (including discounts to council house purchasers) but also by the maintenance and enhancement of advantages available to owner occupiers through anomalies in the taxation system.(2)

There are four general points to be made from this brief review of policy changes. Firstly, the largely technical and financial nature of the changes has meant that there has been little Parliamentary or public debate about their effect. Housing was not an issue in the 1983 election in the way it had been in, for example, February 1974. When the public *did* express a view on housing, it was one of virtual complacency. According to *British Social Attitudes: the 1984 Report*(3) there was a strong feeling that more public money should be spent on health and education, but not on housing. Although pressure groups and, increasingly, local authorities spoke out against what they saw as damaging cuts(4), the general public remained sceptical. The tenants' movement, perhaps divided by the right-to-buy issue, remained generally quiet, except on single-issue campaigns, such as dampness. In short, housing has not been seen as a political priority.

This generalisation is, however, less true in Scotland than in England and Wales, and here I come to the second point. The effect of the trends described is bound to be different in Scotland, where 53% of all households are public sector tenants, from the impact in England where the comparable figure is only 28%. Other significant differences between the two countries exist; for example, council house rent levels are about 30% lower in Scotland, and no Scottish housing association tenants have the right to buy. Scotland maintains elements of its tradition of public renting which is absent from much of England. Nevertheless, the trends reflect a convergence in the housing situations north and south of the border.

Thirdly, the changes have had a profound impact on the nature of the relationship between central and local government, with the balance of power shifting from the latter to the former. This is, of course, not confined to the sphere of housing. But, whereas other areas of local government spending are constrained by general powers, housing is subject to specific controls. In particular, as Arthur Midwinter has described, councils no longer have the freedom to fix rent levels as they choose. Housing is by far the most important function performed by district councils, and the erosion of their freedom of manoeuvre has left councillors angry, frustrated or impotent. 80% of Scotland's council housing is in Labour-controlled districts, but Conservative and independent councils have also expressed their resentment. It remains to be seen whether the future of the central-local government relationship will be characterised by hostile confrontation or resigned passivity.

Finally, and most significantly from the point of view of this paper, Government policy since 1979 has profoundly affected the role to be played by the public rented sector. A combination of the right-to-buy, reduce public sector subsidies, increased rents, increased reliance on means-tested benefits and reduced capital expenditure has created a public sector which would have been difficult to imagine fifteen years ago. Indeed the transformation has been as swift and as radical as any shift in social policy in recent decades. The term coined by commentators to describe the change has been "residualisation", and although cumbersome, it admirably describes what has happened. It is the "process whereby public housing moves towards a position in which it provides only a 'safety net' for those who, for reasons of poverty, age or infirmity, cannot obtain suitable housing accommodation in the private sector. It almost certainly involves lowering the status and increasing the stigma attached to public housing....(It) also involves changes in the terms on which public housing is available."[(5)]

The remainder of this chapter is concerned with the evidence of residualisation of public sector housing in Scotland since 1979. The context is set by the financial and legislative changes already described; but it remains to be seen what the effect of these trends has been in terms of bricks and mortar.

New House Building

The most stark indicator of the health of the public sector is provided by the rate of new housebuilding. Table 1 presents the figures for starts (the most sensitive measure) for both council housing, public sector housing as a whole and the private sector.

TABLE 1

Dwellings Started in Scotland

	Local Authority	**All Public Sector**	**Private Sector**	**All Dwellings**
1969	23,897	31,162	8,640	39,802
....				
1974	16,324	22,258	10,258	32,516
....				
1979	4,858	7,871	15,375	23,246
1980	2,770	6,702	9,766	16,468
1981	1,929	3,936	11,098	15,034
1982	2,583	6,448	12,143	18,591
1983	2,174	3,803	15,337	19,140

Source: *SDD*, Scottish Housing Statistics.
SDD, Housing Statistical Bulletin.

It can be seen that the major decline in the rate of new public sector housebuilding occurred *before* 1979. The abandonment of wholesale clearance policies from the late Sixties accounts for the bulk of the decline: but public expenditure constraints in the Seventies had further reduced the rate of activity. From 1979 to 1983 the downward trend continued. The rate of starts in 1983 was less than a half of that in 1979. Furthermore, an increasing proportion of housebuilding was for so-called special needs (in particular the elderly) rather than general needs as in the past. Interestingly, the last decade marked a reversal of the situation which has prevailed since 1919, in which Scotland built *proportionately* more public sector houses than the rest of the UK. In 1983, Scotland's rate was only 8.1% of the UK total.

Building for the private sector has risen since 1980 in response to the demand stimulated by the Government for low-cost owner occupation, although the picture has been complicated by fluctuations in the availability and price of credit. But the response has not been as enthusiastic as might be expected and does not compensate, overall, for the decline in public sector construction since 1979. Supply factors, such as local shortages of suitable land partially account for this situation, but the main explanatory factor is the limited scope for extending owner occupation downmarket by way of new building. With the average price for new houses in Scotland at Spring 1984 standing at £31,000[(6)], and with much cheaper options available to those exercising the right-to-buy, new private house building cannot be expected to rise much above the levels evident in the early 1980s. Nevertheless, private sector house building has, since the mid-1970s, overtaken the public sector, a reversal of the pattern of the previous fifty years.

Sales

The supply of public sector housing is also affected by the level of sales. Table 2 shows the effect of the introduction of the right-to-buy in October 1980.

TABLE 2

Sales to Sitting Tenants

	Local Authority	All Public Sector
1979[1]	642	1,670
1980[1]	2,938	6,488
1981[2]	6,803	11,043
1982[2]	10,772	14,965
1983[2]	11,883	17,473

1 Includes small number of houses sold other than to sitting tenants.

2 Based on incomplete returns.

Source: *SDD,* Scottish Housing Statistics
SDD, Housing Statistical Bulletin

Not all sales, of course, have taken place under the right-to-buy provision. Homesteading, improvement for sale to individuals and to developers have grown in importance, although the scale is still relatively insignificant.(7)

Right-to-buy sales account for less than 4% of the 1979 council housing stock (the proportions are much higher for SSHA and the New Town Development Corporations). One can be tempted to conclude that the impact is marginal; certainly, the level of sales is significantly less than in England and Wales, and must disappoint those who in 1979 envisaged a wholesale transfer of ownership in Scotland from the public sector to individuals. But it would be a mistake to minimise the effects. The differential impact of council house sales has now been well documented, especially in England(8), but increasingly also in Scotland.(9) The (as yet) unpublished findings of the Scottish Office report on the subject confirm the fears of those who argued in 1979 that tenants exercising the right-to-buy would be concentrated in particular areas, with repercussions throughout the council sector.

Firstly, the level of sales is much higher in some local authorities than in others, as shown in Table 3.

TABLE 3

Distribution of Sales by Selected Districts, October 1980–December 1982

	Number	Percentage of Stock Sold
Badenoch & Strathspey	97	9.0
Stewartry	228	8.8
Western Isles	219	8.7
Orkney	134	8.3
North-East Fife	583	7.3
Kincardine & Deeside	257	7.1
Bearsden & Milngavie	129	6.7
....		
Motherwell	302	0.8
Glasgow	1265	0.7
Monklands	189	0.7
Clydesdale	52	0.5
Dundee	217	0.5
Clydebank	32	0.3

Source: *SDD*, Housing Statistical Bulletin, Sales of Public Sector Housing, February 1984.

The table shows two pronounced correlations: sales are higher in rural and (less markedly) suburban areas than in urban areas,and are higher in those areas with an initially *low* level of council housing. Thus it is in, for example, Bearsden and Milngavie and Badenoch and Strathspey that sales are significant, rather than (say) Glasgow or Motherwell. This pattern is even more pronounced at a local level: analyses of sales in authorities as disparate as Banff and Buchan[10] and Glasgow[11] show that some estates or communities have been virtually unaffected by the right-to-buy, while others have been transformed.

The second clear point to emerge concerns the types of houses sold, and this goes a long way to explain the geographical pattern described above. In almost all authorities (Edinburgh was a partial exception) sales have been concentrated in semi- detached and terraced housing (89.5% of all sales), particularly those built in the 1920s and since 1965. These houses represent the cream of the housing stock, and their sale substantially affects the image, in qualitative terms, of public sector housing. On the other hand, sales of flats and maisonettes, which make up half the housing stock, account for only 10.5% of all sales.[12] Similarly, sales have been concentrated among family houses (especially four-apartment) rather than smaller dwellings which are predominantly flatted.

A full analysis of the effect of council house sales would include a financial appraisal from the local authority's point of view. Suffice it to say, in passing, that the receipts from sales (prices currently average £9,343, after the average 44% discount has been taken off) *have* improved the cash-flow situation of authorities suffering cut-backs in their capital expenditure allocations. But income is nowhere near enough to allow the *replacement* of the houses lost, and when measured against the income lost by way of rent foregone, the overall long-term financial effect of sales is certainly against the local authority interest.[(13)]

However, the main concern here is to highlight the effect on the supply of public sector housing. The combined effect of reduced rates of house building, a limited amount of demolition, and losses through sales, has been that the size of the public sector housing stock has diminishing, from 1,090,000 in 1981 to 1,049,000 in 1983. The effect in certain localities is more pronounced. As a result, shortages are emerging which belie the picture presented by global statistics suggesting that there is more than enough housing to go round.

Indicators of housing need are always difficult to interpret. But there can be little doubt that the 15,000 applications made to local authorities under the Housing (Homeless Persons) Act 1977 in Scotland each year understate the real homelessness problem, as most single people and childless couples are not covered by the legislation. Shelter (Scotland) found that numbers on council house waiting lists grew from 144,000 in 1981 to 156,000 in 1982. While questions have been raised about the validity of this measure, there can be little doubt that the upward trend reflects the growing shortage of council housing, of the appropriate type, size and location.

An addditional perspective can be gained from projections covering the next few years. Projections made in 1979 covering the period up to 1991 suggest a percentage increase in the number of households in Scotland from 1.80m to 1.90m. By far the largest component of this increase was an anticipated 22% increase in the number of single person households.[(14)] For this category alone, there is a need for 7,000 additional houses every year until 1991. Given the limited purchasing power of single people in particular,a substantial part of this additional need must be met by the public sector. A housing policy which emphasises transfers of ownership *within* the stock, at the expense of additions to the stock, will not be able to satisfy these needs.

Modernisation

The above discussion has examined the quantity of public sector housing. However, judging from the content of local authority Housing Plans, and the public statements made by both politicians and professionals, the issue of quality is at least as important, and perhaps more so. Expenditure constraints have affected both modernisation programmes (capital expenditure) and repair expenditure on the Housing Revenue Account. There is a grey area between the two categories, and some authorities (Glasgow being the most notable) have taken advantage of this by switching repairs expenditure from capital to revenue and vice versa, as circumstances warrant.

The existing public sector housing stock poses a wide variety of problems, depending on the type and date of construction. Over 70,000 council houses built before 1939, are still to be modernised. Modernisation in these cases normally consists of replacement of kitchen and bathroom fittings, rewiring, the provision of heating systems, window replacement and structural repair to varying extents. Costs vary greatly, but full modernisation can be expected to cost over £10,000 per unit. This has been substantially reduced in Glasgow by the adoption of the Tenants Grants Scheme, but three-quarters of the savings here were attributable to a reduction in the work content.[15] However, many of the houses so modernised, particularly those built under the relatively generous standards of the 1920s, remain popular, and can be expected to provide good quality accommodation for many years.

Much more intractable problems are posed by council houses of non-traditional construction in the years immediately before, but particularly after the Second World War. About 30,000 non-traditional houses built between 1945 and 1955 require to be modernised. In the case of houses built under such systems as Orlit, Airey, and BISF, major structural work may be required to make the houses safe.

A third group of problems is posed by 1960's systems-built houses, particularly those forming part of high-rise or deck-access blocks. The problems arise from the uncritical adoption of inappropriate designs and construction methods in an attempt to boost house construction towards Government targets. Design problems were often exacerbated by expensive or inadequate heating systems. Hutchesontown in Glasgow, Whitfield in Dundee and Wester Hailes in Edinburgh all illustrate variations on this theme. In some cases, demolition has proved to be the alternative favoured by councils at a loss as to how to make the houses habitable.

Much of the debate about modernisation has centred on dampness. This single issue has probably occupied more Parliamentary time than any other aspect of housing over the last five or six years. Dampness may take the form of penetrating damp, which is particularly acute where exposure to wind-driven rain coincides with construction defects. Much more widespread, however, is condensation dampness, which affects an estimated one council house in five in Scotland. Whereas the blame for condensation has often been put on the way people live, there is now much wider acceptance that it is the product of design and construction of the house, the means of ventilation, and the heating system. Legal authority was given in 1982 to this interpretation by a court decision under the Public Health (Scotland) Act 1897, where Renfrew District Council were held to be responsible for condensation in modernised council houses in Johnstone because of their failure, among other things, to consider the cost of running the central heating system provided.(16)

Campaigns fought by the Johnstone tenants and other groups, and mounting public concern about the causes and extent of dampness, prompted an investigation by the Select Committee on Scottish Affairs into the subject in late 1982. The investigation, which involved the collection of evidence from a wide range of bodies, was interrupted by the 1983 General Election. But a report – albeit one which merely reflected the state of the discussion at the time of the dissolution of Parliament – was eventually produced in February 1984.(17)

While not as hard hitting as many critics (and some members of the Committee) would have liked, the Report does recognise that damp living conditions are "a major social evil", and that "it is unreasonable to blame tenants for problems which arise because their living habits are those common in society generally, or because they cannot afford to pay for heating, or because their homes are badly designed or built". In sympathy with the majority of witnesses, it called for a house condition survey, and an injection of resources specifically to deal with the dampness problem; they estimated £500 million was required to cure the problem of damp in Scottish council houses. On both issues, the Government has not moved, raising important questions about the effectiveness of the Select Committee machinery.

Exchanges between local and central government also have occurred on the subject of asbestos. Asbestos is found in many elements in the construction of houses, particularly as pipe lagging, in ducted heating systems, and in wall panels. Recognition of the health hazard it presents and concern about the extent of its use in the Fifties and Sixties has prompted local authorities to ask for more resources to get rid of asbestos in their council houses. As with dampness, the Government's response has been to leave it to councils to determine expenditure priorities within the limits set by their capital allocations.

Repairs

Spending on repairs funded by the Housing Revenue Account increased until 1982, but has since fallen slightly in real terms as HRA expenditure has been squeezed. As buildings deteriorate and expectations rise, the dissatisfaction felt by tenants over levels of repairs increases. The incidence of vandalism and environmental dereliction are particularly important in undermining the morale of tenants of an estate. Yet, in the present circumstances, councils feel they are running hard to stand still.

With resources scarce, they have turned to new measures to improve the efficiency of the repairs service. The trend away from routine response repairs towards cyclical repairs on a planned basis is widespread, and, as in the case of the Scottish Special Housing Association, planned maintenance can achieve a high level of sophistication. Computerisation can assist in the reporting and ordering of repairs, and better liaison between housing and the technical departments can improve the quality of the service. A few authorities have sought to change the division of responsibility between landlord and tenant as regards repairs, but there is limited scope for this without encroaching upon the landlord's legal responsibilities.

The Government's response has been to introduce a statutory right under the Tenants' Rights etc (Scotland) (Amendment) Act 1984 for tenants to undertake repairs that are the landlord's responsibility and to reclaim a proportion of the costs from the landlord. There are practical obstacles to such a scheme; in particular, the tenant needs to have cash in hand to pay for the repair, has to engage the contractor, and generally acts as the agent for the local authority. Take-up, based on the experience of the Northern Ireland Housing Executive, will not be large, and will not bring substantial cost savings. The main significance of the statutory right to repair is that it changes the formal nature of the landlord-tenant relationship, which has hitherto been based on the common law and statutory duties on the landlord to maintain houses. The new position is ambiguous, and the changes cannot be to the tenant's advantage.

Council House Management

Much of the negative image of council housing stems from the style of council house management long prevalent throughout Scotland, based on authoritarian assumptions and the denial of rights and information to tenants.[18] To the extent that this is a problem of attitudes rather than resources, it might be expected that innovations in housing management would be unimpaired by the current resource crisis. Many improvements in practice can be introduced at little or no cost, notably those involving the way the housing service is presented to the public. It is disappointing therefore to find that, in defiance of the spirit of the Tenants' Rights Act, a large number of local authorities publish their allocation rules in terms which are confusing, intimidating or generally negative[19], and that tenancy agreements are often difficult to read and refer to, and fail to describe all of the tenants' rights.[20] Clearly, many councils do not feel it necessary to "sell" their service. It is hardly surprising, therefore, that tenants feel frustrated and sometimes hostile.

But advances have been made. The concept of a decentralised housing service, in an attempt to get away from the monolithic town-hall image, has gained acceptance in such councils as Glasgow and Edinburgh. Communication between headquarters staff and those in area offices is crucial if decentralisation is to be more than window-dressing. In this, computerisation is vital. While a few councils have taken full advantage of the information revolution, others have been slow to recognize that routine aspects of allocating houses and ordering repairs can be left to the computer, leaving staff free to concentrate on the tasks which require personal contact.

Bringing the housing service closer to the public has taken other forms. Some critics of public sector housing management argue for a much greater degree of tenant involvement in decision-making. The right for tenants to be consulted on matters affecting them, included as part of the equivalent English legislation, was omitted from the Tenants' Rights Act. But as compensation, the Government set up the Tenant Participation Advisory Service in Scotland which has promoted the idea of tenant involvement in decision-making to those councils who have been prepared to listen. The trouble is that "tenant participation" means very different things to different people, ranging from better and fuller information to tenants (West Lothian's Tenants' Handbook is agood example of what can be done) to the setting up of management co-operatives (in which Glasgow District Council and SSHA have taken the lead). But there is little evidence of any fundamental shift in the landlord-tenant relationship. The participation model represented by the community-based housing associations of Glasgow represents the closest Scotland comes to changing the authoritarian patterns of the past; yet, as they evolve, these associations tend in practice to lose the democratic decision-making structures which characterised their infancy.

A more sensitive housing management service requires better training and education of staff. Here, Scotland has made significant advances since 1979, albeit from a deplorably low base level. The importance of staff training at all levels has been recognised by the setting up in 1980 of the Scottish Housing Training Unit of the Institute of Housing, partially funded by local authorities. Its work includes the running of courses in management skills as well as specific aspects of housing policy. The shortfall of professionally qualified staff in housing in Scotland – a 1977 Report found only 97 qualified staff, against a conservatively estimated requirement of 350[(21)] – has been addressed by the establishment of courses at the Universities of Stirling, Glasgow and Heriot-Watt. This must be a positive trend. But better facilities and more generous staffing levels are required to convert higher levels of training into a better housing service for tenants. At heart, the improvement of housing management is constrained by resources.

Rents

An explicit part of the Government's stance on council housing has been its efforts to raise rents, by persuasion and administrative pressure rather than by direct rent fixing (see Arthur Midwinter's chapter). Although many local authorities have resisted this pressure, and attempted to minimise rent increases, the overall effect has been for rents to rise considerably faster than inflation since 1979. Average rents in 1984 were £513.42 p.a., compared with £255.61p.a. in 1979, an increase of 101%. Although rents are still almost a third below English/Welsh averages, this does constitute a move away from the traditional Scottish low rent policy.

Rising rents in combination with unemployment, and, in many sectors of the population, falling real incomes, have led to a sharp increase in rent arrears, at least until 1983. Accurate figures on arrears are difficult to find because of differences in rent accounting methods, but Glasgow, for example, had arrears amounting to 14% of collectable rent in 1983.[(22)] While this rise has caused alarm in some quarters, there has been a new awareness of the causes of arrears. A Scottish Office report in 1980 stated unambiguously that poverty was the principal cause of rent arrears, and that there was little evidence of fecklessness or deliberate refusal to pay rent.[(23)] This message has at least begun to be understood by councils who are increasingly likely to investigate a tenant's financial circumstances before resorting to eviction proceedings. A change in attitude has also been encouraged by the provisions in the Tenants' Rights Act which required courts to be satisfied that it is reasonable to evict a tenant (for rent arrears or any other of the other grounds specified) before it grants an eviction order. The impact of the Act is discussed by Adler and Himsworth in their chapter in this book. However, it would be misleading to attribute too much to the legislation. Many local authorities and most sheriff courts have followed the letter but not the spirit of the 1980 Act.

The rise in rent arrears has been stemmed by the introduction of housing benefits in 1982-83, because most council tenants on supplementary benefit (certificated cases), now have their rent paid directly to the council by the DHSS. In other respects, however, the housing benefit system has completely failed to live up to expectations. In particular, it has done nothing to simplify a chaotic system which treats households on similar incomes in very different ways, depending on whether or not they are in employment. Local authorities, who in 1982 resisted the over-hasty introduction of the scheme, have found housing benefits to be an administrative nightmare, particularly in making payments to private tenants. 812,000 households in Scotland (590,000 of them tenants) receive housing benefit, almost half of all households.[(24)] Yet take-up is still a problem, and eligible households must number about a million. This reliance on means-tested assistance, subject to the complexities, vagaries and reductions in benefit levels which at present characterise the system, has implications for the way housing costs are met, in particular in the public sector.

This leads me to return to the concept of residualisation. The replacement of general subsidies to council housing by a means-tested form of support for the poor does much to promote the welfare image. For those who do not qualify for housing benefit, rising rents provide an incentive to tenants to buy, thereby gaining access to the fiscal benefits of owner occupation. Thus concentrating subsidies on the poorest tenants plays an important part in changing the relative position of council housing and owner-occupation.

Conclusion

Having reviewed the trends in evidence, it is possible to make some observations about the future of council housing in Scotland.

The evidence of residualisation is unambiguous, although it would be inaccurate to take 1979 as the start-date for the trend. Falling levels of investment, rising rents, subsidies and incentives to owner-occupiers, a concentration of the poorest households in the public sector, and a reliance on means-tested assistance within the public sector all contribute to a transformation of the role of council housing. The most recent developments indicate, if anything, an acceleration of the trend. The Public Expenditure White Paper indicates a further 12% drop (in money terms) in housing expenditure in Scotland between 1983/84 and 1985/86, with rate-fund contributions the most likely area for enforced reductions. The Tenants Rights etc (Scotland) (Amendment) Act 1984 indicates, in relation to the right-to-buy, that the Government is envisaging a "more-of-the-same" policy, with quite significant extensions in the discount arrangement expected to fuel a new boom in house sales. Perhaps the most explicit statement yet of the Government's view on tenure is provided by the Building Defects Act, which provides for 90%-100% reinstatement grants to those former council tenants who have bought specified system-built houses with structural defects, while offering no assistance to councils to carry out similar work to identical houses which remain in council ownership.

The emphasis on extending owner-occupation at the expense of the public rented sector, and the growing disparity in levels of financial assistance to occupiers in the two sectors provide evidence that current Government thinking is overwhelmingly concerned with tenure. The reasons for this emphasis are complex, but perhaps have more to do with promoting a certain ideology based on individual ownership and minimal state involvement, rather than simply reducing public expenditure. The danger is that in following this course of action, the economic and social costs are being ignored.

The crucial point is that tenure change cannot on its own improve housing conditions or satisfy housing need; only increased investment can do that. Increasing rates of owner-occupation merely redistribute housing resources, and the pattern of that redistribution is on the whole regressive. International comparisons are illuminating as shown in Table 4.

Most of the best-housed nations in Europe have rates of owner-occupation similar to that of Scotland (37%) and below that of Great Britain (56%) (1981 figures). By contrast, those countries with high rates of owner-occupation have, in general, some of the poorest housing conditions.[25] Looked at in this light, the pursuit of the property-owning democracy seems a rather quixotic enterprise.

Other concerns can be expressed about the growth of owner-occupation. Firstly, in an attempt to lower the cost of entry to owner-occupation, construction standards are being sacrificed, particularly in relation to space. Only time will tell if the houses provided in the Government-inspired private building mini-boom of the 1980s will retain their value.

TABLE 4

Percentage Rates of Owner-Occupation in Selected European Countries

	Date of Information	% Stock Owner-occupied
Bulgaria	1970	82
Ireland	1979	76
Greece	1970	72
Yugoslavia	1971	71
Spain	1970	64
Netherlands	1977	41
West Germany	1978	36
Sweden	1970	35
Switzerland	1970	28
East Germany	1970	27
USSR	1970	23

Source: United Nations: Major Trends in Housing Policy in EEC Countries, Economic Commission for Europe, 1980 and Building Societies Association, Housing Tenure, 1983.

Secondly, owner-occupiers on low incomes are the least able to meet the repair and improvement costs associated with down-market property. They are also exceedingly vulnerable to fluctuations in the mortgage interest rate, such as that experienced in July 1984. The financial advantages of owner-occupation are only fully realised by those on secure incomes sufficient to purchase sound houses whose capital appreciation is guaranteed.

Thirdly, the popularity of owner-occupation and council house sales in particular is in very large part attributable to the financial incentives being offered. In theory, sales could be further extended by increasing the discounts, thus ensuring a continued flow of capital receipts for recycling. The further this process goes on, the less sense it makes economically, as assets are being sold at prices which do not reflect their value to the community. Hitherto, the concern with capital receipts has ignored consideration of the value of the assets being disposed of.

Finally, the growth of owner-occupation is likely to be very expensive in the long-run. Mortgage interest tax relief in Scotland now costs the Government an estimated £160m by way of revenue foregone. This figure is rising rapidly, and on a *per capita* basis is about three times as much as is paid out to council tenants in Housing Support Grant and rate fund contributions. The alternative way of assessing subsidies to owner-occupiers, through exemptions from investment taxes, would show an even higher cost to the nation. It is quite clear that the policy objective of increasing owner-occupation is being bought at enormous public expense.

Current housing policy is thus inefficient and inequitable. Pressure for reform has grown in recent years, from bodies as diverse as the Policy Studies Institute[26] and Shelter.[27] The virtually unanimous view is that housing finance needs a thorough overhaul, embracing the taxation system as well as housing subsidies as conventionally defined.

But what would emerge from such a review? It is quite clear that the country cannot return to some mythically halcyon days before the term residualisation was invented; reverting to 1975 levels of expenditure on housing would be prohibitively expensive. In any case, the change in the popular image of council housing over recent years is probably irreversible. If the public sector in housing is to escape the welfare stigma, it must follow new directions which do not fit easily into the tenure pattern we have grown to accept. For example, Forrest, Lansley and Murie argue against a recreation of the previous structure of tenure, in favour of a form of "municipal home ownership", loosely based on the Swedish model, to be achieved by a rechannelling and reorientation of subsidies.[28]

It remains to be seen whether such fundamental reform could ever be adopted as a manifesto item by choice by any political party (the alternative scenario of reform being forced on an unwilling Government on grounds of economic necessity is perhaps more likely). Any proposal which involves increasing the tax burden on owner-occupiers is unlikely to appeal to an electorate dominated, in Britain, if not in Scotland, by owner-occupiers. Certainly, the Labour Party, the traditional supporter of the public sector, has shown itself unwilling to address itself to the sorts of reforms which would encourage its revival. In a recent discussion paper, the Scottish Council of the Labour Party stated the view that "any Labour Party policy on housing must tackle this divergence (in the distribution of subsidy) *not by hitting house owners,* but by restoring financial aid to those who rent their houses" (my emphasis).[29] Yet it is difficult to see how any reform which does not address itself to the privileges enjoyed by owner-occupiers can ever make sense of our housing system.

References

1. The right to buy and other changes to public sector housing law are well described in C. Himsworth *Public Sector Housing Law in Scotland* Planning Exchange, 1982.

2. See, for example, S. Goss and S. Lansley, *What Price Housing?* Research Report 4, SHAC, 1982.

3. Social and Community Planning Research, *British Social Attitudes: the 1984 Report* Gower, 1984.

4. See, for example, Shelter (Scotland) *Dead End Street,* 1981, and the press statements made by (among others) the Scottish Federation of Housing Associations, the Institute of Housing and the Convention of Scottish Local Authorities.

5. P. Malpass and A. Murie, *Housing Policy and Practice*, Macmillan 1982, p.174

6. Halifax Building Society, *House Price Index*, Regional Bulletin No.2, 1984.

7. N. Armstrong, "The Promotion of Owner-occupation by Scottish Public Housing Agencies" in D. Alexander (ed) *Housing in Scotland, Some Current Issues,* University of Stirling, 1984.

8. For example, R. Forrest and A. Murie *Monitoring the Right to Buy 1980-1982*, Working Paper 40, School for Advanced Urban Studies, 1984.

9. For example, F. Twine, "Council House Sales in Aberdeen" in D. Alexander, (ed) *op.cit.*

10. Banff and Buchan District Council Housing Plan, 1982.

11. Glasgow District Council Annual Housing Review 1983.

12. Scottish Development Department, *Statistical Bulletin,* June 1984.

13. For an analysis of the financial effect of council house sales, see B. Kilroy "The Financial and Economic Implications of Council House Sales" in J. English (ed) *The Future of Council Housing,* Croom Helm 1982.

14. Scottish Development Department, *Scottish Housing Statistics* 13, 1981.

15. H. Jones, P. Graham and D. Wilkinson, *Glasgow Tenants Grants Scheme: An Assessment*, Central Research Unit, Scottish Development Department, 1983.

16. J. Gilbert, C. Orr and S. Hashagen, *The Tenants Handbook*, Scottish Consumer Council/Assist, 1983.

17. Scottish Affairs Committee, *Dampness in Housing* Volume 1, House of Commons Paper 206-1, 1984.

18. P. Gallagher, "Ideology and Housing Management" in J. English (ed) *op.cit.*

19. Shelter (Scotland), *Council House Allocation in Scotland*, 1982.

20. G. Atherton, *Terms of Tenancy*, Scottish Consumer Council, 1983.

21. Scottish Housing Advisory Committee, *Training for Tomorrow*, Scottish Development Department, 1977 (Muir Report).

22. Glasgow District Council *Annual Housing Review*, 1983.

23. D. Wilkinson, *Rent Arrears in Public Authority Housing in Scotland* Central Research Unit, Scottish Office, 1980.

24. For a full discussion of the problems of housing benefit, see Shelter (Scotland) submission to DHSS *Review of Housing Benefits*, 1984.

25. D. Donnison and C. Ungerson, *Housing Policy*, Penguin 1982.

26. J. Ermisch, *Housing Finance, Who Gains?* Policy Studies Institute, 1984.

27. Shelter, *Housing and the Economy*, 1982.

28. R. Forrest, S. Lansley and A. Murie, *A Foot on the Ladder*, Working Paper 41, School for Advanced Urban Studies, 1984.

29. Labour Party (Scottish Council), *Scotland's Housing Crisis*, 1984.

POLICY SUCCESSION IN A SCOTTISH QUANGO: THE SCOTTISH SPECIAL HOUSING ASSOCIATION 1937-1984

JOSEPH J HOGAN
SENIOR LECTURER IN PUBLIC ADMINISTRATION
ROBERT GORDON'S INSTITUTE OF TECHNOLOGY, ABERDEEN

HUNAIN M ALQADDO
RESEARCH STUDENT
ROBERT GORDON'S INSTITUTE OF TECHNOLOGY, ABERDEEN

Throughout the course of its existence the Scottish Special Housing Association (SSHA) has made a vital contribution to the implementation of a succession of housing and regional economic policies for Scotland. Today, the SSHA owns some 92,000 houses throughout Scotland, making the Association the owner of the second largest stock of housing in Scotland. Despite its manifest importance to Scottish housing the SSHA has not yet been the subject of an extensive academic study.(1) The purpose of this chapter, therefore, will be to make a start towards filling this gap. Accordingly, we will first present a definition of the SSHA and a survey of its main work during its first forty years. Secondly, we will cover the recent activities of the Association. In doing so we will thereby provide a brief case study of how recent housing policies for Scotland, which are covered in more detail in other chapters of this edition of the *Scottish Government Yearbook*, have affected this particular public housing organisation.

1. Defining the Scottish Special Housing Association

The Association is a non-departmental and non-ministerial agency of the Scottish Office that since its establishment in 1937 has been utilised, on behalf of the Secretary of State for Scotland, to assist the implementation of housing and regional economic policies for Scotland by designing, building and then managing houses throughout Scotland. The SSHA is governed internally by a Council of Management consisting of a Chairman, a Deputy Chairman and up to five other members. The members of the Council are appointed by the Secretary of State for Scotland and serve for a term of three years that is renewable at the invitation of the Secretary of State for Scotland; Council members are also paid for their part-time work. The Council of Management meets for eight to ten times a year and is responsible for ensuring that the policies and activities of the Association are in line with government policies and procedures. In practice the Association's day-to-day activities are managed by a full-time General Manager, who is appointed by and accountable to the Council of Management, and the Secretary of the Association who, like the rest of the SSHA's salaried staff, is a full-time civil servant. Despite definitional problems with the term, the SSHA is accurately described as a Scottish "quango" which the Secretary of State for Scotland uses to supplement the work of Scottish local authorities and to undertake special work which falls outside the responsibility of any Scottish housing authority.

In performing this function the SSHA designs, constructs, rehabilitates and modernises houses using the services of its own Building Department or, when secured on a competitive tendering process, those of private contractors. The Association also builds houses on an agency basis for a range of government bodies in Scotland, which in the past has included the construction of homes in isolated parts of Scotland for keepers employed by the Northern Lighthouse Board and for employees of the Forestry Commission working in similarly remote areas. The SSHA also builds houses on an agency basis for Scottish local authorities, if called upon by the Secretary of State for Scotland to do so, when they cannot obtain competitive tenders from commercial builders. This facility was used for the first time in 1956 when the Building Department obtained the tender from Inverness County Council to build houses at Caol and Corpach to provide homes for workers with the newly-constructed paper and pulp mill of Wiggins Teape. In all, over 10,000 houses have been erected on an agency basis by the Association. The houses erected for the Association remain in its ownership and are subject to its management. By 1980 the SSHA owned nearly 100,000 houses.

In financial terms the SSHA is a non-profit making Government Sponsored Company. The Association is established under the Companies Act as a company limited by guarantee but having no share capital. As such its funds are generated from government sources. The Association's revenue (or recurring) expenditure is financed from rent income and from annual subsidies and grants by the Treasury that are earmarked for purposes that have been approved by the Secretary of State for Scotland. Most of the SSHA's revenue budget is spent on loan charges, house maintenance programmes, and financing the management (including staff) costs of the Association. The SSHA's capital budget is financed entirely by the Treasury, is at the request of the Secretary of State for Scotland and must be approved by Parliament. The limit on capital advances to the SSHA has been progressively increased as a direct result of its expanding activities; the present statutory limit sanctioned by Parliament is £750 million. Capital advances are interest-bearing, and are repayable over definite, fixed periods. The borrowing period for building new houses is sixty years and because of recent high interest rates the SSHA has sought various ways to reduce its capital demands, such as financing major modernisation programmes from its revenue account. Monies generated from the sale of houses to tenants or clients when the SSHA acts as a construction agent also contributes to financing its work.

As a public agency the SSHA is accountable to a department of the Scottish Office, with the department exercising day-to-day control over the Association on behalf of the Secretary of State for Scotland. Over the years the specific department and the nature of its controls over the Association has changed. When first established the SSHA, which initially bore the name of the Scottish Special Areas Housing Association Limited, was intended to assist the Commissioner for the Special Areas in Scotland in promoting schemes to alleviate unemployment in places designated as distressed (hence 'special') areas.[(2)] In fact the Commissioner was an official of the Department of Health for Scotland, which exercised responsibility for controlling the SSHA's finances and for approving the allocation of construction programmes in the special areas. The SSHA's activities were extended by the Housing (Scotland) Act of 1944 to permit the Association to build houses, as directed by the Secretary of State for Scotland, in any part of Scotland. The 1944 Act and the Housing (Scotland) Act of 1946 entitled the SSHA to receive Treasury subsidies and grants subject to the approval of the Secretary of State for Scotland and the controls of the Department of Health. Pursuant to this legislation the Council of Management was required to submit to the Department quarterly financial statements. In 1958 the Department's controls were extended to include oversight of the annual process of setting rents for SSHA's tenants.

When the Scottish Development Department (SDD) was established on 1st July 1962 the new department was given responsibility for exercising control over housing policy in Scotland. The relationship between the SSHA and its new departmental overlord was eventually detailed in a formal agreement signed between the two bodies on 10th April 1967. Under this agreement the SDD exercises detailed control over most of the SSHA's activities, including the approval of house construction contracts, building plans, the remuneration of employees, rent reviews and the procedures for selecting tenants for accommodations owned by the SSHA. In the following year the Department began to stipulate the number of houses that could be built for different purposes each year and set a system of indicative costings for pricing the various construction activities of the

Association. The extent of the SDD's financial and other controls over the Association has increased in line with the housing and public expenditure policies of recent governments, and will be considered later in this chapter.

In practice the Association has proven itself to be a flexible instrument of Scottish central government. Over the years the SSHA has been given different remits in line with changes in government housing and economic policies, and we will now turn to outlining the Association's main contributions to these policies between 1937 and 1977.

2. The First Forty Years: 1937-1977

In order to reduce unemployment in the special areas it was necessary for the SSHA to adopt a method of construction that could be used successfully by unskilled operatives. This demand led to the adoption, from Holland, of the 'no-fines concrete' construction technique, which consisted of concrete made only with the larger particles of aggregate cemented together without sand or 'fine' aggregate. The resultant concrete was poured into prepared forms, which enabled a gang of men to construct a three-room house in four days, employing only two or three skilled tradesmen in a gang of fifty workers. To implement this technique the SSHA set up its own Building Department and, in early 1939, began a programme of building 2,000 houses in the special areas. This programme was abandoned with the outbreak of war, when the SSHA was directed to provide housing for special wartime needs. In this role the SSHA built wartime accommodations for workmen moved to Balloch, Johnstone and Hamilton to undertake essential work, constructed Post Offices at, for example, Dunfermline and Kirkwall to handle mail for Royal Naval personnel, and constructed hostels for evacuated families at Bridge of Weir, Milngavie and Neilston. By the end of the war the SSHA had built, mainly in the West of Scotland, 2,829 houses, of which close on 1,700 houses were owned by the Association.

In 1944 the Association was instructed to resume work on the housing projects which had been abandoned in 1939 as preparation for a vigorous role in the post-war housebuilding programme. The main remit of the SSHA was to build houses as quickly as possible for the 'general needs' programme. Thus the Association was empowered and provided with the necessary finances by the 1944 and 1946 Housing (Scotland) Acts to build houses in any district of Scotland which the Secretary of State for Scotland determined was in need of assistance with its house construction programme. The 'general needs' programme required a sharp increase in the personnel and the finances of the SSHA's Building Department, which also utilised innovative construction techniques to reduce the costs and time involved in building new houses. By the early 1950s the Building Department was building two houses for every hour of the normal working week. A total of 46,000 houses had been erected when the 'general needs' programme was terminated in 1972. In addition the SSHA undertook, between 1949 and 1960, a special housebuilding programme for the National Coal Board to facilitate the movement of miners and their families from exhausted pits to new coalfields. A total of 10,000 houses had been built by the Association for the National Coal Board when this programme was completed in 1960.

In 1953 the Clyde Valley Advisory Committee decided that the rehousing and housing density problems of Glasgow would have to be tackled by both dispersing large numbers of Glasgow citizens to overspill housing developments outside the city and by redeveloping housing in the centre of Glasgow. Over the ensuing years the SSHA made a major contribution to both programmes. The Housing and Town Development (Scotland) Act of 1957 empowered the Association to supplement the work of Scottish local authorities by building overspill communities for Glasgow Corporation. The largest single community development for this venture was erected at Erskine; smaller communities were constructed at Hamilton and Little Earnock. To redevelop the centre of Glasgow the SSHA assisted the Central Glasgow Redevelopment Area programme by building multi-storey housing blocks of up to twenty-six storeys in height. As part of both programmes the SSHA also developed green field recreation facilities for tenants. Both programmes comprised the main bulk of the Association's work between 1959 and 1969, with the SSHA having constructed over 12,000 homes in places as far afield as Dunbar, Arbroath and Fort William when the programmes were completed in 1980.

In the early 1960s the SSHA's primary role shifted once more, this time to supporting the economic expansion programme proposed by the government in its White Paper – 'A Programme for Development and Growth in Central Scotland' – of 1963. The programme was designed to generate industrial growth in selected communities in Central Scotland, with the New Town Development Corporation and the SSHA sharing the main responsibility for constructing economic expansion houses. To supervise the house construction programme the Secretary of State for Scotland appointed the 'Houses for Industry Committee', consisting of representatives from the Scottish Development Department, the Department of Trade and Industry, the Department of Employment and the SSHA; the Housing (Scotland) Act of 1964 empowered the Association to build homes for the venture to relieve the pressure on local authorities, who were already overloaded with their own housing programmes, in Central Scotland. A particular feature of the SSHA's contribution to the programme was the construction of quality housing for in-coming managers, senior executives and professional workers to offset a lack of quality housing in the private sector. Between 1966 and 1972 the Association constructed 10,000 houses for this venture, including the construction of housing estates in Linwood (to support the Rootes car plant), Erskine and Tweedbank.

The 'Houses for Industry Committee' in 1973 proposed a construction programme of 14,000 houses (to be built between 1973 and 1977), with the focus of construction switched from Central to North and North East Scotland to support the development of the oil and gas industries. A large proportion of these houses were built in the Moray Firth area, Aberdeen, Peterhead and other communities in the region for incoming workers employed in the new industries. By 1977 this programme was slowing down due to a combination of the oil and gas boom levelling off and the difficulties experienced, particularly in the Aberdeen area, in obtaining suitable sites for house construction. Homes were also built in the Shetlands for workers engaged in knitwear and fish processing and in the Borders for the wool industry. A total of just over 10,000 houses had been constructed for this phase of the economic expansion programme by 1981.

3. Recent Developments: 1977-1984

For most of its first forty years the SSHA had contributed to the implementation of housing and regional economic policies for Scotland by quickly building houses in green field sites throughout Scotland. During the second half of the 1970s the construction work of the Association underwent a basic shift from building community housing schemes to undertaking major redevelopment work in inner city areas for Scottish local authorities and the planned modernisation of its own housing stock. In part, this new role was a by-product of the post-war emphasis on quantity rather than quality in mass housing construction projects, an emphasis that gave rise to the legacy of a deteriorating stock of housing in the ownership of Scottish local authorities and the SSHA; concentrating on new build schemes in green field sites also meant that the problems of inner city blight, particularly regarding housing constructed during the inter-war years, was neglected. On the other hand, the British economy moved into a recession during the mid-1970s that reduced demand for economic expansion housing projects (particularly in the Borders region) and led, in time, to deep cuts in the provision of public expenditure for house construction purposes.

The policy underpinnings of the Association's new role were first laid down in a memorandum from the Scottish Development Department in 1975, with the justification for a parallel change in Scottish housing policy coming in the form of a Green Paper – 'Scottish Housing' (A Consultative Document) – that was published in June 1977. The Scottish Development Department's memorandum directed the Association to undertake redevelopment and modernisation rather than new build work. The Green Paper supported this change on a national level by arguing that the post-war housing shortage had largely been eliminated in Scotland, and pointed Scottish housing policy in the direction of a programme of planned improvements in inner city housing. In addition, the Green Paper announced the commencement of a small 'Special Needs' programme for building homes to meet the housing needs of, for example, the disabled, the elderly and single (particularly young) people.

In accord with the SDD's memorandum the SSHA embarked on a Redevelopment Housing Assistance Programme (RAP) to assist Scottish local authorities, particularly in Glasgow, in regenerating their inner city housing by both building new houses and rehabilitating old ones. At first the SSHA was directed to build and upgrade a total of 2,650 houses for RAP, with the Housing (Amendment) (Scotland) Act of 1976 providing the Association with the necessary funds to assist Scottish local authorities in expediting their attack on low housing standards. By early 1979 the programme had been increased, with the Association now allocated a total of 10,290 improvements, to be completed in 1983, in the housing stock of over twenty District Councils throughout Scotland.

A key feature of the Association's contribution to RAP came in the form of participation – along with the SDD, the Scottish Development Agency, Strathclyde Regional Council, Glasgow District Council, the Greater Glasgow Health Board, the Manpower Services Commission and the Housing Corporation – in the Glasgow Eastern Area Renewal Project (GEAR). This programme, which sought to regenerate comprehensively the community of East Glasgow, involved the SSHA in building 1,500 new homes, carrying out the rehabilitation of 800 properties and undertaking various environmental improvement schemes for the project. To facilitate its work on GEAR, which involved liaison and negotiations with many government bodies, the Association opened a new Regional Office (West) in Glasgow in early January 1977.

Coincidentally with RAP the Association commenced a programme to modernise comprehensively housing in its own stock that had been erected twenty-five or more years ago. Most of these houses had been rapidly and economically constructed to tackle the post-war housing shortage, but had come to suffer from marked condensation and insulation problems, with their tenants (particularly those in steel-frame houses built in the immediate post-war years) complaining that their homes were very expensive to heat because of excessive heat-loss problems. In July 1975 the SDD approved a proposal from the Association to undertake a major modernisation of its steel-frame houses; the modernisation programme was expanded in 1977 to cover 11,636 houses of many different types in its own stock. These major modernisation projects were directed at entire blocks of houses that were considered to be in need of extensive modernisation work, such as re-wiring old electrical installations, replacing kitchen and bath facilities, improving their heating system, replacing gutters and lead water mains, and upgrading the roof and wall insulation; the actual work undertaken varied between different types of housing. In addition, a programme of minor modernisations, such as installing new external doors and replacing individual items of sanitary wear, was approved for houses that were individually considered, as a result of yearly inspections made in the course of a planned maintenance routine that was introduced in 1970, to be in need of work.

In the event the actual extent of the Association's redevelopment and major modernisation work fell significantly short of the targets planned and approved by the government between 1975 and 1979. For example, only 4,200 houses had been built and 1,660 units modernised for RAP by the end of the 1982-83 fiscal year, as compared with the planned target of 10,290 improvements. The reasons for the shortfall are found in the combined effects of economic recession, attendant changes in the government's public expenditure policies, and the difficulties experienced by the SSHA in implementing the redevelopment and major modernisation programmes.

The OPEC oil embargo in 1973 provoked a sharp increase in the rate of inflation that, amongst other consequences, greatly increased the costs of materials and labour for house construction. For example, the cost of building a standard house for the SSHA rose from £5,470 at the end of 1971 to £16,699 by June 1977. Such rapid cost inflation created considerable stress on the economy and the government's public expenditure programme. As a central plank of its programme for tackling Britain's economic recession the newly-elected Conservative Government in June 1979 imposed a system of cash limits on public expenditure that led to deep cuts in the SSHA's capital expenditure allocation from the 1980-81 fiscal year onwards. Under the new constraints on capital spending the Association's planned programme of capital expenditure projects was cut by around 40 per cent, over the 1981-84 fiscal period, from the levels projected when determining the SSHA's capital budget for fiscal 1979-80. To ensure that the SSHA's work was in line with the government's spending policies the SDD laid down, on 1st April 1980, a detailed plan for the Association's future activities. The plan established the level of new starts for the SSHA's new build, redevelopment and modernisation programmes. Thus, new build starts were set at 469 units for fiscal 1982-83, as compared to 1,614 starts made in fiscal 1979-80. As a result of the cuts made in the SSHA's planned capital programme a total of £57.9 million was removed from its capital expenditure budget between the 1981-82 to 1983-84 fiscal years.

Problems inherent in the redevelopment and major modernisation programmes also contributed to reducing the SSHA's capital budget work in the 1980s. The redevelopment programme encountered significant delays in gaining compliance from participating government bodies, private organisations and individuals for the infrastructure planning, site acquisition and clearance phases. Comparable delays were further experienced in obtaining the support of Tenants Associations and individual tenants, who normally had to be rehoused to permit work on their homes, for the building phases of both the redevelopment and major modernisation programmes. Working simultaneously on both schemes meant that the SSHA experienced significant logistical problems in moving labour and materials between different sites throughout Scotland. As a consequence of these factors the Association did not spend all the monies allocated in its annual budgets for work on the redevelopment and major modernisation programmes, and these 'savings' were part of the cuts made in the SSHA's planned capital expenditure budget for the 1980s.

The Association's actual capital spending since the 1979-80 fiscal year demonstrates the impact of the new constraints upon public spending. With the exception of fiscal 1982-83, which will be discussed later, the SSHA's capital spending has been reduced below the level for fiscal 1979-90 (see Table 1). By contrast the Association's revenue spending has increased by over 30 per cent between the fiscal years of 1979-80 and 1982- 83, with the increase reflecting the growth of the SSHA's modernisation work. As Table 2 indicates, reduced capital spending is reflected in a declining construction and redevelopment role for the Association. As such the new goals laid down between 1975 and 1977 for Scottish housing policy and the public expenditure policies of the present Conservative Government have reinforced each other to shift the primary role and work of the Association from house construction to the management, modernisation and maintenance of its own stock of housing. The Association, in line with an instruction – dated 13th January 1983 – from the SDD, now performs a residual housing construction role for the 'Special needs' programme.

For fiscal 1982-83 the SSHA was actually allocated a capital expenditure budget of £43.6 million. The out-turn capital spending budget of £59.9 million for fiscal 1982-83 is due to an unexpected injection of £18.2 million above anticipated levels from sales of the SSHA's houses to sitting tenants; an underspend of £1.9 million reduced the Association's capital spending from £61.8 million to £59.9 million. The sale of its houses to sitting tenants has been a prominent feature of the Association's recent work. The house sales programme began, under 'voluntary procedures' laid down by the SDD in July 1979, some time before the Tenants Rights, Etc., (Scotland) Act of 1980 gave sitting tenants the statutory right to purchase their homes from the Association.[3] During the 1979-80 fiscal year the SSHA sold 80 of its houses to sitting tenants, and a further 8,842 houses were sold during the 1980-81 to 1983-84 fiscal period; 3,200 house sales are planned for fiscal 1984-85. In accord with its position as an implementing agency of government policy the SSHA has been directed to pursue a vigorous role in the area of house sales to demonstrate the utility of this policy to other government bodies, particularly Scottish local authorities. Indeed, this 'mission' can be expected to continue as long as the Tenants Rights, Etc. (Scotland) Act of 1980 remains on the statute book.

TABLE 1

Annual Capital and Revenue Spending (in £ millions) of the SSHA over the 1970-1983 Fiscal Period

	70/1	**71/2**	**72/3**	**73/4**	**74/5**	**75/6**	**76/7**	**77/8**	**78/9**	**79/80**	**80/1**	**81/2**	**82/3**
Revenue Spending	11.1	13.0	14.9	16.8	19.0	25.7	34.0	43.5	53.4	57.9	64.9	71.5	80.9
Capital Spending	14.9	13.1	10.0	12.6	25.8	35.8	36.4	41.1	30.1	47.2	46.8	44.8	59.9

Source: SSHA

TABLE 2

Annual Completion Rates (in individual dwelling units) for the main Construction Programmes of the SSHA over the 1976-84 Fiscal Period.

	76/7	**77/8**	**78/9**	**79/80**	**80/1**	**81/2**	**82/3**	**83/4**
Modernisation	148	803	1044	1484	1562	953	1603	1853
RAP	–	290	280	620	1024	1466	452	327
Economic Expansion	2099	1347	593	222	195	–	14	98
Total new building	3188	2304	2245	1530	1383	1591	550	511

Source: SSHA

Cutbacks in the capital budget of the Association and the re-orientation of its work provoked a slimming down of SSHA staff, with the effects first being felt by the Building Department. This department had been established in 1938 to build that portion of the SSHA's new build work that had not been secured, through a competitive tendering process, by private construction companies; funds for the department are provided in accordance with the provisions of various Housing (Scotland) Acts. In accordance with Treasury requirements, the Building Department's accounts are kept separate from those of the SSHA to afford a basis for comparing the Department's work and costs with firms in the private sector. Indeed, the Building Department is treated as a separate organisation and its tenders, to the Association and other government bodies, are closely examined by the SSHA (particularly the Technical Division) and its supervising government department to ensure that the costs are competitive with the prices in the private sector. In practice, the SSHA's supervising government department has required the Building Department to obtain, on average, 20 per cent of its work from competitive tenders, with the remainder obtained via negotiations with the SSHA and other government agencies at rates approved beforehand by the SSHA's supervising government department.

During the post-war boom period for the housing construction industry the Building Department quickly expanded in size and generated profits on its construction work. But the OPEC oil embargo led to severe inflation in the costs of the housing industry that, when combined with the widespread practice in the construction business of tendering fixed-price contracts, led to deficits in the ledgers of the Building Department of over half a million pounds for each of the 1973-74 and 1974-75 fiscal years. The deficits led to the abandonment of fixed- price contracts and the adoption of actual cost tenders, but the Department's volume of new build work was severely reduced by the cuts in its capital programme. In addition the Local Government Planning and Land Act of 1980 imposed further constraints on both the capital and maintenance work of the department. This piece of legislation requires the Building Department, and its counterparts in local authorities, to tender on the open market for any new build programme costed at more than £50,000, for maintenance work costed at more than £10,000, and to generate a profit of not less than 5 per cent on its annual capital turnover. Although the Act empowers the Building Department, and other direct labour organisations in the public sector, to spend profits (in the same fiscal year in which they were generated) that exceed the 5 per cent provision, the legislation injected a great degree of uncertainty into the future operations of the Building Department, which, when combined with the cuts in its capital programme, contributed to reducing the staff of the department.

The contraction process began in the Autumn of 1979 when the SDD directed the Association to undertake a comprehensive review of manpower levels in the Building Department, basically to reduce the department's staff to levels compatible with the planned construction programme of the department. Over the next three years the department's salaried staff was reduced from 233 to 93 employees, while the number of operatives (comprising workers hired, and paid at hourly rates, for individual construction projects) was reduced from 1,749 to 977 workers between 1979 and 1982. In the process many units of the Building Department were amalgamated, with several branches of the department, as was the case with four supply depots, being closed. The cutbacks firmly re-oriented the department towards work on modernisation and maintenance programmes, with the Association now having most of its new build work undertaken by private construction firms. For example, in fiscal 1982-83 a total of 544 houses were built (mainly to complete work on the SSHA's construction programmes that were authorised in the early 1970s) by private construction firms for the Association, whereas only 12 houses – as compared to 1,296 in fiscal 1975-76 – were erected by the Building Department. The adjustments in the staff and work of the department succeeded in converting the Building Department into a profit-making organisation. In each financial year of the 1980-83 fiscal period the department generated profits on its capital programme, with the profits for fiscal 1982-83 on its capital work standing at £788,000 on an annual capital turnover of £9,831,000; in fiscal 1982-83 a profit of £271,000 was gained from a turnover of £7,641,000 on the department's maintenance budget.

Adapting to the tight discipline imposed by fiscal cutbacks and the new goals of successive governments for Scottish housing policy required a comprehensive re-organisation of the SSHA's organisational structure. As the construction work of the SSHA increased during the post-war years the SSHA evolved an organisational structure that was suited to a vigorous house- building role. This structure consisted of a Technical Division, the Building Department and a Housing Management Department, with each unit responsible, respectively, for handling the different demands of the design, construction and the management phases of the house construction process. In addition, an Administrative Division and a Finance Department provided the other units with a range of central staff services and conducted necessary negotiations with various government bodies in Scotland. In practice, the Association's structure was a functional one in that it was organised to meet the different requirements of the construction process by devolving responsibility for each phase to separate, specialist units. But precisely because the Association was vertically divided into separate units the organisational structure was not compatible with the new management role of the SSHA. This new task requires close co-ordination between the various units of the SSHA in order to manage a stock of housing that is physically located in different communities throughout Scotland and consists of varying types of houses with widely contrasting (especially regarding modernisation work) local needs. This defect was quickly recognised by the senior officers and the General Manager of the Association, who obtained the approval of the Council of Management (in mid- 1979) to conduct a fundamental review of the SSHA's structure to make it compatible with its projected tasks. This review was approved by the SDD, but was subject to the requirements that any re-organisation did not increase the number of senior posts nor exceed the planned establishment budget for the Association.

Following preliminary discussions between senior officers on the type of structure needed the Association decided, in February 1981, to commission the management consultants firm (in Edinburgh) of Urwick, Orr and Partners Limited to examine the organisational structure of the SSHA and to recommend changes in the light of the Association's projected role and workload. The Urwick group, who had conducted a similar review of the Northern Ireland Housing Executive, worked in close conjunction with the SSHA's senior staff (who organised a working party to liaise with the deliberations of the Urwick group) and submitted their final report in June 1981.

The report's recommendations paralleled the views of the Association's senior managers in proposing the establishment of a number of Regional Management teams who were to be charged with the responsibility for comprehensively managing and delivering a range of services to the local tenants of the SSHA's stock of housing. These regional units, which were to be organised on the principle of managing housing stocks of similar size, were to be headed by a Regional Manager and staffed with personnel drawn from the Technical, Finance, Housing Management and Administrative units of the SSHA. In line the SSHA's Technical, Finance, Housing Management and Administrative units were to be re-organised into Directorates with field officers attached to the regional units and a central staff (located in the SSHA's headquarters in Edinburgh) office that would provide supporting services to the regions and ensure that Association policies are implemented at the regional level. In effect, the report recommended the adoption of an organisational blueprint under which the regional units would become the operational arms of the Association with the responsibility for meeting the different needs of the

SSHA's tenants.

To provide the regional teams with clear direction concerning the policy positions of the Association the report recommended the establishment of a central Policy Board. This Board would consist of the General Manager and the heads of the new Directorates, and would be responsible for preparing internally formulated policy proposals for consideration by the Council of Management, with the Council's decisions subject to the approval of the SDD. In addition, the report proposed the establishment of an Executive Board, consisting of the members of the Policy Board plus the individual Regional Managers and the Manager of the Building Department, to convert official Association policy into operational programmes. Finally, the report proposed significant reductions in the staff of the Technical Department (to reflect a decline in the Association's construction work) and lesser reductions in other units.

The work of the Urwick group was completed with the submission of their final report. The senior managers and the Council of Management of the Association then developed the proposals into a series of changes that were finally approved for implementation by the SDD in May 1981. In short time, Association staff were redeployed to work in either the three Regional Housing teams – a North and a South Region (both with their headquarters in Edinburgh) and a West Region managed from Glasgow – or the four central directorates. The regional units, which are sub-divided into twenty-one Area Housing teams, are multi-disciplinary teams, consisting of staff drawn from all but the Finance Directorate, and are responsible for a full range of services – including rent collection, house sales and lettings – to their tenants and for managing maintenance, modernisation work and liaising with the local authorities within their jurisdictions. In line with their comprehensive management task the Regional Managers are responsible for revenue and capital expenditure programmes within their regions. Today the regional teams manage 78,200 houses and conduct negotiations with the individual Scottish local authorities who manage a total of 13,800 houses on behalf of the Association. The Executive Board met for the first time in July 1982 with the Policy Board commencing its work in early 1984 after the re-organisation programme had been fully implemented. Finally, the salaried staff of the Association (excluding the Building Department) was reduced from aroung 1,400 staff in mid-1979 to close on 1,100 staff by the end of 1982.

In practice, the re-organisation devolved a substantial degree of authority to the regional teams in order to manage the day-to-day local operations of the SSHA, while the central directorates, the Building Manager, the Secretary (who is now the head of the Administration Directorate), the General Manager and the Council of Management provide the local units with support services and are also responsible for making and overseeing the implementation of Association policies, subject to the approval, on behalf of the Secretary of State for Scotland, of the SDD. Although it is too early to comment on at this stage, the functioning and the consequences of the re-organisation will provide fertile materials for future studies of the Association.

Conclusion

Over its life the SSHA has demonstrated itself to be a flexible instrument of Scottish Central Government by building and rehabilitating houses to supplement the work of Scottish local authorities, and by undertaking special work that falls outside the authority of other government bodies in Scotland. However, dependence on government policies makes the Association vulnerable, as its recent history underlines, to changes in governments and government policies. One of the main consequences of recent government policies for housing in Scotland has been to draw the Association much closer to the supervision of the SDD. Indeed, the SSHA is now subject to such tight controls, particularly through the annual budgeting process, over its finances and planned programmes of work by the SDD that some doubts may be cast over its status as a non- departmental agency of the Scottish Office. Although the SSHA is, by its nature, a responsive agency, the Association has recently sought to increase its input into determining its future programme of work. Since November 1983 the Area Housing teams have been developing 'Area Housing Plans'. These plans will serve as the basis for determining, at the regional level (by October 1984) a comprehensive housing strategy for the SSHA that will be discussed with the SDD when deciding the Association's capital expenditure allocation for fiscal 1986-7. While it is again too early to assess this strategy, it must be remembered that, in the long run, governments and their policies to change. Should a future government decide to increase its efforts and spending in the area of housing policy for Scotland, then the SSHA, as an implementing agency of government policy, can be expected, as it has in the past, to benefit by playing a vigorous role.

References

1. Academic studies of Scottish Government and housing policies for

Scotland have only devoted a few paragraphs to the SSHA. To date, the main study of the SSHA is *A Chronicle of Forty Years, 1937-1977,* which was published (to commemorate the fortieth anniversary of the SSHA in 1977) by Macdonald Printers (Edinburgh) Limited for the Association. The study was prepared from materials researched by David H Halley, formerly Secretary and Solicitor to the Association, and SSHA staff. The contents of this chapter are based on published government documents, published and unpublished SSHA materials, and interviews with many of the senior staff of the Association.

2. In 1939 the name was changed to the Scottish Special Housing Association Limited, and in 1969 the work 'Limited' was dropped because some Tenants' Associations and Local Authorities took the word to indicate that the Association was a profitmaking commercial enterprise.

3. Under the Heath government, the SSHA sold 410 of its houses to sitting tenants during the 1973-4 fiscal year.

TENANTS IN ARREARS: A NEW ROLE FOR THE SHERIFF COURT?*

MICHAEL ADLER
DEPARTMENT OF SOCIAL ADMINISTRATION
UNIVERSITY OF EDINBURGH

CHRIS HIMSWORTH
DEPARTMENT OF CONSTITUTIONAL AND ADMINISTRATIVE LAW
UNIVERSITY OF EDINBURGH

Introduction

The biggest single change introduced by the Tenants' Rights, Etc. (Scotland) Act 1980 (in this article abbreviated to the Tenants' Rights Act or the 1980 Act) was the creation of the public sector secure tenancy. This was used to introduce that package of rights, known as the Tenants' Charter, including the right to a written lease, to sub-let or take in lodgers, to carry out repairs, alterations and improvements and, above all, the right to purchase from the landlord authority. These rights, which are similar to those granted to public sector tenants in England and Wales by the Housing Act 1980, apply to all secure tenancies. At their core is security of tenure itself, the grant to the public sector of rights parallel to those enjoyed for many years in the private sector under the Rent Acts. The essence if this

* The authors would like to acknowledge the financial support of the Scottish Development Department for funding a research project on the implementation and impact of section 15(1) of the Tenants' Rights, Etc (Scotland) Act 1980. They would particularly like to thank Scott Kerr for his very substantial contribution to the research. The views expressed in this paper are those of the authors alone and do not represent those of the Scottish Development Department or indeed of anyone else.

security is the protection given to tenants by the limits imposed upon the grounds available to the landlord for recovery of possession. This has been very important for private sector tenants and, despite the misgivings of many in local government, the same benefits have now been extended to the public sector. The local authority argument had alwats been that they could be trusted to use their powers as landlords reasonably and that such powers were needed in order to ensure satisfactory housing management.[(1)]

Whatever the strength of the arguments on each side of this issue, the introduction of public sector security may not in one respect be of enormous practical significance. A court order was always necessary before a local authority's notice to quit could be enforced and local authorities were not, in any event, in the habit of wholesale ejection of tenants. The only circumstance in which local authorities did raise very large numbers of actions against tenants was in the case of tenants with rent arrears.[(2)] Since arrears with the payment of rent remains a ground for possession under the 1980 Act, no fundamental challenge has been made to the powers of landlord authorities.

Three changes were, however, introduced. In the first place, section 14 of the Act introduced a procedure which required that before proceedings could be taken against a tenant, notice in a new statutory form had to be served. This replaces the old notice to quit. Thereafter, proceedings continue to be by way of summary cause in the sheriff court. The second change is that, in addition to the need to establish that arrears of rent are owed, it must appear to the court that it is "reasonable" for an order for recovery of possession to be made. Even before the court makes a final decision on the case, and this is the third change, the court may "as it thinks fit, adjourn proceedings... for a period or periods, with or without imposing conditions as to a payment of outstanding rent or other conditions". This power to adjourn proceedings is contained in section 15(1) of the 1980 Act and replicates an equivalent power available to the court in private sector proceedings. It was the use made of this power to adjourn which provided the main focus of a research project we have recently completed for the Scottish Development Department.[(3)]

It had been thought that the insertion of this new power to adjourn might be important in two ways. In the first place, it could create a new role for the sheriff court. The court would no longer be confined to a process of merely "rubber-stamping" the landlord's application followed by the automatic issue of decree of ejection. Instead the court would be able to play a more active role by withholding the award of decree in appropriate cases and becoming involved in a process of mediation between the landlord and tenant to decide the terms and conditions upon which a tenancy would continue – at least for a time.

The second way in which this power might prove important is that if the issue of decrees was no longer automatic, housing authorities might face delays and difficulties and pressure might be put upon them to work out a different relationship with defaulting tenants. It would still be one underpinned by the ultimate sanction of dispossession authorised by the court but one in which a more "managerial" approach to the problem of rent arrears might develop.

These two possible developments are, of course, related. Both are concerned with the long-standing question of how to handle rent arrears, with the causes of rent arrears, with preventative action which may be taken and with measures which are appropriate once arrears have accumulated. Recent official thinking has been that preventative rather than curative measures are to be preferred and that court proceedings are not the most rational response to the arrears problem.(4)

An initial suspicion that the most significant fact about section 15(1) in the first two years after its introduction in October 1980 was that it was not actually being used prompted the commissioning of the research. An early impression had developed that it was perhaps only in the Edinburgh sheriff court that sheriffs were adjourning proceedings at all and one important question was, therefore, to discover systematically whether this was the case. We were also concerned to find out the effects, if any, of the use of adjournment in any court that used the power upon tenant, landlord and court. Assuming different levels of use of the power to adjourn, we also wanted to explain why some courts had and others had not resorted to it. Beyond that, the research enabled us to speculate more widely upon the policy implications of this legislative attempt to introduce the courts into a process in which they had not previously played a strong role.

What we did was to select ten sheriff courts in different parts of the country and the eighteen housing authorities (fifteen local authorities, two new town corporations and the SSHA) in the areas covered by those courts.(5) There were then four parts to the research. Firstly, for a period in 1982, we took directly from the court records the number of public sector actions for recovery of possession which had been raised together with details of the parties, whether or not the tenant was present or represented in court and the outcome.(6) If, in any instance, the outcome was not final, i.e. if there had been an adjournment or some other continuation of the proceedings, we traced subsequent "callings" in the case to discover the final decision of the court.[7] Secondly, and this time from the housing authorities, we sought statistics on the number of tenancies they had, the number of notices of proceedings they had issued in a year, the number of actions actually raised and the eventual number of evictions carried out. We were able to compare these figures with directly equivalent figures collected from all Scottish housing authorities in 1978.[8] These two exercises were to provide us with a substantial amount of hard data about actual practice in 1982 in both courts and housing authorities. To enable us to gather further information and to interpret these initial statistical findings, we also, thirdly, conducted interviews with sheriffs and sheriff clerks and, fourthly, with those housing officials most directly concerned with the collection of rent arrears in their authorities.

The use by sheriff courts of their power to adjourn under section 15(1)

The primary result of the research was to confirm previous suspicions and to establish that it was indeed the case that in the spring of 1982 (eighteen months after the Act came into effect in October 1980) very little use was being made in the courts of the power to adjourn proceedings for recovery of possession. Over half (54%) of the cases in our sample of 948 court actions were disposed of at the first calling by the grant of an immediate decree of ejection. The remaining actions were disposed of by decree for expenses only (the principal sum having been settled) (18%) or by dismissal (the outstanding debt having been settled in full) (10%). A further 10% of cases were continued for technical reasons. In only 5% of all cases were proceedings adjourned under section 15(1) of the 1980 Act. Not only was the number of cases adjourned very small but all were confined to one court – the Edinburgh sheriff court. In the spring of 1982, no other court in our sample of ten courts was making any use at all of the power to adjourn.

This finding must, however, be qualified in two ways. In the first place, subsequent interviews showed that a pattern of adjournments had become established in the Glasgow sheriff court by mid-1983. It is possible that the position had changed in other courts too. The other qualification which should be mentioned is that whilst adjournments under section 15(1) were infrequent and confined to one court, there were in some other courts alternative devices used to achieve a deferred outcome of a related sort. In the Airdrie court, for instance, there was quite substantial use of the "continuation *sine die*" according to which, on the pursuer's motion, the action would be held in abeyance pending satisfactory rates of payment of arrears negotiated between the pursuer landlord and the tenant.[9]

Attendance as a pre-condition of adjournment

Why was it that in the Edinburgh court, and later in the Glasgow court as well, the power of adjournment was being used whereas, in the other courts, it lay dormant? By the summer of 1983 the Edinburgh and Glasgow courts had become quite unlike the others. The answer, revealed initially in the court records we examined and subsequently in interviews with sheriffs in the two courts, lies in the very close relationship between the number of tenants who attended or were represented in court and the number of adjournments which were granted. Attendance at court did not imply any high degree of forensic sophistication. All that was required to obtain an adjournment in the Edinburgh or Glasgow court was that the tenant (or his/her representative) was physically present to request an adjournment rather than immediate ejection and made an offer acceptable to the authority which would then be ratified by the court. Periods of adjournment were typically for six weeks. Representation of tenants in these two courts was only rarely by a solicitor. Much more usually it was by a spouse, close relative, social worker, councillor, or representative of an organisation such as Shelter.

Another difference which had emerged in the Edinburgh and Glasgow courts was that a sheriff rather than the sheriff clerk or his depute presided. Under the Sheriff Court Summary Cause Rules it is permissible for sheriff clerks to sit and, before the 1980 Act, this had been the usual practice in possession cases.[10] Since the court had virtually no discretion to deny authorities their remedy, the role of the court had become wholly appropriate for delegation to the sheriff clerk. In the majority of courts we looked at this practice had continued. In the absence of tenants as defenders, the grant of decree continued to be almost automatic. Some courts occupied a half-way position in that the sheriff, rather than the sheriff clerk, did sit but business continued to be almost entirely uncontested and interventions by the sheriff were extremely rare. (In one court, in anticipation of changes which the 1980 Act was expected to bring about, the sheriff replaced the sheriff clerk on the bench but, after a few months during which no change took place, the sheriff once again gave way to the sheriff clerk.) Another half-way position was taken up in a court where the sheriff clerk continued to sit but was himself presiding over a court in which increasing numbers of tenants were beginning to turn up ("it takes a while for the punters to realise there is something in it for them"), some negotiation between the housing authority and tenants took place in court and any difficult cases were referred to the sheriff.[11] Otherwise, however, the picture was one of great contrast between that majority of courts in which very few tenants turned up and it mattered little if they did so, the sheriff clerk continued to sit and business remained "as usual" and, on the other hand, the Edinburgh and Glasgow courts in which the sheriff sat, large numbers of tenants appeared nearly all of whom were granted adjournments as a matter of routine at the first calling and many of whom reappeared to be granted further adjournments at second (and subsequent) callings. In these two courts at least the impact of section 15(1) was being quite sharply felt.

How to produce a greater use of the powers of the court

The passing of the 1980 Act was insufficient to ensure its implementation. Insofar as the Act authorised courts to adjourn proceedings, it was merely permissive in character. It did not impose a statutory duty upon courts to adjourn or even to consider adjournment *ex proprio motu*. Furthermore courts enjoy an independence and a distance from government which makes them immune from executive encouragement or persuasion. We were told that courts do not receive guidance from, for instance, the Scottish Courts Administration on the mode of implementation of a new Act. Moreover, it was clear that the Scottish Development Department could not issue a circular, as it might to local authorities, inviting from the courts the response which, in policy terms, it might wish to see. Thus, the initiative for any change in court behaviour has to come in adversarial proceedings from one or other of the parties themselves. Courts are necessarily reactive rather than proactive agents of change. Even if there were a positive desire by sheriffs to become involved in the adjournment procedure under the 1980 Act, even if courts themselves wished to shed the old image of the rubber stamp (and we did hear support for this in many courts outside Edinburgh and Glasgow) it would still be necessary for one of the parties to the proceedings to invite the court's participation.

The pursuers, i.e. the housing authorities, would have little incentive to persuade the hitherto passive courts to adopt a more active stance – it is extremely unlikely that any housing authority would invite upon itself the additional trouble involved. That is not to say that housing authority personnel could see no advantage at all in the participation of courts in the collection of rent arrears. Most housing authorities did recognise that the threat of eviction was a serious matter and one which should be controlled by a court. Thus, we were told of the need for the court to ensure fair play and to provide a form of back-stop protection against the possibility of utterly arbitrary behaviour by a housing authority. But, by and large, they had clearly been satisfied with the role of the court prior to the passing of the 1980 Act.

Housing authorities have considerable experience of dealing with tenants in arrears. Realistically, what they are looking for is an accommodation between themselves and their defaulting tenants under which the tenants, following negotiations, will aim to pay off debts by instalments over a relatively long period. They are aware that immediate payment of substantial arrears is usually impossible. They know that eviction itself does not ensure payment nor, in most cases, is it a politically acceptable option. But the threat of eviction held out by an authority holding a decree issued by a court is generally regarded as the necessary back-drop to serious negotiation with tenants. It is widely believed that such a decree forces new priorities upon tenants regarding the payment of different debts to the advantage of the landlord authority. In the case of one housing authority only, we did come across a positive welcome for the practice of tenants appearing in court on the grounds that tenants are so much "in awe of the sheriff" that agreements reached in court and backed up by an adjournment are more likely to stick than attempts to reach an agreement out of court under threat of eviction. It would have been interesting to see whether tenants regarded appearance in court in the same light. For the most part, however, authorities saw negotiation between themselves and their tenants as something to be carried on in private with a decree or threat of a decree in the background. They could see no advantage in further participation by the court nor in the tenants' attendance at court. Half the authorities (nine out of eighteen) said that they thought tenant attendance was a bad idea and that they discouraged it.

If, therefore, there is to be a request for an adjournment under section 15(1) it is clear that this calls for an initiative by or on behalf of the tenant and the presence or representation of the tenant in court. Logic supports our empirical finding that courts will grant adjournments only when tenants are present and ask for them. Thus the principal reason for the slow and patchy implementation of the 1980 Act is that nothing was done to encourage tenants to appear in person and for this the government must, as author of the reform, accept the main responsibility. In fact, the Act created a participatory vacuum which has only been filled in rather special circumstances, for example, where there was already a tradition of attendance in the heritable property court (Edinburgh is the case in point) or where pressure from tenants could be generated with the assistance of pressure groups like Shelter, rights agencies like the Castlemilk Law Centre, community associations and sympathetic social workers and councillors (as has occurred in both Edinburgh and Glasgow). Could it have been otherwise? We believe it could have been and that if the government had given greater encouragement to tenants participation in the new procedures, a different result would have been achieved. Given the antipathy of most authorities towards legislation which they quite reasonably viewed as likely to make life more difficult for themselves, it was not to be expected, initially at least, that they would use their own initiative to encourage tenants to appear in court. However, the government could have prepared a clear statement of the tenant's right to security of tenure which positively encouraged tenants who were subject to court action to go to court and could have required housing authorities to serve this on the tenant together with the (highly formal and therefore largely incomprehensible) notice of proceedings and (subsequently) with the summons to appear in court. The problem is not a new one and has been successfully overcome in other contexts.[(12)] Without such encouragement, it is unlikely that attendance will ever become the norm in those parts of the country where pressure group activity is not sufficient to mobilise housing authority tenants.

This interpretation quite deliberately places great weight upon attendance by tenants in court as the principal key to the analysis of differential use by courts of their powers to adjourn. This, in turn, becomes the key to understanding court behaviour and attitudes more generally. There appears to be a very close relationship between attendance by tenants in court and not only the use of adjournment but also the appreciation by courts of a stronger more interventionist role. Although there may be other routes to a changed function for the court (perhaps including legislative intervention to ensure that the sheriff himself conducts proceedings) increased attendance by tenants would be the most important single catalyst.

The role of the courts in relation to rent arrears and evictions

If the course were to be adopted of promoting increased attendance by tenants in court and thus, we argue, increased use by courts of their own power of adjournment, this would be upon the assumption that such a development would be in the best interests of housing policy in this area. Is this necessarily the case? Are the particular characteristics of private sector security which were taken off the statutory peg to be used in the public sector directly transferable in this way? Is there any reason to believe that a stronger, more interventionist role for the sheriff court is the best way forward?

If we were to take the sole purpose of the moves towards public sector security in the 1980 Act to be either simply a sop to public housing as a counterbalance to the right to buy or, on the other hand, a symbolic grant of a Charter with "rights" and "security" as merely pieces of propaganda, then the actual effectiveness of provisions such as section 15 of the Act would not be very important. The desired result will have been achieved simply by putting public sector security on the statute book.

Again, if the aim of creating a role for the courts was solely that of making life so much more difficult for housing authorities that they would be forced to adopt more managerial, more preventative procedures for dealing with the problem of rent arrears, then this would seem to be a rather cumbersome and indirect way of achieving that purpose. In any case, if this objective had been paramount, the government could have reissued Circular 2/1974[(13)] or launched some other initiative to promote "good practice". Only five of the eighteen authorities in our study claimed that they had altered their procedures as a result of the Act. In each case, this appears to have resulted in a greater emphasis on early intervention and the adoption of a more managerial approach to the problem of rent arrears. The five authorities concerned included two where changes in policy were introduced at least partly in response to changes in the practice of the courts; and three where policy was changed independently of the courts. Thus, some housing authorities reviewed their policies without being provoked into doing so by changes in the practice of the courts. The five authorities did not include two authorities which raised actions in courts which had started to grant large numbers of adjournments. Clearly, changes in the practice of the courts did not necessarily give rise to changes in the housing authorities' procedures for dealing with tenants in arrears. Political ideology,[(14)] professional inclination and commitment and the human, machine and cash resources available would appear to be much stronger determinants of a housing authority's approach. Most authorities are committed to some degree of preventative action on arrears although the emphasis they place on preventative policies as against court action varies a great deal.

On the other hand, the main point may have been to involve the sheriff court more strongly not simply to create greater problems for housing authorities and thereby to encourage them to a more preventative approach to arrears management, but because a stronger role for the courts would have a positive utility of its own. Looking at experience so far presents obvious difficulties and limitations. The main one is that, with only two courts using the Act, we can look only to the practice of those courts and the experience of the authorities using them. Moreover, we are still very much in the early days of the Act and full development of its use (if, indeed, that has yet been achieved) has been delayed even in the Edinburgh court and, to a much greater extent, in the Glasgow court. This brevity of experience is extremely important because there is every reason to believe that the full consequences of introducing successive adjournments of proceeedings against tenants will be cumulative in their effect. Instead of tenants' cases being called and disposed of finally within seconds they may now be called on two, three, four or more occasions each demanding more time of the court. One feature of the Edinburgh court, in sharp contrast with those courts where adjournments are not being ordered, is that court sittings devoted to public sector heritable property cases have doubled.

This additional cost in time and resources to the court system is not, however, the most important consideration. The principal question is whether policy advantages are accruing. Here again we run into difficulties due to the limited experience of adjournments and also, in our own case, problems we encountered with our research. We should have liked to have been able to examine, for example, whether levels of rent arrears in the authorities we examined had been affected by the introduction of the 1980 Act or differentially affected according to the court area in which authorities operated. It may be that this sort of calculation will, in time, become a possibility but, for us, there was only an unreliably short period available and severe methodological difficulties in isolating the new procedures under the Tenants' Rights Act from other significant variables, such as increases in unemployment and the introduction of housing benefit. The other possibility would have been to follow through individual case studies of tenants subject to court proceedings to try to ascertain the effects of successive court hearings and to compare the effects on their arrears of adjournments and decrees. This is something we had hoped to examine but housing authorities were unable to provide us with the necessary follow-up information. Thus, there is really no way of saying what has been the impact on rent arrears of the adoption by the Edinburgh and Glasgow courts of new procedures as compared and contrasted with the operation of "traditional" procedures in other courts. However, we were led to believe that, in Edinburgh, in many cases where successive adjournments had been granted followed by an apparently successful sist of proceedings (i.e. a long-term suspension of the case), the sist had eventually been recalled and a decree of ejection granted. If this occurred on a substantial scale the overall effect of adjournments may have been simply to delay for some months the order that would otherwise have been granted very much earlier. As we have said, eviction is only very rarely carried out, but if a delayed decree is all that has been achieved, a question mark must surely be placed over the whole exercise.

Other questions are being asked in the courts themselves. Even though we found that sheriffs in both Edinburgh and Glasgow recognised the importance to tenants and their families of arrears proceedings and considered that they as sheriffs had an important role to play in them, they nevertheless expressed doubts about the task which was required of them. Sheriffs are "generalists" in that they move on a rota system between criminal work and civil work including the summary cause court. They are, therefore, not able to develop any particular specialist experience of rent arrears or related issues but are exposed to them when their turn comes round. There is some unhappiness in this role. We were told that arrears work was "not really judicial business". Sheriffs are there in a sense to protect tenants but as a result of being there get involved in a process of "horse trading" for which they have little liking. Asked about the grant of eviction decrees, they saw with regret that decree was inevitable if the tenant did not appear and the housing authority did not withdraw. They lack an inquisitorial role. It seemed clear that, although this did not come over very strongly from the sheriffs themselves, they were not operating in a court fully equipped to assess the appropriateness of payment terms which might be imposed upon tenants when adjournments are granted. An "agreement" reached in court between pursuer and defender would almost always be acceptable. Asked about the (very rare) event of the "reasonableness" of an eviction being questioned in court, one sheriff told us of his regret about the lack of any clear statutory guidelines. Reasonableness is nowhere defined and the interpretation of this term therefore depended upon the personal views of the sheriff concerned. If there were twelve sheriffs, then twelve different interpretations of reasonableness and thus twelve different social policies could be applied.

It was clear that this and other issues had been discussed informally between sheriffs but judicial individuality of approach nonetheless was paramount. There was a wish to establish a practical day-to-day response to questions of adjournment and eviction rather than to develop a clear policy collectively held. We had a strong feeling of a storm being weathered by the courts before a new and hopefully less burdensome solution emerges.

Improvements to existing procedures

Experience in the courts so far is only one guide towards appropriate future change. We are bound to ask more theoretical questions about what the role of the courts in relation to rent arrears should be. Even to attempt to discuss this issue presents difficulties – but at the same time considerable fascination! Essentially they are the difficulties of defining and isolating the "problem" of rent arrears and then of identifying appropriate solutions. The problem of what to do about rent arrears is inextricably linked with questions about rent, rent rebates, wider relationships between public landlords and their tenants, and public sector housing itself. It is related to general questions of debt and its remedies which extend much wider than rent alone. It is part of the problem of economic recession and the systemic debt that goes with it.

It is also important to distinguish between rent arrears as an individual problem to be solved or mediated on a case-by-case basis and as a mass problem which demands across-the-board solutions. Steps taken to solve the one may contribute not at all to the other. More specifically, attempts to achieve individual justice between a landlord and a tenant may bear little relationship to mass justice between landlords as a whole and tenants as a whole. Such considerations bring us closer to questions concerning the role of the courts. It is essential that before one invokes the aid of the sheriff court (or, indeed, any court or tribunal) to take on a specific task in a world full of complex relationships and before oneattempts to monitor the "success" of that court, one must have some clear understanding of what is being demanded of it. Only then does it become possible to discuss who should constitute the court – whether they should have legal or other skills; whether it should be a court (such as the sheriff court) of general jurisdiction or one confined to but specialised in other housing issues; what powers it should have; whether it should be restricted to legal or jurisdictional review; or whether, on the other hand, it should have wider powers to consider and apply principles of housing policy and practice.

Important as these questions are, they range much too wide for consideration in the present context. We mention them here simply to indicate that, in focussing now on issues of a narrower compass, we do so in the knowledge that the broader questions remain. We assume for present purposes that substantially the same legal relationships between public sector landlords and their tenants will continue; that rent will be demanded; that rent arrears will accumulate; and that recovery of posession as a final sanction on the authority of a court (or tribunal) will remain.

This having been said, we think it is helpful to approach the question of the role of the courts in relation to arrears and evictions through a comparison with the role of the courts in relation to divorce. In a seminal article entitled "Bargaining in the Shadow of the Law",(15) Robert Mnookin and Lewis Kornhauser argued for a new way of thinking about the role of the law at the time of divorce. Instead of imposing solutions from above, they argued that the primary function of contemporary divorce law should be to provide a framework for divorcing couples to determine for themselves the distribution of rights and responsibilities after the dissolution of their marriage. This process, by which the parties would be empowered to create their own legally enforceable commitments, was referred to as "private ordering". According to Mnookin and Kornhauser, spouses should be encouraged to negotiate with each other on the understanding that, if they failed to reach an agreement, the court would impose its own resolution which might be less favourable to either or both parties. Thus the function of law is only partly to adjudicate when the parties are unable to agree, but also, and perhaps more importantly, to provide the framework in which the parties can themselves reach agreement. In the light of this model we wish to consider the following questions. First, does section 15(1) facilitate a private ordering in which the housing authority and the tenant can "bargain in the shadow of the law" and reach an agreement (which is subsequently ratified by the court) to pay arrears by instalments; secondly, is this the right role for the courts and, thirdly, if not, what is the right role?

One assumption of Mnookin and Kornhauser's argument is that private ordering would take place outside the courtroom and that the parties would not go to court until they have reached an agreement with each other and are ready to have this "rubber stamped" or unless they are unable to do so. These assumptions clearly do not apply to rent arrears cases since, in the two courts where tenants appeared and the statutory provisions of the Tenants' Rights Act were being implemented, most offers to pay were made and accepted (or not) in the court itself. Indeed, once the summons had been served, at least one housing authority refused to accept offers by tenants to pay in instalments unless these were made in court. However, our interviews with sheriffs and housing officials, as well as observation in those courts which made regular use of section 15(1) powers to grant adjournments, did suggest that the parties seemed to understand the likely limit on payments which would be acceptable to the court, and made their offers with this in mind. Thus, most (but not all) offers were accepted. A further assumption is that the parties should have a good deal of information about each other but this was clearly not the case. The housing authority may know something about the tenant's income and household circumstances but its representatives in court are unlikely to know very much about the tenant's outgoings or general state of indebtedness or about salient details of the tenant's domestic situation. In any case, at first calling, whoever presides over the court is unlikely to know anything about the tenant. At second and subsequent callings, the tenant may be asked to explain why he or she has not been able to keep to the terms and conditions previously agreed upon but such information as is elicited is likely to be incomplete and unsubstantiated. Moreover, the court is likely to be ignorant about the policies and procedures of the housing authority or its dealings with the tenant. All this would not matter if the two

two parties were roughly equally matched but this is obviously not the case. Neither would it matter if they were equally able to act in their own best interests but this is clearly not the case either. Housing authorities have all the advantages of the "repeat player" (they know the ropes and are able to play the situation to further their interests) while the tenants have all the disadvantages of the "one-shotter" (and regularly lose out on the grounds of their inexperience).[(16)]

For private ordering to offer a more attractive "solution" to the problem of rent arrears, the law would have to provide a more fully elaborated legal framework in terms of which the parties could seek to reach agreement. In particular, it would need to provide guidelines for the payment of arrears by instalments and give some indication of what the concept of "reasonableness" as applied to the grant of a decree of ejection is supposed to mean. Since what is meant by "reasonableness" in this context is a question of social policy, its meaning would have to be spelled out in the legislation and not simply left for each sheriff to decide in his/her own way. However, even with these innovations, it is not clear that the law would be able adequately to protect the public sector tenant.

The fact that the two parties (public sector tenants and housing authorities) are so unequal, and that public housing authorities cannot necessarily be trusted to protect the interests of their tenants provided a very powerful justification for legal intervention and effectively distinguishes disputes between public sector landlords and tenants from those between husbands and wives. Mnookin and Kornhauser's argument that spouses should be allowed to make mistakes because, on balance, they are more likely than judges to know what is best for themselves and because, on the whole, they will make fewer mistakes, may be quite plausible but the analogous argument simply does not hold in relation to public sector landlords and tenants. Thus the court must be able to intervene and impose its judgement on the parties even when they agree, if that agreement runs counter to the interests of either party. (It is to be expected that the court would intervene most often to protect the interests of the tenant but it might also, on occasion, need to intervene to protect the interests of the public authority and the general public, e.g. where the authority has clearly accepted a much lower level of payment than the tenant can afford.)[(17)] For this to be possible, the court (and not just the housing authority) would require tenants to provide details of their financial and personal circumstances, and housing authorities to provide information about their policies and procedures in relation to rent arrears and their attempts to contact the tenant. This would, of course, represent a considerable departure from current practice and make considerable demands on the time and resources of the courts but, in our view, such innovations are necessary if the courts are to play an effective role in encouraging housing authorities to adopt preventative measures, and to seek a balance between the interests of the individual tenant and the public authority.

Alternatives to existing procedures

In the previous section we proposed a number of innovations to the existing (summary cause) procedure which were intended to make that procedure more effective. In this final section, we refer very briefly to some alternatives to this procedure. In theory, they could take three forms: administrative hearings, similar to Aberdeen's Arrears Sub Committee[(18)] and strongly advocated by one of the housing officials we interviewed; a specialist tribunal or panel dealing with rent arrears and related matters suggested to us by two housing officials, and a specialist housing court. Of these three proposals, administrative hearings attended by representatives of the housing department and, if possible, by representatives of other agencies, e.g. social work departments and the DHSS, could be well placed to investigate the causes of the tenant's financial problems, give advice and negotiate payment by instalments but, because they would be inside rather than outside the authority, they could not provide an effective safeguard for tenants or subject the housing authority to critical scrutiny. A specialist tribunal or panel would presumably be rather less formal than a court and, as such, it might encourage more tenants to attend. Apart from this, the main differences between a specialist tribunal or panel dealing with rent arrears and related matters and a specialist housing court are in terms of the breadth of jurisdiction and the standing of the associated personnel. A housing court would be presided over by a housing judge and he/she and the other officials would be expected over time to become proficient in all matters relating to housing. Although this is a somewhat radical proposal which is unlikely to meet with immediate approval, proposals for a housing court were put forward as long ago as 1937 and are widely supported by organisations representing landlords as well as tenants. Moreover the case for a housing court (in England and Wales) was recently accepted by the House of Commons Select Committee on the Environment in its report on the private rented sector.[(19)] Our own view is that such a court might provide an ideal environment for an independent body to carry out the sorts of tasks outlined above but that a specialist tribunal or panel could be equally effective.

It would clearly be premature to make concrete proposals for institutional change in one direction or another. On the other hand, we are left with the strong feeling – surely incontestable in the light of our findings – that the procedures initially established by the 1980 Act have been far from successful. We further feel, however, that, although adaptation of the present system may hold out some hope for improvement, the limitations inherent in the adversarial, generalist and yet jurisdictionally confined sheriff court are too great.[20] The transplant of this aspect of the institutions of private sector security into the public sector is unlikely ever to be entirely successful. We, therefore, feel certain that a prima facie case for much more substantial change has been made. However, the case for such a change would have to be based upon research across fields much wider than our own. Nevertheless, our present hunch is that the time of the specialist housing tribunal or court will surely come.

References

1. The 1977 Green Paper (the Labour Government's consultative document on housing in Scotland) noted that public sector housing authorities took the view that "as responsible public bodies, they should not be inhibited in carrying out their management functions, particularly where difficult tenants are involved, that they in practice do secure evictions on the same grounds as private landlords, and that statutory security is unnecessary if they are to have a statutory responsibility to house the homeless". See *Scottish Housing : a Consultative Document,* Cmnd 6852, HMSO, 1977, para.9.21

2. In 1977/78, the last time a complete count was taken, there were 33,568 actions for recovery of possession of heritable property (including 6,550 joint actions for recovery and payment); 25,480 decrees were obtained; and 1,053 evictions carried out. See Diana Wilkinson, *Rent Arrears in Public Authority Housing in Scotland,* Scottish Office Social Research Study, HMSO, 1980, Table 3.4. Our own research in eighteen housing authorities suggests that over the period 1977/78 to 1981/82 the number of actions raised and decrees granted fell slightly and that there was an 18% reduction in the number of evictions carried out. Some housing authorities increased their use of court procedures and evictions while others made less use of these measures.

3. A full report of the research *Public Housing, Rent Arrears and the Sheriff Court : a study of the early implementation and impact of the Tenants' Rights, Etc. (Scotland) Act 1980* is to be published by the Scottish Development Department as a C.R.U. Paper.

4. See Joint SDD/SWSG Circular 2/1974 *Measures to reduce rent arrears*

and prevent evictions and the recommendations in Diana Wilkinson, *op.cit.*, Chapter 8.

5. The ten sheriff courts were chosen to represent the range of sheriff courts in Scotland. They included the courts serving three of the four cities (Aberdeen, Edinburgh and Glasgow), two other courts serving predominantly urban areas in Strathclyde (Airdrie and Paisley), two courts serving large towns and their hinterland (Kirkcaldy and Perth) and three courts serving predominantly rural areas (Arbroath, Lanark and Selkirk). The eighteen housing authorities which raised actions in these courts represented the entire range of Scottish housing authorities in terms of size, urban-rural characteristics and styles of housing management.

6. Housing authorities raising less than 25 actions during February 1982 were sampled continuously from January 1982 until at least 25 cases were obtained; those raising more than 25 but less than 100 actions in February 1982 were continuously sampled until the next highest threshold of 50, 75 or 100 cases was obtained; while housing authorities raising more than 100 actions in February 1982 were sampled using an appropriate sampling ratio until 100 cases were obtained. Thus the minimum number of cases per authority was 25 and the maximum 100.

7. Final court decisions included decrees for recovery of possession, decrees for expenses only, decrees of dismissal, continuations *sine die* (used only in the Airdrie court) and sisted cases, unless we were aware that the case had been recalled during the period of study.

8. The 1978 data are reported in Diana Wilkinson, *op.cit.*

9. It would appear that the granting of continuations *sine die* on the pursuer's motion preceded the passing of the Tenants' Rights Act.

10. See Act of Sederunt (Summary Cause Rules, Sheriff Court) 1976 (S.I.476), Rule 18(1).

11. In several of the courts which were normally presided over by a sheriff clerk or a depute (and it may well be the case that it applies to all of them) we were told that defended or otherwise difficult cases (or, in the case of Aberdeen cases where the defender was represented by a solicitor) were routinely referred to the sheriff.

12. A good recent example is the Court of Session's public information leaflet on "do it yourself divorce" which merited a consumer award for

plain writing.

13. *op.cit.*

14. Although there was no apparent relationship, among the eighteen housing authorities in our study, between political control and an authority's approach to rent arrears and evictions, changes in political control may lead to changes in policy. A recent example was the decision of Edinburgh District Council soon after the Labour Party gained control in May 1984 to abandon the use of eviction in cases of rent arrears.

15. Robert Mnookin and Lewis Kornhauser "Bargaining in the Shadow of the Law : The Case of Divorce", 88 *Yale Law Journal* (1978), pp.950-997. See also Robert Mnookin's article with the same title in 32 *Current Legal Problems* (1979), pp.65-103.

16. See Marc Galanter "Why the 'haves' come out ahead : speculations on the limits of legal change", 9 *Law and Society Review* (1974) pp.95-160. See also Galanter's critique of Mnookin and Kornhauser in Mauro Cappelletti (ed) *Access to Justice in the Welfare State,* Badia Fiesolana, Firenze (Florence) 1981, pp.147-181.

17. A number of housing officials expressed the view that where tenants appeared in person, the courts frequently accepted unsubstantiated claims, gave the tenant the benefit of the doubt and cosseted tenants by giving them longer to pay than they required.

18. In Aberdeen, the Arrears Sub Committee (chaired by the Convener of the Housing Coimmittee and attended by representatives of the Social Work Department) considered all arrears cases, after service of notice of proceedings and, in many cases, before commencement of court action. Most tenants (we were told 80-90%) appeared in person before the sub committee. The sub committee, which sat once a month centrally and once a month in a decentralised area office, investigated the causes of rent arrears, discussed tenants' financial problems, gave advice and tried to negotiate payment of the debt by instalments with tenants.

19. *First Report of the Environment Committee,* HC 40-1, 1982.

20. For an assessment of the sheriff court and its possible strengths in administrative matters, see the *Report of the Grant Committee on the Sheriff Court,* Cmnd 3248, 1967, Part III.

TRENDS IN HEALTH POLICY: LESSONS FROM AN INTERNATIONAL PERSPECTIVE[1]

ALEX ROBERTSON
DEPARTMENT OF SOCIAL ADMINISTRATION
UNIVERSITY OF EDINBURGH

At the time of its inception in 1948, it was widely believed by planners, politicians, practitioners and the public that, following a period of initial heavy usage as the backlog of hitherto untreated illness received attention, the scale and cost of the National Health Service would decline as the amount of illness in the population was reduced. This expectation itself reflected two fundamental, related and erroneous assumptions. First, health 'needs' were construed as finite. Once the barrier of cost had been removed, and the needs arising from untreated sickness had been dealt with, only a maintenance level of medical provision would thereafter be required. Second, the path to health was presumed to lie through the provision of medical services. It was assumed that, by achieving the effective deployment of and universal access to medical resources through the administrative unification of available services, a high level of health would be guaranteed.

To take the latter point first, it is something of a truism that what the NHS provides is in fact a national *sickness* rather than a national *health* service. The efforts of the NHS, in other words, are concentrated on dealing with diseases once they have appeared, rather than on the development of policies for the prevention of disease and the promotion of positive health. In this respect, the UK shares a common pattern with other Western countries. The last forty years have seen the most dramatic expansion ever in medical knowledge and technology. This expansion has emerged within, and tended further to consolidate, the dominance of clinical medicine. An important consequence of these developments has been that medicine has become increasingly specialised and dependent on (expensive) hospital-based facilities (Mechanic[2]; Illich[3]). As against this, the work of McKeown[4], Powles[5], Illich[3] and Smith[6] indicates that the contribution of clinical medicine to the dramatic decline in the rate of mortality from infectious diseases over the last century has in fact been relatively small. According to these authors, this reduction can be attributed largely to improvements in nutrition and the general living standards of the populations of developed countries, rather than to medical interventions, including immunisation programmes (although these again emerge as more important than advances on the clinical front).

With reference to the notion that health needs are finite, experience subsequent to the NHS's introduction has demonstrated this assumption to be false. One of the most important trends to have emerged in developed countries during the course of the present century has, as indicated above, without doubt been the transformation that has taken place in the patterns of illness which befall the populations of such nations. As infectious diseases have abated, so especially has infant mortality diminished and the proportion of the population surviving into the middle and later years of life expanded. Medicine has in consequence now increasingly to cope with the mainly chronic and degenerative conditions which beset old age. Tuberculosis, influenza, typhoid and diphtheria have been supplanted by cancer, rheumatism, arthritis, afflictions of the respiratory tract, mental disorder and heart disease as the main problems calling for medical attention in industrialised societies (e.g. Omran[7], Lalonde[8], Parry[9], Milio[10,11]. As opposed to the relatively brief and normally well-defined (acute) disease process of infectious illness, degenerative diseases are chronic as to duration, insidious in their onset, and irregular and episodic in their manifestation of symptoms (Wadsworth et al.[12]).

These developments have profound implications for both the content and the shape of medical services in advanced societies. Zola and Miller[13], for example, point out that 'success' in treating chronic conditions tends to be judged by relative rather than absolute criteria. Traditional notions of 'disease' and 'health' lose most of their relevance (see also Oldham[14]). Improvement rather than complete cure becomes the target of medical intervention. Concepts of 'adaptation' and of behaviour which is more or less 'successful' given the context in which the patient has to act, take the place of more categorical notions. The medical contribution to dealing with such problems may largely be defined as those of support, maintenance and repair, rather than of recovery and cure (Mustard[15]).

Contrary to the expectations of its founding fathers, therefore, the NHS has seen neither a reduction in the 'need' for its services, nor a decline in the proportion of national resources requiring to be spent on it. In fact, and in common with all other countries of the Western world, the United Kingdom has, over the last thirty years, had greatly to expand the proportion of her Gross National Product that is devoted to expenditure on health (e.g. Ehrlich[16], Maxwell[17], Wing[18], Swedish Institute for Health Economics[19]). Apart from the change in illness patterns and the (in part) resultant increase in demand for medical services, any attempt to provide a satisfactory explanation of these trends would clearly also require to note the advances – indicated above – which have taken place in medical technology, and the cost of providing such facilities; the labour-intensive nature of medical care, coupled with the rise in manpower costs of the last several years; and the rise in public expectations of what constitute acceptable standards of care for groups like the mentally ill, the handicapped and the elderly who have often been neglected in the past. It may, however, be worth adding that the UK has been rather more successful than most countries in containing the rate of that increase – probably in large part because such decisions are taken within a political arena, as part of the annual budget allocations, in which the claims of health care must vie with other appeals for expenditure priority (e.g. Klein[20]).

Policy Responses

The pressures generated by these financial and medical demographic trends have elicited two general types of response from health care systems. First, is a series of attempts to cater for increased (or at least undiminished) levels of demand whilst holding the cost of the service constant – essentially through better management of those services – as is obviously reflected in the approaches criticised by David Hunter and Robin Milne in their chapters in the present volume (see also Bevan et al[21]) and through improving the 'effectiveness' and 'efficiency' of existing treatments (Cochrane,[22]), McLachlan[23], Clark and Forbes[24]). In recent years, of course, the claim has also been advanced that these objectives might best be attained by expanding the private sector for medical care. The second approach – reducing people's dependency on health services – has been a development primarily of the last few years. One aspect of this has been the emergence of initiatives designed to promote 'self-help' in dealing with medical problems (Robinson and Henry[25], Hatch and Kickbusch[26]). Second, is a range of preventive strategies, introduced with varying emphases and in various settings internationally, which will form the main focus of the remainder of this paper.

Prevention and Degenerative Disease

The potential for preventive programmes in dealing with degenerative disease has been widely acknowledged within the NHS. The consultative document on 'Prevention and Health'[27], prepared jointly by the Health Departments of Great Britain and Northern Ireland outlines historical trends and regional and social-class variations in different types of disease, together with some of the scientific, ethical and other issues related to the development of preventive strategies. The Scottish Health Education Group (formerly the Scottish Health Education Unit) and the Health Education Council have done valuable work in promoting and conducting research and evaluation on health education activities, identifying priority areas for health education at national level and drawing up programmes of health education for promotion both nationally and locally (Yarrow[28], Woodman[29], Billington and Bell[30], Billington et al[31], Sutherland[32]). Among other things, the Scottish Health Education Unit produced various reports on patterns of alcohol use, particularly among young people, and was followed by the DHSS with a discussion document on 'Drinking Sensibly'[33]. Interesting discussion papers have also been produced on safer pregnancy and childbirth[34] and avoiding heart attacks[35].

When, however, one searches for more explicit policy statements, the picture appears rather less impressive. The purpose of the SHHD[36] memorandum on 'The Way Ahead' was (p.3) to 'set out guidelines for the development of the Health Service in Scotland for the next few years'. The last of the six 'main principles' identified as priorities is the:

> 'encouragement of preventive measures and the development of a fully responsible attitude to health on the part of the individual and the community'.

But despite a claim that these principles are to be 'developed in detail in the memorandum', the proposals for prevention amount to two paragraphs (*ibid.* pp.19- 20), drawing the reader's attention to the DHSS[27] 'consultative document'; encouraging Health Boards and the Health Education Unit to increase resources for health education; exhorting local authorities to sustain their existing level of commitment to environmental health matters; and, with a comment on the state of Scottish dental health, urging Health Boards and Regional Councils to give serious consideration to the question of fluoridation of water supplies.

The equivalent English document is labelled 'Further discussion of the Government's National Strategy'[37] and devotes six paragraphs to preventive matters, in the course of which it is stated that one of the principal aims of preventive initiatives should be to encourage individuals to accept greater responsibility for their own health. The report stresses the potential role of community health services in the early detection of disease and in giving health advice to individuals. The remaining paragraphs point to the desirability of increasing the number of Health Education Officers; argue that 'every effort should be made' to increase the rate of take-up of vaccination programmes; point to the benefits of family planning and health authorities' responsibility for training staff in this field; and refer to the preventive role of statutory and voluntary social services in work with children and in giving temporary relief to families caring for handicapped or 'disturbed' relatives (*ibid.*, pp.8-9).

Scottish (and English) preventive strategies are therefore based on attempts to change individual behaviour through health education; support for vaccination and environmental health services; and statements about the need for integration between health and social work services. Two principal conclusions perhaps emerge from this review. First, and even allowing for the complexity of the issues the documents are addressing, the 'strategies' appear as sets of modest, discrete and not terribly well-connected elements which seem likely to provide only partial coverage of the problems they are addressing. Second, and perhaps reflected in the first, is the fact that the search for appropriate responses tends to be conducted within the limits set by existing administrative/service structures and responsibilities.

The UK health services are not of course alone in the relative paucity of their present policies for preventing chronic disease (e.g. German Federal Centre for Health Education[(38)]). But in the case of Scotland at least, there is perhaps some cause for surprise in the total lack of any reference to developments in two nations – Canada and Norway – with which this country has traditionally had rather close links, and in which innovative and interestingly-contrasted approaches to health promotion are currently being implemented. Let us compare these two separate developments and discuss their potential relevance for preventive policies in Scotland.

An International Comparison

The Canadian Approach

The Canadian Government's publication of its 'working document' on *A New Perspective on the Health of Canadians*[(8)] represented an undoubted landmark in thinking about preventive strategies for dealing with the health problems of developed countries. The document is remarkable for its vigour of expression and for the general clarity of its analysis, as well as for its willingness to accept and promote what are at one level fairly radical conclusions.

The 'New Perspective' essentially presents a plan for the health of the Canadian people. It proposes a shift in approach from that which informed previous reports on health care policies in Canada. These had been primarily concerned with the organisation and provision of health services[39,40]. The 'New Perspective' focuses on the causes of health and illness as these relate especially to Canada, and their implications for the prevention of illness and the development of programmes for the promotion of (positive) health.

Lalonde's report proposes a conceptual framework for health care – the 'Health Field Concept' – which outlines the directions from which health problems should be approached, and which is presented as a workable basis for the development of health services in any country. Health services are placed in the context of the 'Health Field', which is seen as comprising four broad sets of elements which affect an individual's health. The component parts of this health field are[8,pp.31-32]:

(a) *Human Biology* – defined as 'all those aspects of health... which are developed within the human body as a consequence of the basic biology of man and the organic make-up of the individual'. It includes the various body systems, genetic inheritance, the processes of maturation and ageing, etc.

(b) *Environment* – which 'includes all those matters related to health which are external to the human body and over which the individual has little or no control'. In addition to such factors as pollution and control of the quality of food and drugs, this element also recognises the importance of stress and the effects of rapid social change as factors in ill-health.

(c) *Lifestyle* – which consists of all of the 'decisions by individuals which affect their health and over which they more or less have control'.

(d) *Health care organisation* – which is seen as comprising 'the quantity, quality, arrangement, nature and relationships of people and resources in the provision of health care'.

The health field concept offers several advantages as a framework for understanding health problems. First, it points to the importance of factors other than health services within the field of health. Second, it is comprehensive, in that health problems can be traced to one or other of these elements, or to a combination of them. This means that, in principle, it becomes possible to plan health policies more effectively, with due recognition of the potential contribution of the different elements to health problems and solutions. Third, the notion of a 'health field' permits one to analyse the relative significance of each of the four elements, as well as the interactions between them, as causal factors in illness and death. Planners of preventive programmes can thus focus attention on the factors that are most important for any given problem. The document cites the example of death from traffic accidents, in which analysis indicates that the main factor is risks taken by individuals (lifestyle) with lesser importance given to the design of cars and roads (environment) and the availability of emergency treatment (health care organisation). Related to this is a fourth feature, in that the health field concept permits a further sub-division of factors. With traffic deaths, for example, the influence of lifestyle can be further disaggregated to the risks associated with driving under the influence of alcohol or drugs, carelessness, failure to wear seat belts, and speeding.

The health field concept thus provides an original and important tool for the determination of policies and priorities. It has the potential for identifying unexpected or hitherto unrecognised factors in the causation of death and illness. In particular, it places health services in a broader context and so allows one to make a rational assessment of the extent to which investment in them, relative to other elements, is likely to produce an effective return. Within such a framework, public policy can also be co-ordinated; so that the work of government departments responsible, for example, for roads and industrial developments can be related in a systematic way to the concerns of those departments more explicitly concerned with health, rather than leaving those relationships to proceed in the *ad hoc* and fragmented way in which developments have traditionally tended to take place.

Priorities and Strategies

With its emphasis on prevention, the Lalonde document undertook an analysis of the major causes of premature death in Canada by re-analysing mortality statistics for 1971. In order to do this, the report introduced a new concept, that of potential years of life lost, or PYLL (Lalonde[8], Chapter 3; see also Romeder and McWhinnie[41]). A death occurring between the ages of 1 and 70 is, by the Lalonde definition, a premature death, with the number of years before the age of 70 at which a death occurred giving the PYLL figure. Thus, a man dying of lung cancer at the age of 44 would contribute 26 (70 – 44) PYLL to the total for the appropriate disease category.

An analysis using this measure identifies ischaemic heart disease, road accidents and other types of accidents as the three main causes of premature death among males; for females, the main factors were motor vehicle accidents, diseases of the respiratory system, and other types of accident. Because all of these result to some degree from known factors in the environment, lifestyle and human biology, it is argued that, if the health of the Canadian nation is to be enhanced, it will be necessary to shift the balance of effort and commitment away from simply providing health services, towards a more preventive policy. It is, however, argued in addition (Lalonde[8], p.37) that the shift of emphasis towards attacking the causes of illness will not jeopardise existing commitments to the provision of services. If the incidence of illness can be reduced by prevention, then the cost of present services will decline. The problem is seen as a collective one, in that the causes of illness are thought to be embedded in Canadian society, and the cost of their treatment shared throughout society. Consequently, solutions will involve the entire nation.

Working therefore towards the two broad objectives of (a) reducing health hazards for 'high-risk populations' and (b) improving the accessibility of good health care facilities for those whose present access is unsatisfactory, it is suggested that the health field concept leads to five broad categories of strategies for future action. These strategies are (Lalonde[8],p.66 et seq; see also Gellman et al.[42]):

(i) *A health promotion strategy,* which comprises a set of twenty three more specific strategies aimed at informing, influencing and assisting individuals and organisations to accept more responsibility for their own health. More specific strategies involve programmes of education on nutrition; intensive use of recreation facilities; identification of high risk groups in the population; and the development of a home fitness test (the Fitkit) to enable Canadians to evaluate their own physical state.

(ii) *A regulatory strategy,* which is aimed at using the regulatory powers of the Federal Government to reduce hazards to health and encouraging and assisting the various provincial governments to use their legislative powers to the same end. The eight more specific strategies drawn together under this heading include such proposals as regulations for improving the nutritional content of food; laws governing the use of seat belts; and increased control over health hazards from pollution, radiation, etc.

(iii) *A research strategy,* designed to help discover and apply the knowledge required to solve health problems. The fifteen strategies suggested for inclusion under this rubric essentially relate to the development of a research programme on the underlying causes of fitness, sickness and death; the development of more effective statistical indicators; and research on the relative effectiveness of different forms of health care provision and approaches to changing behaviour.

(iv) *A health care efficiency strategy,* the objective of which is to help the provincial governments (which of course in Canada enjoy a high degree of autonomy from the Federal Government, having primary responsibility for administering their own systems of health care within broad Federal standards) reorganise their health care systems so that the three elements of cost, accessibility and effectiveness 'are balanced in the interests of Canadians' (Lalonde[(8)]p.66). It comprises twenty suggested strategies, which cover such possibilities as financing health care in such a way as to provide incentives for providing satisfactory care at the lowest cost; training programmes for various types of health professionals; and the introduction of measures, including the use of expert committees, to diminish the time between the development and application of knowledge.

(v) *A goal-setting strategy,* comprising seven suggested strategies with the purpose of setting specific targets for health improvement, and improving the efficiency of the system of health care. These targets include specified reductions in the incidence of mortality and morbidity from particular diseases, with specific dates by which such reductions are to be achieved; setting standards for both the mental and physical care systems; and the extension of national nutrition standards to include definite recommendations on safe levels of intake for hazardous substances occurring naturally in food.

An Evaluation

Given the two general objectives of reducing health hazards and improving the accessibility of health care, the health field concept accordingly made it possible to develop a conceptual framework comprising five main strategies and seventy four specific proposals within which health issues can be analysed in full perspective, and health policy developed for future years. From the point of view of prevention, the approach suggested is to identify those members of the Canadian population who are at high risk in relation to major health problems, and to devise programmes aimed at reducing these risks. The route to the achievement of these goals lies, with the guidance provided by the health field concept, through the application of knowledge, faith and political will; and a concerted effort by professions, scientists, education, government, industry, voluntary associations and private citizens (*ibid.* p.63). Several points need to be made about this analysis. Let us concentrate first on the health field concept.

Although human biology is included in the health field, and comment is made on the crucial role it plays in dealing with such costly diseases as arthritis, diabetes, atherosclerosis, cancer, mental retardation, genetic disorders, and congenital malformation, the discussion of this element is not really expanded very much further. The analysis therefore effectively concentrates on environment, lifestyle and health care organisation.

It is therefore at least implied that the development of preventive policies around the area of human biology will at this stage be heavily dependent on further basic research. At present, it would seem that the most likely path for the development of policy related to human biology traverses the territory of genetic research. Knowledge about the inheritance of genetic disorders resulting in serious disease makes it possible, through genetic counselling, contraception and therapeutic abortion, to reduce the incidence of serious genetic disorders. According to McKeown[4,43] there are three sets of issues which need to be considered before wholeheartedly attempting to develop preventive programmes. These relate to questions of ethics, effectiveness and desirability. Under the ethical question, would it be right (morally or otherwise) to control human breeding? Genetic programmes are in danger of reducing human beings to the status of objects, and this raises religious and other objections.

From the point of view of effectiveness, McKeown points out that knowledge is at present very obscure. How many conditions, for example, are due to a single gene? And if conditions are recessive or polygenic, how effective are counselling or other kinds of programmes likely to be? How meaningful is it, for example, for potential parents to be told that they have a one in four, or a one in eight, etc. chance of producing a genetically-disordered offspring? McKeown also makes the point that mutation is not an insignificant factor, though not the most common element in genetic disorders. Again, this points to the inadequacy of knowledge in this area at present. Finally, McKeown suggests that it is worth at least raising the question (closely related to the ethical issues alluded to earlier) of whether it is desirable that a society should aim to control its breeding in such a way as at least to increase the proportion of genetically well-endowed people; and potentially, to restrict its further progeny to those with what are deemed to be 'acceptable' genetic characteristics.

Whilst it is obviously important, from a scientific point of view, that research on these matters should continue, the issues pointed to above would seem seriously to undermine the preventive potential of genetic approaches.

Environmental concerns transcend the traditional public health measures of sanitation and immunisation, and protection from pollution and harmful consumer goods. Aspects of rapid social change are included as necessary for a full environmental analysis. For example, the economy is on the one hand linked to attitudes causing ill health and death, which are considered (Lalonde[8], p.5) the 'dark side of economic progress'; whilst on the other hand, and in particular in relation to occupational health, the 'protection of economic activity' should form 'a healthy balance' with concern for (*ibid.*) the 'quality of the environment and life' to foster individual development. This represents a move into territory identified by the (Canadian) Royal Commission on Health Services[39] as important, but beyond its terms of reference. Action over environmental causes is seen as beyond the individual's ability and is thus accepted by the Lalonde report as the responsibility of the state.

Life style is the 'aggregation of decisions by individuals which affect their health and over which they more or less have control'(Lalonde[8] p.32). In consequence (*ibid.* p.26):

> 'individual blame must be accepted by many for the deleterious effect on health of their respective lifestyles. Sedentary living, smoking, over-eating, driving while impaired by alcohol, drug abuse and failure to wear seat belts are among the many contributors to physical and mental illness for which the individual must seek some responsibility and for which he should seek correction'.

It is, however, accepted (*ibid.*pp.36-36) that it is often difficult to separate environmental influences from individual choice, because the former can influence the latter. Yet, a perspective on health policy which holds a person responsible and consequently able to choose expresses (*loc.cit.*):

> 'faith in the power of free will, hobbled as this power may be at times

by environment and addiction'.

Thus, in the interests of fostering individual freedom, but with an eye to the influence of the environment, and despite the difficulties of isolating the two as independent forces, the individual is held responsible.

This is an immensely important point. The range of measures available to governments in their attempts to change people's eating, exercise, smoking and other habits essentially consists of legislation, taxation and persuasion. With respect to legislation, there is of course a continuing debate over the rights of individuals to choose to indulge in 'unhealthy' or high-risk activities such as driving without a seat belt or crash helmet, and of the rights of governments to penalise them for doing so; but one does not wish to enter into that argument here. Fiscal measures are of course widely (if rather unsystematically) used; although McKeown[43] makes the interesting point that the potential for the differential use of subsidies for 'healthy' products and taxes on 'unhealthy' products has been nothing like sufficiently recognised. But while recognition is given in the Canadian document to such fiscal and legislative possibilities, by far the greater emphasis in the argument and in the development of programmes since its publication has been on changing life style through the 'softer' approach of advertising and persuasion.

There has of course been considerable discussion over the relative merits of attempts to effect lifestyle changes through 'blanket' programmes of advertising aimed at all members of the community, as opposed to identifying 'high-risk' groups of individuals in the community and concentrating one's efforts on them (see, for example, Stern et al.[44], Blackburn[45], Farquhar et al.[46], Breslow[47]). The Stanford Three Cities Project[46] indicated that substantial changes could be introduced in life style through a general programme of advertising (backed up in certain cases by instruction and discussion) throughout a community; whilst the Multiple Risk Factor Intervention Trial (the 'Mr Fit' programme) indicated the success of the selective approach with high-risk individuals. As demonstration projects, however, both of these experiments suffer from the fact that no follow-up investigation was conducted, to determine how permanent or otherwise are any changes produced by such methods; and Gray and Blythe's[48] review of health education programmes leads them to be rather pessimistic about their effectiveness (see also certain of the papers in Billington and Bell[30] and Billington et al.[31]).

Two sets of issues are raised by such approaches. First, is the obvious and basic problem of knowledge. This is recognised, of course, in the specification within the 'New Perspective' of a research strategy. Given the complexity of the aetiology of most degenerative diseases – with what seems likely to be a multifactorial pattern of causality in most instances (Oldham et al.[(14)], Morris[(49)], Wadsworth et al.[(12)]) – and given also that one has to depend on fairly complex inferences from probabilistic statistical data, is one ever likely to acquire a sufficiently secure knowledge-base to provide an indisputable foundation for any preventive programme (see, for example, DHSS[(27)]pp.66-68; Mustard[(15)], Mettlin[(50)])? The health-risks associated with such substances as cholesterol, sugar, saccharine and refined white flour have been identified and repudiated with equal fervour. Convincing statistical arguments can still be advanced even against the assertion that smoking causes lung cancer. This problem is recognised in the working document[(8)],pp.57-8:

> '...many of Canada's health problems are sufficiently pressing that action has to be taken on them even if all the scientific evidence is not in. The Chinese have an expression 'moi sui' which means to 'touch, to feel, to grope around'. It reflects a deliberate approach to innovative and creative action even when scientific certainty and predictability are in question'.

Whatever type or mixture of lifestyle prevention programmes one adopts, however, one must surely also relate these to environmental factors. To attempt to change individual behaviour through personal persuasion alone is to take a rather naive and atomistic view of the position of the individual in society. Thus, one has at least to take note of the possible effects of peer-group pressures and commercial advertising on individual choices – as is in fact acknowledged in the 'New Perspective' (*ibid.*, pp.35-36). In addition, however, there are powerful commercial vested interests which make it at least difficult for individual choice to operate entirely freely. Thus, how effective are strictures against high-cholesterol diets likely to be in countries – like Canada and Great Britain – where the dairy industry is important? With particular reference to Scotland, the same question could obviously be posed in relation to alcohol and tobacco. In addition, campaigns against the consumption of bread made from super-refined flour operate at the very least under a disadvantage in countries where the mass production of such bread has led to economies of scale which make it cheaper than bread made from wholemeal flour (see also Mustard[(15)]).

Compared with such problems lifestyle prevention obviously presents a relatively easy option for governments to tackle. The Lalonde document pins its faith on the ability of knowledge, harnessed to collective effort and commitment to produce desired changes. Ultimately, its stance tends to be politically naive. The history of attempts to implement policies based on the New Perspective's approach tend to highlight this problem (e.g., McEwan[(51)]). Lifestyle change represents the 'soft underbelly' of the health field; and it is to this area that government policies in most countries have tended to be directed, whilst other elements of the health field have been ignored. To anticipate arguments I intend to raise later, the emphasis on 'soft' persuasion-oriented approaches to lifestyle change are obviously attractive to individualistic societies such as Canada (and Great Britain). Current health policies need not only to be based on (limited) knowledge, but must also rely on the support of key groups in society. The Canadian policy is attempting to transcend the interests of the various groups concerned through rhetorical appeals which propose increased health as a national goal.

With reference to the health care system, the basic argument of the New Perspective is that previous emphasis has been on the allocation of cash for illness which has already been experienced. Such services need some improvement in terms of accessibility, efficiency, responsiveness to local needs, and more effective distribution of staff among and within them. But the services themselves are constantly claimed to be of such effectiveness that they need not be changed in order to improve health. Consequently, the main area for improvement in terms both of increasing health and reducing expenditure lies in prevention.

Certain points deserve to be noted about these arguments. First, rather than being based on analyses of the causes of *changes* in morbidity and mortality over the years, the appeal is based on statistical and causal analyses of *illness.* As a result, the question of how much and what kind of impact health care has had on health is never systematically examined. Second, the argument of the document is that health services are no longer the source of health improvement. The question obviously then becomes why? Is it because they are highly effective in dealing with acute illness, but costly and ineffective in dealing with chronic illness? In short, what is the justification for maintaining a commitment to their provision and tying further expenditure on them to reductions, due to changed behaviour, in the number of (degenerative) conditions requiring treatment by the health services? Third, to what extent will the health care system in the future be *caring,* rather than *curing*? How valid will it therefore be to maintain services at their present level? And if chronic illnesses are characterised by slow onset, with patterns of eruption of symptoms which are originally treated as acute illness, but which are very difficult to diagnose; and if the ages affected span from 40 onwards, rather than simply being the elderly, how effective are treatment-oriented services in dealing with them[52]?

Since the commitment is to provide health services in order to meet consumer demand, it would appear that doctors' responsibilities will remain in health care, rather than health promotion. From the above, the relevant questions appear to become: (a) what is the proven effectiveness of health services?; (b) what, if any, is the role of the medical practitioner in reducing demand?; (c) in a situation where demands on the health services will continue to be met, and the doctor remains in the same relationship to the consumer as previously obtained, will this 'new perspective' make for any reduction in expenditure on health services?

Using the very basic distinction between 'process' and 'outcome' evaluation[53], there is no clear indication in the Lalonde text that 'effectiveness' means 'outcome', as distinct from 'process' or organisation of health care. One of the research strategies contains 'effectiveness' in its formulation – an evaluation of mass-screening programmes. But none of the health care efficiency strategies seems to view 'effectiveness' in terms of the ability of treatment to improve health. They deal instead with such matters as accessibility, efficient allocation of human and financial resources, and planning mechanisms.

Assessment

The 'New Perspective' therefore relies upon change in the behaviour of doctors and (more importantly) consumers to slow the rate of growth in health services, while proposing no reduction in the availability of services. It proposes an esssentially voluntary, persuasion-oriented programme, based on changing lifestyle and environment. The Canadian public is being asked to assume a major responsibility for illness and health. The document therefore strongly reinforces a traditional theme of individual responsibility; is apparently new in its support for environmental reform (although, as has been argued above, this is given much less prominence than lifestyle); but encourages both life style and environmental improvements as a means of expanding existing health services, whilst limiting the proportion of the Canadian national income which goes on health.

The working document is therefore caught on the horns of a particularly subtle dilemma. It does appear to be responding effectively to concerns about health care – in terms of both the types and cost of contemporary health problems. But it implies that a causal approach to health care will best serve the individual. The nature of the policy problem is therefore shifted from effectiveness and control, to that of the causes of illness and health. It is accordingly implied that the road to solving modern disease trends and rising health costs is through the expansion of scientific knowledge and a co-ordinated national effort. A social policy is promulgated which seeks to harness and diffuse energy across the whole of Canadian society in order to cope with illness and foster health[(52)]. The problem of power and of vested interest is thereby ignored. The strategy remains primarily individualistic, being limited for the most part to government-initiated programmes in health education. For these reasons, it seems unlikely to succeed. To quote Mustard[(15)] for example:

> 'a nutrition policy developed and started by government will have little impact if done in isolation from the groups concerned with producing and marketing food. If such a policy is to have any hope of success, agriculture, food processing, food marketing, consumer and corporate affairs and other groups would have to be involved. If agriculture goals are set with an economic focus we will not necessarily have the best foodstuffs from a nutrition standpoint. If food processing and marketing also have mainly an economic focus, the same problems occur'.

The Case of Norway

In an article critical of contemporary developments in health policies in the West, Ringen[(54)] (see also Milio[(11)]) also comments that health policies in Norway have shared the same general trend. A Norwegian Ministry of Social Affairs White Paper[(55)], for example, acknowledged that the bulk of health expenditure now goes on supportive services which are not effective in promoting health. Contemporary developments represented a drain on national resources, rather than contributing to an increase in the total amount of social resources: indeed, no more than 0.2–0.3% of the total health budget was at that time (1976) allocated to well-defined preventive activities. In common with their Canadian counterparts, Norwegian health planners conclude that future improvements in health will depend on preventive programmes, rather than on an increase in expenditure upon, or the development of services in, the conventional health sector. And as in the case of Canada, the issue tends to remain at the level of exhortation, but without the elaboration of a set of health strategies such as are outlined in the Canadian document. As with Canada, no specific evaluation is made of the services; nor any suggestion given that reductions should take place in expenditure on these services themselves.

Norway has, however, at the same time been developing a nutrition and food policy, independent of its health policies, whose aims, methods and procedures might well serve as a model for those whose more overt responsibility is for health (Royal Ministry of Health and Social Affairs[55,56]). The policy itself relates to two major concerns (e.g. Ringen[54], Milio[11]). First, is the assumption that certain causal factors can be addressed in order to remedy specific health problems which are believed to be related to nutrition. More specifically, it is assumed that heart diseases can be reduced through a reduction in the cholesterol content of the diet; that dental diseases and diseases of the digestive tract can be remedied by reducing carbohydrates in the form of sugar and by increasing the fibre content of the diet; and thirdly, that a high prevalence of anaemia among women may be remedied by increasing the iron content of the diet.

Second, the nutrition and food policy is also motivated by a concern with the global food situation. Noting that developed countries have a diet characterised by domestic animal products, especially protein, whilst the diet of the peoples of developing countries is characterised by vegetables, especially starches and carbohydrates, the Norwegian policy is attempting to increase Norwegian domestic self-sufficiency in food and thereby reduce demand on the limited supply of foodstuffs on the world market.

By contrast with the individualism of the Canadian policy, with its emphasis on individual responsibility and change of behaviour through persuasion, the Norwegian policy attempts to manipulate the environment in such a way as to make it easier for individuals to make 'healthy' choices. Following, for example, an analysis of cardiovascular disease in Norway from 1951 to 1978 and a review of experiments in Norway and other countries relating to prevention of cardiovascular diseases[56], it is concluded that dietary measures could make for a significant improvement. It is intended that the amount of total energy intake provided by fats should be reduced by about 7% by the year 1990; and that this reduction should be compensated for through an increase in the intake of carbohydrates, whilst sugar consumption as a source of energy should also be reduced. Similarly, the use of polyunsaturated fatty acids in the total fat intake should be increased. The goal is to reduce the ratio of saturated to unsaturated fatty acids, which is at present about 4 : 1, to a level of 2 : 1 by 1990. Similar recommendations relate to the intake of fibre; and reference to the differing experiences of other countries leads the authors to conclude that iron enrichment of the diet would not be justified (*ibid*,p.16).

In order to effect these and other changes, a system of consumer and producer subsidies has been introduced to make 'healthy' foods cheaper than 'unhealthy' ones, along with a variety of regulatory measures designed to outlaw foods which are deemed to be a danger to health. The policy has three components (see, for example, Milio[10],p.180). The first is developing a co-ordinated series of programmes of subsidies aimed at meeting national goals. Given the agreed need to expand Norway's relatively small agricultural sector, subsidies are being made to those involved in food production to invest in commodities which will help develop rural areas. In addition, domestically-produced foodstuffs are subsidised in order to make them cheaper than imported products, provided those foodstuffs contribute to nutrional goals. In particular, it was proposed that potatoes be subsidised as part of the attempt to increase the country's consumption of non-refined carbohydrates, although as yet various problems have prevented the implementation of this suggestion[57]. In order to reduce the consumption of fat, especially of cholesterol and polyunsaturated fats, margarine is favoured over butter and low-fat milk is favoured above whole milk. To reduce the proportion of fat to body-weight among animals, the system also has reduced support for concentrated animal feeds, which has also tended to diminish milk production and encourages the presence of roughage in cattle feed.

The second aspect of the Norwegian policy framework is designed to deal with problems of transferring from one form of agricultural production to another. For example, producers receive investment subsidies to enable them to purchase equipment and expand their total acreage of arable land. Base prices have been established for all products, together with a system of quotas for the production of particular foodstuffs[54].

Thirdly, a health education and information programme is being implemented, which goes far beyond the simple delineation of the health-related effects of different types of foodstuff. Its intention is in addition to improve people's understanding of food production, of the price of food, and of the private and public sector determinants of the kind of food that is available[56,54].

Like the Canadian 'new perspective', the Norwegian nutrition and food policy may therefore be seen as an attempt to apply current knowledge and thinking about the causes of common modern diseases to eradication or reduction of those diseases. However, the Norwegian policy does not commit the error of regarding individuals in isolation from their environment. The flaw at the heart of the Canadian policy is its failure to recognise and attempt to tackle the problem of power.

A recent document has also questioned the effectiveness of medical services in dealing with chronic conditions, as a means of opening a debate about ways of reducing the cost and increasing the effectiveness of those services (J. Grund et al.[(58)]). But with reference to the more specific concerns of this paper, Norway's nutrition policy recognises that consumers cannot effectively make choices on their own. Two major policy means have been identified for the development of the Norwegian nutrition and food policy (Ziglio[(59)]):

(1) An administrative framework which was set up in order to ensure the co-ordination and future continuation of the policy[(55)].

(2) The identification of workable means of implementation, which can be summarised as
(a) consumer education
(b) pricing policy.

In respect of the means of implementation, the nutrition and food policy is sensitive to the needs of three basic 'constituencies', namely, consumers, producers, and Norwegian social organisation. The Norwegian policy is characterised by a consensus approach, recognising and relating to the needs of producers, rather than seeking a crude confrontation with them. By contrast with the Canadian approach which attempts to transcend the interests of different groups by proposing increased health as a national and 'neutral' goal, the Norwegian policy has specified its objectives, then involved producers in the political processes necessary for setting out the procedures to attain them. As Ziglio[(59)] points out, Norwegians are finding that political and economic realities necessitate compromise. It was of course realised from the outset that this would be so. What was not known, and is still not clear, is the extent to which the various factions may be able (and prepared) to compromise.

Conclusions

The Canadian new perspective is based upon an important and highly intelligent analysis of the factors contributing to health. Its ultimate weakness is perhaps its assumption that knowledge obtained from this framework, in combination with goodwill, will be enough to overcome the future health problems of Canadian society. The Norwegian approach is based on a less comprehensive (though no less intelligent) analysis of contemporary health problems, but has placed the need to develop a politically-feasible set of procedures at the heart of its aproach. Any attempt to develop preventive programmes for Scotland would obviously do well to use Lalonde's new perspective as a basis for understanding the boundaries and determinants of the health problems involved, but proceed along policy steps guided by the Norwegian initiative. Since, however, it is always dangerous to abstract social products and processes from their own immediate context, it may be worth ending with one or two caveats – less as reasons for not attempting to implement a strategy along the same lines as the Norwegian approach than as a reminder that such an implementation would need to adapt certain features to a more specificaly Scottish environment.

First, it is important to recognise that the agricultural sector in Norway is a relatively weak factor within the country's economy. By contrast with the large and 'export-oriented' Canadian agricultural system, Norway's agriculture is 'import-oriented'[59]. In situations where agriculture is important for the overall balance of payments (as is the case for Canada) it seems likely that it will be rather more resistant to change, particularly during periods of economic recession. In this respect, Norway was in a much easier position, at the time of the formulation of its Nutrition and Food Policy, than was Canada to make its agricultural policies consistent with the objectives of a policy for health. In this connection, Milio[11], for example, observes that the political action for creating structural changes was implemented at a time of growing uncertainty over essential foreign food imports and when new oil wealth became available (see also Milio[60], pp.176-178).

Second, Norway has a number of structural and political characteristics which perhaps make it much more possible to implement a policy of this kind than would be the case in many other countries. Ringen[54], for example, points out that the population is only 4 million and is extremely homogeneous in its social, ethnic and attitudinal characteristics. With respect to the agricultural sector, there has been an active relationship between farming organisations and the government over a number of years, where the latter has attempted to exert a degree of control over future developments, through a structure and tradition of decision-making built on participation by a whole range of interested parties in discussions and decisions, with an emphasis on achieving consensus policies which satisfy the main needs of the dominant groups involved, but which are also acceptable to parties with a less central stake in the isue (see also Milio[11]). In addition, almost all wholesale production and distribution of foods is done through producers' co-operatives, so that a structure for co-operation between farmers and the government has been cultivated over a long time; and this, according to Ringen[54] has probably, more than anything else, made the nutrition policy possible.

Finally, there is a factor more specifically related to our own internal political situation. A government which subscribes to the same sentiments as those voiced by Mr William Ross in 'The Way Ahead', but wedded to a rhetoric of individual initiative and responsibility seems unlikely to embrace such a policy with much enthusiasm. Consumer subsidies, for example, are not part of the current government's policy repertoire. At best, it might therefore be expected to continue its present rather lukewarm support for health education, with added superficial invocations of the notion of individual responsibility for health. But this final element is not immune to change and the two previous points merely underline the fact that we must appreciate that health promotion programmes need to integrate the question of health into a wider social, economic and political context. The potential for influencing lifestyle, and thus in the long term for improving or maintaining health, lies in the capacity to cope with such uncertainties and difficulties(59).

References

1. This paper is based on an article by the same author entitled 'Salute e politica sanitaria: tendenze presenti e sviluppi futuri', which appeared in G. Bertin, M. Niero and E. Ziglio (eds) *Politiche di Welfare State e Modelli Decisionali*, Unicopli, Milan, 1983.

2. D. Mechanic, 'The growth of medical technology and bureaucracy: implications for medical care', *Health and Society*, 55 (1977), pp.61-78.

3. I. Illich, *Limits to Medicine,* Penguin, Harmondsworth, Middlesex, 1977.

4. T. McKeown, *The Role of Medicine: Dream, Mirage or Nemesis?*, Nuffield Provincial Hospitals Trust, London, 1976.

5. J. Powles, 'On the limitations of modern medicine', *Science, Medicine and Man,* 1 (1973), pp.1-30.

6. F.B. Smith, *The People's Health, 1830-1910*, Croom Helm, London, 1979.

7. A.O. Omran 'Changing patterns of health and disease during the process of national development'; in G.L. Albrecht and P.C. Higgins (eds) *Health, Illness and Medicine: A Reader in Medical Sociology*, Rand McNally, Chicago, 1974.

8. M. Lalonde, *A New Perspective on the Health of Canadians: A Working Document,* Information Canada, Ottawa, 1975.

9. M. Parry, 'Health care' in R. Underwood (ed) *The Future of Scotland*,Croom Helm, London, 1977.

10. N. Milio, *Promoting Health through Public Policy*, T.A. Davis, Philadelphia, 1981, ch.2.

11. N. Milio, *Primary Care and the Public's Health: Judging Impacts, Goals and Policies,* D.C. Heath & Co., Lexington, Mass., 1983, ch.2.

12. M. Wadsworth, W. Butterfield & R. Blaney, *Health and Sickness: the Choice of Treatment,* Tavistock, London, 1971.

13. E. Zola & R. Miller 'The erosion of medicine from within' in E. Freidson (ed.) *The Professions and their Futures,* Free Press, New York, 1975.

14. J. Oldham, G. Pickering et al. 'The nature of essential hypertension'; *Lancet,* 1 (1960), pp.61-78.

15. J.F. Mustard, 'Health, Health Care and Public Policy', paper delivered to the Canadian Club on 11.1.77.

16. D.A. Ehrlich (ed.), *The Health Care Cost Explosion: Which Way Now?*, Henry Dunant Institute, Bern, 1975.

17. R. Maxwell, *A Simple Man's Approach to Health Economics,* London, 1977.

18. A Wing, 'The impact of financial constraint', in G. Scorer and A. Wing, (eds), *Decision-Making in Medicine: the Practice of its Ethics,* Edward Arnold, London, 1979.

19. Swedish Institute for Health Economics, *The Costs of Health Care: Trends and Determining Factors,* Report No.3, Lund, 1981.

20. R. Klein, *The Politics of the National Health Service*, Longman, London, 1983, ch.4.

21. G. Bevan, H. Copeman et al. *Health Care: Priorities and Management,*

Croom Helm, London, 1979.

22. A. Cochrane, *Effectiveness and Efficiency: Random Reflections on Health Services,* Nuffield Provincial Hospitals Trust, Oxford, 1972.

23. G. McLachlan (ed), *A Question of Quality?: Roads to Assurance in Medical Care,* Nuffield Provincial Hospitals Trust, Oxford, 1976.

24. E.M. Clarke and J.Q. Forbes, *Evaluating Primary Care,* Croom Helm, London 1979.

25. M. Robinson & E. Henry, *Self-Help and Health,* Martin Robertson, London, 1977.

26. S. Hatch & I. Kickbusch (eds.), *Self-Help and Health in Europe: New Approaches in Health Care,* World Health Organisation, Copenhagen, 1983.

27. DHSS, *Prevention and Health: Everybody's Business: A Reassessment of Public and Personal Health,* HMSO, London, 1976.

28. A. Yarrow, "Scotland", in German Federal Centre for Health Education, *Health Education in Europe: Organisation, Activities, Research Projects, Professional Preparation, Plans for the Future,* International Journal of Health Education, Geneva, 1972, pp.15-18.

29. G.W. H. Woodman, "England, Wales and Northern Ireland", in German Federal Centre for Health Education, *op.cit.*, pp,4-15.

30. D.R. Billington & J. Bell (eds), *Attitudes and Health Education,* Scottish Health Education Unit, Edinburgh, 1978.

31. D.R. Billington, J. Bell, M. Gass & C. Maxwell (eds), *Research in Health Education,* Scottish Health Education Unit, Edinburgh, 1979.

32. I. Sutherland (ed.), *Health Education,* Allen and Unwin, London, 1979, chapters 1 & 12.

33. DHSS, *Prevention and Health: Drinking Sensibly. A Discussion Document,* HMSO, London, 1981.

34. DHSS, *Prevention and Health: Reducing the Risk: Safer Pregnancy and Childbirth,* HMSO, London, 1977.

35. DHSS, *Prevention and Health: Avoiding Heart Attacks,* HMSO, London, 1981.

36. SHHD, *The Health Service in Scotland: The Way Ahead,* HMSO, Edinburgh, 1976.

37. DHSS, *Priorities in the Health and Social Services: The Way Forward,* HMSO, London, 1977.

38. German Federal Centre for Health Education, *op.cit.*

39. Royal Commission on Health Services, *Report*, (3 vols), Queen's Printer, Ottawa, 1964.

40. Department of National Health and Welfare *Task Force Reports on the Cost of Health Services,* (3 vols.), Queen's Printer, Ottawa, 1970.

41. J-M. Romeder & J.R. McWhinnie, *The Development of Potential Years of Life Lost as an Indicator of Premature Mortality,* Canadian Department of National Health and Welfare, Ottawa, Long Range Health Planning Staff Paper.

42. D. Gellman, G. Lachaine et al. 'The Canadian approach to health policies and programs', *Preventive Medicine,* 6 (1977), pp.265-75.

43. T. McKeown, 'Health and humanism', in G. McLachlan (ed.) *Problems and Progress in Medical Care, 5th Series,* Nuffield Provincial Hospitals Trust, Oxford, 1977.

44. M.P. Stern, J.W. Farquhar et al. 'Results of a two-year health education campaign on dietary behaviour', *Circulation,* 54, (1976), pp.826-33.

45. H. Blackburn, 'Coronary disease prevention. Practical approaches to risk factor changes', *Advanced Cardiology,* 20 (1977), pp.1-9.

46. J.W. Farquhar et al. 'Community education for cardiovascular health', *Lancet,* 1 (1977), pp.1192- 95.

47. L. Breslow, 'Risk factor intervention', *Science,* 200 (1978), pp.908-12.

48. M. Gray & M. Blythe, 'The failures of health education', in P. Atkinson

et al. (eds), *Prospects for the National Health,* Croom Helm, London, 1979,

49. J.N. Morris, *The Uses of Epidemiology,* Livingstone, Edinburgh, 1967.

50. C. Mettlin, 'Prerequisites of successful lifestyle intervention', *Social Science and Medicine,* 13A (1979), pp.559-62.

51. E.D. McEwan 'Have Lalonde's health-care ideas died of neglect?', *Toronto Financial Post,* 14.10.78; p.6.

52. M. McGuire, *The 'New Perspective" and Group Interests,* unpublished M.A. thesis McMaster University, Hamilton, Ontario, 1977.

53. A. Robertson and J. Gandy 'Policy, practice and research: an overview', in J. Gandy, A. Robertson and S. Sinclair (eds), *Improving Social Intervention: Changing Social Policy and Social Work Practice through Research,* Croom Helm, London, 1983.

54. K. Ringen, 'The "new ferment" in national health policies: the case of Norway's nutrition and food policy', *Social Science and Medicine,* 13C (1979), pp.33-41.

55. Royal Ministry of Health and Social Affairs, *On Norwegian Food and Nutrition Policy,* Report No.32 to the Storting (1975-76), Oslo, 1976.

56. Royal Ministry of Health and Social Affairs, *On the Follow-Up of Norwegian Nutrition Policy,* Report No.11 to the Storting (1981-82), Oslo, 1981; pp. 1218.

57. I am grateful to Erio Ziglio, graduate student in the Department of Social Administration at Edinburgh University, for providing up-to-date information from his current research on this matter.

58. J. Grund, P.F. Hjort et al. *Helseplan For 1980 Ara,* Gyldendal Norsk Ferlag, Oslo, 1982, ch.5.

59. E. Ziglio, 'The Canadian and Norwegian approaches to health promotion policy'. Unpublished seminar paper, Department of Social Administration, University of Edinburgh, March, 1984.

60. N. Milio, 'Promoting health through structural change: analysis of the origins and implementation of Norway's farm- food-nutrition policy', *Social Science and Medicine,* 15 A (1981), pp.721-34.

THE LURE OF THE ORGANISATIONAL FIX: RE-REORGANISING THE SCOTTISH HEALTH SERVICE

DAVID HUNTER
DEPARTMENT OF COMMUNITY MEDICINE
UNIVERSITY OF ABERDEEN

For the second time within a decade the National Health Service has been reorganised and a third restructuring, albeit of a more limited nature, is in the offing. Events in Scotland have lagged behind those elsewhere in the UK, have followed a different course and have resulted in slightly different outcomes. The intention in this chapter is not to describe in great detail the nuts and bolts of the arrangements that have taken root. Some of this detail and the problems confronting the fifteen Scottish Health Boards in implementing the reforms are presented in another chapter. This chapter attempts to trace the origins of the latest reforms, describes their underlying philosophy and pinpoints where they differ from the rest of the UK. In so doing, the narrative provides a commentary on aspects of health policy-making in Scotland which is conducted in a wider UK arena where the central department in London, the DHSS, takes the lead.

The developments reviewed here focus on two separate, though related, reform initiatives. The first is directed towards the actual organisational structure of the Health Service; the second is concerned in large part with the managerial culture and the processes encased by these structures. Each is considered in turn and a third section assesses their significance for future health policy and for health care in Scotland.

Structural Reform

Between 1974 and 1984 the structure of the Scottish Health Service comprised three levels below the central department, as shown in the Diagram. From mid-1984 the structure comprised two levels below the central department. Ten of the fifteen health boards, i.e. the multi-district areas, were affected by the changes. While the actual changes are of some interest, much more interesting is the rationale underlying them and the process of their adoption which makes for a curious saga of hesitancy, lack of direction and policy reversal. If, as has been alleged,[1] policy-making is as much about puzzlement as power then the 1984 reorganisation of the Scottish Health Service bears ample testimony to the salience of this view.

To understand events in Scotland over the past four years it is necessary to say something about those in England. As will become clear what happened in Scotland was a direct result of what happened in England; the same holds for Wales and Northern Ireland.

Not long after the NHS was initially reorganised in 1974 rumblings were heard from various quarters about the disaster it was proving to be. It was alleged, mainly by sections of the medical profession, that Sir Keith Joseph, then Secretary of State for Social Services, had created a bureaucratic Leviathan that was in danger of collapsing under its own weight. Criticism centred on the number of management tiers ('shed a tier' became a well-worn cliche in Health Service circles in the latter half of the 1970s), on the inflated number of administrative staff (i.e. the dog was getting smaller while his tail was growing bushier), on the remoteness of appointed bodies from the communities they served, and, by no means least, on the system of consensus management whereby decisions lay in the hands of teams of officers from the four main disciplines: administration, finance, medicine and nursing. There are those who maintain that the only way to manage a complex undertaking like the NHS is through multi-disciplinary consensus teams;[2] others, who were vocal in the late 1970s, argue that consensus management is a negation of good management and that its introduction into the NHS in 1974 was the outcome of an 'implicit bargain'[3] between the government and a suspicious medical profession jealously guarding its interests which it believed would be threatened by any form of chief executive system of management. Moreover, those belonging to this school of thought argue that the very nature of the NHS (chiefly its complexity and its multi-professional composition) which has led to great opposition to chief executives also happens to be the very reason why they are required.[4] This debate is returned to later in the chapter.

It is hard to know whether the discontent over reorganisation was merely the frustration with their lot felt by some displaced groups who yearned for the cosy familiarity of a structure many had known for twenty years or more. There is no doubt that the 1974 reforms opened up decision-making to other groups. The duopoly, or cosy cabal, of administrators and doctors gave way to a management team concept involving other disciplines. Moreover, the purpose of the 1974 reforms was to replace the former tripartite structure comprising local authority health services, primary care and hospital services with a more unified structure to enable integrated care to be provided to people whose needs transgressed professional and organisational boundaries. It should also be stressed that while the reorganised NHS was not enthused over by everyone in Scotland there was far less overt hostility towards it than was the case in England. In part this may have been because it was simpler but other reasons were probably important, too, including a healthier resource base in Scotland compared with England and a scale of activities generally which was claimed to be more manageable and which could be conducted more informally.

In England the rumblings became sufficiently loud for a Royal Commission to be set up in 1976 only two years after the NHS had been reorganised. The Commission's remit was to look at the management of the NHS, a Herculean task which was handled competently if not with aplomb. It reported in 1979[(5)] by which time the Labour Government had been replaced by a Conservative administration. While in Opposition, the Conservatives had begun to form very clear ideas about what they saw as being wrong with the NHS and what they saw as the cure. Whereas the Royal Commission advocated a gradualist, evolutionary approach to reforming aspects of the structure in certain health authorities, the government sought a more dramatic remedy that would involve the entire NHS. Their thoughts on the matter were set out in a consultative document, *Patients First*, published in late 1979.[(6)] It payed homage to the Royal Commission's recommendations but in general ignored most of what the Commission had to say. Clearly Ministers had already made up their minds and the Commission's report was only invoked where it bolstered their ideas.

Hard on the heels of the English consultative document came versions for the rest of the UK. In contrast to the English paper, the Scottish one[(7)] was very thin – seven pages of text compared with twenty-five pages – and gave the appearance of being a 'knee-jerk' response to the English document. Whereas the English paper produced a firm rationale for the proposed reforms based on notions of *laissez-faire,* devolution and flexibility with a strong desire to loosen the centre's reins on the periphery, the Scottish paper lacked this dimension. It did not even have a thematic title. What was proposed for the NHS across the UK was a simplification of the structure: superficially, only the details and the titles differed in the four parts of the UK. In Scotland it was proposed to retain the fifteen health boards but in the ten boards with district structures it was suggested that many, if not all, of them should abolish these and establish units of management.

In England the changes proposed were more substantial: the area tier of management below region was to be shed and a new district authority level created below it which would more or less correspond to the then existing district management teams,. The new districts, however, were to be not merely management bodies but were to be member bodies responsible for policy-making and planning activities. Details of the arrangements below districts were to be issued at a later stage although three general principles were outlined: (a) maximum delegation of responsibility to hospital and community services; (b) no managerial tier between the hospital and community services level and the district level; and (c) hospital staff, other than clinical staff, to be accountable to the hospital administrator and not to district level managers (i.e. functional management in services like catering, laundries and cleaning was to be curtailed somewhat to reduce fragmentation).

The Scottish consultative paper was a curious document. Although reference was made to the Royal Commission, the opening paragraph made it clear that the Scottish Secretary of State's statement was triggered by the Secretary of State for Social Services' action in producing *Patients First*. More curious still was the strategy favoured for restructuring. If *laissez-faire* was the name of the game it reached extremes in Scotland where the ten health boards with districts (see Appendix for details of these) were asked to review their arrangements 'with a view to abolishing districts'. It was accepted that in a handful of cases boards would wish to retain districts and it was a matter of these boards stating their retaining reasons for the *status quo*.

In Scotland an option would have been to remove the area health boards, which, strictly speaking, are comparable to the area health authorities in England which were abolished in 1982, and centre operations on districts or on new authorities to be of a size somewhere between areas and districts. However because abolition of health boards would have entailed a considerable upheaval and because the areas had, in the government's view, worked well since 1974 it was decided to leave boards intact. In other respects the document kept close to its English counterpart from which it took its cue.

Within the NHS there was no real enthusiasm for a second

reorganisation in under a decade and, despite repeated assurances from Ministers, the upheaval that ensued was inevitably greater than had been predicted. Progress was swifter in England where a timetable was laid down and the new district health authorities assumed their responsibilities on 1 April 1982. In Scotland events proved to be more protracted than elsewhere in the UK and the main changes have only fairly recently been completed in some boards. A firm timetable was not set for Scotland at the start.

In England a circular[(8)] appeared in July 1980 setting out the government's decisions about restructuring. Area health authorities and health districts were to be replaced by district health authorities. Below districts, services were to be organised into units of management comprising an administrator, a nurse and a senior member of the medical staff. Units could be organised in a number of ways: a large single hospital, the community services of a district, client care services, maternity services, geographical areas, or a group of hospitals. It was up to the new districts to produce plans for units which would then be approved by the regions.

In Scotland a circular appeared almost a year later in March 1981.[(9)] This followed two statements in Parliament by the Secretary of State on progress in Scotland. The first of these, in July 1980, referred to the division of opinion among health boards over the fate of districts. Three out of the ten boards with districts favoured their abolition and were later joined by another two. The other seven, the so-called 'Magnificent Seven' (later reduced to five), opted to retain a district structure. The second statement, in March 1981, had nothing new to say beyond the fact that discussions between the Department and health boards were in progress. Decoding the language, this meant that the discussions had run into difficulties and progress had ceased.

The circular itself reaffirmed the Secretary of State's desire to see districts abolished or, if this was not possible, their number reduced. In other respects, in particular the emphasis on strong unit management, the circular followed the English one.

The impatience with some health boards and the future of their districts which could just be detected in the Scottish circular came to a head in November 1983 when the Secretary of State announced to Parliament in response to a question[(10)] that *all* health boards were to operate without districts and were to be so instructed forthwith. Significantly, and somewhat curiously, the decision was taken with the concurrence of health board Chairmen including those from the five boards intent upon retaining districts. The extent to which Chairmen gave their agreement willingly or with reservations is not clear. The Secretary of State may have enlisted their support in order to legitimise the decision in the eyes of those managing services and to avoid, or minimise, a hostile reaction to the abolition of districts. In short, the room for manoeuvre available to Chairmen might have been very limited.

The Secretary of State alleged that 'adopting a common form of organisation will also provide a firm basis for consideration of the recommendations of the NHS Management Inquiry led by Griffiths ...' (see below). The circular[11] which followed went further, asserting that the Secretary of State was 'in no doubt that the elimination of districts ... will contribute to the pattern of strong unit management recommended by the Griffiths Report'. The circular gave other more immediate reasons for the abrupt switch from a *laissez-faire* to a directive stance. In the period since the first circular it had become evident 'that the revised management structures being devised by individual health boards would create excessive disparities between them, and bring about considerable difficulties for both management and staff'.[12] A key problem was reaching agreement on Whitley Council gradings. It seems surprising that these problems had not been anticipated, a reflection, perhaps, of the lack of thorough preparation in Scotland for the second reorganisation.

The ten health boards with districts were required to establish units of management which would be 'coherent and discrete areas of management responsibility, forming a distinct management level to which substantial decisions can be devolved'.[13] A firm date – 1 April 1984 – was set for implementation of the reforms by the five health boards which had originally planned to abolish districts. An extension of two months was given to the other five boards which had hastily to draw up plans for units. From June all health boards were to be uniform only varying in the number and type of units they decided to establish.

How are these various moves in the second round of the reorganisation game to be interpreted? And what alternative options were available? At one level the moves can be seen as evidence of the lack of enthusiasm in the SHHD for a further reorganisation, an absence of clear thinking about what was wanted and as the consequence of ending up with a structure of health boards some of which would have two tiers below them (districts and units) while others would have just one tier comprising units some of which would resemble in all but name the districts they were replacing. At another level the history of events illustrates how difficult it is in practice to allow complete flexibility over structures, posts and gradings when there exist powerful counterpressures, in the shape of Whitley Councils and professional bodies, for consistency and uniformity not only between but also within the four countries making up the UK.

The five health boards which initially decided to retain districts did so either on grounds of size (Glasgow and Lothian), geography (Highland), or a combination of both (Lanarkshire and Tayside). But with ten boards either already without districts or intent upon abolishing them the pressure was on the remaining 'recalcitrant' boards to fall into line whatever their reasons for retaining districts. Had a number of boards been permitted to retain districts then this would have made an already anomalous situation even more anomalous. Scottish districts would have resembled English districts in name only. Unit administrators below districts would have been a quite separate species from their counterparts in other boards or South of the Border. Doubtless such factors were in part responsible for the pressure exerted upon all boards to remove districts although, as mentioned above, this still left Scotland in a different position from that taking shape elsewhere.

There were many administrators who were of the opinion that the government had dismissed too readily a review of area health board boundaries and functions. The Scottish Division of the Institute of Health Service Administrators (IHSA) commented on the proposals in April 1980 and 'doubted the validity of the premises on which the proposals to retain existing areas and abolish their districts were based'.[(14)] The IHSA described the area boundaries as a compromise beween planning requirements and operational management and argued that a case could be made for reconsidering the boundaries.

Whatever the arguments for or against districts, the Scottish Health Service as it now stands is in some respects unique in the UK.[(15)] With the abolition of districts there is a preponderance of areas very much larger than the average-sized district health authority (DHA) in England. This carries with it potential span of control problems particularly in Glasgow and Lothian which are the biggest day-to-day health management bodies in the UK (see Appendix).[(16)] Moreover since there is no regional tier in Scotland health boards must assume a wider range of responsibilities than the English DHAs. Other regional functions are run by the SHHD or by the Common Services Agency which is jointly managed by the Department and by the health boards (see Diagram).

One way of removing the anomalies created by choosing to axe districts would have been to recast health board boundaries but, as noted earlier, this course was rejected on the grounds that a major upheaval was to be avoided. However, in his first Parliamentary statement in 1980, referred to above, George Younger, the Secretary of State for Scotland maintained, as he had done in the consultative paper, that 'the changes to be made in district organisation and management levels below area will have substantial implications for staff'. In his second statement in 1981 he referred to the five boards without districts 'where the scope for major structural change does not exist' thereby clearly suggesting that the abolition of districts was more than just an exercise in fine-tuning. For some people in the health service this admission effectively demolished the argument for not examining health board boundaries which the government, in its 1979 consultative paper, had decided was not on the agenda for discussion.

Concern over the size of area health boards arose because of what was happening in England at the time. Most of the 194 English DHAs cover populations of about 200,000 with large authorities, i.e. 500,000 and over, being the exception. In Scotland, Greater Glasgow Health Board covers a population of over one million and Lothian a population of three quarter million. On the basis of figures produced in Parliament on the size of English DHAs, Rees[(17)] contrasted the position with what was happening in Scotland. Only 6% of DHAs have populations over 400,000 compared with 50% of health boards (excluding the three island boards); 70% of DHAs fall within the population band 100,000 to 300,000 compared with only 26% of Scottish boards; 75% of the districts in Scotland covered populations of between 100,000 and 300,000. On the basis of these figures it was thought that the Scottish *districts* or, in some cases, amalgamations of districts should form the basis of new authorities.

Of course an increase in the number of health boards would probably have brought forth calls for a regional tier in order to achieve complete parity with England and to return Scotland to a pre-1974 type of structure comprising regional boards and boards of management. Between 1948 and 1974, the NHS across the UK was more uniform than it became after 1974.

Apart from the merits or demerits of focussing attention on districts, there were two central weaknesses in the government's case for reorganising the NHS in Scotland. First, whereas in England savings in management costs were a major factor in the desire to simplify the structure this was not the case in Scotland. Even if one were sceptical of the claims being made in England that management costs might be reduced by up to 10%, it at least provided a firm political rationale for the upheaval that did not depend exclusively on unsubstantiated theoretical organisational gains from shedding a tier. As administrators in Scotland argued, why proceed with major reform if no savings were likely to be realised and if the other benefits were uncertain to say the least. The effect upon morale and the disruption of services could hardly be justified. Even allowing for an element of safeguarding jobs, this view cannot be dismissed lightly given the inevitable distraction from arguably more important matters that any reorganisation brings in its train.

But the chief cause for dismay in Scotland over restructuring was the admission by the then Health and Social Work Minister, Sir Russell Fairgrieve, that 'with England having to do it we felt on balance we should do it'.[18] Sir Russell went on record saying that 'while we don't like in Scotland necessarily to trail in England's coat tails the fact is that England was having a look at the thing after six years. It was really felt on balance that we ought to look at the structure in Scotland as well because we were quite convinced there could be some improvement'. The Minister hypothesised that if Scotland enjoyed independence he would probably not have gone ahead with reorganisation.

The above account of events in Scotland between 1979 and the present time is an endorsement of Keating and Midwinter's[19] argument about policy-making generally in Scotland that 'if an issue comes up through the UK network or arises simultaneously in England and Scotland, (the Secretary of State's) discretion will be more limited'. The role of the Scottish Office becomes largely reactive responding to initiatives from the 'lead' department (DHSS) in London rather than grasping initiatives itself. Creativity in the Scottish Office seems confined to administrative means rather than to policy ends.[20] The restructuring of the Scottish Health Service is a good illustration of this management style. It appears, too, as if the changes about to occur in the management of the NHS in Scotland may provide a further illustration. Before describing events in this area, and by way of concluding this subsection, a brief review of the current structural position in the Scottish Health Service is in order.

By the middle of 1984, all health boards had their units of management in place; while doubtless scars remain the wounds caused by the reorganisation itself, and more especially by the way it was handled, have practically healed. Units present opportunities for improved management but they also open up the possibility of conflict within boards. In most boards some of the former districts have merely been relabelled units (e.g. Grampian and Tayside have done this in the case of two of the three former districts in each board). In devising units, services that were combined under the former districts have been divided. For example in Dundee with a population of just under 200,000 three units have been created to replace the district: psychiatry, general hospitals, geriatrics and community services. This division of activities is probably no worse than any other (with the possible exception of organising services on a client group basis which may aid planning across services) but it could create difficulties in achieving co-ordinated care for groups like the elderly who straddle all three units. It means that professionals will in future have to deal with three sets of unit management groups, and four officers within each unit, instead of just one district management group as before.

It is, of course, far too early to assess, or pass judgement upon, the new arrangements but there are grounds for concern that they may not achieve their aim of improved decision-making. Significantly, both circulars sought to impress upon health boards that the principle of the integration of hospital and community based services – a primary objective of the 1974 reorganisation – be maintained. Proper co-ordination between units in respect of these services was to be ensured. The very fact that the government deemed it necessary to insert a statement to this effect suggests that it foresaw potential problems at this interface through the creation of units. As the Appendix shows, the boundaries of the old districts in some health board areas matched the corresponding local government districts. Some units (e.g. re-labelled districts) will continue to share these under the new arrangements. But in many cases, in part because units are not all based on geographical criteria, the mismatch in boundaries is now more apparent. For instance, the former South District of Grampian Health Board has been replaced by five units in contrast to two local government districts. In Dundee, where the health district and local government district shared common boundaries, there are now three units. Of course most local government community services are the responsibility of the regional tier the boundaries of which, with the exception of Strathclyde, are coterminous with health board boundaries. But housing is a district responsibility and social work divisions often match district boundaries. Since most contact between health and local authorities occurs between boards and regions the absence of common boundaries below this level is unlikely to make a great deal of practical difference. What it may do, however, is set back attempts to promote closer links at levels below health boards and local authority regions.

Another issue is the extent to which units will be granted the devolution ostensibly sought by Ministers in terms of controlling budgets and decision-making. The issue of devolved decision-making was a key one in the former area/district structure, especially in the smaller boards, and it remains to be seen how prepared boards will be to stand back and allow units to manage. This has become a major issue in England because the original philosophy of local discretion has undergone a quiet revolution. While vestiges of the old rhetoric remain in Ministerial speeches the catchwords are no longer 'flexibility' and 'local discretion' but 'efficiency' and 'accountability'. They signal a fundamental shift in the running of the NHS in England. An interventionist stance has been assumed by the central department which has replaced the former *laissez-faire* stance. The reasons for this shift cannot be considered here but have been set out by the author elsewhere.(21) Its implications for the new districts and units seems to be that regions are reluctant to allow districts too much freedom and, in turn, that districts are reluctant to let go of units. Span of control problems make it very difficult for regions to control districts and for districts to control units but it is precisely because of a concern over loss of control that regions and districts may be reluctant to devolve responsibility. However if units are not granted freedom to manage they will cease to be credible, authoritative bodies and run the risk of being bypassed in favour of districts in England and health boards in Scotland.(22)

The *volte face* that took place in England is not apparent to such a degree in Scotland where initiatives to strengthen the centre's grip on the Service have not been replicated. Nevertheless it remains to be seen whether units of management will function as intended. Unless they do the case for reform will not have been met.

Managerial Reform

Not content with merely trying to get the structure right, the government has more recently directed its energies to the internal management of the NHS. Once again events in Scotland are inextricably bound up with events in England and, as with structural reform, have lagged some way behind.

In February 1983, the Secretary of State for Social Services appointed Roy Griffiths, Chief Executive of Sainsbury's, to lead a small team with the remit 'to give advice on the effective use and management of manpower and related resources in the NHS'. The NHS Management Inquiry took about six months and a twenty-four page typescript, the Griffiths Report, was published in October 1983.(23) The Inquiry was confined to England although the team visited the central departments and health authorities in Scotland and Wales. In a Parliamentary statement, the Secretary of State for Scotland made it clear that he would be seeking to apply Griffiths to Scotland and that the first stage would involve publishing a discussion document. As mentioned already, the Minister claimed that one reaon for finally instructing all boards to abolish districts was to pave the way for implementing Griffiths' proposals for strong unit management. After almost six months delay the discussion document[24] was published in June 1984 with comments to be submitted by the end of September. The reasons for the delay are not known. One possibility is that the SHHD decided to wait upon events in England before making its move. Such caution probably reflected the DHSS's own reluctance to move too swiftly on Griffiths after an initial burst of enthusiasm on the part of the Secretary of State for Social Services. Once again, the SHHD took its 'lead' from the DHSS.

Although confined to England, clearly what Griffiths has to say is of relevance across the UK especially if it is being acted upon beyond England. The report combines diagnosis with prescription. The thrust of its argument is that the NHS suffers from 'institutionalised stagnation', the result of a labyrinthine consultation process and a system of consensus management teams which gives the right of veto to each team member. Apart from the Secretary of State there is no manager, or managers, within the Service who can at the end of the day say 'the buck stops here'. There is a notable 'lack of a clearly-defined general management function throughout the NHS'.[25] Consequently in the Inquiry team's eyes 'the NHS is so structured as to resemble a "mobile": designed to move with any breath of air, but which in fact never changes its position and gives no clear indication of direction'.[26] Griffiths' observations are divided between the central department and the health authorities at region and district. He also comments on unit management. He does not mince his words when considering the role of the central department. There is 'a danger of over-organisation' with the centre 'too much involved in too many of the wrong things and too little involved in some that really matter'. Authorities 'are being swamped with directives without being given direction'[27] which makes it difficult to implement major initiatives or achieve change.

Not surprisingly Griffiths brought a business perspective to bear on the NHS and was intent upon emphasising the similarities between NHS management and business management, a view that is very much in keeping with the spirit of the times. But his diagnosis is broadly shared by many both inside and outside the Service even if differences of opinion exist over parts of it. For instance, consensus management has given rise to considerable comment and to sharp differences of opinion. Whereas Hunter[28] in a study of management practices in two Scottish health boards in the mid-1970s did not find any great enthusiasm for consensus management, Schulz and Harrison[29] in their survey of management teams in England found 'widespread support for the practice of consensus decision-making'. But although Griffiths was firmly of the opinion that consensus management 'can lead to 'lowest common denominator decisions' and to long delays in the management process' he did not wish to replace consensus management *in toto*. Without detailing precisely what might be involved, a general manager was 'to harness the best of the consensus management approach and avoid the worst of the problems it can present'.[30]

The House of Commons Social Services Committee conducted a brief inquiry into the Griffiths Report and concluded that 'the general critique contained within the Report commands general assent'.[31] But the Committee was less happy with some of the prescriptions to deal with the condition diagnosed. Four of the proposals merit comment. They are, first, to establish a Supervisory Board within the DHSS, chaired by the Secretary of State and charged with the oversight of the NHS; second, to set up an NHS Management Board under the direction of the Supervisory Board to 'give leadership to the management of the NHS'[32] and to cover *'all existing NHS management responsibilities in DHSS'*;[33] third, to introduce a general manager at all levels – region, district and unit – to be drawn from any of the four disciplines currently represented on consensus management teams – administration, finance, medicine and nursing – and to be appointed from within each authority; and, fourth, to involve clinicians closely in management by, *inter alia*, developing management budgets.

Rare in government, the Secretary of State for Social Services moved quickly on Griffiths particularly in respect of the reforms at the centre. If the issue of general management took longer to resolve than was at first thought desirable this was partly because of the need to consult opinion in the Service and because of strong opposition to the idea from powerful interests like the British Medical Association. Consequently conclusions on the Griffiths Report were not announced in England until early June. These were published in guidance to health authorities.[34]

The government has opted for the appointment of general managers at all levels while allowing health authorities some flexibility over the precise details and timing of implementation. But they will not be able to deviate from the principle. General managers will for the most part be full-time. Combining the general management function with other duties is not thought to be desirable although it may be permitted at unit level to encourage clinicians tp apply for posts provided other duties take second place. In England, general managers, drawn from inside and possibly from outside the NHS, are to be introduced at regional and district health authority levels as soon as possible, and at hospital and unit level by the end of 1985. Ministers are at pains to point out that there is 'no question of throwing consensus management out of the window. Consensus is vital to the management of any organisation ... but this should not mean that decisions are ducked or avoided'.[35] General managers will be on fixed-term contracts – 3-5 years in the first instance and annually thereafter. Further management training for clinicians is to be given a high priority.

In a Parliamentary debate[36] on the Griffiths Report in early May 1984 Norman Fowler, Secretary of State for Social Services, reported that the Supervisory Board had already been established. Under his chairmanship, it brings together key people both in and beyond the DHSS, including the Permanent Secretary, Chief Medical Officer, Chief Nursing Officer (an omission from the Griffiths Report, and Roy Griffiths himself. A Management Board is being established with a full-time Chairman recruited by open competition and acting as a fourth Permanent Secretary at the DHSS accountable for hospital and community services expenditure. Under its Chairman, the Board will be responsible for all the DHSS's work in relation to the management of the NHS – finance, personnel, service planning and so on. A personnel director is to be appointed to the Management Board. Pending the emergence of the Board, an NHS management group has been active in the Department 'to provide a better focus within the existing structure'.[37] To overcome fears that these new Boards might interfere with, or dilute, Ministers' accountability to Parliament, Norman Fowler has sought to assure MPs that the two Boards do not have separate corporate status and that their arrival does not herald increased involvement by the Department in the affairs of the Service. The Chairman of the Management Board, like the other Permanent Secretaries, will be directly accountable to the Secretary of State. He will not, as some would have wished, enjoy even the degree of independence and departmental detachment enjoyed by the chairmen of nationalised industries.

In the Scottish consultative paper, the Secretary of State accepts the principles underlying the analysis in the Griffiths Report and believes they apply to the Scottish Health Service. He wishes to see the identification of general managers at both health board and unit levels. The timetable for the changes is considerably lengthier than the English one. It is divided into three phases: phase 1, the appointment of general managers at board level, to be completed before the end of 1985; phase 2, the examination of unit structures, management information and budgeting systems prior to the introduction of the general management function at unit level, to be completed by the end of 1986; and phase 3, the strengthening of the management function at unit level, with no time limit given.

The bulk of the Scottish consultative document is taken up with a detailed description of the functions of general managers at board level. It is considerably more thorough than the English circular which in any case, and as mentioned already, places much more emphasis upon the general management function at unit level. The Scottish document lists thirteen different responsibilities which would be part of the post. The Secretary of State also goes to great lengths to ensure that the general manager's overriding responsibility for the sound management of public monies allotted to the board should be clearly established. The Secretary of the SHHD, as Accounting Officer for the health vote, would delegate part of his authority to the general manager who would be required to appear before the Public Accounts Committee (PAC) to answer questions on matters arising from the financial performance of his board. Indeed, the general manager would be directly accountable to the PAC since he would be required to sign the board's annual accounts. It is not clear if general managers in England are to shoulder similar responsibilities. Either way it seems curious that the Scottish document should go into such fine detail on this point. Whatever the reasons, the implications for the ability of units to operate freely are potentially profound. If the general manager at board level is faced with the prospect of appearing before the PAC, which has taken a tough and uncompromising line on variations in performance in the NHS, insisting on the need for tighter central control (see next section), it is hard to imagine unit general managers flourishing in such an environment. This could be one reason why the Secretary of State for Scotland is lukewarm about the general management function at unit level.

In contrast to the plans for England, the introduction of general managers at unit level in Scotland seems less than clear. The vigorous policy being pursued south of the border has given way to a vaguer, more cautious and more relaxed approach. Although a general commitment to general managers at unit level is contained in the discussion document, 'at this stage the Secretary of State does not propose a specific timetable for the complete introduction of the general management function at this level' since he '... is not committed to this particular approach in every case.'(38) The document goes to great lengths to pacify the professions, particularly the medical profession: 'while the introduction of the general management function at unit level will affect the roles of individual professional managers, it is not (the) intention to weaken the existing involvement of professional staff in management.'(39) In England the importance of general managers at unit level as being vital to the success of the whole reform strategy is stressed in the circular. 'The primary objective for health authorities in implementing the (Griffiths)

Report's recommendations must therefore be to achieve changes at unit level and below. If there were no observable improvement in services at that level, in the eyes of patients and the community, within three to five years, then there would have been no point in making changes at DHA level or above'.[40] There appears to be a significant difference of emphasis on this point between Scotland and England although it is possible that the Scottish circular which will follow the discussion period will adopt a tougher approach. Another, albeit slight, difference in emphasis can be detected over the fixed terms for general managers. Appointments should be for five years and should be renewable which is in contrast to the English arrangements.

At the centre in Scotland the changes being implemented (i.e. not open to discussion as happened in England some seven months or so earlier) are fairly limited and do not greatly disturb the status quo. A Supervisory Board has been set up with the Minister for Health and Social Work as the Chairman with a membership including the Secretary, the Chief Medical Officer and the Chief Nursing Officer of the SHHD, the Chairman of the Planning Council, individuals with relevant experience of private sector management, and the holder of a new post for NHS Management and Finance. No Management Board as such is being established but a new Under-Secretary post (Management and Finance) has been created and filled. The equivalent of the role which in England has been given to the chairman of the NHS Management Board (not yet appointed), the occupant of the post is in charge of a reorganised and strengthened group of divisions in SHHD concerned with NHS management, planning, finance and performance monitoring. This group was formerly the Planning Group (see Diagram). Unlike England, the Scottish equivalent of the Management Board is not being led by a chief executive, or general manager, appointed from outside the civil service.

In sum, the changes proposed for Scotland are in line with the plans now being implemented in England. In keeping with previous reorganisations, there are subtle variations and shifts in emphasis reflecting different circumstances and interests. But the overall thrust of what is likely to happen is virtually the same.

It is, therefore, almost certain that in Scotland the government will broadly follow England in the move to appoint general managers whatever the consultation process may reveal on the subject. It is hard to see how Scotland could for long remain out of step if general managers are to become the norm in the NHS in England. While fairly marginal variations in administrative arrangements are tolerated in different parts of the UK,[41] differences of this magnitude would be unlikely to exist for long. So it can be fairly safely assumed that general managers will be appointed in health boards and, over a longer period, in units.

The general management function will have the most profound implications for health care management if it succeeds. It is a little ironic that Scotland waited upon events in England before issuing proposals because in fact the arguments in favour of chief executives for the NHS were originally ventilated in Scotland some eighteen years ago[42] and it is possible that the Griffiths team had the benefit of access to this work. The Farquharson-Lang Report was concerned with improving the administrative practice of hospital boards in Scotland and much of the managerial philosophy and quest for greater efficiency and effectiveness which emerged forcefully as central themes in 1974 can be found in this Report. It called for increased standards of management ability from officers and recommended the establishment of a chief executive post at each type of board to be filled either by a professional or medically qualified administrator, the determining factor in selection being ability and not professional qualifications. Like Griffiths, the Farquharson-Lang Committee had industrial organisations in mind when considering the relevance of a chief executive for the NHS. 'We see no fundamental difference in principle between the hospital service and other forms of organisation within which highly skilled experts exercise a considerable degree of independent judgement, subject to direction on broad policy determined by a board and interpreted for them through a general manager'.[43] For Farquharson-Lang the choice was a clear one which is echoed in the Griffiths Report. 'The advantages of a single channel of management and administration seem ... clearly to outweigh the possible disadvantages'.[44] Just as the Griffiths Report said much that was true also of Scotland, so Farquharson-Lang said much that applied to England and Wales. But in the mid-1960s the proposal for a chief executive 'was quickly seen to have fallen on fallow ground even in Scotland'.[45] Since then all official statements on the management of the NHS have consistently either rejected the case for a chief executive, as in England, or have avoided any mention of the subject, as in Scotland.

The implications of Griffiths for the medical profession will be equally profound if they materialise. The intention is to make doctors more aware of the costs they incur every time they decide upon a course of treatment. Without actually confronting clinical freedom head on, Griffiths (and now the government) wants doctors to participate more closely in the preparation of management budgets. Some commentators[46] do not think Griffiths makes sufficient inroads into clinical freedom and believe it will survive largely intact as a result. They see it as a 'fatal flaw' in the Report which will severely limit its impact upon practice.

An Assessment

As the title of this chapter attempts to convey, the NHS has been subjected to numerous organisational fixes since its inception. The rapidity with which these have been applied has increased since 1974 although England has borne the brunt of the battery of new initiatives. The pace of change has been considerably slower in Scotland and, indeed, many of the non-structural reforms that have taken root in England over the past few years, like privatisation and contracting out 'hotel' services, performance indicators, annual review meetings between Ministers and regional health authority chairmen and Rayner-type scrutinies of particular areas of administration, to name just a few, have not been reproduced in Scotland either in any guise or pursued with the same vigour. It is not clear why this should be so; there does not appear to have been a previous period in the NHS's history when there was such a marked divergence in policy style between Scotland and England despite a general tendency for Scotland to follow England's lead on major developments.

While the major developments described earlier have been applied in both countries, the enthusiasm for them in the SHHD is far less evident than in the DHSS. Moreover whereas all the initiatives launched in England combine to form a reasonably coherent strategy with fairly clear philosophical underpinnings, developments in Scotland have been less obviously coherent or ideological. They have occurred more haphazardly and cannot really be seen as components of a blueprint or grand design. The George Younger/John Mackay ministerial team at the Scottish Office shows little of the reforming zest and zeal regularly displayed by Norman Fowler and Kenneth Clarke at the DHSS where scarcely a week passes without at least one major policy announcement, whether it be the activities of general practitioners, links between the public and private health care sectors, or whatever. This is not necessarily a desirable way of proceeding, especially if the pronouncements are contradictory, but it is of interest to note the rather different policy and managerial styles evident in the two countries.

It remains to be seen whether all this hectic activity does more than merely heat up the system and offer a costly distraction from arguably more important concerns but it is of some significance that the initiatives launched in England have a more explicit and full-blooded ideological basis than the more faint-hearted approach evident in Scotland where notions of 'paying lip service' and 'going through the motions' spring readily to mind. There may be other factors at work, however, which are less immediately obvious in England and practically invisible in Scotland. All the initiatives being pursued have as their common theme the drive for efficiency and improved control over resource use. If little or no new money is to be made available to the NHS, then the only alternative is to use existing resources more efficiently in order to create the means for new developments or simply to stand still. As Day and Klein[(47)] have said, it is 'the vision of a NHS that could stretch scarce resources by improving the quality of management'.

The Treasury and Public Accounts Committee (PAC) are keeping a wary eye on health spending and unless the DHSS can be seen to be doing all it can to improve the husbandry of resources then they will draw the conclusion they have drawn before, i.e. that there is too much slack (and fat) in the Service, and act accordingly. It was the wrath of the PAC[(48)] in 1981 which triggered the *volte face* on reorganisation in England mentioned earlier although this was not the only factor. A Green Paper[(49)] published by the Treasury in March 1984 states clearly that 'the Health Service needs to achieve continuing efficiency improvements, from higher productivity and *better management*, following the example of private industry in recent years'. Elsewhere the paper states that while demands for additional spending in some policy fields will be no more than special pleading there will be genuine demands for increased spending which must be financed by reductions in programmes of lower priority, or by further efficiency savings. The NHS is in the frontline of increasing demands because of an ageing population, increasing affluence and rising expectations, the switch from institutional to community care and medical advances. It seems that the Treasury's unswerving gaze upon the DHSS has deflected attention from the situation in Scotland although almost one-third of expenditure within the Scottish Secretary's responsibility goes on health and personal social services. This, coupled with a healthier resource base and higher per capita spending on health, has probably sheltered Scotland from the full brunt of the cold winds blowing between the Treasury in Whitehall and the DHSS at the Elephant and Castle. Another factor disguising the situation may be the way in which the block grant for Scotland is assembled which may make it less easy for the Treasury to monitor closely what is happening within the individual spending programmes that go to make up the block grant.[(50)]

At a broader level, deeper environmental influences are at work. The

'Business Society' ethic is presently in vogue and manifestations of it in the health field are the Griffiths Report and numerous other initiatives designed to reinvigorate public sector management. The Business Society favours the private sector and self-help and is suspicious of public sector activities. The NHS is caught up in a wider debate about the future of the welfare state and public provision. Although not immune from this debate, the Scottish Health Service seems less central to it than the Service in England. From a geopolitical perspective, distance may have its virtues and may have the effect of reducing the potency of the rhetoric that fills the Whitehall/Westminster arena.

Of the two sets of changes that have either taken or will be taking place in Scotland the Griffiths Report and its proposal for general managers is potentially the most significant development. It will only be so, however, if it impinges directly upon the *process* of management. If it is no more than a role change or a minor structural modification then the chances are that nothing of real substance will change. It has been argued that Griffiths 'wants to change the culture. He is trying to do a very much bigger task than just appointing a general manager'.[51] If he succeeds then the way may be open to tackle some of the deep-seated and pervasive problems in the NHS which have remained resistant to the ministrations of successive governments. Among these is the oft-repeated aim of giving greater priority to certain client groups than they have received in the past and to shift the balance of care away from hospital, or institutional, care to community care.[52] It is here that another of Griffiths' proposals becomes crucial, namely, the involvement of clinicians in management.

As has been mentioned, doctors' daily decisions commit resources and often the sums involved are not negligible. Whatever other changes take place, whether at unit level or above, will be rendered irrelevant unless the actual process of incurring expenditure at the sharp end of the Service is disturbed and modified. Doctors cannot be dictated to but they can be guided and required to justify explicitly their commitment of resources. At present they tend to make decisions in an implicit manner with no apparent consideration of alternative uses. Again, because of the historically healthy resource base in Scotland, including health care manpower, the pressures for improved clinical management are less acute. But they are there nevertheless and can be expected to intensify. A note of caution must be sounded. Just as structural or managerial reforms have been deemed panaceas for the ills of running a complex organisation so there is a danger of clinical budgeting and costing being included in the same category. Making doctors more cost-conscious and ultimately more efficient and cost-effective are laudable aims but while these approaches have merit in some situations they can, if not handled with sensitivity, have major shortcomings. Care of the elderly is one area where the sensitive application of economic techniques is required otherwise one quickly reaches a position expressed vividly by Woody Allen: 'death is a great way to cut down on expenses'.[(53)] Economic and costing techniques have their uses but they do not provide the final 'single bullet' solutions to clinical priorities that some of their proponents envision.

If Griffiths, and government initiatives based on his Report, can help alter the climate in which managers and doctors operate and raise consciousness then he will have succeeded in an area which has defeated many before him. And if management *is* about to take a new direction then what was advocated for Scotland in 1966 by Farquharson-Lang may finally be about to be put to the test. But if Griffiths does not succeed then the well-worn cliche about the NHS being over-administered and under-managed will remain in 'good currency' as a valid judgement on the condition of health care management not only in Scotland but throughout the UK. At the same time the *limits* of administration should not be overlooked: perfect administration like perfect competition is an illusion. Misguidedly, general management could be regarded as the latest panacea to a range of deep-seated problems. Health care management is on trial. In the midst of all the activity could it be that this further round of reorganisation will be nothing less than yet another cruel diversion from the central policy issues confronting the NHS and health care? Although the lure of the organisational fix is forever present it is to be hoped not.

HEALTH SERVICE ORGANISATION: SCOTLAND 1974-1984

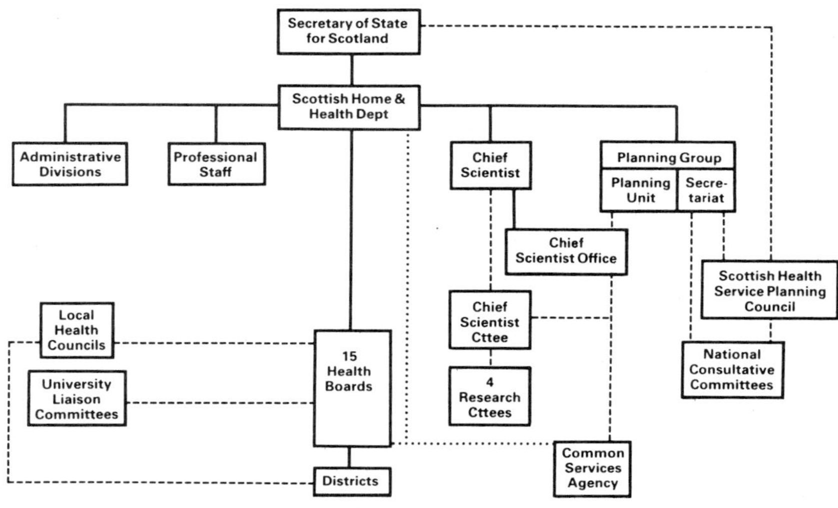

Note: Below Districts, until 1984, were units and/or sectors for day-to-day operational purposes. After June 1984 all Health Boards replaced Districts with Unit Management Groups (UMGs). Some UMGs retain the same boundaries as former Districts; others are closer in type and size to former units and sectors.

APPENDIX

HEALTH BOARD DISTRICTS

Board	HB District	Local Government District
Argyll & Clyde	Argyll & Bute	Argyll & Bute
(Population: 452.4)*	Dumbarton	Dumbarton
	Inverclyde	Inverclyde
	Renfrew	Renfrew
Ayrshire & Arran	North Ayrshire & Arran	Cunninghame
(Population: 374.1)		Kilmarnock & Loudoun
	South Ayrshire	Cumnock & Doon Valley
		Kyle & Carrick
Borders	(Single district)	Tweeddale
(Population: 100.5)		Ettrick & Lauderdale
		Roxburgh
		Berwickshire
Dumfries & Galloway	(Single district)	Wigtown
(Population: 144.2)		Stewartry
		Nithsdale
		Annandale & Eskdale
Fife	East Fife	North East Fife
(Population: 340.2)		Kirkcaldy
	West fife	Dunfermline
Forth Valley	Falkirk	Falkirk
(Population: 273.0)	Stirling	Stirling
		Clackmannan
Grampian	North	Banff & Buchan
(Populataion: 483.0)		Gordon
	South	City of Aberdeen
		Kincardine & Deeside
	West	Moray
Greater Glasgow	Western	Part of City of Glasgow
(Population: 1001.8)		Bearsden & Milngavie
		Clydebank
	Eastern	Part of City of Glasgow
	Northern	Part of City of Glasgow
		Strathkelvin

Board	HB District	Local Government District
	South Eastern	Part of City of Glasgow Eastwood
	South Western	Part of City of Glasgow
Highland (Population: 192.0)	North	Caithness Sutherland
	South	Badenoch & Strathspey Inverness Lochaber Nairn Ross & Cromarty Skye & Lochalsh
Lanarkshire (Population: 570.1)	Monklands/Cumbernauld	Cumbernauld Monklands
	Hamilton/East Kilbride	Hamilton East Kilbride
	Motherwell/Lanark	Lanark Motherwell
Lothian (Population: 746.1)	North Lothian	Part of City of Edinburgh East Lothian
	South Lothian	Part of City of Edinburgh Midlothian
	West Lothian	West Lothian
Orkney (Population: 18.9)	(Single district)	(Single district)
Shetland (Population: 25.9)	(Single district)	(Single district)
Tayside (Population: 396.8)	Dundee Angus Perth & Kinross	Dundee Angus Perth & Kinross
Western Isles (Population: 30.6)	(Single district)	(Single district)

* Population figures at June 1981 (in thousands).

References

1. H. Heclo, 'Social Politics and Policy Impacts' in M. Holden Jr and D.L. Dresang (eds.), *What Government Does* (Beverly Hills: Sage Publications, 1975).

2. See, for example, R. Schulz and S. Harrison, *Teams and Top Managers in the National Health Service,* King's Fund Project Paper No.41 (London: King's Fund Centre, 1983).

3. R. Klein, 'Policy making in the National Health Service', *Political Studies, 22,* No.1, March, 1974, pp.1-14.

4. See, for example, D.J. Hunter, 'Cometh the NHS Chief Executive?' *Hospital and Health Services Review, 79,* No.6, November, 1983.

5. Royal Commission on the National Health Service, *Report*, Cmnd. 7615 (London: HMSO, 1979).

6. Department of Health and Social Security (DHSS), *Patients First* (London: HMSO, 1979).

7. Scottish Home and Health Department (SHHD), *Structure and Management of the NHS in Scotland* (Edinburgh: HMSO, 1979).

8. DHSS, *Health Service Development: Structure and Management,* Health Circular HC (80) 8, July 1980.

9. SHHD, *Structure and Management of the NHS in Scotland,* NHS Circular No.1981 (GEN) 14, March 1981.

10. Appendix 1 to SHHD NHS Circular No. 1983 (GEN) 27, Parliamentary Question and Answer, 10 November 1983 (see note 11 for full reference to circular).

11. SHHD, *Structure and Management of the NHS in Scotland: Abolition of District Level of Management,* NHS Circular No. 1983 (GEN) 27, December 1983, paragraph 10, p.3.

12. *ibid*, paragraph 3, p.1.

13. *ibid,* paragraph 6, p.2.

14. R.R.W. Stewart, 'Scottish restructuring: institute view', *Health and Social Service Journal,* 24 April 1981, p.467.

15. P.M. Rees, 'Getting a grip on boundaries', *Health and Social Service Journal,* 29 May 1981, p.632.

16. W. Farquhar, 'Reorganisation in Scotland – the end or the beginning?', *Hospital and Health Services Review, 80,* No.1, January 1984, pp. 20-21.

17. Rees, *op.cit.*

18. S. Halpern, 'Scottish restructuring', *Health and Social Service Journal,* 3 April 1981, pp.374-5.

19. M. Keating and A. Midwinter, *The Scottish Office in the United Kingdom Policy Network,* Studies in Public Policy No.96 (Glasgow: Centre for the Study of Public Policy, University of Strathclyde, 1981).

20. R. Parry, 'Scotland as a laboratory for public administration', paper prepared for 6th annual conference of the PSA United Kingdom Politics Work Group , Glasgow, 1981.

21. D.J. Hunter, 'Centre-Periphery Relations in the National Health Service: Facilitators or Inhibitors of Innovation?' in K. Young (ed.), *National Interests and Local Government,* Joint Studies in Public Policy 7 (London: Heinemann, 1983). For a different view, see D.K. Nichol 'Current issues in administration: a more centralised bureaucracy?' *British Medical Journal, 288,* 28 April 1984, pp. 1317-9.

22. I. Wickings (ed.), *Effective Unit Management* (London: King Edward's Hospital Fund, 1983).

23. *NHS Management Inquiry* (Leader: Roy Griffiths), (London: DHSS, October 1983).

24. SHHD, *The General Management Function in the NHS in Scotland: Proposals for Discussion* (Edinburgh: SHHD, June 1984).

25. *NHS Management Inquiry, op.cit.*, paragraph 4, p.11.

26. *ibid,* paragraph 8, p.12.

27. *ibid.*, paragraph 6, p.12.

28. D.J. Hunter, 'Cometh the NHS Chief Executive?', *op.cit.*

29. Schulz and Harrison, *op.cit.* p.21.

30. *NHS Management Inquiry*, *op.cit.* paragraph 15, p.17.

31. House of Commons Social Services Committee, *Griffiths NHS Management Inquiry Report*, First Report, Session 1983-84, HC 209 (London: HMSO, 1984), paragraph 4, p.vii.

32. *NHS Management Inquiry, op.cit,* paragraph 3, p.3.

33. *ibid,* paragraph 4, p.4.

34. DHSS, *Health Services Management: Implementation of the NHS Management Inquiry Report,* Health Circular HC (84) 13, June 1984.

35. DHSS Press Release, 'Griffiths Report – Health Authorities to Identify General Managers', 84/173, 4 June 1984, p.3.

36. Hansard Weekly Reports, *Parliamentary Debates,* House of Commons, 4 May 1984, column 647, p.340.

37. *ibid,* col. 648, p.340.

38. SHHD, *The General Management Function in the NHS in Scotland:...', op.cit.*, paragraphs 6.1 and 5.1.

39. *ibid,* paragraph 6.2.

40. DHSS, *Health Services Management:..., op.cit.*, paragraph 6, p.2.

41. D.J. Hunter, 'Organising for Health: The National Health Service in the United Kingdom', *Journal of Public Policy, 2,* Part 3, August 1982, 263-300.

42. SHHD, *Administrative Practice of Hospital Boards in Scotland* (Chairman: Farquharson-Lang), (Edinburgh: HMSO, 1966).

43. *ibid,* paragraph 211, pp.63-4.

44. *ibid,* paragraph 212, p.64.

45. B. Watkin, *The National Health Service: The First Phase 1948-1974 and After* (London: Allen and Unwin, 1978), p.105.

46. A. Ludbrook and G.H. Mooney, 'Clinical freedom, efficiency, and the Griffiths Report', *British Medical Journal, 288*, 4 February 1984, pp.420-1.

47. P. Day and R. Klein, 'The mobilisation of consent versus the management of conflict: decoding the Griffiths report', *British Medical Journal, 287,* 10 December 1983, p.1813.

48. House of Commons Public Accounts Committee, *Financial Control and Accountability in the NHS,* Seventeenth Report, Session 1980-1, HC 255 (London: HMSO, 1981).

49. HM Treasury, *The Next Ten Years: Public Expenditure and Taxation into the 1990s,* Cmnd. 9189 (London: HMSO, 1984), paragraph 39, p.15.

50. P. Madgwick and R. Rose, 'Introduction' in P. Madgwick and R. Rose (eds.), *The Territorial Dimension in UK Politics* (London: Macmillan, 1982).

51. House of Commons Social Services Committee, *op.cit.,* paragraph 244, p. 80.

52. A.M. Gray and D.J. Hunter, 'Priorities and Resource Allocation in the Scottish Health Service: Some Problems in 'Planning and Implementation'', *Policy and Politics, 11,* No.4, 1983, pp.417-437.

53. Quoted in J. Avorn, 'Benefit and Cost Analysis in Geriatric Care: Turning Age Discrimination into Health Policy', *The New England Journal of Medicine, 310,* No.20, 17 May 1984, p.1297.

REORGANISATION AND INDUSTRIAL RELATIONS IN THE NATIONAL HEALTH SERVICE IN SCOTLAND[1]

JOHN W. LEOPOLD and P.B. BEAUMONT
UNIVERSITY OF GLASGOW

Introduction.

The long drawn-out dispute in 1982 saw industrial relations in the National Health Service at an all-time low. That dispute was the first to involve in a united way all of the many sub groups of staff employed in the NHS – administrative and clerical, nursing, ancillary, para-medical, technical, works and doctors. The decade of the 1970s had seen a steady build up to this situation; a dramatic growth in trade union and professional association membership and organisation; various groups of health service staff taking industrial action for the first time; and difficulties associated with a relatively strict enforcement of incomes policy. Industrial relations in the NHS were also characterised by an extremely centralised bargaining system through one general and eight functional Whitley Councils; a relatively under-developed personnel and industrial relations management function; inter-union competition and rivalry between trade unions and professional associations.[2]

In the aftermath of the 1982 dispute, industrial relations in the NHS have somewhat faded from the public eye. But developments are taking place in four particular areas – reorganisation of the NHS in Scotland, privatisation, expenditure cuts and the possibility of the recommendations of the Griffiths Report being introduced into Scotland[3] Each of these issues will be examined in this paper, but central consideration will be given to the process of reorganisation as through this some of the dominant problems and concerns about the way the NHS is managed can be examined. These include the relationships between the government, via the Scottish Home and Health Department, and the fifteen Scottish health boards; the relationships between the health boards as employers and their employees; the complex inter-relationships between trade unions and professional organisations; and the role of the personnel function in the management of the health service.

Reorganisation of the NHS in Scotland

The details of the policy which led to the reorganisation of the NHS in Scotland are dealt with in David Hunter's chapter and need no further elaboration. Rather we will concentrate on the substantive issues that had to be settled between management and staff interests once the decision was taken to remove districts. These included the timing of reorganisation; the oversight of grading levels of senior posts in the new structures; the shape of the new structures; the arrangements for slotting in and competition for the new posts; the arrangements for officers displaced by the restructuring; appeals procedure and details of a premature retirement policy. Some of these points were for negotiation, others consultation; some on an all-Scotland basis involving all the relevant trade unions and professional organisations, others at a health board level, sometimes with all organisations, sometimes only with those representing a particular category of staff. It is a complex picture which we will attempt to analyse under the headings outlined above, relating the events to the central features of the industrial relations system in the NHS.

The Impetus Towards Reorganisation

Following the publication of *Patients First,*[(4)] which outlined the Conservative government's philosophy for the management of the health service in England and Wales, the Scottish Home and Health Department issued its consultative paper *Structure and Management of the National Health Service in Scotland.*[(5)] The health service in England had three tiers of organisation – regional, area and district and *Patients First* proposed, among other things, the removal of the area tier. Scotland, on the other hand was essentially a two tier system, area and district, but five of the fifteen health boards operated without districts. The remaining ten health boards had between two and five districts, giving a total of twenty-nine districts in the country as a whole. The decision to create districts was an administrative act of the health boards at the time of the 1974 reorganisation; in Scotland only the health boards are statutory bodies.

The government's aims for reorganisation in Scotland at this stage can be summarised:

1. Boards should work towards removing districts and replace them by units of management, but those boards which felt that this was not possible could make a case for their retention.

2. Management arrangements at local level should be strengthened with greater delegation of authority and responsibility to units of management.

3. Local functional managers of non-clinical support services were to become accountable to unit administrators not to area functional managers.

These basic aims were later confirmed in March 1981 when the SHHD issued its circular on reorganisation.(6) Health boards were still permitted to be flexible in their implementation of the circular. The size and shape of the new units of management were left to local circumstances and no date was prescribed centrally for the reorganisation.

The laissez-faire approach in fact meant that a number of boards, Argyll and Clyde, Grampian, Greater Glasgow, Highland, Lanarkshire, Lothian and Tayside decided to devolve greater responsibility to unit management within a framework of districts. Three boards, later known as the 'first wave' boards, Ayrshire and Arran, Fife, Forth Valley, decided at an early stage that they would remove districts, while Borders, and Dumfries and Galloway health boards, although not having districts, also proceeded to revise their management structure in line with the philosophy of maximum devolution to units. Between March 1981 and the autumn of 1983 two boards, Argyll and Clyde and Grampian shifted into the removing districts camp, but then Argyll and Clyde changed its decision yet again and this, as we shall see, precipitated a directive approach by the Secretary of State.

Although the first wave boards examined their structures and produced proposals for new units, some based on geography, some on functional specialities, some on a mixture of these two basic principles, a period of uncertainty, confusion and frustration ensued in the attempts to designate a date for reorganisation and in establishing the staffing arrangements for the new posts. The Secretary of State's hoped for implementation date of April 1982 proved impossible to achieve. Meanwhile, in England the new District Health Authorities took over on 1st April 1982, and the Welsh reorganisation was effected a year later.

The staffing arrangements for England and Wales were jointly determined by management and staff interests in the General Whitley Council, with details for specific staff groups being negotiated in the appropriate functional Whitley Council. A new mechanism was established to deal with arrangements for reorganisation in Scotland, the General Whitley Council, Reorganisation Sub-Committee (Scotland). Representation on the staff side of this body was via the functional Whitley Councils which eliminated any potential difficulties of TUC affiliated unions refusing to sit on the same body as non-TUC professional organisations. This committee met three times, in July October and December, 1983.

There was, however, a basic difference of opinion between management and staff over the timing of reorganisation; management favoured an early date because two years had passed since circular 1981 (GEN) 14 was issued, while the staff side favoured a later date so that all boards could move simultaneously. Initially a compromise date of 1st April 1984 was agreed; posts affected by reorganisation which became vacant were frozen and the first wave boards proceeded with local consultation and negotiation.

It is worth noting at this stage that not all organisations involved in the health service actually favoured the proposed reorganisation in Scotland. Trade unions and professional associations felt that it was an unnecessary imposition on Scotland from London and, moveover, that it was stimulated by political prejudice rather than any logical approach to the efficient management of the service; the prejudice that the service was over-administered and that therefore the number of administrators should be reduced. As we have seen a number of health boards had decided not to remove districts and when Argyll and Clyde health board again changed its decision and decided not to remove districts, the laissez-faire approach of the Scottish Office turned to compulsion and direction.

The Secretary of State's announcement that boards would be instructed to remove districts came in the form of a written answer to a parliamentary question on 10th November 1983.[(7)] The details soon followed in a circular.[(8)] But this was direction from the centre without the direct hand of the Secretary of State. Both the parliamentary answer and the circular clearly stated that the decision followed a meeting between the Minister for Health and Social Work and the health board chairmen and had "the concurrence of the chairmen". This is further evidence of the growing power and influence of the chairmen, some of whom in this instance were party to a decision which was not the policy of their health board. The parliamentary answer also reflected the latest development in health service management thinking in England – the Griffiths Report.(9) The Secretary of State took the view that a common form of organisation would provide a firm basis for consideration of Griffiths – a point to which we shall return.

The compulsory removal of districts threw the timetable into disorder. Those boards which were well on the way to meeting the 1st April 1984 deadline did not want to be held up. As they had all decided in principle to abolish districts some two years earlier many senior management posts had been left unfilled or were held by people 'acting up' one or more grades. On the other hand those boards which now had to devise new structures needed as much time as possible. The staff side of the Reorganisation Sub-Committee (Scotland) favoured a late common date, although there was some division as to what date was actually feasible and indeed a minority of the trade union representatives wanted to meet the Secretary of State and argue the case against compulsory removal of districts in all boards. The final compromise was that the first wave boards would proceed on 1st April, 1984 the others would reorganise by 1st June 1984, but that no board could make appointments to reorganised posts from outwith their own board until such time as all boards were ready to proceed to the round of appointments for officers 'displaced' as a result of reorganisation. Thus the first wave boards had to wait at least two months with vacant posts before being able to appoint displaced officers from outwith the boards, and in practice the delay was much longer. In effect it could be argued that through this device the staff side achieved their objective of a common date at the point where it mattered – when competition for posts moved to an all-Scotland basis.

The Overview of Gradings

The delay in fixing an implementation date for Scotland did have an advantage in that the experience of reorganisation in England and in Wales was available to management and staff sides alike. Indeed the principal agreement, that on staffing arrangements which determined the procedures for filling posts, was reached in the General Whitley Council prior to the first meeting of the Reorganisation Sub-Committee (Scotland). One vital issue which both the English and Welsh Authorities had had to deal with was the question of ensuring that there was consistency of grading of senior posts in the new structure. In England this task had been undertaken by the Regional Health Authorities, whereas in Wales the task was undertaken by chairmen of the Welsh Health Authorities on an informal basis. What device would be used in Scotland?

The need for some overview of gradings arose because the decision on what exactly should replace districts was left to health boards to determine. This was consistent with the devolutionary philosophy of the restructuring exercise, but in marked contrast to the 1974 reorganisation when the Scottish Home and Health Department authorised all the senior grades. But the devolved approach had the danger that grading drift could emerge and similar posts in different health boards could be graded differently. Grading drift is seen by the Department as against the interests of the taxpayer to the extent that people are paid more than the appropriate rate for doing a similar job.

The initial proposal by management was to use MAGOG, the Management Group on Gradings. Created in 1981 as MGAFGS, the Management Group on Administrative and Finance Gradings, its remit was extended to senior nursing grades in April 1983. MAGOG was a way of devolving collectively to health authorities grading control based on a system of job evaluation so as to achieve consistency. It was intended to operate both in normal circumstances and in the context of restructuring. Its creation and the extension of its remit were both agreed by health board chairmen who also agreed that boards would comply with the Group.

There were some fears from within the service that MAGOG would not be able to cope with the demands that restructuring would have placed on it, and that involvement in restructuring could undermine MAGOG's role as a grading review mechanism. Even more fundamental objections came from the staff side. Firstly, the trade unions opposed MAGOG anyway because it is a unilateral management job evaluation technique with no trade union input, and secondly because in the context of reorganisation the use of MAGOG to evaluate grades would cut across the agreements on grading reached jointly through the Whitley system.

A new ad hoc body then emerged – the Scottish Chairmen's Grading Committee, subsequently known as the Fyfe Committee after its own chairman, Mr. W.S. Fyfe, the chairman of Ayrshire and Arran health board. In the first instance the Fyfe Committee comprised the chairmen of the five first wave boards; two members from the mainland single district boards; three assessors, a board secretary, a treasurer and a chief area nursing officer and was serviced by a secretariat of two drawn from serving health board officers. Later chairmen from the other boards were added. Like MAGOG, but unlike many similar exercises in private industry, there was no staff side input.

The Fyfe Committee was granted full delegation of power to ensure consistency of grading by the Secretary of State. Thus he could claim that any grading decisions arrived at by the Committee were not those of the Secretary of State, nor of the SHHD, but of the boards themselves acting collectively through their chairmen. The service as a whole had been given the responsibility of policing the decisions of individual health boards.

The role and powers of the Fyfe Committee were the subject of debate in the Reorganisation Sub-Committee (Scotland) and the staff side were assured that its task would be equivalent to that done by the Regions in England and that it would not impose decisions. On the other hand the Department circular on the Committee makes it clear that unless boards can supply further information to justify their grading then the decision of the Fyfe Committee stands.

Clearly with these two contradictory views problems would arise if, and when, the Fyfe Committee overturned any grading submitted to it by boards. This indeed happened. The situation is further complicated by the fact the boards discussed their structures and gradings with their staff locally. The trade unions take the view that these discussions took the form of negotiations and that the grading structure finally reached was in effect negotiated agreements, especially as they were agreed within the context of the reorganised structure costing no more than its predecessor, and in the light of functional Whitley Council agreements on grade indication factors. The Department took the view that local talks were only consultative and that the boards acting in concert through the Fyfe Committee took the final decision and that is the one which has to be upheld. Each board was represented on the Committee through its chairman and could therefore not justifiably object to the decisions reached.

Many boards, however, did find themselves in an awkward situation when the Fyfe Committee altered gradings. Their staff sides were arguing that Fyfe was only advisory and therefore boards ought to honour their agreements with the staff side. In some cases boards did re-submit, but usually without success, and the ad hoc mechanism had no appeal channel built into it, although the original MAGOG proposals did allow for disputed gradings to be the subject of discussions betwen the board and MAGOG and for final resolution by the SHHD. With Fyfe, however, reasons for changing gradings were not given to boards. Individual officers, on the other hand, have a right of appeal on the grading attached to their post under existing Whitley agreements, and staff sides are threatening a number of individual appeals once the new structures are in operation. Such appeals are likely to be strongly resisted by the Department on the grounds that it was the health boards themselves who agreed to accept the Fyfe Committee's verdict on the grade, rather than their own original view. Indeed the Department felt it necessary to caution health boards against premature appeals and urged them to allow a reasonable time to elapse for new posts to become fully established and post holders to settle in.[(10)]

Lack of Coterminous Structures

It is not yet clear how many posts actually had their grading proposals altered (and some were upgraded), but it does appear that a disproportionate number were nursing posts rather than administrative or finance ones. This relates to another feature of the structures a number of health boards have determined – administrative, finance and nursing units of management are not coterminous.

Boards were given a free hand to determine their own structures by the SHHD, and did so in consulation with their staff interests. Some boards, such as Ayrshire and Arran evolved a structure that was largely based on functional specialities; others, such as Forth Valley based the structure largely on geography. The norm, however, has been to draw up structures based on a mixture of functional speciality and geography.

With the removal of districts the previous management body, the District Executive Group (District Administrator, District Finance Officer, District Nursing Officer, District Medical Officer) ceased to exist. In its place came the Unit Management Team which comprises the Unit Administrator, Director of Nursing Services and a senior member of the medical staff and usually, but not always, the Finance Officer. The fact that what is understood by a 'unit' varies according to the staff group concerned may indeed pose some difficulties when the new structures are functioning. It is not clear in situations where two nursing units relate to one administration unit, whether the two Directors of Nursing Services will be part of a unit team with the administrator covering both nursing units, or whether the administrator will be part of two unit teams, or indeed whether the DNS of the smaller unit will only relate to a unit team via another DNS.

To fit in to the philosophy of devolved power and responsibilities, the administrative units had to be of such a size to attract salaries which would in turn attract competent senior managers, but at the same time be close to the delivery of patient services. Finance units are related to budgets and there tend to be fewer finance units than administrative units in all the structures that have been evolved. The problematic area, however, was nursing. Where administrative units were determined by functional speciality – acute services, geriatric services, psychiatric services – then it was relatively easy to have nursing units to match them. The difficulty lay with what to do with two particular services – maternity and community. The first is characterised by relatively small numbers of beds and staff; the second by geographical spread. In some administrative units one or both of these services were subsumed within larger units; in other boards they constituted a separate unit.

On the nursing side, however, the nurses who worked in these services are generally represented by separate organisations from nurses in other areas – the Royal College of Midwives for maternity, and the Scottish Health Visitors Association for community. These organisations see themselves as professional associations rather than as trade unions, and in their view it was vital for the future well being of their profession that separate maternity and community units existed for nurses, so that midwives and health visitors could aspire to become Directors of Nursing Services for their respective specialties. The pressure to have these separate units was particularly strong in Greater Glasgow where the agreed structure comprised eleven administrative units, nine finance and nineteen nursing. The RCM was outraged at Lanarkshire Health Board's proposal not to have a separate midwifery unit.

The corollary of being separate was that the small maternity and community units tended to attract lower gradings when assessed by the Fyfe Committee, and indeed in some cases the removal of maternity from a larger general nursing unit threatened the grading of that post as well. Thus it is the nurse organisations which are most affected by and concerned about the grading reversals of the Fyfe Committee.

While the particular interests of the RCM and the SHVA pressed them towards separate units, the main professional organisation for nurses, the Royal College of Nursing, strongly favoured coterminous units, particularly with the spectre of the Griffiths Report in the background. This proposed general managers in the units and if these were to be drawn from the existing second in line officers in units, then nursing would be at a distinct disadvantage if nursing units did not match administrative or medical ones.

While Greater Glasgow presents the most extreme picture, the situation in the rest of Scotland varies markedly. In some boards all the maternity and community services were grouped together to form reasonably large units which attracted relatively high gradings for both nurses and administrators, but where separate small maternity and community nursing units exist the gradings are generally low. While this may create a limited career structure for midwives and health visitors in their own speciality, it does mean that senior nurse managers will continue to be drawn from the general and psychiatric areas.

Consultation/Negotiation at Health Board Level

The question of timing, the overview of gradings and staffing arrangements were dealt with at national level, but a number of issues arising out of reorganisation were dealt with at health board level. The mechanisms developed for dealing with local consultation and negotiation were essentially the same throughout the country. Initially meetings were held between management and all the staff interests in the board but with the NALGO branch secretary always acting as the local staff side secretary, as was the case nationally. These were based on ad hoc reorganisation committees rather than on existing joint consultative committees and thus got round the problem, which exists in many boards, of TUC and non-TUC organisations refusing to sit together in the same committees. Once consultation had taken place on structures, the large all-embracing committees broke down into smaller groups dealing with particular categories of staff.

The essential issue to be decided was which new posts were for slotting in and which for competition and the agreement on staffing arrangements clearly stated that this was a mattter for negotiation at board level.[(11)] Slotting in was where the job was virtually unchanged and the post holder continued to undertake substantially the same duties; competition was for posts where a number of detailed definitions were met. These agreements are designed to give existing board employees the first opportunity to be appointed to the new posts and to minimise the number of officers displaced by the reorganisation. An additional agreement gave personal protection of salary and conditions of service for a specified number of years for officers whose posts were downgraded as a result of reorganisation.

Local negotiations had to take place within the confines of agreements on equivalent grade and substantial promotion which were reached in the relevant functional Whitley Councils. There was some delay in reaching this agreement for administrative and clerical staff as the staff side insisted that Board Secretary and Treasurer posts should be subject to competition as these posts had all been upgraded by one main scale to reflect new responsibilities. Management resisted this for some time, and in the absence of a firm agreement the first wave boards proceeded locally on the basis of the management offer, which reflected the agreement which had been used in England some two years previously.

One specific area where representation from staff interests led to changes in board plans for restructuring concerned the establishment (or not) of area posts for professions supplementary to medicine e.g. physiotherapists, speech therapists, radiographers. In some boards such posts were established for one or more of these professions, usually on a part time, part managerial, part clinical basis. One exception to this was the attempt to establish area radiographer posts. This was opposed by the BMA which argued that the responsibility for radiography lay with clinicians and a dangerous conflict could arise if radiographer managers were appointed. This is but one reflection of a continuing conflict between doctors and a range of medical related professions which have responsibilities and duties in similar areas.

Generally these local negotiations seem to have operated smoothly through the special reorganisation committees that were established which were made up of all organisations, both trade unions and professional associations. What potential might there be for such arrangements to continue?

The TUC unions' basic objection to the presence of non- affiliated organisations is that they undermine the possibility of developing common staff side positions because their views on matters such as privatisation, financial cutbacks and overseas patients are so diametrically opposed to those of the TUC unions. Indeed some trade union officers would go as far as to argue that it is only the trade unions which are interested in the overall service that the health service provides, whereas the professional associations are largely and primarily interested in their profession. Thus the trade union view is that the arrangements for reorganisation were a one-off arrangement which came to an end once reorganisation was in place. Indeed negotiations on procedural agreements for the new structures are taking place in the existing joint consultative committees rather than the reorganisation committees. Without the common purpose of reorganisation it is unlikely that TUC and non-TUC organisations will work together. This will be particularly so as issues such as Griffiths, privatisation and financial cutbacks come to the fore in the autumn; issues on which the TUC and non-TUC organisations are divided.

Personnel Management and Industrial Relations in the New Structures

District Executive Groups operated on a consensus basis, with collective responsibility for running services, budgets, and personnel matters. In effect any one chief officer had a power of veto over the others. Consensus management has been under fire for some time; accused of 'lowest common denominator decisions' and of long delays in the management process.[12] The thrust of reorganisation is towards individual accountability and responsibility, although some element of collaborative team working is expected from unit teams. Second in line officers will have control of budgets and resources and will also have responsibility for industrial relations at unit level including the power to dismiss.

With the removal of districts the twenty District Personnel Officers were also removed. The essential dilemma facing boards in reorganising the personnel function was whether to centralise at area level or to decentralise to the units. If unit personnel posts were established it was unlikely that they would attract senior gradings and hence would not attract senior experienced people to the posts. On the other hand if all the personnel resources were centralised at area headquarters then all sorts of problems and difficulties could arise and possibly grow at local level if assistance and advice was not readily on hand.

Most boards have evolved a compromise whereby there will be a personnel presence at unit level, but these officers will essentially be dealing with the personnel administration aspects of the function – appointments, recruitment, contracts of employment, terms and conditions of service, and while providing some limited industrial relations advice, the burden of this work will be undertaken by unit administrators and area personnel departments. The latter have been strengthened by drawing in the former DPOs and allocating responsibility for developing policies to specific officers. In some cases the area personnel department has been further strengthened by the appointment of additional officers with special responsibility for industrial relations policy. Thus the intention is to have the area personnel department developing policy and guidelines and, indeed, training for the new unit managers who now have industrial relations as a major element of their responsibility. This centralised policy and advice service is supported by unit personnel officers dealing with the more routine aspects of the personnel function.

It remains to be seen whether this structure can overcome a problem which existed previously in multi-district boards of policies being interpreted in different ways in different districts, and of trade unions seeking to level up practice in all districts to the level of the best. If anything, with the multiplicity of units which now exist in *all* boards the potential for variation increases and thus places additional responsibility on both unit managers and central personnel policy makers and advisors.

One controversial point in this reorganisation of the personnel function has been the question of the need for separate nursing personnel officers. Under the district structure, Senior Nursing Officers (personnel) existed in a number of districts, but there was evidence that their duties largely fell into the personnel administration category and when industrial relations issues were to the fore the District Personnel Officer became heavily involved. There has therefore been considerable pressure to establish a unified personnel service at unit level. In some boards this has been achieved; in others it is still a matter of controversy.

The devolution of the power to dismiss to single officers, rather than the consensus management group has concerned trade unions. They felt that the consensus system meant that any one chief officer wanting to dismiss an employee had first to justify their position to three other senior managers, and that this often tempered what might have been ill-advised decisions. In Glasgow in particular the trade unions attempted to press that the authority to dismiss should be vested in more than one officer. Their concern was that errors in judgement would be made by senior managers which from the trade union point of view would have to be challenged through the appeals mechanism. If individual senior managers were frequently the subject of appeals this would result in a situation where the board would either have to dismiss the appeal or dismiss the senior manager. While private companies might be inclined to the latter, it was feared that health boards may opt for the former.

Displaced Officers and Premature Retirement

A central concern of the staff sides was that the reorganisation should not lead to compulsory redundancies. Boards had to achieve their reorganisation in such a way that the new structures cost no more than the old, and their targets for reducing management costs, set in 1982, were adhered to.[(13)] The General Whitley Council agreement on staffing arrangements protected those officers displaced from their employing boards by ensuring that they had first opportunity for posts in other boards at the first stage of all-Scotland competition. When the second wave of boards commenced reorganisation at the end of 1983 it was agreed that this stage could not commence until all boards had completed their internal process. Thus the first wave boards would have to wait until at least 1st June, or longer if any board had not completed its internal processes.

In the event the number of displaced officers was relatively few; about a score on the administration and finance side, somewhat less for nurses, but they did cover the entire range of the grading structure. The small number was largely because posts likely to be affected by reorganisation were left unfilled or filled by officers in an acting-up capacity even before the formal agreement specified that this must be the case after 1st August 1983. In fact a number of first wave boards were unable to fill all their unit posts and began the reorganised system on 1st April with key posts vacant, despite attempts by at least one board to obtain a special dispensation from the agreed staffing arrangements timetable. Overall, at the end of the internal stage of the process there were more unfilled posts than displaced officers, although the grades and specialisms of these did not necessarily match. Some boards chose to retain officers in a supernumerary capacity until such time as a suitable vacancy arose.

In order to try and coordinate the lists of displaced officers and vacant posts a clearing house was established which came into operation in July and even at that stage some boards were still holding up the process as they had not made appointments to their new unit posts. The net effect of these delays and uncertainties was that open competition for vacant posts did not take place until October and in some boards key posts in the new structures were unfilled for over six months.

A notorious feature of the reorganisation in England had been the massive number of premature retirements over and above that estimated by the DHSS; 435 compared to 2,830.[14] In January 1984 the SHHD estimated that some 200 posts at District level would be directly affected by reorganisation but that it was not possible to estimate accurately the number likely to come forward for early retirement.[15] Anxious that the public criticism of the situation in England was not repeated the Department embarked on an informal estimate of likely premature retirements with the Area Personnel Officers' group. In Scotland individual applications had to be vetted by the health boards and submitted to the Department for approval. In this way a stricter control was kept in the number of premature retirements.

An SHHD circular in 1983 stressed that there was a need to demonstrate where the reduncancy was occurring to justify a retirement claim and that the call upon the superannuation fund had to be totally justified. This letter was later the subject of a staff side complaint in the Reorganisation Sub-Committee as in their view this was the SHHD exceeding the terms of a Whitley Council agreement. Notwithstanding this, the Department continued to interpret the agreement in a very rigid way in Scotland, to the extent that a number of officers seeking premature retirement, but whose cases were not immediately accepted by the SHHD, had to apply for posts they did not really want, and to which boards did not really expect to appoint them, in order to remain eligible for premature retirement.

By the end of the first stage of reorganisation some fifty five applications for premature retirement had been approved. It was expected that the proportion of early retirers/total staff employed would be even lower in Scotland than Northern Region which had the lowest proportion of premature retirements in England. A number of applications were rejected either because the applicant was too young or because subsequently they were offered posts, and two of the rejections were the subject of an appeal by the relevant trade union.

Cat and Mouse

While reorganisation has been the focus of events in the NHS in Scotland, privatisation, cuts and, most recently Griffiths have been the key words in England and Wales. Until June 1984, these issues were rather dormant in Scotland, partly because attention and energy has been directed towards reorganisation, but partly because of different attitudes and policies of health boards in Scotland to them. While health boards used reorganisation to justify their delay in responding to the Secretary of State's September 1983 circular on privatisation, equally the Department was slow to produce a promised discussion paper on Griffiths in Scotland. This cat and mouse response ended abruptly when the document on Griffiths was produced on June 6th[(16)] and some two weeks later boards were instructed to put some of their services out to tender.[(17)]

Privatisation

In the summer of 1983 health boards were requested to test the cost effectiveness of catering, domestic and laundry services by putting them out to tender, and to report to the Department by April 1984.[(18)] Compared with England little progress has been made in contracting-out services in Scotland. Boards were treading cautiously, partly out of a concern not to rush into changes which might be regretted later, partly from a belief that the in-house service is best and partly from a fear of industrial action by unions whose members would be affected.

What happened between the autumn of 1983 and the spring of 1984 was that boards examined those areas of the services under threat in which costs were above average. Such areas have been, with trade union approval, thoroughly examined by work study teams and in some cases bonus schemes introduced in the belief that this would improve efficiency and make the service less vulnerable to outside tender. In short the threat of privatisation has enabled boards to reach agreement locally with trade unions to improve efficiency, sometimes at the cost of jobs, in areas which management had long felt required change but in which they had not been able to implement it. In return there was an understanding that boards would not proceed with privatisation.

Although aware of these developments, Ministers were not satisfied. Hence the circular instructing health boards (except Island boards) to put services for their headquarters and at least two hospitals out to tender by the end of 1984 and to prepare a three year programme for other services. Significantly this decision followed discussions between the Minister for Health and Social Work and health board chairmen.

Trade unions in the NHS and the Labour Party were immediate and strong in their condemnation of the circular. NUPE discounted the alleged savings to be made from privatisation and saw the decision as a political, ideological act. A campaign of active resistance was called for. The STUC, through its health and social services committee, pledged to fight the decision and to co-ordinate the trade union response. In August the main TUC unions involved obtained legal advice that the circular was not mandatory on boards. This opinion, combined with considerable trade union activity helped Fife Health Board not to put the services out to tender, but instead to seek full co-operation with all parties to make savings and increase efficiency under Board managerial control. Fife were the first board to decide on the issue and their decision has since been challenged by the Minister, but the Fife decision remains a significant one from the unions' point of view in that the chairman of Fife Health Board is also the chairman of the Ancillary Staffs Whitley Council. Since the Fife decision in August some other boards have followed suit, whereas others are pressing ahead in putting the required services out to tender. Privatisation will be the dominant issue in health service industrial relations in the autumn of 1984 and beyond.

Griffiths

The Griffiths Report on management in the NHS recommended, inter alia, the appointment of general managers at each level of management. The government accepted the recommendations and were proceeding to implement them in England.(19) In Scotland, the Secretary of State was in general agreement with the principles underlying the Report's recommendations, but the SHHD promised a discussion document early in 1984 before proceeding. The date for this was progressively put back and the document only appeared in early June calling for comments by the end of September. While again reorganisation proved a convenient excuse for the delay, it was clear that there was not a unified view among all the professional interests in St. Andrews House.

The Secretary of State favoured the appointment of general managers at board level by the end of 1985, but at unit level there is to be an examination of unit structures, management information and budgeting systems prior to the introduction of general managers. This examination is to be completed by the end of 1986. General managers are to be appointed "on the basis of the criterion of the best person for the job, regardless of discipline" and "might be, but need not be, drawn from existing chief officers."[20]

The professional organisations whose members will be affected by the appointment of general managers are opposed to the plan.[21] A major concern is where the new general managers will be drawn from and how such a general manager would relate to the professional and clinical responsibilities to the chief officers in each management area. It is in those boards without coterminous units that most problems in this area will arise and this is primarily why the Royal College of Nursing was particularly concerned about such structures. What chance have nurses got of becoming general managers if nursing management is divided between two or three units, whereas administrators and doctors command large budgets and staff resources? What authority will non-nursing general managers have over nursing managers?

The trade union responses to the Social Services Committee expressed concern about the removal of consensus management. We have already seen that the change from districts to units has ended consensus management at that level and has led to problems on the question of the authority to dismiss. The appointment of general managers at health board level will pose similar questions there. The relationship of the personnel officer to top management may need reviewed. Should the APO continue to be responsible to the board secretary, or should his or her role as personnel officer to the whole board be emphasised by making the line of accountability direct to the general manager? A whole number of detailed questions about how the general manager will actually operate remain unanswered and while some points may be clarified during the consultation process, many will only be answered when general managers are actually in post.

Financial Cuts

While financial cuts and closures have been the focus of much trade union activity and opposition in England, this has not been the case to the same extent in Scotland. During 1983 there was a one percent cut in resources, but this was later reinstated and Scottish boards were not subject to forced staffing reductions as their English and Welsh counterparts were in September 1983.[22] Where financial savings are being made by boards they are not dramatic. It is largely a case of new things not happening; a ward not opening, a building not being upgraded, a facility not being developed. Therefore there are few concrete issues for the trade unions to focus on and attempt to rally their members and the public around, although protests are made as each new saving exercise is announced.

At an all-Scotland level, the Scottish Trade Union Congress initiated the Scottish Health Service Campaign, calling for a real two percent growth in health service spending to cover the changing age profile of the population and developments in medical technology. This campaign has involved trade unions, local authorities, health councils and health consumer groups. A network of thirty local committees held over fifty public meetings throughout Scotland in the spring of 1984. A petition calling for the two percent real growth raised 250,000 signatures, and was presented to the Prime Minister on 27th June 1984. The steering committee of the Campaign recognises that its task is a long-term one and intend campaigning for the NHS through the lifetime of the present Conservative government and possibly beyond.

Summary and Conclusions

Issues about the management of the National Health Service and its industrial relations remain to be settled. The autumn of 1984 will see the questions of privatisation, cuts and Griffiths to the fore in public debate in Scotland and their resolution during 1985 will merit future study and analysis.

Debate on the reorganisation process has largely been confined to the service itself although some of the decisions on management structure will clearly have implications for service delivery. After all the philosophy of *Patients First* and its Scottish counterpart was to move decision making closer to the point of service delivery. But the precise impact on patient services which the multi-variant unit structures will have remains to be seen, particularly in those boards which had concluded earlier that they should retain districts.

Our main concern has been the way in which this reorganisation has been brought about and the implications for industrial relations. The reorganisation in Scotland has also had implications with regard to the relationship between health boards and the SHHD. In this the role of health board chairmen has become decisive. The Secretary of State claims that the decision to remove districts in all boards was not taken by him, but by the chairmen. This raises fundamental questions about the powers of chairmen and their accountability to boards, which in turn raises questions about democracy and accountability of health boards themselves. For example, the STUC are concerned that their nominees on health boards have been reduced from 40 to 19 since the Conservatives took office in 1979. Two boards, Forth Valley and Lothian now have no STUC nominees. Similarly the creation and use of the Chairmen's Committee on Gradings is further evidence of the growing power of chairmen. Its operation has left a number of aggrieved organisations and individuals in its wake; and the formal elements of appeals mechanisms may yet come under strain if a large number of gradings are appealed. There is legitimate concern that the Whitley Council machinery and its agreements on grading criteria, and the capacity for staff interests to agree matters such as structures and gradings locally, have been circumvented by the use of the Fyfe Committee.

Otherwise at the health board level consultation and negotiation appear to have operated satisfactorily. In particular the slotting in and competition arrangements for posts in each board have gone smoothly although there have been examples of disappointment, frustration and bitterness when some individuals have not been appointed to particular vacancies. It is unlikely that there will be any compulsory redundancies resulting from reorganisation. While consultation and negotiation took place on an all-staff interest basis, it is unlikely that staff sides comprising both TUC and non-TUC organisations will continue in existence at the end of the reorganisation process. Reorganisation has been seen by most parties involved to be a special case, where the common purpose involved has drawn together the staff side and indeed management. This is not to say that there have been no differences but that these have in most cases been resolved. The experience of the Reorganisation Sub-Committee (Scotland), however, may well prompt the staff side to press for the establishment of a Scottish Whitley Advisory Committee to deal with Scottish issues in the future. However, the fundamentally political issues of privatisation and cuts will again find the TUC and non-TUC organisations opposed. Industrial relations in the National Health Service will therefore continue to be both interesting and controversial.

References

1. The research on which this paper is based was financed by a grant from the Scottish Home and Health Department. We acknowledge the assistance of those trade union and professional association officials, health board officers and SHHD civil servants who were interviewed, and Ann Adamson who transcribed tapes. The views expressed, however, are entirely the responsibility of the authors.

2. For overviews and summaries of these points see N. Bosanquet, *Industrial Relations in the NHS – the search for a system,* King Edward's Hospital Fund for London, London 1979. A.S. Sethi and S.J. Dimmock (eds), *Industrial Relations and Health Serevices,* Croom Helm, London 1982. TUC Health Services Committee, *Improving Industrial Relations in the National Health Service,* TUC, London, 1981. John W. Leopold and P.B. Beaumont, *The Development and Operation of the Personnel Function in the National Health Service in Scotland,* University of Glasgow, 1984.

3. DHHS, *NHS Management Inquiry,* DHSS, London, 1983.

4. DHHS, *Patients First,* London, HMSO, 1979.

5. SHHD, *Structure and Management of the National Health Service in Scotland,* Edinburgh, HMSO, 1979.

6. SHHD *Structure and Management of the NHS in Scotland,* NHS Circular 1981 (GEN) 14.

7. *Hansard* 1288. 711 November 1983, p.118.

8. SHHD *Structure and Management of the NHS in Scotland: Abolition of District Level of Management* NHS Circular 1983 (GEN) 27.

9. DHHS, *NHS Management Inquiry, op. cit.*

10. SHHD, *Grading Arrangements and Reviews following NHS Reorganisation* SHHD/DS (1984)30.

11. SHHD, *NHS Reorganisation: Staffing Arrangements (Scotland)* Advance Letter (GC) 8/83.

12. DHHS, *NHS Management Inquiry, op. cit.* p.17. For a fuller discussion of the pros and cons of consensus management see Steve Harrison, 'Consensus Decision-Making in the NHS – A Review', *Journal of Management Studies,* 19, 4, 1982.

13. SHHD, *Management and Administration Costs 1982-5,* NHS Circular 1982 (GEN) 12.

14. House of Commons, Committee of Public Accounts, *Premature Retirements in the National Health Service,* London, HMSO, 1984.

15. *ibid* p.23/4, 27.

16. SHHD, *The General Management Function in the National Health Service in Scotland: Proposals for Discussions,* Edinburgh 1984.

17. SHHD, *Use of Commercial Contractors by the NHS,* NHS Circular 1984 (GEN) 14.

18. SHHD, *Use of Commercial Contractors by the NHS,* NHS Circular 1983 (GEN) 13.

19. Parliamentary Debates, The Secretary of State for Social Services, 25 October 1983, 4 May 1984, 4 June 1984. DHSS, *Health Services Management Implementation of the NHS Management Inquiry Report,* Health Circular HC(84)13.

20. SHHD, *The General Management Function op. cit.*

21. For a statement of the views of a number of professional organisations and trade unions see House of Commons, Social Services Committee, *Griffiths NHS Management Inquiry Report,* London, HMSO, 1984, 209 parts i – iv.

22. See for example *Observer* 2/10/83, *Guardian* 18/1/84.

OPTION APPRAISAL IN THE SCOTTISH HEALTH SERVICE*

ROBIN G. MILNE
DEPARTMENT OF POLITICAL ECONOMY
UNIVERSITY OF GLASGOW

> "This does not imply a radical change in the more traditional methods of control. The main use of financial appraisal is still to stimulate the judgement of those who initiated the project in the first place".(1)

> "...this is not a new idea. It is being used I suppose to describe the more rigorous and more developed methodology used in the application of an old idea which is that before one embarks on an expensive major capital project one should look at both capital and running costs of it and alternative ways of providing the service. We would say that in our major programme which began in the '60s we always endeavoured to do that; though perhaps with less rigour than we might have done".(2)

Introduction

The purpose behind 'option appraisal' is to make the best use of resources at the government's disposal from the point of view of all parties and not simply from that of the government department with funds to spend. Proposals may previously have been appraised one way or another. The distinctive feature of 'option' appraisal is to introduce the economic element in a "more rigorous" way. Such evidence as we have suggests that the few occasions when option appraisal has been applied have been to prospective capital schemes. Whilst this is where choices are often most visible, in fact the principles are as applicable to assets already in public ownership as to those to be acquired(3), and to programmes involving recurrent expenditure (i.e. revenue allocations) as to those involving the capital budget.

Option appraisal within the Scottish Health Service has the appearance of the 'flavour of the month'. Yet as the first quote shows, within the public sector as a whole, the principles implied by option appraisal can scarcely be regarded as novel; indeed they have been applied to the nationalised industries since 1962.(4) However, the general acceptance of these principles within the NHS has been a long time coming, although there are a few notable exceptions about which more will be said later. Certainly that acceptance was long after 1969 when all investment in the public sector was to have been covered.(4) The long delay is explicable in terms of the past tendency to appraise only major capital proposals in a formal manner and, in the case of the NHS, this has usually meant in effect appraising hospitals. Hospitals, according to a senior civil servant with experience of both, have a complexity comparable to aircraft carriers.(5) The long delay before the economic element in option appraisal was given formal expression may, therefore, seem excusable. The same excuse would not, of course, apply to the more 'straightforward' investment decisions.

Times have changed, and minor as well as major capital expenditures are expected to be appraised in terms of the Treasury's current guidelines.(6) The Scottish Health Service – the fifteen health boards and the Common Services Agency – are to be given notice by the SHHD that *all* capital expenditures must be appraised this way, the the SHHD is preparing a manual to assist them to do so in the appropriate manner. The Treasury's approval is required for the more expensive hospital projects funded by the SHHD, whether from its own National Capital Programme or from the ordinary capital allocation the SHHD distributes to the health boards. In January 1983 hospitals costing £2 million or more would have required the Treasury's approval in principle.(7) The SHHD is responsible for the appraisal of the others and, in turn, delegates some of that responsibility to the health boards.

In early 1984 the health boards were responsible for capital schemes funded from their Ordinary Capital allocation if they cost (a) £1 million or less in total if no net increase in clinical resources were involved, (b) £500,000 or less in total if a net increase in clinical resources were involved, (c) £150,000 or less in respect of building costs alone, and (d) £100,000 or less for schemes which had a predominantly engineering context. Schemes not covered by (a) to (d) would invariably have required the approval of the Building Division of the Common Services Agency. Schemes not covered by (a) and (b) would have required the approval of the SHHD as well. The limits are shortly to be raised again. No such approval has been required on complex medical equipment, however expensive; although the SHHD has had to be notified of the intention to purchase equipment costing more than £100,000 and orders must be made through the Supplies Division of the Common Services Agency.[8] In recent years the SHHD has retained about half its capital allocation and has been responsible for appraising its use. The Building Division also used to have a responsibility for monitoring the health boards' maintenance programmes, but this was formally transferred back to them in 1979.[9]

At the time of writing 'option appraisals' have been carried out on three major capital proposals. In two cases – the provision of facilities for acute services for Fife Health Board and of facilities for the mentally handicapped for Dumfries and Galloway Health Board – economic advice came from the Health Economics Research Unit (HERU) at the University of Aberdeen. In the case of the third – the provision of facilities for the elderly for Lanarkshire Health Board – assistance came from Strathclyde Business School at the University of Strathclyde. It is my general impression that those within the Scottish Health Service still feel they have not acquired sufficient expertise to incorporate the economic element in appraisals without such external assistance as HERU has offered; though this lack of confidence may be dispelled once the SHHD manual for appraising proposals has been published and its contents are fully appreciated.

Option appraisal has generated a lot of interest and activity in the Scottish Health Service, yet the two statements at the head of this paper suggest its impact on the decision reached is likely to be marginal. The two statements deserve to be considered, if only because of their authoritative sources and their common view from different perspectives of public service. C.D. Foster, author of the first statement, writes as a professional economist after several years' experience of applying appraisal at the Ministry of Transport (under the sympathetic leadership of Barbara Castle). The author of the second source is A.L. Rennie, who at the time was Secretary to the SHHD, and replying, under examination, to the Committee of Public Accounts to the prospect of implementing option appraisal.

On the face of it their remarks are surprising, especially the one coming from the SHHD which referred to practice in the 1960s and not to 1981 when it was made. The Treasury admits that "...much of the work of a typical appraisal can be carried out competently by officials of *any* discipline...".[10] But the Treasury adds that they need "proper training", and that "specialists" are also needed. Two specialist groups specifically identified are economists and accountants.[11] However, until recently, the Scottish Health Service has been short of them both.

No economists have been employed in the SHHD or the Common Services Agency in their capacity as economists. Nor has been SHHD or the Scottish Health Service made much if any use of economists employed elsewhere in the Scottish Office. However, since 1977 the SHHD has funded HERU 'inter alia' to provide economic advice to itself and the Scottish Health Service.[12] Since 1979 HERU has also run nine month correspondence courses in Health Economics; and altogether a hundred staff employed by the Scottish Health Service have completed it[13], and would have learnt something about option appraisal as a result. Whether they acquired the "proper training" the Treasury argues is necessary is another matter. Certainly health board officials seem highly nervous at the prospect of option appraisal, and to be leaning unduly on external sources. Finally, in April 1984 HERU set up a consultancy service to facilitate the commissioning of major studies requiring its assistance.[14]

Management accountants have been employed throughout the Scottish Health Service since its reorganisation in 1974. But in a couple of respects their training falls short of the Treasury's guidelines. Without "proper training" they would tend to ignore the impact of proposals outside the Scottish Health Service. In addition, they tend to think of valuing costs and benefits in accounting terms and not as economists. The Treasury's guidelines clearly demand the latter.[15]

If the advice of professional economists and (management) accountants had not been available in the 1960s, how can the Secretary's statement be justified? It is our answer to this historical question which provides the basis for assessing what impact 'option appraisal' may be expected to have. Several sources were used. Officials from the SHHD and Scottish Office, including Mr A.L. Rennie himself, the Building Division and a health board, and members of HERU have been interviewed. Use has also been made of the SHHD circulars and its various publications although, of course, there is no guarantee that the statements of intention contained in them have been carried out. One set of sources not used, but available for example to the Controller and Auditor General, is the SHHD's and health boards' documentation of appraisals. However this last set of sources is recognised to be an unreliable indication of how thoroughly proposals were appraised as the appraisals were rarely fully documented. These sources are used to assess how fully each of the Treasury's guidelines had been implemented.

The Treasury's Guidelines

In the course of time the Treasury has added to its list of guidelines to be included in the appraisal of projects. The list started with discounting (Treasury, 1973), and the latest pamphlet identified another five. A list of the six is given below in the order of their application in an appraisal. In 1982 the DHSS produced a pamphlet of its own to translate the Treasury's guidelines into terms more familiar to NHS officers.[16] Some regional health authorities have produced pamphlets of their own, and the SHHD has one scheduled to appear later this year (1984).

The list of guidelines

1. The selection of options.
2. The identification of *all* costs and benefits.
3. The quantification of costs and benefits where possible.
4. Discounting, using the Treasury's test discount rate.
5. The adjustment for risk and uncertainty.
6. Backchecks and monitoring.

As was mentioned above, these guidelines are to be applied to *all* capital projects, whether or not their eventual approval in principle must be obtained from the Treasury or the SHHD. There are, however, two major exceptions. First, the DHSS made it clear to the Public Accounts Committee that it did not expect *clinical activities* to be subject to 'cost-benefit analysis'.[17] Cost-benefit analysis is a highly specific form of appraisal[18], one which assumes that the costs *and* benefits of proposals can be valued in financial terms. This may be a reasonable requirement for commercial proposals, but is hardly to be accepted readily for proposals which involve saving, say, lives.

Other forms of appraisal, such as cost-effectiveness analysis, are possible which would satisfy the Treasury[18] but can there be many clinical activities which offer more than one option to achieve the *same* outcome and so *avoid* the problem of measuring their respective benefits? For example, the treatment of chronic renal failure by dialysis or transplant in both cases raises life expectation, but of a very different quality. So much has been recognised in cost-effective analyses of this treatment.[19] Fortunately, in this choice the less costly method, where a choice is medically justified, also offers the better quality of life. But one cannot predict so convenient an outcome and, if the chronic renal failure example is indeed the exception, then the exemption of clinical activities from cost-benefit analysis is likely to exempt the majority from *any* serious sort of economic appraisal. It is noteworthy that the DHSS has appraised a limited number of clinical activities, but their economic content is regarded as "one factor taken into account by DHSS working groups considering whether such services should be introduced nationwide".[20] In addition, economic appraisal seems to be gathering some support from the medical profession itself.[21]

The second major exemption is *strategic decisions.*[22] Quite what is meant by the term 'strategic' has never been precisely defined, but the following example may help illustrate its meaning within the Civil Service. The decision to build a hospital is a strategic decision; the decision on its siting is not, and would be considered suitable for option appraisal. It would seem that (national) priorities, such as those contained within the SHAPE Report for the Scottish Health Service[23] are another example of a strategic decision. Certainly they are not based on a full economic appraisal.[24] As the authors of the report admit, they adopted "...a pragmatic approach, in which value judgements would necessarily play a *particularly large* role...".[25] Priorities defined this way are liable for, and arguably deserve the same criticism as was directed at the members of the Royal Commission on the Third London Airport. They recommended one among several possible sites, but did not consider whether a third one was needed in the first place.

Three of the six guidelines – the first, fifth and sixth – are ones which any government department or independent authority might be expected to adopt. The external pressure of the Treasury would hardly seem necessary, since their adoption would assist the departments in securing such goals as they may have. For the remainder of this section we indicate the role of these three and the extent they have been taken up. Only then do we turn to the three remaining guidelines – the second, third and fourth.

The Selection of Options

The obvious reason for selecting several options is the fact that the one first thought of might not be the one eventually preferred. It is clearly this guideline that the Secretary to the SHHD had in mind when referring to past appraisals of major capital proposals. But, as we hope to show, the value of comparing different options depends on whether the other guidelines in the list are also included. If they all are, then it would by no means be obvious which one would eventually be preferred until the appraisal were well in hand if not completed. Unfortunately, the Secretary did not indicate in 1981 which, if any, of the other guidelines were regularly included in the appraisals.

This is not the place for a full analysis of the options open to those running the health service. But a number of observations can be made which point to the need for certain improvements. The first observation is that *many* options do not necessarily involve clinical activities, although academic 'health' economists have tended to focus on this exempt group. Thus Williams[(26)] refers to choices in the *type* of treatment for a given disease (kidney dialysis or transplant), to choices in the *place* of treatment (as an in- or out-patient for the removal of varicose veins), and to the choices in the *time* of treatment (mass miniature radiography for the early diagnosis of pulmonary tuberculosis). Drummond[(27)] summarises over one hundred such studies which have been published. Many more are now available. The field of non-clinical activities has been largely unexplored by this group of economists although this omission is not likely to last long now that option appraisal requires formal adoption.

Second, the choice of option is directly related to the *objective* of the proposal. Ideally that objective should be expressed in terms of the outcome of the proposal, say, of lives saved, care of the elderly, and so on. Until recently the Scottish Health Service's objectives were only in terms of the provision of facilities, say, of the number of beds by type per capita. In the end the options have to be expressed this way, but an examination of the quantitative guidelines used by the Scottish Health Service suggests no full formal analysis of both the costs and benefits of providing the facilities.[(28)] Norms expressed in terms of throughput, say of admissions per capita, are hardly more appropriate. Recently, however, there has been a move in the right direction in that objectives are also being defined in terms of programmes which usually refer to specific client groups such as the elderly.[(29)] This comes closer to the final output of health services although, in doing so, one also comes closer to evaluating clinical activities which have been declared exempt from cost-benefit analysis. However, if this sleight-of-hand is allowed to pass then sets of facilities can be selected, each of which best meets the objective of its respective programme given that programme's budget allocation. It is this approach which was adopted in appraising the proposal by the Dumfries and Galloway Health Board to make local provision for the mentally handicapped.

Third, it is too rarely recognised that the scale of provision, whether it be of facilities or the programme's budget, can be varied. The DHSS manual, for example, makes no explicit reference to this possibility.[(30)] Yet if the scale of provision is not considered among the options, then the Scottish Health Service may find itself making recommendations not very different from one made by the American Cancer Society that more than

$47 million be spent to identify a person with cancer of the colon.[31]

The Secretary to the SHHD recently elaborated the extent to which options were considered when the Hospital Plan for Scotland, first published in 1962, was developed and implemented. In the first place, the regional hospital boards were asked to make a set of proposals which would take into account what catchment population the hospital would serve and the related problem of where it be sited. In addition, they were asked to consider whether functions, like maternity care, should be located at a single hospital or provided separately. More recently, decisions whether to build the hospital in phases or all at once have had to be evaluated. The quality of the evaluation no doubt was variable, but the intention was clear: to aim at functional efficiency which, in the context of acute facilities, meant sufficiently large developments to offer specialist services on a 24 hours a day basis.

At the same time the SHHD, as the Department of Health for Scotland became, itself made several appraisals whose eventual purpose was a set of design guides for hospital departments and health centres. The hospital departments covered were wards[32], accident and emergency departments[33], and outpatient departments.[34] In each case the aim was functional efficiency, by which is meant the initial definition of the functions of the department in question and a design solution which was thought would perform them most efficiently in terms of the resources available. The SHHD also has had access to a series of similar studies produced by the DHSS. The SHHD and DHSS virtually ceased publishing their series of design guides and hospital planning notes on reorganisation in 1974. Those that had been published, however, have had an important place in the subsequent design of hospitals and health centres.

The next stage is construction. The responsibility for this, in the case of hospitals, lay with the regional hospital boards, until reorganisation. Then responsibility was shifted to the newly created Building Division of the Common Services Agency, which took over many of the staff originally employed by the boards. Again after reorganisation, and probably to some extent before it, each proposal was appraised with an economic element in mind. Two particular sets of choices had an explicit economic content: the choice of fuel, introduced in 1965[35] and more recently the choice between building new and upgrading existing buildings.[36] Many other options would have been considered, several with an implicit economic content such as the choice of orientation and shape of a building, and options in the building elements such as the choice between flat and pitched roofs.[37]

Risk and Uncertainty

We turn now to the second guideline the SHHD might be expected to implement without pressure from the Treasury to do so. Risk and uncertainty are inherent in most proposals. They are least important for proposals to replace existing facilities. They become more important when the provision of existing facilities is extended. They become most important when an entirely new programme is proposed. In the last case there may be little idea of its take-up by patients or of its benefit to them. But in all cases, even when existing facilities are replaced, risk and uncertainty cannot be avoided where the outcome of the proposal extends into the future. Thus the quite straightforward decision to replace a boiler involves the choice of fuels, whose relative cost could change.

The Treasury suggests the use of sensitivity analysis as the means to cope with risk and uncertainty. It does not avoid the problem they cause, but it does indicate the extent to which the preferred option depends on the assumptions made. Ideally the selected option should be clearly preferred for all reasonable assumptions. If it is not, then judgement is required even in those cases where economic criteria alone would dictate the selection of options.

We have only limited information on the extent to which risk and uncertainty were taken into account. It is our impression that at the earliest stages in the proposal, the regional hospital boards and their successors the health boards took little or no account of it. The next stage is the design guides and hospital planning notes produced by the SHHD and the Scottish Hospital Centre. An examination of them gives no suggestion that risk and uncertainty were taken into account either. Certainly none have been taken for the last stage of construction.(38)

Backchecks and Monitoring

The purpose behind this guideline is to learn from past mistakes. A systematic approach to this guideline requires an explicit statement of the objectives of the proposal and the assumptions behind the option eventually selected.

There is evidence of some willingness to put this guideline into practice. The first stage involves a set of proposals made by the regional hospital boards and then by the health boards which have the SHHD's approval. The outcome – the Hospital (subsequently the Health) Plan for Scotland – has been publicly revised several times. Thus the original Plan for Scotland[39] published in 1962 had 'revisions' and 'reviews' to it published two and four years afterwards, respectively.[40] Revisions, usually accompanied by additions to the existing scheme, have been periodically announced.[41] The latest revision, unlike its predecessors focuses on the bed requirements of individual health boards, and does not go so far as recommending particular schemes whose approval now depends on 'option appraisal'.[42] Even this latest effort recognises its own estimates will need periodic revision.

There is also evidence of revisions by the SHHD and one of its agencies, the Scottish Hospital Centre, to their published hospital planning notes and design guides. We have identified six 'design in use' studies which have been published. Three were reviews of the operation of the hospital as a whole,[43] two reviewed ward designs,[44] and one reviewed the design of health centres.[45] Shortcomings of existing designs were identified and corrections to them were made. However this work of 'backchecks and monitoring' lapsed when it was delegated to the Building Division due to a lack of resources to do it and of first hand information on maintenance costs to test the assumptions.[46] The regional hospital and health boards have also had a similar responsibility,[47] but it would appear not to have been carried out regularly if at all.

Conclusions

Three of the six guidelines indicated by the Treasury for inclusion in an *economic* appraisal of proposals might reasonably be expected to be adopted by the SHHD and the Scottish Health Service. Our analysis indicates they have a useful role, though it should be made clear that in the cases of these three there is nothing specifically 'economic' about them. *Any* appraisal might include all three. To make the appraisal economic and satisfy the Treasury's goal of an efficient allocation for the benefit of *all* parties it is necessary to include the three other guidelines as well. Their role will be evident in due course.

There is mixed evidence for their adoption. There is no evidence of a systematic approach to risk and uncertainty. In the early days of the 1960s, when the major capital programme took off, there was a willingness to consider a variety of options in a systematic way and to check the practical value of proposed design solutions. However this work was largely at the initiative of the SHHD. It is not clear that the SHHD carried the regional hospital boards with them; and on reorganisation this enthusiasm seems to have evaporated. The same choices continue to be appraised, and there is little evidence of a willingness to expand the list. One might therefore hope the Treasury's initiative will have an impact on the implementation of all three self-serving guidelines.

The Identification of all Costs and Benefits

The Treasury is quite clear that the appraisal of proposals should include *all* important costs and benefits, those falling on the private as well as the public sector, and not just on the organisation responsible for them.[(48)] In this way an efficient allocation of resources from the point of view of *all* begins to be possible.

It is hardly to be expected that, without prompting, the SHHD and the Scottish Health Service would use this information in a way completely contrary to their own interests. Nevertheless, the obvious willingness to consider several sites for buildings suggests their receptivity to the interests of others. Just how far the SHHD and Scottish Health Service are willing to go in this direction partly depends on there being channels for the interests of others to be expressed and whether trading is possible. This section concentrates upon these possibilities.

First it should be recognised that the structure of the SHHD and Scottish Health Service guarantees points of contact between them and other interest groups. In the end, the SHHD and the Scottish Health Service are accountable to the Secretary of State for Scotland and through him to Parliament, where the interests of other groups can also be represented.

Second, since reorganisation of the NHS the Secretary of State has been advised by the Scottish Health Service Council, whose membership is drawn from all the major professional groups and from each health board and university with a medical school as well as from the SHHD.[(49)] The Council, for example, was consulted on the original statement of national priorities,[(50)] and was responsible for drafting the (revised) SHAPE Report published four years later.[(51)]

Third, there has been a continuing practice of involving several bodies with an interest in the NHS in its running. Before reorganisation the local authorities ran the community health services, and nominees from a variety of bodies were members of the regional hospital boards and boards of management. Many of the latter became members of the newly constituted health boards. Hunter[(52)] identified "local authorities, trade unions, voluntary bodies, business groups, churches and professional associations" as bodies with nominees on health boards selected by the Secretary of

State. Health boards with a medical school also have a university representative.

These nominees are expected to represent the interests of patients, though there might be some doubt about how far they would carry out this obligation. Imagine, for example, the situation of a trade unionist, from the National Union of Mineworkers, when told that solid fuel was *not* the preferred choice after an appraisal by the Building Division.

The role of health boards is to "deal with major policy, strategic planning decisions, the broad allocation of resources and matters of substantial interest to the community".[(53)] Hunter,[(54)] drawing on a study of two health boards between 1975 and 1977, has cast serious doubt on their ability to do so. First, he states that members were unclear as to what was actually required of them, although their "enthusiastic" reception of the initial statement of priorities in 1976 suggests this impotency should have been short-lived. And second, he suggests that the health board officers tended to dominate the thinking of members because the former had the advantages of greater time, expertise and resources at their disposal. This problem is less easy to correct, but it depends on the debatable assumption that officers take the role of 'masters',not 'servants' to their members.

Fourth, a variety of bodies have existed with whom the regional hospital boards, and their successors the health boards have been expected to consult. Thus the regional hospital boards were expected to consult local authorities, NHS Executive Councils and other interested parties when proposing a building scheme.[(55)] And health boards have also been expected to consult local authorities, the new constituted local health councils (about which we have more to write shortly), area professional consultative committees, staff associations, and any others with a "valid" interest when decisions involve the change in use of premises or their closure.[(56)]

Fifth, since the reorganisation of the NHS in 1974 there have been improvements in the machinery of negotiation between the health boards and the local community and local authorities. The first has come through the establishment of local health councils,[(57)] whose geographic boundaries of responsibility usually coincided with the district health authorities then in existence.[(58)] Like health board members, local health council members are nominated, not elected. Local authorities select their own nominees; and the health boards select the nominees of voluntary agencies, trade unions, and other bodies with an interest in the health services in that particular community. Local health council members are also expected to represent the interests of the community as a whole and not the bodies which nominated them. Finally, they are also unpaid.[59]

Whilst the composition of the membership of local health councils and health boards have much in common, they have been assigned different roles. As noted above, the health boards are expected to set priorities. Councils, on the other hand, are expected to act as a channel of communication between their health board and the local community, in both directions. They also have an advisory and monitoring role. For example, among the topics considered suitable for their examination are the quality of health services provided, plans for new services and changes in the use of existing services, facilities for patients, waiting lists and the co-operation between the health service and the related local authorities services.[60] The investigation and reporting on individual complaints (which is the responsibility of the Ombudsman) and on the clinical treatment of individuals (with is the responsibility of the professions) are the only topics expressly excluded from the consideration of the councils, though they can advise individuals how and where to make their complaints.

The resources at the health council's disposal are meagre. As noted above the members are unpaid, and their contributions must be fitted in with their several other commitments and, because they often serve voluntarily in other capacities, such free time as they can give to their local health council must be very limited. The members have the services of a paid secretary and access to health board papers relating to the interests of their council, but not much more. In the financial year 1982-83 the Greater Glasgow Health Board spent £93,000 on its five health councils out of a total revenue allocation of £370 millions.[61]

The second improvement is in the machinery of negotiation between the health boards and local authorities. It will be remembered that there are local authority nominees on the health boards and local health councils, and that local authorities must be consulted by the health boards when the use of premises is to be changed or they are to be closed. Nevertheless, it had been felt, prior to the reorganisation of the Scottish Health Service (in 1974) and local government (in 1975) and afterwards, that the existing machinery left much to be desired and that joint liaison committees should be set up between the two bodies which would involve their members and senior officers.[62] Three years later committees were set up in most parts of Scotland.[63]

Consultation is costly in time and effort. Yet it can offer positive benefits if handled in a sensible way. Consultation can draw out the special knowledge of the interested parties and so improve the decisions reached. Thus the local health council members may be more aware of the problems of physical access to the several proposed sites for a new health centre. Consultation can also act as a channel to communicate information, and so avoid misunderstandings and make proposals more acceptable. For example, a change in the use of premises may give a false impression that redundancies are expected, whereas in reality no redundancies are intended. Finally, consultation can help resolve the conflicts of interest that are bound to arise. Even if give-and-take is not possible in respect of any particular proposal, it may be feasible for a series of proposals over a period of time.

We test the willingness of the SHHD and the Scottish Health Service to take account of the interests of them, even at some cost to themselves, by reference to the patient's geographic access to facilities. Judged by the principles for the design of casualty and accident departments(64) and the original Hospital Plan for Scotland(65) patient convenience was very low down on the list of priorities. What mattered was functional efficiency, with facilities being concentrated so that 24 hours a day care, of high quality, could be provided. Only occasional concessions were made to those living in peripheral areas such as Fort William, Dunoon and Oban. This ordering of priorities was still to be found some ten years later in the SHHD's design guide for health centres,(66) where the recommendations continued to be based on the size of the catchment population to be served and not its access to alternative facilities as well.

Yet a change in emphasis has occurred. First, the Borders are to have a new district general hospital, even though the catchment population will be smaller than a similar hospital in the central belt of Scotland, and *consideration* is being given to a similar facility in Dunfermline instead of the continued reliance on hospitals in Edinburgh. Second, the SHHD has revised its recommendation in the design guide for health centres so that health centres with smaller catchment populations than previously may have X-ray facilities if access is otherwise difficult to obtain.(67) The policy was, for example, recently implemented in Ullapool. Finally, an analysis of the provision of out-patient clinics at health centres in Scotland indicates that patient convenience was a consideration, even at some cost to the health boards and consultants.(68)

Consultation can, however, only go so far, at least as judged by existing shortcomings. Thus we find patients in hospital who do not need the medical and nursing services it offers, because there is no suitable place to discharge them to; and there are others in the community who could benefit from just such hospital services if only accommodation were available. This leads to the sixth solution to trading between the Scottish Health Service and other bodies, which is particularly appropriate for conflicts of interests. This solution lies in the definition of the respective responsibilities of the various bodies. The SHHD has gone some way to doing this for the Scottish Health Service.[(69)] However it is not known how far other bodies have gone in the same direction.

The definition of responsibilities, whilst helpful, is not the complete answer in practice. As the SHHD recognises it has interests that can "overlap" or be "complementary" to other bodies like the local authorities and voluntary agencies, which can make a division of responsibilities that is acceptable to all difficult to achieve. It was to overcome this problem,[(70)] and to encourage local authorities to take over their responsibility for those no longer requiring continuous nursing and medical care, that in 1980 the SHHD earmarked some of its own funds to help finance projects set up and run by local authorities. These funds came under the general title of 'support finance'.[(71)]

The SHHD finances up to 60% of the capital costs and, initially, up to 60% of the revenue costs which tapers off after five years. Thereafter the local authority would be responsible for the full financial cost of the proposal. The proposals are submitted by the health boards, but none of the earmarked funds are allocated to them. The financial estimate for 'support finance' in the year 1982-83 was £2 million. However, as can be seen from the table, five of the fifteen health boards still had no schemes in operation and only half of the allocation was spent.[(72)] In the following year £2.7 millions was spent and it would have been much higher still had not Strathclyde Regional Council continued its opposition to participation.

Another cash transfer scheme which will modify the conflict of interests between the Scottish Health Service and local authorities where their interests "overlap" and are "complementary" is a development in Supplementary Benefit provision which took effect in November 1983. It is now possible for local authorities and health boards to relieve themselves of the financial responsibility of persons eligible for supplementary benefit who have been admitted to a registered nursing or residential home on or after the date when the new provision took effect. Since registration rests with the health boards (for nursing homes) and local authorities (for residential homes) their only constraint would, superficially, seem to be the availability of suitable (private) accommodation.

In conclusion, consultation can lead to better and more acceptable decisions being made when more than one party is involved. But conflicts of interest are inevitable. These can be resolved by negotiation, if the various parties have something to negotiate. And the willingness of the SHHD to use financial incentives in the Scottish Health Service's relations with local authorities is a move in this direction although, for one reason or another, the response of local authorities has been less than enthusiastic. However, the Treasury expects more than a 'quid pro quo'. It expects its agents, including the SHHD and the Scottish Health Service, to be prepared to take decisions against their own interests if they thereby serve the general interest. It is perhaps expecting a lot, yet in recent years there is some evidence of this accommodation with the Scottish Health Service in circumstances that were not forced upon it by the Treasury. One may expect the accommodation to be still more evident in proposals that have required the Treasury's approval.

The Quantification of Costs and Benefits

As far as possible all important costs and benefits should be quantified, preferably in financial terms and based on the economist's concept of 'opportunity cost'.[(73)] This concept values resources in terms of their best alternative use, and not necessarily in terms of what is paid for them. For practical purposes the Treasury accepts the two are approximately equal in value,[(74)] though there are notable exceptions to which we make some later reference.

The requirement to include *all* important costs and benefits can involve putting values not only on those borne by the Scottish Health Service but also on others, such as local authorities and other groups identified in the previous section. To contain this section within reasonable bounds we examine the application of the opportunity cost concept to the Scottish Health Service's own activities. Parallels with other bodies will be evident, but it is not our purpose to indicate them. Our general conclusion is that past deficiencies in the application of the concept of opportunity cost have largely been removed, although one important one still remains.

The overwhelming expenditure by the Scottish Health Service is on goods and (labour) services, and the Treasury has accepted valuing them in terms of their market prices is an acceptable measure of their opportunity cost.[(75)] To this extent there is no practical difference between economists and other professional groups, in particular accountants, engineers and surveyors, when putting a value on the resources used.

Where practice differs between economists and the other professional groups is in their valuation of resources – in this case (equipment), land and buildings – already in the possession of the Scottish Health Service.

Economists would expect these assets have an income or realiseable value inputed to them just as much as would actually occur if they were not in its ownership. Ideally, the ownership of an asset should make no difference to the value of its best alternative use. It is a criticism of past practice that it once did, and may still do so. Those responsible for their use may, nevertheless, have valued them as an economist would, given the circumstances they faced. Thus if they treated property as though it were a 'free good', then more likely than not, for them, it had *no* alternative use. There can be little doubt that this 'misuse' of property arose from the constraints put on its realisable value on the open market, so that the opportunity cost to the user was (much) less than it could have been. As we now show these constraints have largely been removed, and hopefully the distortions that went with them.

Three distinct kinds of constraints can be identified. The first is the requirement, when property is to be developed, that first refusal be given to other government departments, then to local authorities, and only then may the property be put on the open market. This requirement was removed in 1979, and property may go straight onto the local open market.[76] The second constraint is the *free* transfer between government departments. This was removed in April 1983, and now the full market price must be paid.[77] The third constraint is the inability of the Scottish Health Service to obtain planning *permission* from local authorities for property it might wish to dispose. It could obtain a planning *opinion*, but this is less binding on the local authority and so worth less to any prospective buyer. Thus, in 1967, one property was valued at £30,000 in its current use as agricultural land, but might have been worth £1.75 million with planning permission for its commercial development.[78] There had been some uncertainty as to the ability of government departments to obtain planning permission.[79] But the government has accepted its desirability, and necessary legislative changes have been introduced to remove any further ambiguity.[80]

The removal of these three constraints means that the SHHD can obtain the full open market price on such property as it wishes to dispose. Equally it must pay this price for any it acquires, even from another government department. As a result one may not only hope, but also expect the Scottish Health Service to make better use of its property from the point of view of society as a whole. However, the removal of these constraints will not effectively bring together the different perspectives of economists and other professional groups such as accountants, engineers and surveyors in valuing assets in the Scottish Health Service's possession.

Given these past constraints, it is to be expected that the SHHD and Scottish Health Service would have property surplus to their requirements. The problem then comes in identifying it. In some cases the surplus may arise from the SHHD's own National Building Programme and be self-evident. But others will be less obvious to the SHHD and may only be known to the health boards. And if one recognises that some property is *under* used, and to that extent is also surplus to requirements, then the need to obtain 'grass roots' information becomes even more important.

The DHSS has taken a variety of measures to obtain this information,[81] but the Scottish Health Service has largely relied on financial incentives by agreeing to return to the health boards part or all of the proceeds from the sale of their property. This scheme was introduced in 1977 when the full amount up to £30,000 per sale was returned.[82] The limit has subsequently been raised: to £60,000 in 1981 and to £100,000 in 1984.[83] Information on the sums returned to the various health boards in the financial year 1982-83 is given in the table. It will be seen that all but four of the fifteen health boards benefitted to some extent, but that the sums involved were trivial in relation to their final (revenue plus ordinary capital) allocation. The SHHD also put restrictions on the use of these funds to conform with the national programme of priorities.

Parliament also imposes constraints on the use of the funds it votes. Generally, funds it votes for any given year must be spent that year and may not be spent later. In addition, funds voted for specific purposes must be spent on that purpose and not on any other. Since spending decisions within the SHHD and Scottish Health Service tend to be implemented at the health board level and below, it is easy to imagine the distortions that can arise. For example, rather than have a large shortfall of expenditure in relation to its allocated budget, one health board suddenly approved the purchase of a body scanner at a cost of £400,000, whose subsequent annual revenue consequences were estimated to be £50,000.[84] Equally, the lack of 'virement' – the ability to transfer funds between votes – can bring a mismatch between revenue and ordinary capital allocations with, say, sufficient funds to build facilities but insufficient funds to run them.

In practice, however, the system of financial control is more flexible than the Parliamentary votes would suggest. First, the SHHD votes comes within the Scottish Office general vote, and the Secretary of State ha discretion in allocating its share of that total prior to obtaining Cabinet approval. Its share can be subsequently adjusted – though not the overall total – only with the Treasury's prior approval. In the past that approval has usually been given.

Second, whilst the hospital and community health, but *not* the family practitioner[85] services are cash limited, the SHHD has allowed health boards a limited ability to shift funds between financial years. Since the financial year 1976-77 the health boards have been allowed to 'carry-forward' underspending up to 1% of their combined total of revenue and ordinary capital allocations.[86] As one would expect, under cash limits health boards which have exceeded their allocations have had the full amount deducted from the following year's allocation. The health boards have also been able to shift funds between financial years in a more planned way, with their ability to 'bank' or 'borrow' funds with the SHHD. These funds are protected against inflation. However, the SHHD has required to be notified of the health boards' plans within one month of the beginning of the financial year and, in recent years, the health boards only knew their initial allocations less than one month before the financial year began. It is important to appreciate that both these schemes to transfer funds between financial years are an arrangement internal to the SHHD. The department itself is subject to the Treasury discipline of cash limits.

Data on the extent of 'carry forward' to the next (1983-84) financial year, and on 'banking' and the final allocations in the current (1982-83) financial year by health board and for all health boards are given in the table. It will be noticed that two health boards overspent their approved budget, in the Western Isles case by an extent which was purely accidental; and three were close to the 1% limit. Overall £4.3 million was underspent, 0.38% of the final allocation. Seven of the fifteen health boards used the 'banking' facility with the SHHD: six to defer expenditure, and one to bring it forward or to draw upon accumulated balances. Marginally less, £3.5 million, was credited to health boards for future expenditure this way than from the 'carry forward' arrangement.

The restriction on the transfer of funds between votes is also more flexible than the Parliamentary votes would suggest. It has already been noted that the Treasury is receptive to requests for transfers of funds between votes, so long as the cash limits total is not exceeded. In addition, the SHHD in effect allows the health boards 100% 'virement' – i.e. the full transfer of funds – between their revenue and ordinary capital allocations. Earmarked funds are excluded, of course, but they are trivial in magnitude compared with the health boards' total allocations. Non-cash limited family practitioner services are also excluded for the obvious reason that the SHHD would then lose control over health board expenditure completely. In recent years the SHHD has allocated about half its capital budget to the health boards, although the proportion varies widely from year-to-year. The total allocated is distributed between the health boards on the same principle as their revenue allocations, i.e. using the SHARE formula.[(87)]

Data on the ordinary capital allocated to health boards and on that actually spent are given in the table for the financial year 1982-83. Only three health boards spent less than their allocation, and six exceeded their allocation by more than 20%. Combining all health boards, expenditure exceeded the amount allocated by 15%. Marginally more use was made of 'virement' than either 'carry-over' or 'banking' to redistribute the health boards' allocations. Combining all three schemes of transfer, then for all health boards some 1.05% of the final allocation was effectively carried overto the next financial year which would not have been possible without 'carry-forward' and 'virement'. For some individual health boards this proportion was much larger: for example, it was 2.37% for Argyll and Clyde Health Board.

The final financial constraint is on the unit costs of construction, referred to as 'departmental cost allowances'. They have a long history. The levels are set by the SHHD, with reference to negotiations between the Treasury and the DHSS, and apply to *all* capital schemes however financed and approved. They are intended to contain capital expenditure without the need to review, in detail, individual schemes before their approval. The only *regular* revisions to the departmental cost allowances are for significant and permanent increases in building costs for the industry as a whole. No trade-off between the allowance set and its revenue consequences is permitted, and the incentive to innovate must be greatly dampened. No moves have been made to remove this constraint.

The discussion so far has concentrated on the extent to which the signals to those making decisions about the use of resources within the Scottish Health Service reflect the full opportunity cost of these resources.

Finally we turn briefly to the extent to which the benefits of proposals – in so far as they are the outcome of proposals – are properly valued in the Scottish Health Service. Usually, in fact, they are not measured at all. First, there is the problem of knowing what the outcome is likely to be. When that is known, the problem of valuing it remains. These two problems largely explain the exemptions given to strategic decisions and clinical activities from option appraisal and cost-benefit analysis, respectively, before their approval in principle.

It is the position of this paper that such an attitude is unduly restrictive. Whilst there is no answer economists can give to measuring the outcome of health services, they have much experience in putting a value on it, once it is known. Perhaps the attempts at putting a value on human life[(88)] can hardly expect to gain universal acceptance just yet. But there are many other benefits from medical intervention or care whose valuation would be much less contentious: for example, the saving of travel *time* as well as travel costs to patients by decentralising the provision of facilities.

In conclusion, we have every reason to expect that the real cost of resources within the Scottish Health Service is now recognised by those using them, or at least by others responsible for their use. To that extent better decisions should now be made. The only exception identified is the continued use of department cost allowances which limit the unit costs of construction. However, caution must be exercised so that assets in the ownership of the Scottish Health Service are not assumed to be free in any evaluations of proposals. Finally, the inability and unwillingness to measure the benefits of programmes is a severe and, to some extent, an unnecessary constraint on the range of proposals which have an economic element in their proposal. Economists need to be given a freer hand so that the effect of this constraint can be reduced and option appraisal be more widely adopted.

Discounting

When the Treasury originally recommended investment (i.e. option) appraisal for the public sector it was discounting it had in mind, rather than any of the other guidelines identified in this paper, and it was to be applied only to the nationalised industries. The reasoning is that the nationalised industries did not have direct access to the capital market, as did the private commercial sector, but instead obtained funds indirectly and on more favourable terms. Given the implicit assumption that the two sectors were in competition for limited capital finance, it was felt necessary to impose some sort of economic as well as financial discipline. One method chosen was to require the nationalised industries to secure a rate of return on their investment thought to be at least comparable to that obtained in the private sector. The rate required is referred to as the 'test discount rate' and represents, in effect, the opportunity cost of capital employed by the nationalised industries. This reasoning has not changed, even when, as in 1969, the request to discount was extended to *all* public sector investment,[(89)] including that funded through the SHHD. The exemption of strategic decisions and clinical activities from option appraisal means that in the Scottish Health Service discounting will serve the useful but rather limited role of screening out options whose additional capital requirements fail to satisfy the test discount rate.

The test discount rate has been changed periodically, and is set assuming constant prices, i.e. no inflation. Initially it was 8% per annum: in 1969 it was changed to 10%; and in 1978 it was changed to 5% and to 7% when a cost-*benefit* analysis of a public service such as the Scottish Health Service was involved.[(90)] For practical purposes 5% is now used for almost *all* proposals by cental government, except by the Department of Transport in its appraisal of roads.

In the sub-section on the selection of options, three sets of choices were indicated. We assess the use and importance of discounting for each of them in turn. The first set of choices made by the regional hospital boards, and their successors the health boards, concerns the catchment populations to be served, the site for the hospital, its mix of facilities and the phasing of its construction. Even if the capital and full revenue consequences of each option had been estimated in financial terms, it is unlikely that discounting was used to make the estimates commensurable. It is probably only recently, with the new styled 'option appraisal' that *both* parts of the appraisal have been included. However, the past omission of discounting in the appraisals is unlikely to have made much difference to the eventual choice except the last named one, the phasing of construction.

The second set of choices concerns the design of hospital departments and health centres. Again the study groups would have been conscious of the capital and revenue consequences of the different options. But, again, it is doubtful whether discounting came into the picture in a formal manner. The design guides and hospital planning notes still form the basis of health service planning, and any serious errors as a result of past omissions are now embodied in current conventional wisdom.

The third set of choices concerns the building of the facilities. It is in this respect that discounting is known to have been used in a systematic if limited way for a number of years. Two choices where discounting has been given a central role are the choice of fuel[(91)] and the choice between building new or upgrading an existing facility.[(92)] Discounting is part of the training of engineers and surveyors just as much as for management accountants. This is not to say that they are very familiar with it; and the manual produced by the DHSS,[(93)] to show how widely it could be used, has been available to engineers and surveyors in the Scottish Health Service. However, the existence of cost allowances has been a severe deterrent on their use of discounting on a day-to-day basis. There is little point in evaluating metal versus wooden frames if the cost allowances exclude the former.

Some Concluding Remarks

This paper opened with two quotations, both from experienced civil servants and both suggesting that option/investment appraisal may be expected to have a modest impact. What does our review of the experience suggest for the Scottish Health Service?

Option appraisal is the title given by the SHHD (and DHSS) to the set of Treasury guidelines intended to introduce an economic element into the appraisal of proposals. Three of the guidelines are the type that independent agents, whether the health boards or the SHHD itself, might be expected to adopt. In the early 1960s the SHHD and the regional hospital boards did consider a limited variety of options, but there is little evidence that the list has been extended. The SHHD and the Scottish Hospital Centre also appraised many of the design solutions for their efficiency, but this process of backchecks and monitoring seem to have largely disappeared on reorganisation. It is hardly done at all now for individual schemes, as is required. Such evidence of its continuance, as exists, is the periodic revision of bed requirements. Finally, there is no evidence of adjustments being taken for risk and uncertainty. In respect of all three guidelines there seems room for improvement, and the Treasury's reminder of their value should not be ignored.

The three remaining guidelines are specifically economic in their content. The requirement to include *all* costs and benefits has already been met, to some degree, and the Scottish Health Service has shown some willingness to serve the interests of other parties at its own expense. A proper valuation of these costs and benefits would indicate if they have gone too far in this direction or need to go further. There has been an improvement in that valuation in respect of its own resources, with three notable exceptions: the continued application of cost allowances to capital expenditure and the exemption of strategic decisions and clinical activities. The exemption of clinical activities is unduly restrictive. The DHSS has begun to recognise its value. More importantly, so has the medical profession. The door to the economic evaluation of clinical activities is not shut; it is only its hinges which are stiff. Rather less, however, can be said for the willingness of the Scottish Health Service to put a correct value on the resources of others, even when it is sensitive to the impact its programmes may have on them. However, the new styled option appraisals are a movement in the right direction, because they identify explicitly some of the limits these values should have. Do individual patients living in Fife justify an additional £500 of expenditure to obtain acute in-patient care in Dunfermline rather than in Edinburgh,[(94)] even if other issues are also involved? Finally, several professional groups employed by the Scottish Health Service have been taught about discounting; but there is little evidence of the familiarity that comes from its everyday use. Departmental cost allowances may inhibit the engineers and surveyors. But there is less excuse for the (management) accountants. Nevertheless, there has been a noticeable improvement in the use of these specifically economic guidelines compared with the 1960s, even if there is no room for complacency.

Finally, option appraisal can be costly in time and resources, especially for major capital projects of a 'one-off' type. Two years is not an unrealistic estimate for some hospital schemes. No doubt if the time can be spared the exercise could be justified too,. But if appraisals are to be applied to all capital proposals, with the familiar exemptions, then more use must be made of the routine practices adopted by the Building Division, for example in the choice between building new and upgrading existing facilities. This mechanistic approach may seem counter to the spirit behind the original introduction of appraisal – see the Foster quote – but it provides useful information to those, who in the end, must exercise judgement.

Select Financial Statistics 1982-83, by Health Board (£ million)

Health Board	Carry forward to 1983-84	(Banking) borrowing	Sale of land/ buildings	Support finance	Ordinary capital allocation	Ordinary capital spent	Final allocation
Argyll & Clyde	0.264	(1.000)	0.053	–	2.433	3.194	85.6
Ayrshire & Arran	0.354	(0.700)	0.013	0.090	1.997	1.906	57.1
Borders	0.112	–	–	0.165	0.549	0.627	17.0
Dumfries & Galloway	0.303	–	0.019	0.027	0.795	1.312	30.4
Fife	0.140	(0.800)	0.094	–	1.812	1.955	55.5
Forth Valley	0.293	(0.800)	–	0.018	1.470	1.507	54.0
Grampian	0.798	1.000	0.377	0.084	2.727	4.171	103.7
Greater Glasgow	1.514	–	0.093	–	6.444	6.529	316.2
Highland	0.205	(1.128)	0.107	0.026	1.107	0.618	42.7
Lanarkshire	(0.055)	–	0.006	0.023	3.012	3.641	95.4
Lothian	0.289	–	0.286	0.240	4.680	5.384	190.9
Orkney	0.031	–	–	–	0.105	0.088	3.1
Shetland	0.034	–	0.005	–	0.132	0.253	4.0
Tayside	0.380	–	0.094	0.110	2.565	2.924	114.0
Western Isles	(0.336)	(0.031)	–	0.240	0.174	0.487	6.0
All HBS	4.326	(3.459)	1.147	1.023	30.000	34.595	1,175.5

Source: Scottish Office Finance Division 5B

References

Acknowledgements: A large number of people have helped an 'outsider' get some feel for the implementation of option appraisal in Scotland. I should particularly like to record the assistance given me by: C. Forsyth, W.M. Martin and A.L. Rennie (SHHD and Scottish Office); A.W. Foster and G.B. Wilson (Building Division of the Common Services Agency); G. Brown, P. Merrylees, A. Neilston, A.M. Paterson, J.R. Wilson and the Registry (Greater Glasgow Health Board); D. Cohen, J. Henderson, A. Ludbrook and G.H. Mooney (Health Economics Research Unit, at the University of Aberdeen); and A.J. Owen. Whilst those listed and others have undoubtedly shaped this study, responsibility for the views expressed remains the the author alone.

1. Foster, C.D. (1971) *Politics, Finance and the Role of Economics*, London: George Allen & Unwin, p.175.

2. Committee of Public Accounts, 1980-1981, *Report 17* (HC 255), London: HMSO, Q 1500.

3. Appropriation Accounts, 1981-82, Volume 8, London: HMSO, para 36

4. Treasury (1980) *Investment appraisal and Discounting Techniques and the Use of the Test Discount Rate in the Public Sector,* London: HM Treasury, para 8.

5. Committee of Public Accounts, 1980-81, *op.cit.*, Q 1505.

6. Committee of Public Accounts, 1981-82a, Report 28 (HC 417), London: HMSO.

7. Select Committee on Procedure (Finance) 1982-83, Report 1, Volume III (HC 24III), London: HMSO, appendix 11.

8. S.H.H.D. (1979a) Circular NHS 1979 (GEN) 40 "Supply, installation and warranty maintenance of X-ray and other specialised equipment."

9. S.H.H.D. (1979b) Circular SHHD/DS (79) 70 "Estmancode-Estate management, practice code for Scotland. Commissioning of health service buildings".

10. Treasury (1983) *Investment Appraisal in the Public Sector: A Management Guide for Government Departments,* London: HM

Treasury, para 35 (emphasis added).

11. Treasury (1983) *op.cit.* para.36.1

12. The SHHD funded a research project in 1974, which was eventually succeeded by HERU. The person appointed gave occasional advice to the Scottish Health Service on an 'ex gratia' basis, as is currently the case with HERU.

13. Cohen, David (1983) Health Economics Research Unit, University of Aberdeen. Personal communication in October 1983.

14. In addition to HERU, since 1977 the Lothian Health Board has funded an economist at the Department of Community Medicine at the University of Edinburgh, from whom economic advice may be sought; and between 1981 and 1983 Grampian Health Board employed one in its Treasurer's Department.

15. Treasury (1982) *Investment Appraisal in the Public Sector,* London: HM Treasury, paras 3.6-3.26.

16. D.H.S.S. (1982) *Appraisal of Development Options in the National Health Service,* London, DHSS.

17. Committee of Public Accounts, 1981-82b, *Report 17* (HC 375), London: HMSO, para 10.

18. Treasury (1983), *op.cit.* annex A

19. Klarman, H.E., et al. (1968) "Cost-effectiveness analysis applied to the treatment of chronic renal disease" *Medical Care* 6, pp.48-54; and Ludbrook, A. (1981) "A cost- effectiveness analysis of the treatment of chronic renal failure", *Applied Economics*, 13, pp.337-350.

20. Treasury, (1983), *op.cit.* Annex D, para.31.

21. Card, W.I. and Mooney, G.H. (1977), "What is the monetary value of a human life?" *British Medical Journal,* 2, pp.1627-1629; and Jennett, B. (1984), "Economic appraisal", *British Medical Journal,* 2, 88 pp.1781-2.

22. C.P.A., (1981-2a), *op.cit.* Q.3224

23. S.H.H.D., (1980a), *Scottish Health Authorities: Priorities for the*

Eighties Edinburgh: HMSO.

24. Milne, R.G. (1981), "Priorities in the Scottish Health Service: the place of the SHARE Report." in H.M. Drucker and N.L. Drucker (Eds) *The Scottish Government Yearbook, 1982* Edinburgh, Paul Harris, pp.207-236.

25. S.H.H.D. (1980a), *op.cit.* para VI 3, emphasis added.

26. Williams, A. (1974), "The cost-benefit approach", *British Medical Bulletin* 30(3) pp.252-256.

27. Drummond, M.F. (1981), *Studies in Economic Appraisal in Health Care*, Oxford, Oxford U.P.

28. Milne, R.G., (1981), *op.cit.*

29. S.H.H.D. (1976a) *The Health Service in Scotland: The Way Ahead* Edinburgh: HMSO; and SHHD (1980a) *op.cit.*

30. D.H.S.S. (1982) *op.cit.*, paras 10-11

31. Neuhauser, D. and Lewicki, A.M. "National health insurance and the sixth stool guaiac", *Policy Analysis* 2(2) pp. 175-196.

32. Scottish Home and Health Department (1963a) *Ward Design* (Hospital planning notes No.1), Edinburgh: HMSO; and SHHD (1977b) *In-patient Accommodation* (Hospital planning note no.1), Edinburgh: HMSO.

33. Department of Health for Scotland (1961) *Provision and Design of Casualty and Accident Departments* (Hospital planning notes), Edinburgh: HMSO.

34. S.H.H.D. (1967) *Organization and Design of Out-patient Departments* (Hospital planning note no.6) Edinburgh: HMSO.

35. S.H.H.D. (1965b) Circular SHM 70/1965 "Choice of fuels for hospital boiler plant".

36. D.H.S.S. (1974) DHSS letter dated 30th July "The upgrading and adaptation of existing facilities". Quoted in Owen, A.J. "Health authority capital budgeting: the state of the art in theory and practice", Discussion paper, University of Warwick, April 1978.

37. Wilson, George B. (1984), Building Division of the Common Services Agency. Personal communication in May 1984.

38. Wilson, G.B. (1984) *op.cit.*

39. D.O.H.S (1962) *Hospital Plan for Scotland*, Cmnd 1602, Edinburgh: HMSO.

40. S.H.H.D. (1964), *Revision of Hospital Plan for Scotland,* Edinburgh: HMSO; and S.H.H.D. (1966) *Review of the Hopsital Plan for Scotland* Cmnd 2877, Edinburgh: HMSO

41. Hansard (1970), Written answer, 20th April columns 52-55. Hansard (1971), Written answer, 22nd June, column 275. Hansard (1972), Written answer, 25th April, columns 254-256. Hansard (1977), Written answer, 2nd May, columns 20-27.

42. S.H.H.D. (1984a) *Scottish Health Building Programme: Report of the Capital Steering Group*, Edinburgh: SHHD.

43. S.H.H.D. (1963b), *Vale of Leven Hospital* (Hospital design in use No.1), Edinburgh: HMSO; and SHHD (1965a) *Victoria Hospital, Kirkcaldy* (Hospital design in use No.2), Edinburgh: HMSO; and SHHD (1968) *Bellshill Maternity Hospital* (Hospital design in use No.3), Edinburgh: HMSO.

44. Scottish Hospital Centre (1967) *The Functional analysis of Ward Plans* Edinburgh: SHC; and S.H.H.D. (1969) *The Falkirk Ward* Hospital design in use No. 4), Edinburgh: HMSO.

45. Scottish Hospital Centre (1974) *Health Centre: Design in Use*, Edinburgh: SHC.

46. Wilson, G.B. (1984), *op.cit.*

47. SHHD (1965c), Circular SHM81/1965 "Procedure for preparation and approval of hospital building schemes." para.82; and SHHD (1982a), *Health Building Procurement in Scotland: Procedures Subsequent to Approval in Principle* Edinburgh: SHHD, para 5.24.

48. Treasury (1982) *op.cit.* para.3.4.

49. Levitt, R. (1976), *The Reorganised National Health Service*, London: Croom Helm, p.225.

50. SHHD (1976a), *op.cit.* para.1.6.

51. SHHD (1980a) *op.cit.*

52. Hunter, D. (1980), "Policy-making in area health boards: the role of the board member", in H.M. Drucker and N.L. Drucker (eds) *The Scottish Government Yearbook, 1981* Edinburgh: Paul Harris, pp.156-186.

53. SHHD (1972), Circular HSR(72)C3 "The administrative structure of health boards", para 4.

54. Hunter, D. (1980), *op.cit.*

55. SHHD (1965c) *op.cit.* para.15.

56. SHHD (1975) Circular NHS 1975 (GEN)46 "Closure and change of use of health service premises".

57. The equivalent bodies south of the Border are called 'community health councils'.

58. SHHD (1974b), Circular NHS 1974 (GEN)38. "Local health councils, preparation of schemes". and SHHD (1974c) Circular NHS 1974 (GEN)90 "Local health councils".

59. Only the chairmen of the health boards receive any remuneration for their services.

60. SHHD (1974c) *op.cit.* appendix.

61. Greater Glasgow Health Board (1983), *Statement of Accounts for the year ended 31st March 1983*, Glasgow: GGHB, p.10.

62. SHHD (1977c), Circular NHS 1977 (GEN)59 "Working party report on relationships between health boards and local authorities".

63. SHHD (1980b), Circular NHS 1980 (GEN)5 "Joint planning and support financing arrangements", para 1.

64. DOHS (1961), *op.cit.*

65. DOHS (1962), *op.cit.*

66. SHHD (1973), Design Guide: *Health Centres in Scotland*, Edinburgh, HMSO.

67. SHHD(1976b), Circular CAMO (76)50 "Radiodiagnostic facilities in health centres".

68. Milne, R.G. & Torsney, B. (forthcoming), "Option appraisal and the provision of facilities in health centres in Scotland" (paper submitted for publication).

69. SHHD (1982b), Circular NHS 1982 (GEN)2 "Health board assistance to local authorities by provision of medical services"; and SHHD (1974a), Circular NHS 1974 (GEN)8 "Financial relationships between health boards and local authorities".

70. SHHD (1980b) *op.cit.*

71. The equivalent term south of the Border is "joint finance".

72. Scottish Office (1984) Personal communication

73. Treasury (1982), *op.cit.* para 3.6

74. Treasury (1982), *op.cit.* para.3.6

75. The Treasury (1982, paras.3.8-3.11) has suggested some refinements but they can be ignored for the purposes of this study.

76. Appropriation accounts (1981-82) *op.cit* Vol.8, para.21

77. DHSS (1983), Circular HC(83)22 "Estate management: underused and surplus property in the NHS", para 20.

78. Appropriation accounts, (1974-75), Vol.3, London: HMSO, para 90.

79. Appropriation accounts (1981-2), *op.cit.* paras.38- 39

80. DHSS (1984), Circular DA(84)13 "Crown Land – Planning permission"

81. DHSS (1983), *op.cit.*

82. SHHD (1977d), Circular SHHD/DS (77)1 "Acquisition and disposal of health service property".

83. SHHD (1981), Circular SHHD/DS (81)5 "Disposal of surplus health service property"; and SHHD (1984b), Circular SHHD/DS (84)18 "Acquisition management and disposal of land".

84. Royal Commission on the National Health Service (1978), *Management of Financial Resources in the National Health Service*, Research paper no.2, London: HMSO, p.225

85. They are general practitioners, dentists, pharmacists and opticians.

86. SHHD (1976c), NHS Circular 1976 (GEN)78 "Carry forward of unspent revenue balances".

87. SHHD (1977a), *Scottish Health Authorities Revenue Equalization*, Edinburgh: HMSO.

88. Mooney, G.H. (1977), *The Valuation of Human Life*, London: Macmillan

89. Treasury (1980), *op.cit.* para.3.

90. Heald, D. (1980), "The economic and financial control of UK nationalised industries", *Economic Journal* 90, p.246 and p.248

91. SHHD (1965b), *op.cit.*

92. DHSS (1974), *op.cit.*

93. Department of Health and Social Security (1970) *An Introduction to Present Value Techniques for Engineering and Constructional Economic Comparisons* (Draft supplement to Hospital Technical Memorandum No.), London: DHSS.

94. Henderson, J., McGuire, A. and Parkin, D. (1984), "Acute hospital beds for Fife – 1 Appraisal of options", Health Economics Research Unit, University of Aberdeen, SOAP, No.3.

SUMMARY OF FINDINGS OF MONTGOMERY COMMITTEE OF INQUIRY INTO FUNCTIONS AND POWERS OF ISLANDS COUNCILS

(Cmnd. 9216, April 1984)

ALLAN MACARTNEY
STAFF TUTOR IN POLITICS
THE OPEN UNIVERSITY IN SCOTLAND

I THE POSITIVE RECOMMENDATIONS

General

First, the creation of the islands councils as all-purpose authorities has been a success, and there should not only be no question of reduction in the councils' powers but the opportunity should be taken wherever possible to consolidate, develop and extend these powers. The recommendations are only one stage in a continuing process of development in the local government of the islands. The conclusions should not be regarded as final, nor should they necessarily apply for more than a relatively short period: an argument found unconvincing in 1983 could become thoroughly persuasive in different circumstances some years from now.

In future consultations between the Scottish Office and local authorities, Scottish Office departments should, as a matter of course, give consideration as to whether there might be grounds for asking for a separate islands councils view to be included in any collective response from local authorities; consideration should be given, as a matter of course, to the possibility of highlighting particular aspects which may be of special relevance to the islands, whether or not an islands view is being requested, and, in reaching a decision on these matters, it should be kept in mind that islands councils, both as all-purpose authorities and as local authorities in particularly remote and isolated areas, may be affected not only by proposals which are directed at such areas but also by proposals which are designed with mainland or urban circumstances in mind but which are to be applied to all local authorities. There may be circumstances in which Acts of Parliament should include a provision to allow the Secretary of State to vary their application to the island areas, and such provisions should in future be considered in relation to all Scottish legislation at an early stage in its preparation. The general principle should apply that if powers are needed by all the islands councils these should be given in public general legislation.

The present system of attendance allowances should be replaced by a form of salary for councillors of a fixed annual sum to compensate them for the time they have devoted to all forms of duty as councillor, and also to make up any financial loss they may have suffered. Health Boards in the islands should be instructed to take note of community councils' views, and to consult them on local issues.

The Government should initiate a study to work out a broad policy towards Gaelic involving all interested bodies, with agreed objectives and responsibilities clearly apportioned between local authorities, central government and the other agencies concerned. When this policy is agreed, a system should be developed to allocate resources in accordance with the respective responsibilities assigned for Gaelic. Until that time,steps should be taken to ensure that adequate financial support is made available to the Western Isles Council to ensure that their efforts to promote the Gaelic language may continue.

Block Grant

The Secretary of State's consent to local authorities to incur capital expenditure should be given to the islands councils in the form of a single block allocation, obtained by aggregating the allocations for separate programmes, with the object that the councils take responsibility for managing this expenditure in order to secure the maximum value from their allocations. The aggregated figure should be obtained by the same procedures as at present, under which allocations are separately fixed for each service, and the councils should be told the amount which it is thought appropriate for them to spend on each service. The councils should report their actual expenditure to the Scottish Office in due course in the normal way.

Oil-related Development (Shetland)

Agriculture and Fishing

The Secretary of State should recognise the direct interest of the islands councils in the welfare of the fishing industry in their areas, and they should be included in any local management arrangements.

The Government should ensure that the use of resources obtained by Orkney and Shetland Islands Councils to develop local industries is not constrained in any harmonisation of aids to the fishing industry in the European Community. The islands councils should be able to operate their own schemes of assistance, although it may be necessary to reach agreement between the councils and central government on the types of assistance each may provide.

Assistance to agriculture provided by the Orkney and Shetland Islands Councils through the reserve funds should be allowed to supplement other grants received, if the additional assistance is to meet costs specifically arising from remoteness, such as the cost of sea transport.

Works and Communications

The islands councils should be given powers to operate their own air services, and should be allowed to take over the Civil Aviation Authority aerodromes in their areas.

Orkney Islands Council should take over responsibility for the internal ferry service in their area.

If the islands councils want to extend their control over the imposition of speed limits on the principal roads in their area,the Secretary of State should make the necessary order.

When the ceiling cost for grant purposes for installation of water and sewerage services is reviewed, this should be determined in the light of the fact that new schemes are going to increasingly remote or very small communities, with higher overall connection costs as a result.

Protective and Welfare Services

A system of apportionment of costs for police and fire services based on actual costs incurred in each local authority area should be considered. The Secretary of State should appoint an arbiter to deal with any differences between constituent authorities over the terms of the joint schemes.

The financial burden on the Western Isles Council arising from the costs of the District Court in their area should be removed.

The Scottish Home and Health Department should encourage and improve the operation of liaison committees in fields of common concern to local authorities and the Health Boards, and central government should continue to give support to the islands areas for projects under the support finance scheme.

The provision of the Tenants' Rights, Etc. (Scotland) Act 1980 whose effect is to give teachers who are tenants of islands councils the right to buy their house should be amended to put islands councils in the same position as other education authorities in Scotland, with the requirement being removed that the Secretary of State's consent must be obtained before an application to buy a house is refused.

II PROPOSALS REJECTED

General

We recommend against the establishment of a "Council of the Islands". We also recommend against the proposals made for an advisory committee to the Secretary of State, as a source of advice on islands matters.

It is the view of the majority of us that the proposal for an "islands desk" in the Scottish Office should not be pursued.

Islands council employees should not be allowed to stand for election to their council. There should be no special arrangements for declaration of interests by islands councillors.

The islands councils should not be given powers to amalgamate community bodies such as community councils, schools councils and local health councils.

There should be no change in the arrangements for regulating the activities described by the islands councils as "inimical developments".

Finance, Oil

Additional responsibilities are not to be taken on unless an area can afford to meet some of the costs of the service.

There should be no change in the arrangements for valuation in the islands. There should be no changes in the way the rate burden is distributed between the oil industry and the local (non-oil related) sector within the Shetland community and there should be no special changes in the legislation on industrial derating or the rating of external plant and machinery as a result of its application in the islands.

Economic Development

There should be no transfer of responsibility from the Highlands and Islands Development Board to the islands councils for providing assistance for economic and industrial development or social development. There should be no change in the composition of the Highlands and Islands Development Board.

Islands councils should not be allowed to have direct access to various European institutions that provide financial assistance to local authorities but should continue to channel their applications through central government.

The Secretary of State's crofting estates in the Western Isles should not be transferred to the ownership of the Western Isles Council.

Works and Communications

There should be no change in the ownership of the ferry terminals at present owned by the Scottish Transport Group in the Western Isles, and no change in responsibility for the management of Stornoway harbour.

There should be no changes in the present financial arrangements for expenditure on roads, other than those as a result of the granting of block capital allocations as recommended by the Committee.

There need be no special arrangements for building control in the islands.

There should be no special arrangements for the direct labour organisations of islands councils.

Fire, Police and Health

There should be no separate police or fire authorities for the islands areas.

There should be no change in allocation of responsibility for health service matters between the Health Boards and the islands councils. There should be no change in the methods of appointment of Health Board members.

SUMMARY OF OPINION POLLS 1983/84

ALLAN MACARTNEY
STAFF TUTOR IN POLITICS
THE OPEN UNIVERSITY IN SCOTLAND

This year we rely again on the monthly System Three (Scotland) polls published in the *Glasgow Herald* to indicate the voting intention of Scotland's electorate, between the two national June polls which form a neat, natural point of comparison. Table 1 thus gives the General Election result of 1983 and the Euroelection result of 1984 with the monthly opinion poll figures in between. Table 2 provides a comparison with a separately organised poll (MORI, published in *The Scotsman*).

Table 3 gives the results of the only opinion poll on the constitutional future of Scotland, also undertaken by MORI for *The Scotsman*.

Given the nature of the speculation about the Euroelections, and the inaccurate prophecies publicly made, it is worth drawing attention to the answers to questions asked in advance of the European Parliamentary elections on what turned out to be two key variables: turnout and personality. Maybe some TV pundits should have absorbed the MORI findings before making predictions! To be specific, the impact of personality (already discernible in 1979 *par excellence* in North East Scotland) could be gauged by answers to the question "Do you know the names of any members of the European Parliament who represent Scotland?". Only 35% could name a Scottish MEP, but, of those named, Winnie Ewing (SNP) scored 76%, with Janey Buchan (Labour) coming in second at 10% and Alasdair Hutton (Conservative) third with 6%.

The same poll (MORI, 25th April 1984) asked respondents how likely they were to vote. 27% said they were "certain" to vote and a further 17% said they were "very likely" to vote in the Euroelections; the actual turnout was 33%. By way of comparison, of those polled 54% stated that they were "certain" to vote in the district council elections and 16% said they were "very likely" to vote. Actual district election turnout was 44.%.

Acknowledgements

The *Yearbook* is again indebted to System Three (Scotland), MORI, the *Glasgow Herald* and *The Scotsman* for permission to publish the data in this section. We are grateful to Edinburgh University Audio-Visual Services for graphical presentation.

Technical Note

Percentages have been rounded; "don't knows", refusals and "won't votes" have been omitted. The dates given are those of completion of the fieldwork, rather than dates of eventual publication.

FIGURE 1 VOTING INTENTION (MONTHLY) JUNE 1983 – JUNE 1984
SYSTEM THREE POLLS

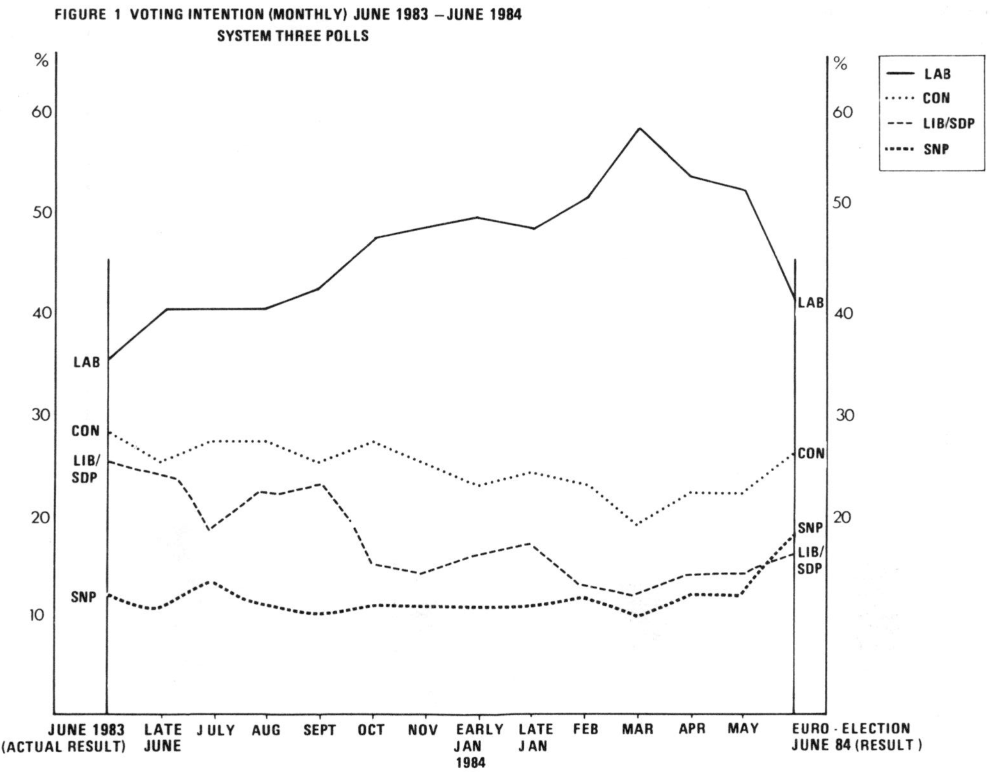

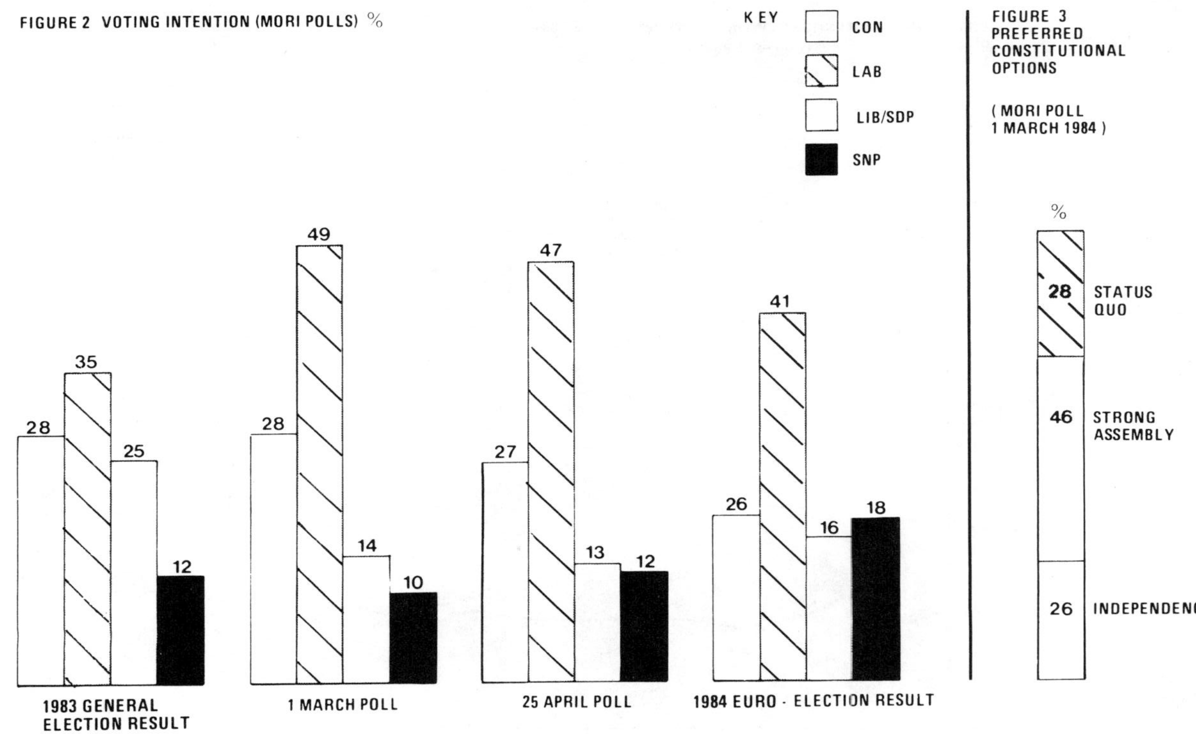
FIGURE 2 VOTING INTENTION (MORI POLLS) %
KEY
CON
LAB
LIB/SDP
SNP
28
35
25
12
1983 GENERAL ELECTION RESULT
28
49
14
10
1 MARCH POLL
27
47
13
12
25 APRIL POLL
26
41
16
18
1984 EURO - ELECTION RESULT
FIGURE 3 PREFERRED CONSTITUTIONAL OPTIONS
(MORI POLL 1 MARCH 1984)
%
28
STATUS QUO
46
STRONG ASSEMBLY
26
INDEPENDENCE

SCOTTISH LEGISLATION 1983

HAMISH McN. HENDERSON
DEPARTMENT OF SCOTS LAW
UNIVERSITY OF EDINBURGH

Election years tend to result in a fairly light crop of legislation, but in 1983 there were actually three more Acts passed than in 1982, although their bulk was less.

Of the sixty public general Acts passed, six were consolidation Acts. Those of interest to Scotland were the *Representation of the People Act*, derived mainly from the Act of 1949; the *Pilotage Act,* consolidating the Acts of the same name of 1913 and 1936, with some material derived from the *Merchant Shipping Act 1979;* the *Litter Act,* bringing together in a dozen sections material scattered through a dozen and a half different sources; the *Car Tax Act* which gathers together in a similar number of sections similarly fragmented material; the very technical *Value Added Tax Act;* and the *Medical Act* which is derived mainly from Acts of the same name passed in 1956, 1959 and 1978.

There were only four "Scotland only" Acts, all passed before the General Election. Two of them are procedurally of some interest. The *Solvent Abuse (Scotland) Act* has the distinction of being one of fewer than a dozen and a half 10-minute-rule Bills that have been successfully enacted since 1945.

The *Divorce Jurisdiction, Court Fees and Legal Aid (Scotland) Act* is the enactment of the first public Bill since the Union of 1707, of which the second reading debate has taken place in Scotland.

Chapter Number

12 *Divorce Jurisdiction, Court Fees and Legal Aid (Scotland) Act* This is really a miscellaneous provisions Act, with four sections of substance, but it is likely to have considerable significance socially throughout the country and economically in relation to the administration of justice.

Less than half a line is sufficient to give Sheriff Courts jurisdiction concurrent with that of the Court of Session in actions of divorce. The Royal Commission on Legal Services in Scotland in its report (Cmnd 7846), published in 1980, had recommended that the Sheriff Court should be given exclusive jurisdiction as a court of first instance in divorce actions. However, the Government, having considered comments which it received on the report, preferred to give pursuers the option. It will be possible to choose the Sheriff Court within whose jurisdiction either party has resided for forty days before the summons is served. Scottish domicile, or habitual residence in Scotland for one year, continue to be requirements.

There had been considerable debate as to whether the extension of the Sheriff's jurisdiction would reduce the cost of divorce actions to the client. The Society of Solicitors in the Supreme Courts had presented the Government with calculations which demonstrated that divorce in the Sheriff Court would in fact prove to be more expensive. But the Government was persuaded by figures based on those in a recent report on the Scottish Legal Aid Scheme, which seemed to indicate that a saving of about one sixth should be achieved.

This provision was due to come into force on May 1, 1984. The simplified procedure by way of affidavit introduced in the Court of Session in January 1983 for divorce based on non-cohabitation for two or five years, where there are no children under sixteen, and no financial claims, and where neither party suffers from mental incapacity, would be extended to the Sheriff Court when the Act came into effect.

The implementation of the fixed penalty procedures of the Transport Act 1982 was expected to lead to a substantial reduction in the workload of Sheriff Courts, and consequently only a small increase in the number of staff and of sheriffs was envisaged.

Chapter Number

12 The general rule that facts alleged in evidence must be corroborated is relaxed in such classes of undefended actions for divorce as the Lord Advocate may prescribe. The clause is similar in language to section 9 of the *Law Reform (Miscellaneous Provisions)(Scotland) Act 1968 (c.70),* which removed the need for corroboration in actions of damages for person injuries. The court may in its discretion call for further evidence. Initially, this relaxation will be restricted to cases proceeding by way of affidavit.

The Secretary of State is given powers to regulate fees and outlays of counsel and solicitors in legal aid case, and in legal advice and assistance cases. When introducing the Bill in the House of Lords, the Lord Advocate pointed out that the placing on the Secretary of State of the duty to regulate fees, where he is responsible for their payment, follows the general pattern on the remuneration of professional services in the National Health Service and elsewhere. Formerly, the High Court of Judiciary had power to prescribe counsel's fees for criminal work, but in practice an informal table was provided by the Faculty of Advocates to the Law Society. In civil matters, fees were regulated by the Court of Session.

Similarly, the Act transfers from the High Court of Judiciary and from the Court of Session to the Secretary of State powers to regulate certain fees paid to courts in criminal and civil proceedings. These fees are designed to contribute towards the cost of running the courts. the Government's policy on the level of costs to be recovered by way of court fees can be studied in the Treasury Minute on the Twelfth Report from the Committee of Public Accounts for the Session 1981-82 (Cmnd 8759).

33 *Solvent Abuse (Scotland) Act* This Act consists of a short textual amendment to Part III of the *Social Work (Scotland) Act 1968 (c.49),* which deals with children's hearings. Section 32 lists eight conditions, any of which, if satisfied, may entitle a children's hearing to impose compulsory measures of care upon a child.

The new condition is that the child has misused a volatile substance by deliberately inhaling, other than for medical purposes, that substance's vapour. The expression "volatile substance" covers more than solvents, so that the legislation applies also to items such as shoe polish and sticking plaster, which are also capable of abuse by sniffers.

Chapter Number

33 "Glue sniffing" has been discussed in Parliament from time to time for a decade and a half and in recent years the problem has become acute. In 1981 there were thirty-three deaths from solvent abuse in the United Kingdom and of these eleven occurred in Strathclyde. Concern was expressed in Parliament during the debates on this Bill that the sale of solvents for the purpose of solvent abuse was not a statutory offence.

However, the decision of the High Court of Judiciary in the case of *Khaliq v. Her Majesty's Advocate* on November 17, 1983 (1984 SLT 137) has removed the need for legislation. It was held that the charge that the accused had sold quantities of solvents, particularly Evostik glue, to eighteen named children and many others, in tins, tubes, crisp packets and plastic bags, for the purpose of inhalation of the vapours of these solvents (knowing that the children would do this, and that the inhalation was or could be injurious to their health or endanger their lives) effectively set forth facts relevant and sufficient to constitute a criminal offence.

39 *Mental Health (Amendment) (Scotland) Act* This is a major Act consisting of a series of textual amendments to the *Mental Health (Scotland) Act 1960 (c.61),* which will facilitate a reprint of that Act in Statutes in Force, or an early consolidation Act. It follows the publication in April 1982 of a consultative paper, "Review of the Mental Health (Scotland) Act 1960", by the Scottish Home and Health Department, and in November 1982 of a "Memorandum on Proposals for the Amendment of the Mental Health (Scotland) Act 1960". Much of the Act parallels provisions in the English *Mental Health (Amendment) Act 1982 (c.51),* which was speedily followed by the consolidating *Mental Health Act 1983 (c.20).*

The Act reflects progress in the diagnosis and treatment of people suffering from mental illness in the last 20 years, and changes in the attitude of society to the rights, or lack of rights, of such people. Only a few highlights are discussed here.

In keeping with modern attitudes, the term "mental deficiency" gives way to the less pejorative expression, "mental handicap", and "defective" becomes a person "protected by the provisions of this section", i.e. s.96 of the 1960 Act. The intention may be commendable, but whether it achieves the desired end is open to doubt. Adults may follow the lead given by Parliament. Children can often be cruel.

Chapter Number

39 The minimum number of members of the Mental Health Commission for Scotland is increased from seven to ten, of whom three must be women. The maximum will in future be left to the discretion of the Secretary of State.

Formerly the Commission had a duty to visit patients "regularly, and as often as they may think appropriate". Now the Commission must visit a patient either during each successive year in which the authority to detain him is renewed, and where no appeal has been made to a sheriff against detention.

The advisory duties of the Commission are extended; in addition to advising the Secretary of State, it must now advise also area health boards and local authorities on any matter arising out of the Act that has been referred to it by the Secretary of State or any of these bodies. In addition it must bring to the attention of the Secretary of State and of any other body, any matter concerning the welfare of patients, which it considers should be brought to their attention.

Under the 1960 Act the Commission had published only four reports. Starting in 1985, it will be required to publish an annual report.

The maximum period of detention for treatment and assessment in an emergency is reduced from seven days to seventy-two hours. This period may be extended for a further twenty-eight days under new provisions added by this Act. This will happen when a psychiatrist reports to the board of management of the hospital that it is appropriate for the patient to be detained for at least a limited period. Where practicable, the consent of the patient's nearest relative or a mental health officer is required, and its absence must be explained in the report. The local authority must arrange for a mental health officer to interview the patient within three weeks of the start of the twenty-eight days, who reports to the responsible medical officer and the Mental Welfare Commission on the patient's social circumstances. This may affect the course of treatment to be followed. The patient has a right to appeal to the sheriff within the twenty-eight days, to order his discharge.

A voluntary patient may be detained by a nurse for up to two hours where it is necessary for the patient's health or safety, or for the protection of others and where it is not practicable to secure the immediate attendance of a doctor to make an emergency

Chapter Number

39 recommendation. This provision is designed to avoid the risk of legal liability of nurses where they seek on medical grounds to restrain voluntary patients from leaving hospital.

Formerly, the initial period of detention of long-term patients was a year, renewable for a further year and subsequently at two-yearly intervals, with the approval of the sheriff. Each of these periods is now halved. The patient may appeal to the sheriff against his detention, once in each period of renewal.

The 1983 Act inserts a new Part in the Act of 1960 dealing with consent of compulsorily detained patients.

The more rigorous forms of treatment require the consent of the patient *and* a second opinion. These forms are surgical operations to destroy brain tissue or its functioning, and other forms specified in regulations, probably hormone treatment and sterilisation. The class was defined in the Review of the (English) Mental Health Act 1959 as being "hazardous, irreversible or not fully established".

Others forms of treatment specified in regulations, and the administration of medicine by any means (after the lapse of three months since the medicine was first administered for the patient's mental disorder) require the consent of the patient *or* a second opinion. This category is expected to include non-hazardous, non-reversible and well-proven methods of treatment by surgery, treatment with medicines and electro-convulsive therapy.

These requirements as to consents and second opinions do not apply to any treatment immediately necessary to save a patient's life, nor to others (not being irreversible or hazardous), immediately necessary to alleviate serious suffering by the patient, or to control violent or dangerous behaviour. Treatments that are not irreversible are similarly permitted if immediately necessary to prevent a serious deterioration of the patient's condition.

In both cases, the regulation-making power ensures flexibility, as knowledge of treatment develops. The responsible medical officer must make a report on the patient before each successive renewal of his detention.

The patient may withdraw his consent to treatment at any time

Chapter Number

39 before its completion. But the Act contains safeguards, permitting continuation of treatment if discontinuance is considered likely to cause serious suffering to the patient.

Medical treatment for his mental disorder, being treatment not falling within the above cases, does not require the patient's consent if it is given by, or under the direction of, the responsible medical officer.

46 *Agricultural Holdings (Amendment) (Scotland) Act* Modern economical developments and recent legislation guaranteeing security of tenure to tenant-farmers and their surviving spouses or children as successors, indefinitely from one generation to the next, have combined to reduce the number of farms available for letting.

In order to try to secure some mitigation of this problem, the Scottish Landowners Federation and the National Farmers' Union of Scotland made joint proposals on rents, arbitration and inheritance. This was followed by the setting-up of a working party by the Department of Agriculture and Fisheries for Scotland to examine and establish the precise intention of these proposals and consider any other relevant matters, with a view to preparing appropriate instructions to the Parliamentary Draftsman for amendment of the Scottish Agricultural Holdings Legislation. This Act is based on the recommendations of the working party.

There are some who may consider the Act to be a public relations exercise of little value, economically or socially, because many landlords are now tempted to take advantage of the provisions of the *Limited Partnership Act 1907 (7 Edw. VII c.24)* and enter into partnerships with those who would have been their tenants. There is then no tenancy to terminate, but a partnership to dissolve.

The substantive part of the Act is in the form of a series of textual amendments to the *Agricultural Holdings (Scotland) Act 1949 (c.75)* and includes a revised version on the ninth schedule to that Act. Some provisions from other statutes are reproduced in the 1982 Act so that they may be conveniently incorporated in a future Statutes in Force reprint, thus relieving some of the pressure of demand for an early consolidation of this code.

The Act begins with establishing guidelines to help the arbiter or the

Chapter Number

46 Scottish Land Court in a question of variation of rent to determine the rent properly payable, disregarding distortions in the market and having regard to the current economic conditions of the relevant sector of the agricultural industry.

The rent review period is reduced from five years – which was rather long during a period of high inflation – to three years, as in England.

The Act preserves the expectations of succession to tenancies entered into before the end of 1983, and so the onus of proving to the Scottish Land Court that the statutory grounds for serving a notice to quit on a successor tenant in fact exist continues to lie with the landlord. But where a tenancy is let on or after January 1, 1984, the onus of disproving them will in most cases lie on the successor tenant. A new ground added in relation to post-1983 leases is that the successor tenant does not have sufficient financial resources to enable him to farm the holding with reasonable efficiency.

The jurisdiction of the Scottish Land Court is extended, so that it may hear an appeal in rent review cases not only on a question of law but also on one of fact, where, because the parties have failed to agree on an arbiter, the arbiter has been appointed by the Secretary of State or (where a Government Department is involved) by the Land Court; where arbiters are appointed by the parties, the arbiter remains final on fact. Many parties may take advantage of existing provisions of the Act of 1949 and concur in invoking the jurisdiction of the Scottish Land Court itself to act as arbiter.

INDEX OF SCOTTISH LEGISLATION

The 1982 Yearbook contains an Index of Scottish Legislation covering the years 1970-1980 (see pages 307 to 312). The 1983 and 1984 Yearbooks updated the Index down to 1982.

Readers may wish to update their copies to cover 1983. The following items should be entered at the appropriate places in alphabetical order.

Abuse, Solvent, 1983 c. 33. Agricultural Holdings, 1983 c. 46. Aid, Legal, etc., 1983 c. 12. Court Fees, etc., 1983 c. 12. Divorce Jurisdiction, Court Fees and Legal Aid, 1983 c. 12. Fees, Court, etc., 1983 c. 12. Health, Mental, (Amendment), 1983 c. 39. Holdings, Agricultural, 1983 c. 46. Jurisdiction, Divorce, etc., 1983 c. 12. Legal Aid, etc., 1983 c. 12. Mental Health (Amendment), 1983 c. 39. Solvent Abuse, 1983 c. 33.

RECENT PUBLICATIONS IN SCOTTISH GOVERNMENT AND POLITICS

C.H. ALLEN
DEPARTMENT OF POLITICS
UNIVERSITY OF EDINBURGH

The list below covers material omitted from previous listings, and material published since the last list in the period 1.6.1983 to 31.5.1984. Where a publisher is not specified, the publisher and author are the same. I would be grateful to be told of any errors or omissions.

1. ADAM SMITH INSTITUTE, *Scottish policy*. London, 1983, 34pp.
2. AGE CONCERN, *Housing facts and figures*. Edinburgh, 1983, 21pp.
3. ALLAN, B (ed), *Making the city work: enterprise and democracy in urban Europe*. Glasgow: Glasgow District Council, 1982, 128pp.
4. ALLAN, N. *Scotland the broken image*. Ottawa: the author, 1982, 70pp
5. ALLEN, C H, "Recent publications in Scottish government and politics", *Scottish Government Yearbook* 1984, 256-77
6. ALPINE, R L W, "The case of whiskey (use of data)", *Understanding the Scottish economy*, ed. K Ingham & J Love, 284-96
7. ANON, "Fiddling while Rome burns", *Local Government Forum* 4 (1983) 12
8. ANON, *Herion abuse in Scotland*. Glasgow: Glasgow University Centre for Urban and Regional Research Discussion Paper 9, 1983, 35pp.
9. ANON, "Migration trends", *Grampian Quarterly Economic Review*, Autumn 1983, 1-17
10. ANON, "Profile of councillors", *Local Government Forum* 4 (1983), 4, 9
11. ANON, "The lost worlds of Scottish politics; an invitation to debate

about the councillors job", *Local Government Forum* 4 (1983), 5-8

12. ANON, *The public sector and urban economic regeneration.* Glasgow: Glasgow University Centre for Urban and Regional Research, Discussion Paper 12, 1983, 43pp
13. ANON, "The Shetland Movement", *New Shetlander* 146 (1983) 20-22
14. ANDERSON, C & NORQUAY, G, "Superiorism", *Cencrastus* 15 (1984) 8-10
15. ARNOT, B, "The threat to the NHS in Scotland: the cuts and privatisation", *Scottish Trade Union Review* 20 (1983)
16. ASHCROFT, B, "Briefing paper: regional industrial development (Cmnd 9711)", *Quarterly Economic Commentary,* 9,3 (1984)
17. ...."The Scottish region and the regions of Scotland", *Understanding the Scottish economy,* ed. K Ingham & J Love, 1973-187
18. ASHMORE, R, *Herion addiction in Edinburgh.* BA dissertation, Edinburgh University Sociology Department, 1984
19. ASHTON, J, "Assembly and alliances", *Scottish Marxist* 28 (1984) 3-5
20. BAIN, A D "Markets for finance", *Understanding the Scottish economy,* ed. K Ingham & J Love, 55-64
21. BALDRY, C et al, "Fighting multinational power: possibilities, limitations and contradictions", *Capital and Class* 20 (1983) 158-67
22. BAUR, C, "The election conundrum", *Scottish Government Yearbook* 1984, 19-26
23. BEGG, H M, *Regional policy: the Scottish experience.* Dundee: Duncan of Jordanstone College of Art, Dept. of Town and Regional Planning, Occasional Paper 13, 1983, 45pp
24. BELL, D, "The labour market in Scotland", *Understanding the Scottish economy,* ed. K Ingham & J Love, 65-73
25. ...."What do indicators indicate?", *Understanding the Scottish economy,* ed. K Ingham & J Love, 273-83
26. BLACK, R M, "Research, intelligence and policy making in Strathclyde Regional Council", *Local Government Policy Making,* 9,2 (1982) 65-70
27. BOCHEL, J & DENVER, D, "The 1983 General Election in Scotland", *Scottish Government Yearbook* 1984, 4-18
28. BOLD, A, "Healing Scotland's divided self", *Weekend Scotsman,* 7.5.83, 1
29. "An open letter on the closed mind" *Chapman,* 35/36 (1983) 2-6
30. BOOTH, S, MONEY, W, & PITT, D, "The Glasgow East Area Renewal project", *Local Government Policy Making,* 9,2 (1982) 47-54
31. BOOTH, S & PITT, D, *A paradox of freedom: interventionism in the Scottish economy.* Strathclyde Papers on Government and Politics 23,

1983, 27pp.

32. ....“Geared up for urban renewal?”, *Scottish Planner* 10 (1983) 2
33. BOUNDARY COMMISSION FOR SCOTLAND, *Third periodical report.* Edinburgh: HMSO, 1983, 2 vols.
34. ....*Report: 1983 review of European Assembly constituencics.* Edinburgh: HMSO (Cmnd 9176), 1984, 38pp.
35. BRAND, J, McLEAN, D & MILLER, W, “The birth and death of a three party system: Scotland in the 70's”, *British Journal of Political Science,* 13,4 (1983) 463-88
36. BRAND, J & MILLER, W, *Study of the British General Election in Scotland.* London: SSRC Report HR 4116, 1980, 108pp.
37. BREITENBACH, E, “Women and work”, *Scottish Marxist* 27 (1983) 809
38. BROOKS, R G, “Scotland's health”, *Understanding the Scottish economy,* ed. K Ingham & J Love, 107-16.
39. BROWN, G & COOK, R, (Eds), *Scotland: the real divide.* Edinburgh: Mainstream, 1983, 256pp.
40. BROWNRIGG, M, “Tourism”, *Understanding the Scottish economy,* ed. K Ingham & J Love, 87-93
41. BULPITT, J, *Territory and power in the United Kingdom.* Manchester: Manchester University Press, 1983, 246pp
42. CALDERWOOD, R, “Strathclyde: an exciting management challenge”, *Local Government Policy Making,* 9,2 (1982) 57-64
43. CAMPBELL, D, “The client-group method of apportioning rates support grant: a challenge to policy planners?”, *Local Government Policy Making,* 9,2 (1982) 80-88
44. CARMICHAEL, K, “Family poverty”, *Scotland: the real divide,* ed. G Brown & R Cook, 145-51
45. CARNIE, J, *Parliament and Scottish ‘issues of conscience’ in the 1970's.* Ph.D. thesis, Edinburgh University, 1983,
46. CARSON, D, *Scottish football.* BA dissertation, Edinburgh University Sociology Department, 1984
47. CARTER, C, *Innovations in planning thought and practice at Cumbernauld New Town 1956-62.* Milton Keynes: Open University New Town Study Unit, 1983, 64pp
48. ....*The evolution of planning at the regional level in Scotland 1945-75.* Dundee: Duncan of Jordanstone College of Art, Dept. of Town and Regional Planning, Occasional Paper 7, 1982, 85pp
49. CARTY, T, “Scottish legal culture and the withering away of the state: a study in MacCormick's nationalism”, *Cencrastus* 14 (1983) 59; reply in *Ibid* 15 (1984), 43-44
50. CENTRE FOR URBAN AND REGIONAL RESEARCH, *Consumer problems and service provision in rural areas.* Glasgow:

Glasgow University, CURR Discussion Paper 14, 1984, 55pp
51. CHAPMAN, K, "Energy resources", *Scotland: a new study,* ed. C M Clapperton (Newton Abbot: David & Charles, 1983), 234-51.
52. CLARK, I R & FENWICK, J M, "Reflexions on Shetland and oil", *New Shetlander* 145 (1983) 27-28
53. CLARKE, W, "Communist councillor", *Scottish Marxist* 28 (1984) 6
54. COLLAXCOT, R A, *A study of the development of general practice in the Scottish islands.* Ph.D. thesis, Leicester university, 1982, 315pp
55. COMMISSION OF THE EUROPEAN COMMUNITIES, *The UK and the EEC: Scotland.* Edinburgh, 1984, 35pp
56. COMMISSIONER FOR LOCAL ADMINISTRATION IN SCOTLAND, *Report of discontinuation of an investigation against City of Glasgow District Council,* Edinburgh, May 1984, 3pp (No.631)
57. ....*Cumnock & Doon D.C.,* Edinburgh, January 1983, 1pp. (No.501)
58. ....*Cunninghame D.C.,* Edinburgh, June 1983, 2pp (No.549)
59. ....*Renfrew D.C.* Edinburgh, September 1983, 5pp (No.569)
60. ....*Stirling D.C.,* Edinburgh, January 1983, 2pp (No.495)
61. *Report of investigation against Argyll & Bute D.C.* Edinburgh, August, 1983, 8pp (No.563)
62. ....*Argyll & Bute D.C.,* Edinburgh, August 1983, 7pp (No.565)
63. ....*Argyll & Bute D.C.,* Edinburgh, October 1983, 13pp (No.586)
64. ....*Banff & Buchan D.C.,* Edinburgh, November 1982, 5pp (No.479)
65. ....*Banff & Buchan D.C.,* Edinburgh, August 1983, 10pp (No.564)
66. ....*City of Dundee D.C.,* November 1983, 6pp (No.587)
67. ....*City of Edinburgh D.C.,* Edinburgh, December 1982, 16pp (No.485)
68. ....*City of Edinburgh D.C.,* Edinburgh, July, 1983, 8pp (No.561)
69. ....*City of Edinburgh D.C.,* Edinburgh, September 1983, 4pp (No.570)
70. ....*City of Edinburgh D.C.,* Edinburgh, October 1983, 2pp (No.577)
71. ....*City of Edinburgh D.C.,* Edinburgh, October 1983, 13pp (No.580)
72. ....*City of Edinburgh D.C.,* Edinburgh, November 1983, 3pp (No.588)
73. ....*City of Glasgow D.C.,* Edinburgh, December 1982, 5pp (No.481)
74. ....*City of Glasgow D.C.,* Edinburgh, January 1983, 5pp (No.494)
75. ....*City of Glasgow D.C.,* Edinburgh, February 1983, 10pp (No.502)
76. ....*City of Glasgow D.C.,* Edinburgh, June 1983, 7pp (No.556)
77. ....*City of Glasgow D.C.,* Edinburgh, July 1983, 6pp (No.560)
78. ....*City of Glasgow D.C.,* Edinburgh, October 1983, 4pp (No.581)
79. ....*City of Glasgow D.C.,* Edinburgh, October 1983, 7pp (No.585)
80. ....*City of Glasgow D.C.,* Edinburgh, November 1983, 6pp (No.589)
81. ....*City of Glasgow D.C.,* Edinburgh, November 1983, 9pp (No.591)
82. ....*Clydebank D.C.,* Edinburgh, January 1983, 11pp (No.493)

83. ....*Clydebank D.C.*, Edinburgh, December 1983, 5pp (No.596)
84. ....*Cumnock & Doon D.C.*, Edinburgh, September 1983, 9pp (No.571)
85. ....*Cunninghame D.C.*, Edinburgh, December 1983, 8pp (No.594)
86. ....*Cunninghame D.C. and Kyle & Carrick D.C.*, Edinburgh, October 1983, 21pp (Nos.578/579)
87. ....*Dumbarton D.C.*, Edinburgh, October 1983, 13pp (No.574)
88. ....*Dunfermline D.C.*, Edinburgh, January 1983, 5pp (No.500)
89. ....*Dunfermline D.C.*, Edinburgh, October 1983, 9pp (No.576)
90. ....*Falkirk D.C.*, Edinburgh, December 1982, 8pp (No.486)
91. ....*Falkirk D.C.*, Edinburgh, June 1983, 10pp (No.551)
92. ....*Falkirk D.C.*, Edinburgh, May 1984, 2pp (No.629)
93. ....*Fife R.C.*, Edinburgh, January 1983, 12pp (No.489)
94. ....*Hamilton D.C.*, Edinburgh, December 1982, 6pp (No.483)
95. ....*Hamilton D.C.*, Edinburgh, February 1983, 9pp (No.503)
96. ....*Hamilton D.C.*, Edinburgh, July 1983, 8pp (No 562)
97. ....*Highland R.C.*. Edinburgh, January 1983, 3pp (No.498)
98. ....*Highland R.C. and Inverness D.C.*, Edinburgh, May 1984, 8pp (No.630)
99. ....*Inverclyde D.C.* Edinburgh, January 1983, 3pp (No.497)
100. ....*Inverclyde D.C.* Edinburgh, June 1983, 20pp (No.554)
101. ....*Inverclyde D.C.* Edinburgh, November 1983, 6pp (No.590)
102. ....*Inverness D.C.*, Edinburgh, August 1983, 10pp (No.568)
103. ....*Kilmarnock & Loudon D.C.*, Edinburgh, August 1983, 6pp (No.567)
104. ....*Kirkcaldy D.C.*, Edinburgh, January 1983, 8pp (No.490)
105. ....*Kirkcaldy D.C.*, Edinburgh, November 1983, 8pp (No.592)
106. ....*Kyle & Carrick D.C.*, Edinburgh, December 1982, 13pp (No.482)
107. ....*Lothian R.C.*, Edinburgh, Januaary 1983, 6pp (No.496)
108. ....*Midlothian D.C.*, Edinburgh, December 1982, 5pp (No.487)
109. ....*Monklands D.C.*, Edinburgh, October 1983, 4pp (No.573)
110. ....*Monklands D.C.*, Edinburgh, October 1983, 8pp (No.582)
111. ....*Monklands D.C.*, Edinburgh, December 1983, 5pp (No.595)
112. ....*Motherwell D.C.*, Edinburgh, January 1983, 5pp (No.491)
113. ....*Motherwell D.C.*, Edinburgh, January 1983, 7pp (No.492)
114. ....*Motherwell D.C.*, Edinburgh, October 1983, 4pp (No.584)
115. ....*Perth & Kinross D.C.*, Edinburgh, September 1983, 8pp (No.572)
116. ....*Renfrew D.C.*, Edinburgh, December 1982, 10pp (No.454)
117. ....*Renfrew D.C.*, Edinburgh, January 1983, 4pp (No.499)
118. ....*Renfrew D.C.*, Edinburgh, October 1983, 5pp (No.583)
119. ....*Stirling D.C.*, Edinburgh, November 1982, 4pp (No.478)
120. ....*Strathkelvin D.C.*, Edinburgh, December 1982, 5pp (No.485)

121. ....*Strathkelvin D.C.*, Edinburgh, November 1983, 10pp (No.593)
122. ....*West Lothian D.C.*, Edinburgh, October 1983, 9pp (No.575)
123. *Report of the Commissioner (Ombudsman) for Local Administration in Scotland for the year ended 31 March 1984.* Edinburgh: HMSO, 1984, 22pp
124. COMMISSION FOR LOCAL AUTHORITY ACCOUNTS IN SCOTLAND, *Accounts... for the year ended March 31 1983.* London: House of Commons Paper HC 69, 1983, 10pp
125. ....*Eighth report.* Edinburgh: HMSO, 1983, 45pp
126. COMMITTEE ON PUBLIC ACCOUNTS, *Hamilton College of Education: disposal of land and building.* Report. London: House of Commons paper HC 122, 1984, 34pp
127. COMMITTEE ON SCOTTISH AFFARIS, *Dampness in housing. Vol.1, Report; Vol.2, Minutes of evidence and appendices.* London: House of Commons Paper HC 206, 1984, 54pp & 322pp
128. ....*Scott Lithgow Ltd: the economic and social consequences of closure. Vol. 1, Report; Vol. 2, Minutes of evidence and appendices.* London: House of Commons Paper HC 207, 62pp & 82pp
129. CONNORS, P, "The condition of the textile industry in Scotland", *Scottish Trade Union Review* 21 (1983) 12, 25-26
130. COOK, R, "Housing and deprivation", *Scotland: the real divide,* ed. G Brown & R Cook, 172-89
131. COOPER, J, "The oil refining industry in Scotland", *Scottish Trade Union Review* 20 (1983) 28-29
132. COR NA GAIDLHLIG, *Language, community and development: the Gaelic situation.* Inverness: HIDB, 1982
133. COWAN, R, "All quiet at Hutchestontown E". *Roof,* Nov/Dec. 1983, 13-14
134. CRAWFORD, C & MOORE, V, *The free two pence: Section 137 of the Local Government Act 1972 and section 83 of the Local Government (Scotland) Act 1973.* London: Chartered Institute of Public Finance and Accountancy, 1983.
135. CRAWFORD, R M, "The economy, the polity and the black,black oil", Scottish Government Yearbook 1984, 137-48
136. CRAWFORD, R, "The electronics industry in Scotland", *Quarterly Economic Commentary,* 9,4 (1984) 78-84
137. CROFTERS COMMISSION, *Annual Report 1982.* Edinburgh:HMSO, 1983, 39pp
138. DAVIES, T & SINFIELD, A, "The unemployed", *Scotland: the real divide,* ed. G Brown & R Cook, 91-106
139. DEPARTMENT OF SOCIAL AND ECONOMIC RESEARCH, *The Motherwell economy: trends and prospects. First report.* Glasgow: Glasgow University DSER, 1983, 39pp

140. ....*The Motherwell economy and labour market. Second report.* Glasgow: Glasgow University DSER, 1984, 410pp
141. DEPARTMENT OF TRADE AND INDUSTRY, *Regional industrial policy: some economic issues.* London, 1983, 142pp
142. DEWAR, D, "Holding the line" (interview), *Radical Scotland*, 7 (1984), 7-9
143. ...."Tory myths and the Scottish economy", *Scottish Trade Union Review* 23, (1984), 10-11
144. DEWHURST, J & LYTHE, C, "Output and employment in the Scottish service sector", *Quarterly Economic Commentary*,9,4 (1984), 69-77
145. DIAMOND, D & SPENCE, N, *Regional policy evaluation: a methodological review and the Scottish example*. Aldershot: Gower, 1983
146. DUMFRIES & GALLOWAY REGIONAL COUNCIL, *Dumfries and Galloway Structure Plan: written statement Feb. 1984,* Dumfries, 1984
147. *Transport policy and programme. Supplement 1983-88.* Dumfries, 1982
148. DUNDEE DISTRICT COUNCIL, *Proposed Dundee enterprise zone.* Dundee, 1982 (?), 48pp
149. DUNLOP, J M, "Cost effectiveness: the project teams approach in Fife Region", *Local Government Policy Making,* 9,2 (1982), 103-106
150. DUNDEE INNER CITY NEIGHBOURHOOD ACTION CENTRE, *Working at home: a feasibility study into the extent, the problems and the future requirements of homeworkers in Dundee.* Dundee, 1984.
151. EDINBURGH S.H.A.C., *Time for a change. Midlothian's allocation policy – a review.* Edinburgh, 1983, 17pp
152. FIFE REGIONAL COUNCIL, *Annual report and financial statement 1982-83.* Glenrothes1984
153. ....*A study into deprivation in Fife: preliminary appraisal.* Glenrothes, 1983(?), 73pp
154. ....*Review of planning documents relating to Fife Region.* Glenrothes, n.d., 105pp
155. ....*Strategic projections 1983.* Glenrothes, 1983
156. FIRN, J R, "Industrial regeneration and regional policy: the Scottish perspective and experience", *Industrial decline and regeneration*, ed. L Collins (Edinburgh: Edinburgh University Dept. of Geography, 1982), 5-19
157. FITZPATRICK, T A, *Catholic secondary education in SW Scotland 1922-72.* Ph.D. thesis, Glasgow University, 1982
158. FORRESTER, C, *From activism to office: women and local*

government in Edinburgh. Glasgow: Planning Exchange, Occasional paper 13, 1984, 21pp

159. FORSYTHE, D, *The rural community and the small school.* Aberdeen: Aberdeen University Press, 1983
160. FRANCE, G H (ed), *'Scottish health authorities priorities for the eighties' and its implementation.* Edinburgh: SHHD, 1981
161. FRASER N, "Scotland and the EEC", *Understanding the Scottish economy*, ed. K Ingham & J Love
162. FYFE, M, "Campaigning with councils", *Scottish Labour Activist* 6 (1983) 4-5
163. GEEKIE, J & KEATING, M, *The Labour Party and the rise of activist democracy.* Glasgow: Glasgow Fabian Society Discussion Paper, 1983
164. GIBSON, P. "Rural housing", *Consumer problems and service provision in rural areas* (Glasgow: Glasgow University Centre for Urban and Regional Research, Discussion Paper 14, 1984)
165. GILLETT, E, *Investment in the environment: recent housing, planning and transport policies in Scotland.* Aberdeen: Aberdeen University Press, 1983, 147pp
166. GLASGOW DISTRICT COUNCIL, *Closure of steelworks at Clydebridge works and Parkhead forge, and possible District Council responses.* Glasgow, 1982, 4pp
167. ....*Factory occupancy study.* Glasgow, 1983
168. ....*Glasgow's special housing initiatives: ways of dealing with difficult to let estates.* Glasgow, Housing Department Research Memorandum 3, 1984, 83pp
169. ....*Social deprivation in Glasgsow,* Glasgow, 1983, 34pp
170. ....*Unemployment in Glasgow by local area, Oct. 1983: research memorandum.* Glasgow, 1984, 16pp.
171. ....*Unemployment in Glasgow: the results of the 1981 Census.* Glasgow, 1983, 6pp
172. G.E.A.R., *GEAR summary statistics 1983.* Glasgow: SDA, 1983, 3pp
173. GLASGOW WOMEN'S STUDY GROUP, *Uncharted lives: extracts from Scottish women's experiences 1850-1982.* Glasgow: Pressgang, 1983, 206pp
174. GLENDINNING, J, REDPATH, G M B & WALKER, R J, *Scottish Office and related departments: review of personnel work.* Edinburgh: Scottish Office, 15257pp
175. GODWIN,D, "Coming clean: corrupted legality in Scotland". *Radical Scotland* 8 (1984) 11-13
176. GRAMPIAN REGIONAL COUNCIL, *Annual report and accounts 198283.* Aberdeen, 1983

177. ....*Forecast of population, employment and housing. 1983 update.* Aberdeen, 1983, 32pp
178. ....*Grampian Region (part) Structure Plan rural area: draft written statement.* Aberdeen, 1983, 106pp
179. ....*Grampian Region (part) Structure Plan rural area: report of survey.* Aberdeen, 1983
180. ....*Grampian Region (part) Structure Plan rural area: written statement, report of survey and consultation report.* Aberdeen, 1984
181. ....*Transport policy and programmes 1983-88.* Aberdeen, 1984, 64pp
182. ....*Transport policy and programmes 1984-89: capital expenditure plan.* Aberdeen, 1984, 20pp
183. GRANT, M, PLANT, M & SAUNDERS, W, *Drinking and alcohol problems in Scotland.* Edinburgh: Scottish Health Education Unit, 1980, 22pp
184. GRANT, N, "Education in rural Scotland", *Consumer problems and service provision in rural areas* (Glasgow: Glasgow University Centre for Urban and Regional Research, Discussion Paper 14, 1984)
185. GRIMES, A, "Pensioners in poverty", *Scotland: the real divide,* ed. G Brown & R Cook, 136-43
186. HANCOCK, K, "Rich man, poor man..(distribution of income)", *Understanding the Scottish economy*, ed. K Ingham & J Love, 151-60; and in *Quarterly Economic Commentary,* 9,1 (1983) 58-64
187. HARRISON, D, "The coal mining industry in Scotland", *Scottish Trade Union Review*, 21 (1983) 30-32
188. HART, T, *Towards a new transport framework: opportunities for change.* Glasgow: Glasgow University Centre for Urban and Regional Research, Discussion Paper 10, 1983
189. HAUG, P, HOOD, N & YOUNG, S, "R & D intensity in the affiliates of US-owned electronics companies manufacturing in Scotland", *Regional Studies,* 17,6 (1983) 383-92
190. HETHERINGTON, P, "Unions hammer on high technology doors", *Scottish Business Insider,* 1,3 (1984) 14-15
191. HIGHLANDS & ISLANDS DEVELOPMENT BOARD, *18th annual report, 1983.* Inverness, 1984, 68pp
192. *Accounts for the year ended 31.3.1983.* London: House of Commons Paper HC 90, 1983, 18pp
193. *Highlands and Islands railway study: summary report.* Inverness, 1982, 30pp
194. HIGHLAND REGIONAL COUNCIL, *Economic review January 1984.* Inverness, 1984, 11pp
195a *Structure Plan: development control policies.* Inverness, 1981, 35pp
195. HOOD, N et al, *Multinational investment strategies in the British*

Isles. London: HMSO, 1983, 389pp

196. HOUSING COOPERATIVES REVIEW COMMITTEE, *Housing cooperatives in Scotland.* Glasgow, SCSS, 1984
197. HOUSING AND URBAN RENEWAL RESEARCH UNIT, *Ethnic minorities in Scotland.* Edinburgh: SDD, 1983, 23pp
198. HUBBARD, G, "Aberdeen's technology gusher", *Management Today,* August 1983, 48-53
199. HUBLEY, T, "Poverty and health in Scotland", *Scotland: the real* ed. G Brown & R Cook, 206-22
200. HUGH-JONES, S, "Living by their wits: a survey of the Scottish economy", *Economist,* 10.9.1983, 3-15
201. HUMES, W M, "Scotland's 'decaying educational mandarinate'", *Chapman* 35/36(1983) 10-12
202. ...."The cultural significance of Scotland's educational system", *Scottish Government Yearbook* 1984, 149-66
203. HUNTER, E, "Women and poverty", *Scotland: the real divide,* ed. G Brown & R Cook, 152-61
204. INGHAM, K, "Foreign firms", *Understanding the Scottish economy,* ed. K Ingham & J Love, 215-36.
205. INGHAM, K & LOVE, J, "Scotland in the UK economy", *Understanding the Scottish economy,* ed. K Ingham & J Love 235-44; and in *Quarterly Economic Commentary,* 9,1 (1983) 52-58
206. ....(ed), *Understanding the Scottish economy.* Oxford: Martin Robertson, 1983, 311pp
207. INDUSTRY DEPARTMENT FOR SCOTLAND, *Scottish input-output tables for 1979. Vol.1: introduction and summary tables.* Edinburgh, 1984, 32pp
208. INVERCLYDE DISTRICT COUNCIL, *Clyde built...no more?* Greenock 1983
209. JOHNSTONE, J, *Scotland through the looking glass.* Glasgow: BBC Radio, 1981, 16pp
210. JOHNES, H (ed), *Population change in contemporary Scotland.* Norwich: Geo Books, 1984, 83pp
211. KEATING, M, "Scottish politics", *Modern Studies Association Yearbook,* 1983, 50-55
212. KEATING, M & MIDWINTER, A, "Current expenditure guidelines in Scotland: a failure of indicating planning", *Local Government Studies,* 10,2 (1984) 21-31
213. ...."The Area Project approach to economic development in Scotland", *Public Administration,* 62,1 (1984) 108-112
214. KEATING, M, MIDWINTER, A & TAYLOR, P, *Enterprise Zones and Area Projects: small area initiatives in urban economic renewal in Scotland.* Glasgow: Strathclyde University Department

of Administration, 1983

215. ....“Enterprise Zones: implementing the unworkable”, *Political Quarterly,* 55,1 (1984) 78-84
216. KELLAS, J, “Scottish politics”, *Modern Studies Association Yearbook* 1982, 34-36
217. KENDRICK, S, “Social change in Scotland”, *Scotland: the real divide*, ed. G Brown & R Cook, 40-65
218. KENNEDY, G, “How much is enough? Defence in Scotland”, *Understanding the Scottish economy,* ed. K Ingham & K J Love, 117-26
219. KEREVAN, G, “Labourism revisited”, *Chapman* 35/36 (1983) 25-31
220. KERNOHAN, R D, “Mrs Thatcher's North Britons”, *Contemporary Review* 243 (Sept.1983) 143-47
221. LAURANCE, J, “Strathclyde's Robin Hood”, *New Society,* 15.12.1983, 455-6
222. LEVER, W F, DANSON, M & MALCOLM, J, *Manufacturing and service industries in inner cities.* Glasgow: Glasgow University Department of Social and Economic Research, 1980, 9pp
223. LEVITT, I, “Scottish poverty: the historical background”, *Scotland: the real divide,* ed. G Brown & R Cook, 66-75
224. LIVINGSTONE, D, “Enterprise or service? (nationalised and state-owned industries)”, *Understanding the Scottish economy*, ed. K Ingham & J Love, 201-212
225. LLOYD, G & MACDOUGALL, B, “A new approach to regional policy?”, *Scottish Planner* 13 (1984) 3
226. LOTHIAN REGIONAL COUNCIL, *Transport policies and programme 1983-88.* Edinburgh, 1983, 18pp
227. LOVE, J & STEPHENS, J, “Ravenscraig: in the melting pot”, *Quarterly Economic Commentary,* 9,4 (1984) 59-60
228. LOVE, J & STEWART, W T, “Scottish trade”, *Understanding the Scottish economy,* ed. K Ingham & J Love, 28-37
229. MACARTNEY, W J M, “Summary of opinion polls of voting intention 1982/3”, *Scottish Government Yearbook* 1984, 242-5
230. MACAVINCHEY, I D, “Economic factors and mortality: some aspects of the Scottish case 1950-78”, *Scottish Journal of Political Economy,* 31,1 (1984) 1-27
231. *Health and economic factors: the Scottish case.* Aberdeen: Aberdeen University Health Economics Research Unit, 1981
232. MACBETH, A, “The government of Scottish education: partnership or compromise?”, *Scottish Government Yearbook* 1984, 167-87
233. McCRONE, D, “Explaining nationalism: the Scottish case”, *Ethnic*

and Racial Studies 7,1 (1984) 129-37

234. ... (ed), *The Scottish Government Yearbook 1984*. Edinburgh: Unit for the Study of Government in Scotland, 1983, 297pp
235. McCRUM, M, *Ethnic minority women in Edinburgh*. BA dissertation Edinburgh University Department of Sociology, 1984
236. MACDONALD, S, "How grows the thistle?", *The Planner*, July-Aug. 1983, 121-23
237. McGREEVY, T E & THOMSON, A W J, "Regional policy and company investment behaviour", *Regional Studies* 17,5 (1983) 305-14
238. MacGREGOR, K, "Crisis for Scottish coal", *Radical Scotland* 8 (1984) 14-15
239. McGUIRE, A, "The regional income and employment impacts of nuclear power stations", *Scottish Journal of Political Economy*, 30,3 (1983) 264-74
240. McILVANNEY, W, "Being poor", *Scotland: the real divide*, ed. G Brown & R Cook, 23-26
241. MacINNES, J, "Bad industrial relations: a Scottish disease?", *MOST*, 31 (1983) 6-8
242. MACKAY, G A & MOIR, A C, *Rural Scotland price survey: report for 1982*. Glasgow: SCC & HIDB, 1983, 28pp
243. MACLENNAN, D, "Housing rehabilitation in Glasgow: progress and impact since 1976", *Housing Review*, Nov.-Dec. 1983, 190-92
244. MACLEOD, A, MAIN, B & RAFFE, D, "The labour market for young people in Scotland", *Employment Gazette*, 91,3 (1983)
245. McNICOLL, I, "North sea oil and gas", *Understanding the Scottish economy*, ed. K Ingham & J Love, 227-34
246. ...."Structure", *Understanding the Scottish economy*, ed. K Ingham & J Love, 3-14
247. McQUEEN, W R, *Movement into and within the owner occupied sector of the housing market*. Edinburgh: Scottish Office Central Research Unit, 1983, 95pp
248. MADIGAN, R, "Women and housing", *Uncharted lives*, ed. Glasgow Women's Study Group, 141-62.
249. MAIN, B, *School leaver unemployment and the Youth Opportunities Programme in Scotland*. Edinburgh: Edunburgh University Dept. of Economics, Discussion Paper
250. MARKUS, T, "Fuel poverty and Scottish homes", *Architects Journal*, 3.5.1979, 1077-82
251. MARLEW, C, *Financing local government in Scotland: an introduction* Glasgow: Planning Exchange, Occassional Paper 9, 1983
252. ....*Financing local government in Scotland: an introduction (revised*

edition). Glasgow: Planning Exchange, 1984, 34pp
253. MARTIN, T, "The Blackhill story", *Strathclyde Studies in Social Work*, Vol.2 (1983?), 35-110
254. MASSIE, A, "The divisions in Scotland", *Spectator,* 5,3.1983. 16-18
255. "What North-South divide?", *Spectator,* 18.6.1983, 9-10
256. MATHER, A S, "Rural land use", *Scotland: a new study,* ed. C M Clapperton (Newton Abbot: David and Charles, 1983), 196-223
257. MIDWINTER, A, "Corporate management in Scottish local government", *Local Government Policy Making,* 9,2 (1982), 91-102
258. ...."Local government", *Modern Studies Association Yearbook* 1982, 9-11
259. ...."Local government", *Modern Studies Association Yearbook* 1983, 16-18
260. ...."Current issues in local government finance", *Local Government Forum* 3 (1983) 6-7
261. ....*The politics of local spending.* Edinburgh: Mainstream, 1984, 115pp
262. MIDWINTER, A, KEATING, M & TAYLOR, P, "The politics of Scottish housing plans", *Policy and Politics,* 12,2 (1984), 145-66
263. MILLAR, A C, *Success or failure? An assessment of Paterson-style corporate management through its implementation in Kirkcaldy District Council.* BA dissertation, Edinburgh University Dept. of Politics, 1984, 29pp
264. MILLER, W L, *Testing the power of a media consensus: a comparison of Scots and English treatment of the Falklands campaign.* Glasgow: Strathclyde University Dept. of Politics, Papers on Government and Politics 17, 1983, 31pp
265. MOAR, L, "Farming today", *Understanding the Scottish economy,* ed. K Ingham & J Love, 74-86
266. MOONEY, G C, *The state, housing and the reserve army of labour: Glasgow 1850-1939.* Glasgow: Glasgow University, Centre for Urban and Regional Research, Discussion Paper 11, 1983, 44pp
267. MORTON, J, "A charmed life", *Local Government News,* Jan. 1984 28-30
268. ...."Community ownership: Scots style", *Local Government News,* May 1984, 12-13
269. NAIRN, A G M, "GEAR: comprehensive redevelopment or confidence trick?", *Quarterly Economic Commentary,* 9,2 (1983) 59-72
270. NAUGHTIE, J, "The year at Westminster", *Scottish Government Yearbook* 1984, 27-35
271. NELSON, F, "Part-time women workers in Glasgow", *Uncharted lives,* ed. Glasgow Women's Study Group, 181-206

272. NORRIS, G M, "Poverty in Scotland 1979-83", *Scotland: the real divide,* ed. G Brown & R Cook, 27-39
273. PACIONE, M, "Neighbourhood communities in the modern city: some evidence from Glasgow", *Scottish Geographical Magazine,* 99,3 (1983) 169-81
274. ...."The temporal stability of perceived neighbourhood areas in Glasgow", *Professional Geographer,* 35,1 (1983) 66-73
275. PATERSON, K, "Adjusted client-group method used for spending guidelines", *Public Finance and Accountancy,* Feb. 1983, 31-34
276. ...."Scotland gets a 2% spending cut", *Public Finance and Accountancy,* Feb. 1984, 27-29
277. PAYNE, G & FORD, G, "Inequality and the occupational structure", *Scotland: the real divide,* ed. G Brown & R Cook, 76-90
278. P.E.I.D.A., *Labour performance of US plants in Scotland.* Glasgow: SDA, 1982(?), 24pp
279. PHILLIPS, K, "What women know", *Uncharted lives,* ed. Glasgow Women's Study Group, 118-40
280. POWER, R, *Scotland and devolution.* Glasgow: Jordanhill College, 1977, 23pp
281. RADICAL SCOTLAND, "Spotlight on Scottish politics: labouring under an illusion", *Radical Scotland* 9 (1984) 7-11
282. RAFFE, D, "Education and class inequality in Scotland", *Scotland: the real divide,* ed. G Brown & R Cook, 190-205
283. ...."Some recent trends in youth unemployment in Scotland", *Scottish Educational Review,* 14,2 (1983)
284. ...."Youth unemployment and the MSC 1977-83", *Scottish Government Yearbook* 1984, 183-222
285. ...(ed) *Fourteen to eighteen: the changing pattern of schooling in Scotland.* Aberdeen: Aberdeen University Press, 1984
286. RAWKINS, P, "Nationalist movements within the advanced nationalist state: the significance of culture", *Canadian Review of Studies in Nationalism*, 10,2 (1983) 221-3
287. REGIONAL STUDIES ASSOCIATION, *Report of an enquiry into regional problems in the United Kingdom*. Norwich: Geo Books, 1983, 142pp
288. ....,SCOTTISH BRANCH, *Regional economic planning in Scotland and comparative regional performance.* Glasgow, 1983
289. REID, M, "Scotland: the new slums", *Scotsman,* 14-16.2.1984
290. REMALLY, S M, *The problems of peripheral communities.* M.Sc. dissertation, Heriot-Watt University, 1979; see section 4
291. RENNIE, F, "Beyond the cringe", *Radical Scotland* 7 (1984) 10-11
292. RHYMER, S, *Religious attitudes of Roman Catholic secondary school pupils in Strathclyde Region.* Ph.D. thesis, Edinburgh

University, 1983, 302pp

293. ROBERTSON, D G, "Education in Scotland in 1984" (review article) *Scottish Government Yearbook* 1984, 223-42

294. ROBERTSON, N, "Oil and the nonoil economy in Scotland", *Scottish Government Yearbook* 1984, 88-121

295. ROSS, A C, "Scotland and the Third World", *Understanding the Scottish economy,* ed. K Ingham & J Love, 225-70

296. ROSS, E, "Devolution", *Beyond Thatcher,* ed. J Lansman & A Neale (London: Junction Books, 1983)

297. ROSS, J M, *Local government in Scotland: some subversive reflections.* Glasgow: Strathclyde University Centre for the Study of Social Policy, 1983

298. ...."The art of the possible", *Radical Scotland* 8 (1984) 7-9

299. ROYAL TOWN PLANNING INSTITUTE/SCOTTISH COUNCIL FOR RACIAL EQUALITY: *Planing in a multiracial Scotland.* London: Commission for Racial Equality, 1983, 18pp

300. SANDILANDS, R J, "Housing schemes and schemes for housing", *Understanding the Scottish economy,* ed. K Ingham & J love, 127-38

301. SCANLAN, S, "Scotland and the Common Agricultural Policy: 1984 and beyond", *Quarterly Economic Commentary*, 9,4(1984) 61-63

302. SCOTTISH CAMPAIGN TO RESIST THE ATOMIC MENACE, *Nuclear-free Scotland campaigners conference report: autumn 1982.* Edinburgh, 1982, 19pp

303. SCOTTISH COUNCIL (DEVELOPMENT & INDUSTRY), *New technology: a Scottish perspective.* Edinburgh, 1980, 38pp.

304. ....*Regional policy review. A consultative paper.* Edinburgh, 1983, 11pp

305. SCOTTISH COUNCIL OF SOCIAL SERVICE (PERTH), *Preparing for the plan*. Perth, 1983

306. SCOTTISH DEVELOPMENT AGENCY, *Accounts for the year ending March 31, 1983.* London: House of Commons Paper HC 7, 1983, 26pp

307. ....*Electronics in Scotland: industry profile.* Glasgow, n.d., 36pp

308. ....*GEAR project report 1983.* Glasgow, 1983

308a ....*Regional policy: the role of a development agency.* Glasgow, n.d., 8pp

309. ....*The Coatbridge Project: project agreement.* Glasgow, 1983, unpag.

310. SCOTTISH DEVELOPMENT DEPARTMENT, *Dumfries & Galloway Structure Plan: proposed modifications.* Edinburgh, 1983

311. ....*Statistical bulletin: unoccupied dwellings: a survey following the 1981 Census.* Edinburgh, 1983

312. ....*Strathclyde Structure Plan: first review and alteration (Secretary of State's approval and modifications)*. Edinburgh, 1983, 16pp
313. ....*Tayside Structure Plan: Secretary of State's proposed modification*. Edinburgh, 1983
314. SCOTTISH EDUCATION AND ACTION FOR DEVELOPMENT, *Bathgate on the edge: a Scottish community in the international economy*. Edinburgh, 1983, 12pp
315. SCOTTISH FEDERATION OF HOUSING ASSOCIATIONS, *Manifesto for the 1984 District Council elections*: Housing. Edinburgh, 1984, 4pp
316. SCOTTISH HEALTH SERVICES PLANNING COUNCIL, *Report for 1982*. Edinburgh: HMSO, 1983, 26pp.
317. SCOTTISH HOME AND HEALTH DEPARTMENT, *Health services research register*. Edinburgh 1983, 26pp
318. SCOTTISH INFORMATION OFFICE, *Local government in Scotland* (Factsheet 28). Edinburgh, 1983, 40pp
319. S.L.A.S.H., *A future for Faifley: a strategy for a problem estate*. Edinburgh, 1983, 37pp
320. SCOTTISH NATIONAL PARTY, *Scottish budget 1984*. Edinburgh, 1984
321. SCOTTISH OFFICE, *Public expenditure to 1985/6: a commentary on the Scottish programme*. Edinburgh, 1983, 67pp
322. ....*Public expenditure to 1986/7: a commentary on the Scotland programme*. Edinburgh, 1984, 110pp
323. SCOTTISH PEAT AND LAND DEVELOPMENT ASSOCIATION, *Survey and recommendations of SPALDA...(on) the I.D.P. development in the Western Isles*. Edinburgh, 1983, 7pp
324. SCOTTISH SOCIALIST SOCIETY, *Scottish Socialist*, No.1-. Edinburgh, 1984-
325. S.S.H.A., *Annual report for year ended 31 March 1983*. Edinburgh, 1983, 40pp
326. SCOTTISH TRADE UNION CONGRESS, *86th Annual report*. Glasgow, 1983, 747pp
327. SCOULLER, J, "'Made in Scotland' (production)", *Understanding the Scottish economy*, ed. K Ingham & J Love, 15-27
328. SCRIMGEOUR, P A & WIGHT, M E, "Manufacturing employment change in the Scottish regions: components of change", *Scottish Economic Bulletin*, 29 (1983) 13-18
329. SECRETARY OF STATE FOR SCOTLAND, *Rate reduction (Glasgow District) 1983-84: a report*. Edinburgh: HMSO, 1983, 38pp
330. ....*Rate reduction (Kirkcaldy District) 1983-84: a report*. Edinburgh: HMSO, 1983, 24pp
331. ....*Rate reduction (Lothian region) 1983-84: a report* Edinburgh:

HMSO, 1983, 28pp

332. ....*Rate reduction (Stirling District) 1983-84: a report.* Edinburgh: HMSO, 1983, 32pp

333. ....*The housing support grant (Scotland) order, 1984: report.* London: House of Commons Paper HC 213, 1984, 12pp

334. ....*The rate support grant (Scotland) order, 1983: report.* London: House of Commons Paper 52, 1983, 2pp

335. ....*The rates support grant (Scotland) order 1984: report.* London. House of Commons Paper 171, 1984, 30pp

336. SHELTER, *Tenants Rights etc. (Scotland) Amendment Bill. Briefing note*. Edinburgh, 1983, 7pp

337. SHETLAND ISLANDS COUNCIL, *Housing plan 1984-89.* Lerwick, 1983.

338. ....*Interpreting Shetland. A strategy for discussion.* Lerwick, 1984, 59pp

339. SHORT, J, "Public finance and devolution: money flows between government and regions in the UK", *Scottish Journal of Political Economy*, 31,2 (1984) 114-30

340. SIMKINS, A, "Scottish weekend school", *Public Finance and Accountancy,* May, 1983, 22-26

341. SIMS, D & WOOD, M, *Car manufacturing at Linwood: the regional policy issues.* Paisley: Paisley College of Technology, Dept. of Politics and Sociology 1984, 94pp

342. SMITH, E A, "Scotland's future development", *Scotland: a new study,* ed. C M Clapperton (Newton Abbot: David & Charles, 1983), 282-300

343. SOCIAL DEMOCRATIC/LIBERAL ALLIANCE, *Towards a new constitutional settlement.* London, 1983

344. SPAVEN, M, *Fortress Scotland: a guide to the military presence*. London: Pluto, 1984, 184pp

345. SPEIRS, B, "Scottish views on the health service", *Scottish Trade Union Review* 20 (1983) 23-24

346. "For a Scottish Assembly", *Scottish Trade Union Review* 19 (1983) 26-27

346a. STEPHENSON, J B, *Ford: a village in the West Highlands of Scotland.* Edinburgh: Paul Harris, 1984, 174pp

347. STEWART, J A, "The relationship between central and local government: recent developments in Scotland", *Local Government Policy Making*, 9,2 (1982) 73-79

348. STRATHCLYDE REGIONAL COUNCIL, *1982 base projections of population, households and housing (Strathclyde Region). Main report.* Glasgow, 1984, 12pp

349. ....*Annual report and financial statement for 1982/3.* Glasgow,

1983, 60pp
350. ....*A social strategy for the 1980's.* Glasgow, 1983
351. ....*Strathclyde economic trends,* No.1-. Glasgow, 1983-
352. ....*Strathclyde Region employment trends to 1987.* Glasgow, 1982, 36pp
353. ....*Strathclyde's budget 1983/4.* Glasgow, 1983, 11pp
354. ....*Strathclyde Structure Plan 1981: monitoring report (1983).* Glasgow, 1984, 58pp
355. ....*Strathclyde Structure Plan. Second review and alteration 1983: consultative draft.* Glasgow, 1983, 215pp
356. ....*Strathclyde Structure Plan: the 'easy read'.* Glasgow, 1983, 36pp
357. ....*Strathclyde Structure Plan 1981: the decision letter and approved policies.* Glasgow, 1983, 36pp
358. ....*Transport policies and programme 6a; 1984-89.* Glasgow, 1984, 158pp
359. SWALES, J K, "Government expenditure and revenues", *Understanding the Scottish economy,* ed. K Ingham & J Love, 163-72
360. ...."Industrial policy in Scotland", *Understanding the Scottish economy,* ed. K Ingham & J Love, 188-200
361. TAYSIDE REGIONAL COUNCIL, *Tayside Structure Plan: Monitoring report.* Dundee, 1983, 60pp
362. THOMASON, E, "Shetland's Council of Social Service: 25 years on", *New Shetlander* 147 (1984) 6-7
363. THOMPSON, P, "Living the fishing: a study in working together", *New Society,* 8.9.1983, 347-50
364. THOMPSON, P, WAILEY, T & LUMMIS, T, *Living the fishing.* London: Routledge, Kegan Paul, 1983
365. THOMSON, A, "Scottish economy", *Modern Studies Association Yearbook* 1982, 36-42
366. "Scottish economy", *Modern Studies Association Yearbook* 1983, 5563
367. TUNEBERG, T, *Skotland: industrier og byer.* Coperhagen: Aschehoug, 1981, 36pp
368. TWINE, F, *Sale of council houses: a case study from Aberdeen.* Stirling: Stirling University Dept. of Housing Administration, Conference on Housing in Scotland, 1984.
369. ...."The low paid", *Scotland: the real divide,* ed. G Brown & R Cook, 107-35
370. WANNOP, U, "Clydeside in transition", *Town Planning Review,* 55, 1 (1984) 34-54
371. WALKER, J, "Freeport Prestwick: behind the decision", *Quarterly Economic Commentary,* 9,3 (1984) 69-70

372. WESTERN ISLES ISLANDS COUNCIL, *Western Isles Structure Plan: report of survey* Stornoway, 1983
373. WILKIE, J, "A Scottish constitutional convention: the door to the future", *Radical Scotland*, Jan. 1984, 16-18
374. WILLIAMS, T D, "Education in Scotland", *Understanding the Scottish economy*, ed. K Ingham & J Love, 139-50
375. WILLS, D, "New images of Scotland: new questions", *Cencrastus* 15 (1984) 40-43
376. WILSON, M, *Tenants associated: a survey of tenants groups in Scotland.* Glasgow: Scottish Consumer Council, 1982, 66pp
377. WOOLFSON, C A, *Working class culture: the work-in at Upper Clyde Shipbuilders*, Ph.D. thesis, Glasgow University, 1982, 817pp
378. WYPER, H, "Scotland against the Tories", *Scottish Marxist* 27 (1983) 3-4, 14
379. YOUNG, R, "A little local inequality", *Scotland: the real divide*, ed. G Brown & R Cook, 223-51
380. "Scottish local government: what future?", *Scottish Government Yearbook* 1984, 36-67

INDEX TO BIBLIOGRAPHY

SECTION 1

SCOTTISH OFFICE MINISTERS

		Private Secretary*
Secretary of State	Rt Hon George Younger MP	John Graham Ext 4001 Assistant: Ms S M McCabe Ext 4034
Minister of State	Lord Gray of Contin (Agriculture and Fisteries, Highlands & Islands affairs)	D Y A McFadyen Ext 4041
Parliamentary Under-Secretaries of State	Michael Ancrum MP (Minister of Home Affairs and the Environment)	Ms J E Morgan Ext 4005
	John MacKay MP (Minister for Health and Social Work)	Miss T S Teale Ext 2100**
	Allan Stewart MP (Minister for Industry and Education)	G J Hetherington Ext 4011

* at New St Andrew's House, Edinburgh EH1 3SX (031-556 8400) except

** at St Andrew's House, Edinburgh Eh1 3DE (031-556 8501)

SECTION 2

REGIONAL COUNCILS

Names and Addresses of Convenors and Chief Officers

	Convener/ Population	Chief Executive	Director of Administration	Director of Finance	Director of Education	Director of Social Work	Director of Planning	Director of Roads
BORDERS Newton St Boswells TD6 0SA 083 52 3301	Tom Hunter (Ind) 101,000	K J Clark		P Jeary	J McLean	D A Macdonald	D P Douglas	R I Hill
CENTRAL Viewforth Stirling 0786 3111	James Anderson (Lab) 273,000	E Geddes	P W Buchanan	J Broadfoot	I Collie	H M Garland	F Bracewell	J F Keith
DUMFRIES & GALLOWAY Council Offices Dumfries 0387 53141	John Jameson (Ind) 146,000	L T Carnegie	G M Sinclair	J C Stewart 0387 62323	J K Purves 30 Edinburgh Rd Dumfries 0387 63822	J W Barbour 8 Gordon St Dumfries 0387 63022	A H Dobbie	H D B Murray
FIFE Fife House North Street Glenrothes 0592 754411	Robert Gough (Lab) 342,000	J M Dunlop		R Venters	I S Flett Wemyssfield Kirkcaldy 0592 62351	M A Gillespie Queensway Glenrothes 0592 756701	W Taylor	R J Stobie (Engineering) Rothesay House North Street Glenrothes 0592 754411

	Convener/ Population	Chief Executive	Director of Administration	Director of Finance	Director of Education	Director of Social Work	Director of Planning	Director of Roads
GRAMPIAN Woodhill House Ashgrove Rd West Aberdeen AB9 2LU 0224 682222	John Sorrie (Con) 490,000	J D Macnaughton	I Miller	T E Carter	J A D Michie	Miss M Hartnoll	T F Sprott	W Turner
HIGHLAND Regional Buildings Glenurquhart Road Inverness 0463 234121	Ian Campbell (Ind) 195,000	R H Stevenson	H Farquhar	J W Bremner	C E Stewart	J G Bailey	R Cameron	G K M Macfarlane
LOTHIAN George IV Bridge Edinburgh EH1 1UQ 031-229 9292	Brian Meek (Con) 749,000	R G E Peggie		B Grosset	W D C Semple 40 Torphichen St Edinburgh EH3 8JJ	R W Kent Shrubhill House Edinburgh EH7 4DP 031-554 4301	G Bowie 1 Parliament Sq Edinburgh EH1 1TU	P J Mason 19 Market St Edinburgh EH1 1BL
STRATHCLYDE Strathclyde House 20 India Street Glasgow G2 4PF 041-204 2900	James Burns (Lab) 2,399,000	R Calderwood		K R V Paterson	E Miller	F E Edwards	H D B Torrance	W S McAlonan
TAYSIDE Tayside House 26-28 Crichton St Dundee 0382 23281	Wm Fitzgerald (Con) 396,000	J A Wallace		I B McIver	D G Robertson	S J Moxley	H Ramsay	A R Mollison

	Convener/ Population	Chief Executive	Director of Administration	Director of Finance	Director of Education	Director of Social Work	Director of Planning	Director of Roads
ISLANDS COUNCILS								
ORKNEY County Offices Kirkwall 0856 3535	Edwin Eunson (Ind) 19,000	H A G Lapsley	R McCullum	R H Gilbert	A Bain	A R Mackinnon	M Sargent	
SHETLAND Town Hall Lerwick 0595 3535	Alexander Tulloch (Ind) 26,000	M Gerrard	P B Regan 31 Commercial St Lerwick	M Green 4 Market St Lerwick	R A B Barnes Brentham Ho Harbour St Lerwick	P Malcolmson 64 St Olaf St Lerwick	G L Mann Victoria Bldgs Explanade Lerwick	
WESTERN ISLES Council Office South Beach Stornoway 0851 3773	Sandy Matheson (Ind) 30,000	R MacIver	D Sinclair	D G Macleod	N R Galbraith 0851 3992	Mrs N E Macleod 0851 3664	J R Haworth	

SECTION 3

DISTRICT COUNCILS

Names and Addresses of Conveners and Chief Executives

	Convenor/Provost	Chief Executive
BORDERS		
Berwickshire	J Evans	R Christie District Offices, Duns TD11 3DU (03612 2331)
Ettrick & Lauderdale	A L Tulley	J D Bell Council Chambers, Paton St., Galashiels TD1 3AS (0896 4751)
Roxburgh	J R Irvine	K W Crammond District Office, High St. Hawick TD9 9EF (0450 5991)
Tweeddale	J Campbell	G Gardiner District Office, Peebles EH45 8GH (0721 20153)
CENTRAL		
Clackmannan	J Millar	A E O'Neill The Whins, Alloa FK10 3KG (0259 722160)
Falkirk	J Docherty	J P H Paton Municipal Buildings, Falkirk FK1 5RS (0324 24911)
Stirling	J Wyles	J Cairns Municipal Buildings, Corn Exchange Road, Stirlingh FK8 2HU (0786 73131)
DUMFRIES & GALLOWAY		
Annandale & Eskdale	R G Greenhow	J A Whitecross High Street, Annan DG12 6AQ (04612 3311)

Nithdale	K Cameron	Municipal Chambers, Dumfries DG1 2AD (387 3166)
Stewartry	J Nelson	W L Dick-Smith Council Offices, Kircudbright DG6 4PJ (0557 30291)
Wigtown	D R Robinson	A Geddes Sun Street, Stranraer DG9 3JJ (0776 2151)
FIFE		
Dunfermline	R Mill	G Brown City Chambers, Dunfermline KY12 7ND (0383 22711)
Kirkcaldy	R King	Town House, Kirkcaldy KY1 1XW (0592 61144)
North-East Fife	D Barrie	D W Anderson County Buildings, Cupar KY15 4TA (0334 3722)
GRAMPIAN		
City of Aberdeen	H E Rae	J M Wilson Town House, Aberdeen AB9 1AQ (0224 642121)
Banff & Buchan	N Cowie	R W Jackson St Leonards, Sandyhill Rd., Banff AB4 1BH (026 12 2521)
Gordon	J B Presley	A C Kennedy 3 High Street, Inverurie AB5 9WA (0467 20981)
Kincardine & Deeside	D J MacKenzie	Miss E M G Cockburn Arduthie Rd, Stonehaven AB3 2DQ (056 92 62001)
Moray	E Aldridge	J P C Bell High Street, Elgin IV30 1BX (0343 3451)

HIGHLAND		
Badenoch & Strathspey	J A McCook	H G McCulloch High Street, Kingussie PH21 1HX (054 02 555)
Caithness	J M Young	A Beattie Council Offices, Wick KW1 4AW (0955 3761)
Inverness	A G Sellar	B wilson Town House, Inverness IV1 1JJ (0463 239111)
Lochaber	C Neilson	A B Blair Lochaber House, Fort William PH33 6EL (0397 3881)
Nairn	H McLean	F T Milne 4 Court House Lane, Nairn IV12 4Dr (0667 52056)
Ross & Cromarty	G D Finlayson	A Cuthbertson County Buildings, Dingwall IV15 9QN (0349 63381)
Skye & Lochalsh	J F Munro	D H Noble Park Road, Portree IV51 9HJ (0478 2341)
Sutherland	Mrs L MacKenzie	D W Martin District Office, Golspie KW10 6RB (040 83392)
LOTHIAN		
City of Edinburgh	J H Mackay	M M Duncan City Chambers, High St., Edinburgh EH1 1YJ (031 225 2424)
East Lothian	T Wilson	D B Miller Council Buildings, Haddington EH41 3HA (062 082 4161)
Midlothian	W Steele	D W Duguid 1 Eskdaill Court, Dalkeith EH22 1DJ (031 663 2881)

West Lothian	D McCauley	D Morrison South Bridge St., Bathgate EH48 1TT (Bathgate 53631)
STRATHCLYDE		
Argyll & Bute	D C Currie	M A J Gossip Kilmory, Lochgilphead PA31 8RT (0546 2127)
Bearsden & Milngavie	R W Robinson	A R Rae Boclair, Bearsden G61 2TQ (041 942 2262)
Clydebank	H Duffy	J M Brown District Council Offices Clydebank G81 1TG (041 941 1331)
Clydesdale	Miss M T Hodgson	P D Daniels District Offices, Lanark ML11 7JT (0555 61331)
Cumbernauld & Kilsyth	J Pollock	J Hutton Bron Way, Cumbernauld G67 1DZ (02367 22131)
Cumnock & Doon Valley	D Shankland	D T Hemmings Lugar, Cumnock KA18 3JQ (0290 22111)
Cunninghame	Mrs T B Beattie	J M Miller Cunninghame House, Irvine KA12 8EE (0294 74166)
Dumbarton	R McNamara	L Mackinnon Crosslet House, Dumbarton G82 3NS (0389 65100)
East Kilbride	G McKillop	W G McNay Civic Centre, East Kilbride G74 1AB (035 52 28777)
Eastwood	Mrs J M Edmondson	M D Henry Cotton Street, Paisley PA1 1LA (041 889 5454)

City of Glasgow	R. Gray	S Hamilton City Chambers, Glasgow G2 1DU (041 221 9600)
Hamilton	S. Casserly	W Johnston 102 Cadzow Street, Hamilton ML3 6HH (0698 282323)
Inverclyde	Sir Simpson Stevenson	I C Wilson Municipal Buidings, Greenock PA15 1LY (0475 24400)
Kilmarnock & Loudon	T Ferguson	R W Jenner Civic Centre, Kilmarnock KA1 1BY (0563 21140)
Kyle & Carrick	G MacDonald	I R D Smillie Burns House, Ayr KA7 1UT (0292 81511)
Monklands	E Cairns	J S Ness Dunbeth Road, Coatbridge ML5 3LF (0263 24941)
Motherwell	J McGhee	J Bonomy P.O. Box 14, Motherwell ML1 1TW (0698 66166)
Renfrew	W McCready	W McIntosh Cotton Street, Paisley PA1 1BU (041 889 5400)
Strathkelvin	R M Coyle	C Mallon P.O. Box 4, Kirkintilloch G66 1PW (041 776 7171)
TAYSIDE		
Angus	A D Welsh	W S McCulloch County Buildings, Forfar DD8 3LG (0307 65101)
City of Dundee	T Mitchell	J F Hoey City Chambers Dundee DD1 3BY (0382 23141)
Perth & Kinross	J M Mathieson	J E D Cormie 1-3 High Street, Perth PH1 5JU (0738 21161)

SECTION 4

DISTRICT ELECTIONS
MAY 1984

Seats won: Percentage of vote in brackets	CON		LAB		LIB/SDP		SNP		OTHERS		Number of Wards Contested: % Turnout	
BORDERS	14	(18.2)	2	(5.6)	5	(16.4)	0	(2.3)	33	(57.4)	20	(44.7)
Berwickshire	8	(42.7)	0	(0)	1	(23.4)	0	(6.3)	3	(27.6)	8	(46.3)
Ettrick & Lauderdale	1	(0)	2	(19.6)	0	(0)	0	(0)	13	(80.4)	5	(45.2)
Roxburgh	5	(13.6)	0	(0)	4	(42.1)	0	(0)	7	(44.2)	4	(35.6)
Tweeddale	0	(0)	0	(0)	0	(0)	0	(0)	10	(100)	3	(55.7)
CENTRAL	11	(19.4)	45	(48.5)	0	(4.8)	9	23.0	3	(4.3)	63	(48.4)
Clackmannan	1	(4.7)	9	(49.7)	0	(4.2)	2	(37.4)	0	(8.1)	11	(47.6)
Falkirk	2	(8.9)	25	(52.8)	0	(1.9)	7	(31.5)	2	(5.0)	32	(45.1)
Stirling	8	(39.8)	11	(42.4)	0	(8.9)	0	(5.3)	1	(3.6)	20	(54.0)
DUMFRIES & GALLOWAY	7	(10.1)	6	(19.0)	4	(8.9)	7	(12.9)	46	(49.1)	42	(45.1)
Annandale & Eskdale	0	(0)	0	(10.8)	4	(26.3)	0	(7.3)	12	(55.6)	9	(44.3)
Nithsdale	7	(22.9)	6	(33.0)	0	(1.7)	6	(20.4)	9	(22.0)	18	(49.2)
Stewartry	–	–	–	–	–	–	–	–	12	(100.0)	12	(45.0)
Wigtown	0	(0)	0	(8.3)	0	(4.3)	1	(11.4)	13	(76.1)	8	(37.7)

Seats won: Percentage of vote in brackets	CON		LAB		LIB/SDP		SNP		OTHERS		Number of Wards Contested: % Turnout	
FIFE	11	(22.3)	54	(39.8)	19	(20.6)	2	(7.0)	6	(10.4)	74	(43.8)
Dunfermline	2	(16.0)	24	(51.4)	6	(14.3)	1	(9.8)	1	(8.6)	26	(43.2)
Kirkcaldy	3	(14.5)	30	(55.3)	3	(9.0)	1	(7.2)	3	(13.9)	30	(41.6)
North-East Fife	6	(41.3)	0	(2.7)	10	(45.3)	0	(3.1)	2	(7.5)	18	(48.3)
GRAMPIAN	15	(19.0)	29	(26.5)	17	(24.2)	8	(6.8)	41	(23.4)	83	(34.9)
City of Aberdeen	8	(21.8)	28	(40.7)	14	(33.6)	0	(11.7)	0	(0.2)	50	(35.3)
Banff & Buchan	1	(7.5)	0	(10.7)	0	(1.4)	5	(25.0)	12	(55.5)	12	(32.9)
Gordon	3	(28.7)	0	(1.9)	2	(25.1)	0	(0)	7	(44.3)	7	(33.8)
Kincardine & Deeside	3	(26.3)	0	(0)	1	(18.3)	1	(2.2)	7	(53.2)	7	(35.6)
Moray	0	(0)	1	(7.1)	0	(0)	2	(11.9)	15	(81.0)	7	(36.1)
HIGHLAND	1	(1.1)	16	(19.9)	4	(2.9)	1	(0.1)	102	(75.9)	40	(45.1)
Badenoch & Strathspey	0	(0)	0	(0)	0	(0)	1	(0)	9	(0)	0	
Caithness	0	(0)	0	(0)	1	(0)	0	(0)	14	(100.0)	3	(44.5)
Inverness	0	(2.2)	8	(25.8)	2	(6.1)	0	(0)	18	(65.9)	16	(41.7)
Lochaber	0	(0)	5	(23.0)	0	(0)	0	(0)	10	(77.0)	7	(51.6)
Nairn	0	(0)	1	(24.2)	0	(0)	0	(1.7)	9	(74.1)	5	(44.8)
Ross & Cromarty	1	(0)	2	(21.0)	0	(0)	0	(0)	18	(79.0)	4	(44.7)
Skye & Lochalsh	0	(0)	0	(0)	1	(0)	0	(0)	10	(100.0)	3	(53.8)
Sutherland	0	(0)	0	(0)	1	(0)	0	(0)	14	(100.0)	2	(66.5)

Seats won: Percentage of vote in brackets	CON		LAB		LIB/SDP		SNP		OTHERS		Number of Wards Contested: % Turnout	
LOTHIAN	28	(27.2)	78	(44.2)	5	(16.5)	4	(8.2)	3	(4.0)	110	(46.7)
City of Edinburgh	22	(32.9)	34	(38.7)	4	(21.5)	2	(4.8)	0	(2.1)	62	(47.2)
East Lothian	6	(39.0)	11	(50.3)	0	(7.9)	0	(0)	0	(2.6)	13	(46.4)
Midlothian	0	(12.1)	14	(56.6)	1	(12.6)	0	(10.6)	0	(8.1)	11	(44.0)
West Lothian	0	(6.3)	19	(56.1)	0	(3.7)	2	(24.1)	3	(9.8)	24	(46.2)
STRATHCLYDE	65	(19.0)	284	(54.1)	18	(10.9)	14	(11.5)	38	(4.6)	383	(44.7)
Argyll & Bute	3	(11.6)	0	(4.2)	0	(0)	1	(8.4)	22	(75.8)	12	(45.2)
Bearsden & Milngavie	6	(44.2)	1	(14.8)	2	(27.2)	0	(2.7)	1	(11.1)	10	(51.8)
Clydebank	1	(5.3)	11	(59.4)	0	(11.1)	0	(21.5)	0	(2.8)	10	(46.4)
Clydesdale	0	(8.8)	6	(43.2)	0	(1.6)	3	(23.5)	7	(21.9)	15	(52.1)
Cumbernauld & Kilsyth	0	(2.9)	8	(56.3)	0	(2.7)	4	(37.1)	0	(1.0)	12	(53.4)
Cumnock & Doon Valley	0	(6.9)	10	(70.4)	0	(9.3)	0	(0)	0	(13.4)	18	(50.2)
Cunninghame	5	(21.9)	23	(56.4)	0	(3.4)	0	(11.4)	2	(6.8)	30	(45.0)
Dumbarton	2	(20.9)	11	(40.2)	1	(15.6)	0	(9.6)	2	(13.7)	16	(50.0)
East Kilbride	2	(12.2)	14	(55.4)	0	(9.9)	0	(20.0)	0	(2.4)	16	(44.1)
Eastwood	10	(57.8)	0	(15.7)	0	(13.7)	0	(6.5)	2	(6.3)	9	(40.7)
City of Glasgow	5	(17.9)	59	(60.1)	2	(11.6)	0	(9.7)	0	(0.6)	66	(40.2)
Hamilton	1	(10.7)	17	(64.9)	2	(16.4)	0	(8.0)	0	(0)	19	(45.2)

Seats won: Percentage of vote in brackets	CON		LAB		LIB/SDP		SNP		OTHERS		Number of Wards Contested: % Turnout	
Inverclyde	0	(4.8)	11	(49.2)	9	(42.8)	0	(3.2)	0	(0)	20	(51.1)
Kilmarnock & Loudoun	3	(23.2)	14	(56.3)	0	(2.8)	1	(17.1)	0	(0.6)	18	(43.6)
Kyle & Carrick	13	(42.9)	12	(42.5)	0	(7.8)	0	(5.5)	0	(1.2)	25	(47.3)
Monklands	2	(26.9)	18	(69.2)	0	(0.7)	0	(1.1)	0	(2.1)	15	(44.7)
Motherwell	3	(15.0)	23	(60.6)	0	(2.2)	2	(11.9)	2	(10.3)	28	(49.7)
Renfrew	5	(18.3)	35	(53.3)	2	(10.3)	3	(16.4)	0	(1.7)	41	(43.7)
Strathkelvin	4	(22.7)	11	(51.8)	0	(9.0)	0	(14.1)	0	(2.4)	15	(48.8)
TAYSIDE	37	(32.9)	31	(30.9)	6	(10.3)	14	(21.6)	6	(4.4)	85	(44.9)
Angus	8	(38.1)	0	(10.6)	0	(2.0)	11	(42.1)	2	(7.1)	19	(43.0)
City of Dundee	15	(25.6)	25	(45.1)	2	(8.6)	2	(17.7)	0	(3.0)	44	(47.1)
Perth & Kinross	14	(43.1)	6	(19.8)	4	(20.9)	1	(11.6)	4	(4.6)	24	(42.3)
SCOTLAND	**189**	**(21.4)**	**545**	**(45.7)**	**78**	**(12.8)**	**59**	**(11.7)**	**278**	**(8.4)**	**902**	**(44.4)**

Source: Election Studies, University of Dundee

SECTION 5

MAJOR POLITICAL AND SOCIAL ORGANISATIONS IN SCOTLAND

1. **Political Parties**

Communist Party, 44 Carlton Place, Glasgow G5 (041 429 2558)

Scottish conservative Party, 3 Chester Street, Edinburgh EH3 7RN (031 226 4426)

The Labour Party (Scottish Council), Keir Hardie House, 1 Lynedoch Place Glasgow G3 6AB (041 332 8946)

Scottish Liberal Pary, 4 Clifton Terrace, Edinburgh EH12 5DR (031 337 2314)

Social Democratic Party, 5 Royal Exchange Street, Glagow G1 (041 221 8871)

2. **Government Agencies**

Crofters Commission, 4-6 Castle Wynd, Inverness IV2 3EQ (0463 23731)

Glasgow Eastern Area Renewal Project (GEAR), Gear Centre, 596 London Road, Glasgow G40 (041 551 0011)

Highlands and Islands Development Board, 27 Bank Street, Inverness IV1 1QR (0463 234171)

The Housing Corporation, Scottish Head Office, 19 Coates Crescent, Edinburgh EH3 7AF (031 226 3153)

Manpower Services Commission for Scotland, 4 Jeffrey Street, Edinburgh EH1 1UU (031 556 0233)

Scottish Development Agency, 120 Bothwell Street, Glasgow G2 JP (041 248 2700)

Scottish Special Housing Association, 37-41 Manor Place, Edinburgh EH3 7EE (031 226 4401)

3. **Industrial and Social Organisations**

Church of Scotland, 121 George Street, Edinburgh EH2 (031 225 5722)

Confederation of British Industry (Scottish Office), 5 Claremont Terrace, Glasgow G3 (041 332 8661)

Scottish Consumer Council, 314 St Vincent Street, Glasgow G3 8XW

(041 226 5261)

Scottish Council (Development and Industry), 1 Castle Street, Edinburgh EH2 3AJ (031 225 7911)

Scottish Council of Social Services, 18/19 Claremont Crescent, Edinburgh EH7 4QD (031 556 3882)

Scottish Trades Union Congress, 16 Woodlands Terrace, Glasgow G3 6DF (041 332 4946)

SECTION 6

EUROPEAN PARLIAMENT ELECTION RESULTS

Electorate and turnout are given in brackets after the constituency name. An asterisk denotes a member of the previous parliament.

		%	% change since June 1983 general election
GLASGOW (518,178; 29.7%)			
*Mrs J. Buchan (Lab)	91,015	59.2	−2.5
Miss S. Chadd (Con)	25,282	16.5	+6.8
C Mason (Lib/All)	20,867	13.6	−6.7
N MacLeod (SNP)	16,456	10.7	+2.9
	Lab majority 65,733		
HIGHLANDS & ISLANDS (307,265; 38.4%)			
*Mrs W Ewing (SNP)	49,410	41.9	+20.2
R Johnston (Lib/All)	33,133	28.1	− 6.1
D Webster (Con)	18,847	16.0	−15.1
J McArthur (Lab)	16,644	14.1	+ 1.1
	SNP majority 16,277		
LOTHIANS (526,068; 35.3%)			
D W Martin (Lab)	74,989	40.4	+5.9
I Henderson (Con)	49,065	26.4	−3.9
J D Mabon (SDP/All)	36,636	19.7	−7.3
D Stevenson (SNP)	22,331	12.0	+4.2
Miss L Hendry (Ecology)	2,560	1.4	–
	Lab majority 25,924		
SCOTLAND MID AND FIFE (528,529; 35.5%)			
A Falconer (Lab)	80.038	42.7	+ 7.9
*J Purvis (Con)	52,872	28.2	− 0.5
Mrs J Jones (SNP)	30,511	16.3	+ 4.3
A Wedderburn (SDP/All)	24,220	12.9	−11.0
	Lab majority 27,166		

SCOTLAND NORTH EAST (548,711; 28.7%)

*J Provan (Con)	53,809	34.2	−0.8
F Doran (Lab)	44,638	28.4	+6.1
D Hood (SNP)	33,444	21.3	+0.5
I Philip (SDP/All)	25,490	16.2	−5.4

Con majority 9,171

SCOTLAND SOUTH (484,760; 33.9%)

*A Hutton (Con)	60,843	37.0	+ 2.9
R Stewart (Lab)	57,706	35.1	+ 4.6
Mrs E Buchanan (Lib/All)	23,598	14.4	−11.6
I Goldie (SNP)	22,242	13.5	+ 4.2

Con majority 3,137

STRATHCLYDE EAST (498,458; 31.1%)

*K Collins (Lab)	90,792	58.6	+ 9.3
G Leslie (SNP)	27,330	17.6	+ 8.0
R Leckie (Con)	24,857	16.1	− 4.2
Ms P de Seume (Lib/All)	11.883	7.7	−13.0

Lab majority 63,462

STRATHCLYDE WEST (499,162; 34.5%)

H McMahon (Lab)	70,234	40.8	+ 5.3
Miss J Lair (Con)	47,196	27.4	− 1.8
Mrs J Herriot (SNP)	28,866	16.8	+ 8.2
D Herbison (SDP/All)	25,995	15.1	−11.3

Lab majority 23,038

SCOTLAND Summary

	1979 European		**1983 General**	**1984 European**	
	Seats	**% Vote**	**% Vote**	**Seats**	**% Vote**
Conservative	5	33.7	28.4	2	25.7
Labour	2	33.0	35.1	5	40.7
Liberal/SDP	0	14.0	24.5	0	15.6
SNP	1	19.4	11.7	1	17.8
Turnout		33.6	72.7		33.1

THE SCOTTISH GOVERNMENT YEARBOOK 1976-7
Ed. by M.G. Clarke and H.M. Drucker
CONTENTS

1. Our Changing Scotland – M.G. Clarke and H.M. Drucker
2. The New Local Authorities – R.E.G. Peggie
3. The Reorganised Health Service: A Scottish Perspective – Drummond Hunter
4. Unemployment and the Scottish Economy – John Firn
5. Political Reactions to 'Our Changing Democracy' – James G. Kellas
6. Accountability, Professionalism and the Scottish Judiciary – The Rt. Hon. Lord Wheatley and Professor D.N. MacCormick
7. Devolving the Universities: Problems and Prospects – The Very Rev. Professor John McIntyre
8. The Economics of Independence – C.R. Smallwood and Professor D.I. MacKay.

THE SCOTTISH GOVERNMENT YEARBOOK 1978
Ed. by H.M. Drucker and M.G. Clarke
CONTENTS

1. Approaching the Archangelic?: The Secretary for State for Scotland – The Rt. Hon. W. Ross, MP
2. The Scottish Development Agency – Dr L. Robertson
3. The Shetland Experience: A local authority arms itself for the oil invasion – J.M. Fenwick
4. Opposition in Local Government – L.M. Turpie
5. Glasgow's Housing Politics – S.F. Hamilton
6. Health and Health Care in West-Central Scotland – D.Hamilton
7. Consultation or Confrontation?: The Campaign to save the Scottish Colleges of Education – Dr Edith Cope
8. Parliament and the Scots Conscience: Reforming the law on Divorce, Licensing and Homosexual offences – R.F. Cook, MP
9. The Failure of the Scotland and Wales Bill: No will, no way – J. Kerr
10. Devolution: The Commercial Community's Fears – D.J. Risk
11. The District Council Elections of May 1977 – J. Bochel and D. Denver

THE SCOTTISH GOVERNMENT YEARBOOK 1979
Ed. by N. Drucker and H.M. Drucker
CONTENTS

THE SCOTTISH GOVERNMENT YEARBOOK 1980
Ed. by H.M. Drucker and N. Drucker
CONTENTS

THE SCOTTISH GOVERNMENT YEARBOOK 1981
Ed. by H.M. Drucker and N. Drucker
CONTENTS

THE SCOTTISH GOVERNMENT YEARBOOK 1982
Ed. by H.M. Drucker and N. Drucker
CONTENTS

SCOTTISH GOVERNMENT YEARBOOK 1983
Ed. David McCrone
CONTENTS

SCOTTISH GOVERNMENT YEARBOOK 1984
Ed. David McCrone
CONTENTS

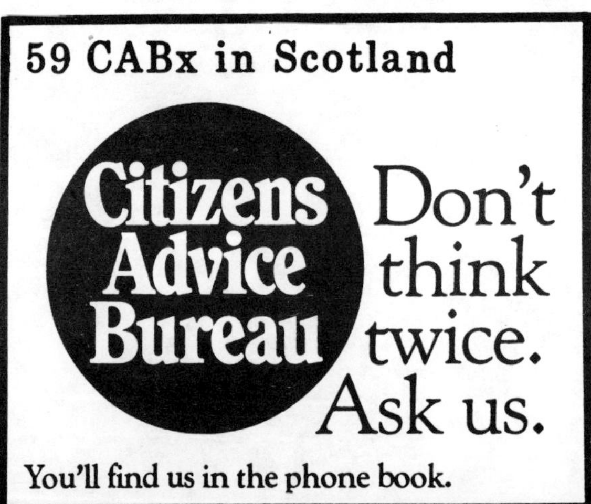
59 CABx in Scotland
Citizens Advice Bureau
Don't think twice. Ask us.
You'll find us in the phone book.